The Cinema of

Adventure, Romance & Terror

The Cinema of

Adventure, Romance & Terror

from the archives of American Cinematographer

Edited by
George E. Turner

Contributions by
Rudy Behlmer
Paul Mandell
Scott MacQueen
George Mitchell
Michael H. Price

THE ASC PRESS
HOLLYWOOD, CALIFORNIA

ISBN 0-935578-09-9

Library of Congress catalog card number 89-083361

Printed in Japan by Dai Nippon Printing Co. Ltd.

First printing 1989

Table of Contents

Acknowledgments

This book was made possible by efforts well beyond the call of duty by Jean W. Turner, who was in charge of production; Martha Winterhalter, art and technical director; Nora Lee, production coordinator; and Matthew C. Lee, special consultant. Ronald V. Borst, Hollywood Movie Posters, provided many of the rarer photos.

Invaluable information and illustrative materials were contributed over a period of years by these individuals, companies and institutions:

L.B. Abbott, ASC; Academy of Motion Picture Arts and Sciences; Bettye Ackerman; Forrest J. Ackerman; Howard A. Anderson, ASC; Robert Armstrong; American Society of Composers, Authors and Publishers (ASCAP); Art Directors Guild; William Bakewell; Noah Beery (Jr.); Samuel Beetley, ACE; DeWitt Bodeen; Karl Brown; Richard H. Bush; Mae Clarke; William Clothier, ASC; Edward Colman, ASC; Pete Comandini; Merian C. Cooper; Stanley Cortez, ASC; Larry "Buster" Crabbe; Marcel Delgado; Reginald Denny; Linwood G. Dunn, ASC; Douglas Fairbanks Jr.; Bernice Fulton; John P. Fulton, ASC; Henry Freulich, ASC; Lee Garmes, ASC; Lillian Gish; Robert Gitt; Dorothy Goldner; Dr. Orville Goldner; John Hall; Vernon Harbin; Seymour Hoffberg, ASC; Alfred Keller, ASC; Donald Kerr; Mario Larrinaga; Joseph LaShelle, ASC; Ernest Laszlo, ASC; Charles Laughton; Archie S. Marshek, ACE; Enzo Martinelli, ASC; Metro-Goldwyn-Mayer Pictures; Paramount Pictures; Richard Patterson; Kenneth Peach (Sr.), ASC; Vincent Price; Charles Buddy Rogers; RKO Radio Pictures; Jean Rogers; Maryvonne Rosse; Ernest B. Schoedsack; Peter Schoedsack; Ruth Rose Schoedsack; Carroll Shepphird; Fred Shepphird; Barry Shipman; Murray Spivack; Clifford Stine, ASC; Kenneth Strickfaden; Richard Tucker; Twentieth Century Fox Film Corp.; United Artists; Universal Pictures; University of Texas, Department of Humanities; Clifford Vaughan; Johnny Weissmuller; Harold Wellman, ASC; Lyle Wheeler; Robert Wise; Harry Wolf, ASC; Fay Wray.

Preface

Those of us who wrote the chapters of this book worked in a haze of nostalgia born of love for the subjects. Yet, none of them is intended as a mere nostalgia piece designed to evoke vanished "good old days." As a matter of fact, most of the films under discussion were made during times at least as trying as those we face today. Gang warfare, famine, epidemics, a world-wide depression, the rise of Hitler and his cohorts, the dust bowl era, racial and religious intolerance, political scandals, wars (including the largest conflict in history), and innumerable other ills were ravaging humanity at the various times when all of these pictures were born.

No, we aren't speaking of "good old days," but of good old movies. They were made for commercial reasons (which only occasionally were realized) and were achieved through the hard work of many artists and craftsmen. Our approach is intended mainly to be informative about the production of these films and only incidentally to express critical opinion.

Nineteen of the following 24 chapters are based upon articles which have appeared in *American Cinematographer.* All of these have been corrected, revised or rewritten, and many new photographs have been added. Five additional chapters have been written especially for this book.

—George E. Turner
Hollywood, 1989

The Cinema of

Adventure, Romance & Terror

1

The Hunchback of Notre Dame

The early 1920s were years of great artistic and technical growth for motion pictures. So many outstanding films were made during that time that it is virtually impossible to pick a single favorite.

Certainly a leading contender is the 1923 *The Hunchback of Notre Dame*, produced at Universal City under the benign dictatorship of the president, Carl Laemmle, and his youthful production executive, Irving G. Thalberg. It has spectacle in the best sense of the word, fine performances, cinematography which set new standards in several respects, steady direction which kept all the sprawling elements of the picture under control, magnificent settings, and faithfulness to the spirit of a literary classic. It was one of the most expensive silent films, costing more than $1,250,000.

Universal at the time specialized in the making of inexpensive program pictures which were sold in packages to exhibitors. These were graded by Laemmle as to importance and quality, the top line product being designated as Universal Jewels, then Junior Jewels, Specials, etc. There was an occasional Super Jewel, meaning a picture so far above the ordinary as to demand special handling, higher rentals and longer playdates. Of this mere handful (which includes *Foolish Wives, Merry-Go-Round, Phantom of the Opera* and *Uncle Tom's Cabin*), Laemmle's favorite and the company's biggest was *Hunchback*.

Lon Chaney and Patsy Ruth Miller as Quasimodo and Esmeralda.

In adapting Victor Hugo's 1831 novel, "Notre Dame de Paris," Perley Poore Sheehan and Edward T. Lowe made many changes, some in the interest of paring the story down to a practical length for the screen, partly to relieve some of the gloom which permeates the novel but would hardly be acceptable to theater audiences of the time, and partly to eliminate Hugo's criticisms of the church.

The film centers around Quasimodo, the deformed bell-ringer of the Cathedral of Notre Dame in Paris, in 1482. He is ordered by Jehan, evil brother of the archdeacon, to kidnap Esmeralda, a beautiful Gypsy dancing girl and ward of the king of the underworld, Clopin. She is rescued by the dashing Captain Phoebus and Quasimodo is sentenced to be lashed in the public square. Esmeralda, taking pity, brings him water and stirs in him a hopeless love. Jehan jealously stabs Phoebus as he embraces Esmeralda. The girl is blamed and sentenced to be hanged in front of Notre Dame. Quasimodo climbs down from the cathedral tower and carries Esmeralda into the sanctuary of the church. Clopin leads his army of beggars, thieves and murderers from their quarter, known as the Court of Miracles, to storm Notre Dame. Quasimodo, thinking they are trying to return the girl to the gallows, hurls building blocks and beams down on them. He finally routs the attack by pouring molten lead onto the rabble. The King's guards disperse the mob as Clopin dies. Jehan now tries to attack Esmeralda in the tower. In rescuing her, Quasimodo is fatally stabbed before throwing Jehan from the tower. Esmeralda learns that Phoebus is alive and that she

Photos by Fred Archer, Jack Freulich, Henry Freulich

Chaney in make-up he designed for the role of Quasimodo.

has been exonerated. As she leaves, Quasimodo tolls the church bells, then dies.

Laemmle and Thalberg agreed that only Lon Chaney could portray Quasimodo. Even while early research was being done by Sheehan in Paris and the physical aspects of the production were being planned, Thalberg was trying to sign the

reclusive actor. Chaney was being difficult because of a grudge against the studio. An agreement was reached late in 1922.

A number of important directors had been considered. Chaney was instrumental in bringing in Wallace Worsley, who had directed him in the Goldwyn production, *The Penalty*. A veteran actor and producer of the New York stage, he became a film director in 1917 and had directed for most of the major studios. *Hunchback* was both his finest work and his last large-scale directorial effort. After it was completed he devoted most of his efforts to the making of travel pictures.

Worsley was aware of Chaney's directorial ability and allowed him to direct some of his own scenes. In staging the gigantic crowd scenes, in which as many as 2,500 extras appeared, Worsley utilized for the first time in motion picture production a public address system. This was the new Western Electric Public Address Apparatus, which made it possible for the director to give orders to actors and crew members in all parts of the vast set. An ex-army officer, George M. Stallings, and ten assistant directors, headed by Jimmy Dugan and Jack Sullivan, helped to control the mass of players. One of the assistant-assistants was a Laemmle relative from France, William Wyler.

Many modern critics have pondered Universal's choice of a comparatively little-known director for a picture which competed (successfully) with the outstanding historical epics of the silent screen. However, a study of the film reveals that *Hunchback* has all the virtues and few of the faults of pictures produced by the better known makers of this type of film: the crowds are handled with great skill, the individual performances are first rate (yet even Chaney is unable to reduce Hugo's concept to a star vehicle), the photographic technique is superior to any picture of its kind of the period, and there is a welcome absence of the dramatic excesses that marred Cecil B. DeMille's films or the exaggerated sentimentality that Griffith so often fell prey to. And if this be heresy . . . .

Elmer E. Sheeley was in charge of set design, with Sidney Ullman as his first assistant. Archie Hall was the technical director in charge of set construction. Stephen Goosson – who designed Shangri La for *Lost Horizon* a dozen or so years later – worked with Ullman and several other artists in a special drafting room over the main stage. Their drawings, which combined the factual with the fanciful, were based upon old prints of the architecture of the period, including a collection of sketches made by Victor Hugo. These designs were translated into plans which were blueprinted and delivered to Hall.

Meantime, 60 workmen hauled in cobblestones from a river 20 miles away and laid them in cement beds – the streets of old Paris. Flagstones were molded in cement and laid in a long row in front of a string stretched between two poles to indicate the front line of the cathedral site. To lay out the cathedral place it was necessary to cut off one flank of a mountain and fill in a large swale.

Carl Laemmle told Hall that the sets should be built as solidly as the real thing, just as had been done previously with the Monte Carlo and Vienna sets for Erich von Stroheim's extravaganzas, *Foolish Wives* and *Merry-Go-Round.* It was his theory that the sets could be used in many other productions, and he was right. They remained in use for four decades, until the cathedral and most of the other buildings were destroyed in a disastrous fire.

The framework was set up by 200 carpenters while sections of the facade were cast in concrete. Finn Froelich, a well known sculptor, was in charge of making the bas-reliefs, embellishments, saints, martyrs and gargoyles that cover the Gothic structure. Before completion the cathedral resembled a huge wooden shed, but when the lumber was removed it had become a replica of the original exterior – or, at least, the bottom 60 feet of it. After masons finished their work, 60 painters added the finishing touches.

At the time of the story, Notre Dame was 150 feet wide and 225 feet high (the spire was added at a later time). Universal's cathedral ended at a point just above the huge arch over the center entrance. To show wider views of the cathedral, the upper portion was constructed as a large-scale miniature which was mounted between the camera and the building and lined up to blend perfectly with the full scale set. The complete cathedral, seen from several angles, defies detection.

Other parts of the building, for use in close-up, were erected at different locations. Part of a tower was built full-scale on a hilltop about one mile away. The hill provided the elevation needed for low-angle shots but, as Patsy Ruth Miller (who played Esmeralda) says, "it was built so that you couldn't hurt yourself if you fell." The Bastille and drawbridge were built about a quarter of a mile from the courtyard. The gardens of the castle were located adjacent to the studio nursery, where the varieties of plants could be moved conveniently. Concrete arches were built over the Los Angeles River, which forms the northern boundary of Universal City, to represent the sewers of Paris. At that time the river bed was not concrete as it is today, and it was used in many pictures. When it appeared as the Seine, the Thames, the Danube or the Mississippi, the semi-arid river often had to be dammed up or even irrigated by the studio fire department.

The principal sets covered 19 acres, 11 for the courtyard and cathedral and eight for streets and the Court of Miracles. The buildings included a castle, a hotel, shops, taverns and houses. Construction took six months. The settings and properties cost about $500,000 – of which $342,869 was for the Place du Parvis set.

In *Movie Weekly* for April 21, 1923, Grace Kingsley describes a visit with Chaney to the set, where they "sat in the 11-acre-square of Notre Dame, facing that wonderful cathedral.

"We had driven up in Lon's Cadillac! Imagine the humble hunchback driving a Cadillac! Around us sprawled or lounged a thousand extras...They were all in bright colors, and they formed a marvelous picture against the backgrounds of church, shops, old-fashioned houses of Paris, which themselves were silhouetted against the green hills of Universal City and the purple mountains in the distance."

Sheehan, co-author of the screenplay, described the atmosphere more poetically in *Cinema Art* of January, 1924:

"The cathedral towers would shimmer in a blue radiance like that of a thousand moons and send back echoes of coyote calls. Wouldn't Victor

This set is a part of medieval Paris being rebuilt at Universal City. At right are cobblestones hauled by wagons from a river 20 miles away.

Hugo have loved all this? I believe so. It was his sort of stuff. It was great and weird. I myself like to believe – and I do believe it – that the great Frenchman's spirit presided over the filming... from the very inception of the idea right up to the premiere opening on Broadway." Sheehan had lived in Paris for 10 years "under the very shadow of the old cathedral" and just around the corner from Hugo's house.

Jack Rumsey, "recently returned from Hollywood," told the New York *Times* (July 1, 1923) that "the immensity of the sets and their accuracy was far beyond the ken of most persons" and that he "felt quite nonplussed when he stood before the great gate of Notre Dame in Universal City... All the atmosphere of Paris was near the cathedral, and every little detail has received attention in making the copy in far off California..."

Sheehan, in addition to his writing duties, worked as a technical supervisor for Worsley. It was

Above: *Part of the cathedral under construction.* Opposite: *Phoebus (Norman Kerry) rescues Esmeralda from Quasimodo.*

he who set the tone for the costuming with this directive:

"We don't think of Christopher Columbus discovering America 'in costume.' We don't allow ourselves to think for a moment of *Notre Dame's* fifteenth century people as wearing grotesque costumes and having queer costumes. No costumes were grotesque to the people who wore them. They were natural, everyday clothes. Our characters must wear their costumes as such. The costumes... will be incidental and the main object is to make them and use them so that the spectator will forget them. They must be incidental – accurate, correct, but inconspicuous."

Three thousand costumes had to be specially made. Planning and measurements were completed about a month before shooting was to begin. A building on the lot, which was 125 feet long with 18 windows, was enlarged to about double that size to handle the large number of costumes to be handed out to the extras at the windows. Around 200 men were necessary to handle wardrobe duties. Col. Gordon McGee, of Western Costume Company, supervised costume research and production. The fancier clothes were worn by characters of the court, the 50 men and 50 women attending the grand ball

Studio artisans sculpt plaster saints for the facade of the cathedral.

at the mansion of Madame Gaundalaurier, Esmeralda, and certain of the Gypsies. The more conspicuous extras were put on the payroll two days early so they could become accustomed to wearing their costumes in order that they would behave on camera as though they were wearing the normal clothes of their day.

The most unusual garb is that of the underworld denizens of the Court of Miracles. Because their home was surrounded by old palaces, these thieves and beggars wore garments pilfered from the nobility, especially during the plague when many of the rich abandoned their homes until the danger had passed. The beggars, therefore, wore the raiment of royalty, however soiled and tattered. The appearance of reality achieved in *Hunchback,* as opposed to the comic-opera look that contributed to the public's dislike of most historical epics, may be traced in large measure to the authentically drab costuming.

Lon Chaney had been a colorful part of the ambience at Universal since its early days, first as an extra and bit player and eventually a featured actor and sometime writer and director. He was one of several actors (others were Jack Pierce, Cecil Holland and C.E. Collins) who stayed busy by bringing their own makeup kits to casting calls and making themselves up on the spot to fit whatever kinds of characters were being cast. Since Universal specialized in Westerns, serials and jungle melodramas, Chaney played many a scar-faced heavy, also appearing as elderly men and paunchy fathers in society dramas.

Chaney, after a salary dispute, left Universal and found greater fame at Paramount, Goldwyn and other companies. When he returned to do *Hunchback* he was a major star, earning the then-munificent sum of $2,500 per week. This picture brought him even greater stature, and when the Metro-Goldwyn company was formed in 1924, he was their first star. He returned to Universal for the last time that year to make *The Phantom of the Opera,* thereafter working for MGM exclusively. He died in 1930 after making his only talking picture, *The Unholy Three.* Ironically, his two most popular pictures were Universal's *Hunchback* and *Phantom.*

Checking in at Universal, Chaney appropriated Dressing Room No. 5, a new one-room shack, with shower, on the front lot. Locking himself in with his makeup kit, two chairs, an iron cot, a wardrobe, a small table and makeup mirror, he worked out the details of Quasimodo. His personal manager, A.A. Grasso, had borrowed for him an old edition of Hugo's book which contained eight drawings of the hunchback by Hugo himself. Using these and Hugo's vivid verbal descriptions, Chaney emerged at length with a Quasimodo which seemed akin to the monstrous gargoyles of Notre Dame.

This initiated a studio tradition regarding No. 5 which persisted until it and similar cubicles made way for more modern structures. Chaney returned there to create *The Phantom of the Opera* in secrecy. In 1928 the room was commandeered by Jack P. Pierce, head of makeup and a great friend and admirer of Chaney. Pierce created there Conrad Viedt's horror makeup for *The Man Who Laughs.* Later he worked in secrecy in No. 5 on Boris Karloff, Bela Lugosi, Lon Chaney Jr. and others who portrayed monsters of various sorts in the studio's

Ernest Torrence exhorts the rabble in a superb night-for-night scene.

popular horror movies of the 1930s and '40s. No. 5 was known as the *Bugaboudoir* and engendered a certain superstitous awe among some of the old-time Universalites.

"When Chaney first put on his makeup – *The Hunchback* is his life's dream and every bit of his 15 years' intensive study of makeup goes into it – Jack Freulich, studio photographer; Henry Freulich, Graflex cameraman with the publicity department; Fred L. Archer, head of the art title department and internationally known for his prize-winning studies, and two other photographers shot photographs simultaneously of the remarkable Quasimodo," *American Cinematographer* reported in February, 1923. This was the first photographic job for the youthful Henry Freulich (later ASC), son of Jack and a celebrated director of photography in later years.

The other major roles were assigned to Patsy Ruth Miller, an excellent young actress who already had played leads in more than a dozen pictures, as Esmeralda; Norman Kerry, who had been in pictures since 1919 and had just scored a big success in another spectacular production *Merry-Go-Round*, as Phoebus; and Ernest Torrence, a tall, lantern-jawed Scottish opera singer, as the beggar-king, Clopin. All three are strong assets to the picture, and Torrence's characterization is almost as compelling as Chaney's. In fact, several who saw the original premiere engagement version have stated that Torrence's role was severely cut when the film was edited for release, and that he dominated much of the long edition, which no longer is available.

Robert E. Newhard, ASC, was named first cameraman (today he would be called director of

Quasimodo on the pillory in Laemmle's Paris.

photography). However, the magnitude of production was such over a long period that almost every other cameraman at Universal had a hand in it at various times, including Charles Stumar, ASC, Stephen S. Norton, ASC, Anthony Kornmann, ASC, Virgil Miller, ASC, Friend F. Baker, ASC, Philip H. Whitman, ASC, and perhaps a dozen others. Only Newhard received screen credit.

A founding member of the ASC in 1919, Newhard had been a cinematographer for about 13 years, having begun as an assistant to Fred Balshofer at the 101 Bison Ranch. He then became one of the earliest special effects specialists, heading an experimental and research department for Thomas H. Ince. One of his most striking efforts was a Billie Burke feature filmed entirely without artificial light by use of mirrors and reflectors. After shooting 14 features for Ince in four years, he worked for Paralta, Frank Keenan, Selznick, Fox, and Goldwyn. He teamed with aviator Frank Clarke in making aerial films, then was called to Universal for his biggest assignment: six months' work on *Hunchback*. It proved his *magnum opus*, a film whose photographic qualities (even in the much-copied 16mm prints which seem to be all that remain) are remarkable even today.

Newhard hailed from rural Pennsylvania and, since boyhood, had been fond of keeping snakes as pets. Snakes were abundant in the grassy and (then) largely undeveloped Universal backlot, and a six-foot gopher snake became Newhard's companion during the last two weeks of shooting. Most of the cast and crew gave the cameraman's friend a wide berth.

Esmeralda is abducted by the Hunchback.

Anthony Kornmann also worked as a first cameraman on many scenes, although it is now impossible to determine which ones. Kornmann was a second unit specialist during most of his career. Hungarian-born Charles Stumar, the most famous of the cinematographers who contributed to the film, was another veteran of the Inceville studio and is believed to have shot some of the softly romantic scenes between Esmeralda and Phoebus. At the height of his career, in 1935, Stumar was killed in an airplane crash while scouting locations. Stephen S. Norton, a diminutive cameraman who at the time had photographed more than 160 features, several serials and innumerable short films, lent his expertise to some of the mob action scenes.

Phil Whitman, another ASC founder, and Friend Baker had been working with designer Sheeley in developing special effects techniques for Universal. They were responsible for the flawless glass shots and hanging miniature effects which completed the job of transforming the backlot into old Paris. They also filmed, at considerable expense, a fantasy sequence depicting Phoebus' fevered dreams during his delirium, which was not used in the final cut because studio executives found it confusing. (Whitman, who eventually switched to directing, is best known for his special effects for Douglas Fairbanks' *The Thief of Bagdad* of 1926, and it was Baker who staged the earthquake for the 1927 *Old San Francisco*).

Virgil Miller considered Chaney "really one of the greatest." Miller said, "I remember when we were both working at Universal and I was getting

Director Worsley and the first public address system used on a movie set. He is flanked by Robert Newhard shooting the domestic negative and Harry McGuire making the foreign negative with their Bell & Howell cameras.

Virgil Miller.

$18 a week and he was getting $35. One day he said, 'Virg, I'm going to hit 'em for a raise.' That encouraged me and I told him I would ask for a raise of $2 a week for myself. We went to Mr. Laemmle and he was refused his raise and so he left Universal. I got my increase and stayed.

"A few years later, with Chaney an established star, the studio wanted him and no one else for *The Hunchback.* He wanted me on camera, so I sat in on the conferences. I was delighted to hear my old friend hold out firmly for an added $35 to be called for in his contract. He got it, too. His checks were made out for $2,535 every week – quite a raise!"

Chaney demanded that Miller should do all of his close-ups. Miller had photographed Chaney in *The Trap* (1922), one of the earliest pictures to use panchromatic film, and Chaney liked the closeups better than those in his other films. Miller was also involved in some special effects and some of the large scale action.

"Once, when Chaney was at the top of the cathedral set and I was down below at the camera, I noticed that he was still wearing his wrist watch," Miller recalled. "I signaled wildly and spelled out 'wrist' in sign language, which he understood because his parents were deaf, and he stuffed the

watch out of sight. After that I always checked him out with the six-inch lens so I got a good close look before we started. I hated to see him have to do the rough scenes over if he didn't have to."

Chaney was himself an enigma. Secretive, uncommunicative and unfriendly much of the time, he could be a staunch friend as well. His first wife considered him an implacable and unforgiving enemy and his son suggested he could be terribly cruel.

"I remember his kindness," Patsy Ruth Miller said in 1985 of her work in *Hunchback.* "I was only 17, and he was extremely kind and very helpful to me, which is certainly not true of all the big stars of that time. He was very serious when working, but had a fey sense of humor. We were working at night on the underworld set and it was about 1 a.m. when they got to my scene. It was dark, foggy, and the klieg lights gave it an eerie look. I had just started when, all of a sudden, a monstrous creature came leaping out from between two buildings and scared the daylights out of me! When I was through screaming I realized it was Lon.

"During preparations for one of the big emotional scenes he said to me, very quietly: 'Remember, my dear, you are an actress. You don't have to live the part, just act it. The point is not for you to cry; make your *audience* cry. You have to be in control of yourself.' When Norman Kerry and I were doing

One of Newhard's memorable night scenes in the Court of Miracles.

11

Phil Whitman.

the scene where he is trying to seduce the Gypsy girl and he's offering me wine and I'm looking calf-eyed, Lon came in off stage and said, 'Oh Mr. Kerry, are my eyes too big for pictures?''

"Lon did a lot of directing on his films. He wasn't a very social man. I *never* saw him out socially, anywhere."

Jackie Coogan, who worked with Chaney in *Oliver Twist* in 1922, described him as "very short, very tan, bowlegged – a rough man, a tough man. A real loner – he made Howard Hughes look like Pia Zadora."

Grace Kingsley found Chaney without makeup "very good-looking, very charming, very well-dressed. You'd never recognize him if you met him on the street.

"'In one way,' he explained, as we watched the extras flock over to the set, 'makeup helps you in putting a characterization over. It aids you in getting into the spirit of the part while you are looking into the mirror, and when you see the interest in the faces of your co-workers. But in another way it hinders.

"'When a makeup is as painful as that which I wore as Blizzard in *The Penalty,* when I had my legs strapped up and couldn't bear it more than 20 minutes at a time – when I have to be a cripple, as in *The Miracle Man,* or have to keep a certain attitude of body as I did in playing Yen Sen in *Shadows,* it sometimes takes a good deal of imagination to forget your physical sufferings. Yet at that the sub-

conscious mind has a marvelous way of making you keep the right attitudes and make the right gestures when you are actually acting.

"'But there's another thing. Though make-up helps the illusion in the minds of the audience, too, still it sometimes requires ten times the concentration to get results when a grotesque makeup is used, inasmuch as the face, in its set lines, must necessarily fail to register many expressions.

"'And when it comes to a character like the Hunchback, which demands that the audience sympathize, despite his repugnant looks – well, it is the hardest part I ever played, that's all.

"'You see, I am following as closely as possible the best-known illustrations of Hugo's novel. Therefore, I am hunchbacked, knock-kneed, have one eye almost entirely closed by a big wart, have a hairy skin, and am altogether repulsive to look at. But this isn't all. I wear a cast that weighs about 50 pounds, and which, doubled up as I am, it is nothing short of agony to carry around.'

"'Can't you take off your makeup and rest once in a while?' I asked.

"'What? When it takes me three hours and a half exactly to put it on?' demanded Lon. 'I should say not! But at that, I cannot stand the makeup longer than six hours at a time. Yet I must not only get interest in the Hunchback; I must get the deepest sympathy for him from my audiences, else he fills my onlookers only with revulsion and disgust. But the thing I dread most of all is not the putting on of the makeup, not even the wearing of it, but the taking it off. See all the hair gone from my eyebrows? Pulled it out taking off my false eyebrows. And my eyelid is all burned from the application of strong glue. Also I'm sure I'm permanently warped about the shoulders from carrying that hump on my back.'"

Actually, there is one major difference in Chaney's Quasimodo and that of Hugo. The author described a giant of a man who had been put together badly. Chaney, being of no more than average size, opted for a misshapen dwarf, a concept the public accepted without complaint. His performance is above criticism, a masterpiece of pantomime investing an initially terrifying creature with endearing qualities. It should be noted that despite his many deformities, the hunchback possesses great strength and agility. Instead of "hamming it up," as actors in heavy makeup often do, Chaney gives the impression that Quasimodo has learned to live with his condition.

Chaney was (secretly) doubled by Universal's serial star, Joe Bonomo, in some of the more

athletic scenes on the tower and in the climb down the facade to rescue Esmeralda.

Quasimodo and Jehan, played by Brandon Hurst.

Historically, the most remarkable aspects of the picture are the lighting and photography of the night scenes, which are far more sophisticated than any previous efforts of this kind. As Harry D. Brown, who headed the lighting crew, said in *American Cinematographer* (October, 1923), "the exact reproduction of the cathedral of Notre Dame on American soil at Universal City ... was in itself a triumph for the motion picture technician, but in spite of all the faithfulness with which the reproduction was executed it could not have been brought to the screen if it were not amply illuminated so that it could be photographed properly.

"There was no precedent by which the electrical engineer or the chief cinematographer could be guided. The entire illumination and proper photography were matters that they themselves had to figure out, and succeed or fail according to their own judgment." Brown stated that "success in film-

ing this record-size set depended basically on the human angle; that is, all the artistic and technical attainments would have been naught had the cinematographic and electrical divisions not worked in harmony so that efficiency in the two departments aided rather than hindered.

"Bob Newhard, a member of the American Society of Cinematographers, ... is an artist of highest quality as proved by his splendid photographic achievement in *The Hunchback.* More than that, he is a prince among men, and during the six months that we worked on the picture there never was a controversy of any kind between the cinematographer and the electrical department, although at times the natural difficulties involved in the making of the picture were such as would test the evenest of tempers. As photography is one of the outstanding features in this production, Newhard cannot be given too much credit for his work.

13

Denizens of the Court of Miracles.

"In the first sequence, that of the 'Festival of Fools,' the illumination had to be of such an intensity that would permit us to shoot the same shots with considerably less light and a great deal more in later scenes. Baskets of burning substances being the source of light, scenes were staged in the dead of night with the buildings all dark and no sign of life, when we had mobs to rush in suddenly from all sides with burning torches, starting bonfires and setting buildings on fire. To light this action atmospherically correct required not only a different intensity of light, but made it necessary to gradually raise the illumination as the mobs advanced on the palace and the cathedral."

Used in filming the festival were 37 sunlight arcs, five GE spots, 154 Winfields and 47 overheads, plus 62 practical arcs for the baskets. Much more complicated was the lighting for the "moonlight and torches" scenes, described by Brown as follows:

"... We started with 15 sunlight arcs and 10 120-ampere spots, the 15 sunlight arcs burning full capacity with 37 sunlight arcs burning at very low voltage. As the mobs advanced with their torches, the voltage was raised to a certain intensity, gradually increasing when they started the bonfires, again raising a little more when the buildings were set on fire, while in the meantime the windows in all of the

buildings were lighting up. By the time the scene had progressed to its height all sunlight arcs were burning at their full capacity, every window was lighted and the entire set was one blaze of light for fully 10 minutes. The total amount of equipment burning was 52 sunlight arcs, 21 GE high intensity spots, 30 120-ampere spots, 47 overheads and 249 Winfields.

"To supply energy to this equipment required seven motor generator sets, two of which were of 300-kilowatt capacity, and three gas-driven power wagons, which gave a total of 24,000 amperes actual load. This energy was distributed to the various parts of the set over approximately five miles of stage cable and feeders, terminating in 16 location switchboards, and from there to the different pieces of apparatus. Energy was transmitted from the main sub-station at the front end of the plant through one mile of 2200-volt feeders."

Earl Miller was chief gaffer in charge of the electrical crew, consisting of 139 men working under nine divisional foremen. Separate crews handled lights and feeders to save time when changing setups. Miller noted that "All during the period of production we had 17 other companies shooting on the lot. We had to furnish them with men and equipment, too, bringing the total to 230 electricians on the payroll and practically all the available equipment in Los Angeles."

Harry Brown was one of the finest electrical experts in the studios. A Spanish-American War veteran, he built the first large electrical signs in America at Atlantic City in 1901, and later pioneered in designing animated signs in Los Angeles. He built the first portable generator and developed the first radioactive machine for the treatment of cancer.

The chief gaffer was Earl Miller, who reminisced about the picture 17 years later, when as chief electrical engineer of RKO-Radio Pictures he worked on a new version of *Hunchback* (in *American Cinematographer* for February, 1940):

"*What* a winter that was; rain, fog, wind and mud – days, weeks, months of it. 'The largest artificially lighted motion picture set in the world,' they told us.

"Believe me, when I recall those foggy cold nights and the miles we walked, night after night, up and down that cobblestone street and out in the mud, I wonder how the picture was ever completed.

"In 1923, incandescent lights were not used for motion pictures. The street set was a few feet longer and wider than the one used in the 1939 version. There were only 56 24-inch sun arcs in the entire industry in Hollywood.

14

"We needed every one for our night shots and Universal arranged to rent all but one. Every night for seven long weeks all the sets in other studios were stripped of 24-inch sun arcs. They were loaded on trucks and hauled to Universal. We used them until 5 a.m., but had to return them to the proper studio and have them set up and ready to burn by 8 a.m. Whenever possible we left the lights on the trucks all night instead of building parallels...

"Every light...was an arc. Some of the 24-inch had automatic feed, but in addition to these there were more than 450 other arcs, all of which were hand fed. All lights had to be trimmed at least twice every night and some three times. Yes, we actually shot every night, all night, for 49 straight nights. At one time (and it *would* be the time it rained the hardest) my crew and I worked five days and six nights straight, rigged all day and shot all night; never took our shoes off; catnapped between shots.

"Finally...the last reel was in the can, and in spite of all the work and worry everyone who worked on or in that picture will tell you that we had lots of fun making it."

C. Roy Hunter, head of the camera and laboratory departments, said that approximately 750,000 feet of Eastman negative were exposed. The

Quasimodo and his treasures.

approximate ASA daylight rating of that emulsion would have been 12. The lenses used were no faster than f:3.5; many were f:4.5 lenses.

Hunter said that "there was one day when the cameras totaled 26. They were grouped in pairs." (It was customary at that time to photograph everything with paired cameras, one of which shot the negative to be sent overseas for the preparation of foreign prints. This effected an enormous saving in shipping and customs costs as compared to sending release prints. Cinematographers were designated as first and second cameramen for this reason.) "The occasion was the engagement of 2500 extras. Unknown to these extras they were to be attacked by 500 horsemen in tin armor and driven onto the steps of the cathedral. The plan was to create a panic. The plan succeeded – in full.

"Every precaution was taken to avoid accidents. First aid stations were established at convenient points, while surgeons and nurses were alloted. The 500 horsemen precipitated a most realistic mob scene when the word was given for them to move in. Terror and pandemonium reigned, speaking truthfully. But the precautions that had been taken worked to a charm. Almost. Of all the close calls and narrow escapes from injury only one required the attention of the surgeons and nurses. And that was a horseman who inadvertently fell from his mount and thereby broke a leg." (*American Cinematographer*, February 1940).

Before the scene with the 2500 extras, 500 horsemen and 26 cameras was shot, Worsley announced that he would demand a retake of the entire day's work should any one of the cameramen fail to get the expected result. This so unnerved one cameraman that, after shooting the slate with his 3" lens, he failed to remove the cap from the 2" lens with which he was supposed to shoot the action. Hunter, upon seeing the rushes, quickly had an extra print struck of the film shot by the camera nearest that of the unlucky cameraman and attached it to the latter's slate shot. When Worsley viewed the rushes, carefully noting the name of the cameraman on each slate, he was forced to admit that every man had performed admirably. Hunter estimated that the scene would have cost about $30,000 to restage – enough money to finance a couple of the profitable six-day Westerns that were Universal's main source of bread-and-butter in those days.

Principal photography, which had begun on December 16, 1922, was completed on June 3, 1923. About 750,000 feet of negative was exposed. Editors Maurice Pivar, Sid Singerman and Ed Cur-

15

Phoebus before King Louis (Tully Marshall).

tiss cut from this an unusually long picture – 12 reels – which would be released to key theaters only at a stage-play ticket price.

Fred Archer prepared the art titles, most which were hand-lettered and illustrated in opaque tempera.

The completed negative was shipped via armored car to the Universal vaults, at 1600 Broadway in New York, around August 1. Accompanied by one of Laemmle's executives, James V. Bryson, and an armed guard, it was insured for $1.5 million, which approximated the actual cost.

One print was struck for the use of Dr. Hugo Riesenfeld, Viennese-born violinist-composer-conductor-empresario, at that time the most famous of the movie theater musical directors. Riesenfeld prepared what he called a "musical setting" – a compilation of classical themes, music composed for adaptation by theater orchestras, and original compositions, which were arranged into a closely keyed accompaniment for the film. French composer Henry Baron won a contest sponsored by Laemmle to compose the main theme, "Chimes of Notre Dame." The music was scored for a symphonic orchestra and also arranged for small ensemble. The published score was made available to theaters which booked the film. Max Winkler compiled a score for keyboard soloists in smaller theaters.

Release prints were printed on Eastman tinted base stocks. This type of color was not intended to resemble what was called *natural color* processes, such as Technicolor or Kinemacolor, but was designed to intensify the changing moods of the drama. The transparent colors of the film base provided a tint under the black and white images – amber for the candlelighted interiors, blue for night effects, peachblow for the romantic scenes, a garish green for the torture chamber and the evil plottings of Jehan, and magenta for the flashback sequence about the kidnapping of Crazy Godule's child. In some instances the images were toned as well, producing a blue on blue for some of the night scenes, sepia on ambertone, and, for the torture scenes, a green tint over a blue tone that is appropriately hideous.

The premiere was held at Carnegie Hall on August 30, 1923. Proceeds were donated to the American Legion's fund drive for a mountain camp for veterans. Regular showings at advanced prices began at the Astor Theater on September 2. The picture received excellent reviews and drew huge crowds. Laemmle was so pleased that he commissioned an Austrian sculptor, A. Finta, to make a bust of Chaney as Quasimodo, which was installed in the lobby in anticipation of a long engagement. A special program was held at the Astor to celebrate the 100th performance on October 22, and another for the 200th showing during an entire week of late December. The picture was about 12,000 feet long during this special engagement, with a running time of 220 minutes. It was later cut to about 10,000 feet.

On February 17, 1924, *Hunchback* left the Astor to begin its first regular price release. Carl Edouarde, musical director of the Mark Strand Theater in New York, assisted by composer-orchestrator Cecil Copping, arranged an entirely new score for a 50-piece orchestra, mixed chorus, soloists and

The dying Quasimodo.

chimes. Domenico Savino composed the "love theme," "Twilight Hour," and classics by Arcadelt, Suk, Delsaux, Fourdrain and others were utilized.

In 1929, plans were formulated to remake *Hunchback* as a talkie, utilizing the same sets and props that had been created for the original. Chaney, now under contract to MGM, was not available to re-create his role, and the other actor considered for the part, Conrad Veidt, returned to his native Germany after hearing his heavily accented performance in the part-talking versions of two other films. The Depression had placed Universal in financial straits which made production of a picture of such scope impractical, so Laemmle had to content himself with a reissue of the original with a new musical score synchronized on disks. Recorded under the supervision of Roy Hunter, the orchestra was conducted by Heinz Roemheld with original music by Roemheld and Sam A. Perry augmented with library music.

Remake plans resurfaced in 1931 with Bela Lugosi as the prospective Quasimodo. A new script was written and during the next four years Boris Karloff, Henry Hull, Peter Lorre and Edward G. Robinson were mentioned as possible Quasimodos. The project was still pending at the time Universal was bought by a group of financiers in March, 1936. With the departure of the Laemmle family and friends, the new owners set about establishing a new image in which Gothic spectacle had no place.

Three years later, *Hunchback* was remade, superbly, by RKO-Radio, with Charles Laughton.

The Hunchback of Notre Dame

RKO built a new cathedral and environs at the RKO Ranch in Encino. A French version, released in the U.S. in 1957, featured Anthony Quinn and Gina Lollobrigida. Anthony Hopkins was Quasimodo in an admirable TV production.

After more than six decades, the 1923 film has attained almost legendary status. Laemmle's long-time right-hand man, Robert Cochrane, said an interesting thing about it a long time ago:

"The great pictures... were, almost without exception, productions which never would have been made if the question of whether or not they should be attempted had been left to a popular vote. You could count in a minute all the people who predicted the great success of *The Hunchback of Notre Dame.*"

—George E. Turner

Carl Laemmle *presents a Universal Super-Jewel production; directed by* Wallace Worsley; *based on the book by* Victor Hugo; *adapted by* Perley Poore Sheehan; *scenario by* Edward T. Lowe; *photographed by* Robert Newhard, ASC; *film editors,* Sidney Singerman, Maurice Pivar *and* Edward Curtiss; *art directors,* Elmer E. Sheeley *and* Sidney Ullman; *added photography by* Tony Kornmann, ASC, Virgil Miller, ASC, Charles Stumar, ASC, Stephen S. Norton, ASC; *photographic effects by* Philip H. Whitman, ASC, *and* Friend F. Baker, ASC; *supervised by* Irving G. Thalberg; *production manager,* George M. Stallings; *sculptures by* Finn Froelich *and* Charles Gemora; *costume supervision,* Col. Gordon McGee; *assistant art directors,* Stephen Goosson, Charles D. Hall; *technical director,* Archie Hall; *continuity,* Charlotte Woods; *production assistants,* Edgar Stein, Capt. Albert Conti; *unit manager,* William J. Koenig; *electrical engineer,* Arthur Shadur; *lighting effects,* Harry D. Brown, Earl Miller; *lighting crew,* Carl Gotham, Bud Garner, G.H. Merhoff, Soldier Graham, Fred Seelock, Eddie Barry, Bert Kohler, Eric von Miessel, Wayne West; *assistant directors,* Jack Sullivan, James Dugan, William Wyler; *art titles,* Fred W. Archer, ASC; *stillmen,* Jack Freulich, ASC, Henry Freulich, ASC; *casting,* Fred Datig; *music (1923) arranged by* Hugo Riesenfeld *featuring special themes by* Henry Baron *and* Sol Paul Levy; *keyboard score (1923) arranged by* Max Winkler; *music (1924) arranged by* Carl Eduoarde *and* Cecil Copping, *featuring "Twilight Hour" by* Domenico Savino; *music (1928) arranged and composed by* Heinz Roemheld *and* Sam A. Perry *and recorded by* C. Roy Hunter; *length c. 12,000 feet; released September 6, 1923.*

Quasimodo, Lon Chaney; *Esmeralda,* Patsy Ruth Miller; *Phoebus,* Norman Kerry; *Clopin,* Ernest Torrence; *Mme. de Gondelaurier,* Kate Lester; *Jehan,* Brandon Hurst; *Gringoire,* Raymond Hatton; *King Louis XI,* Tully Marshall; *Dom Claude,* Nigel de Brulier; *King's Chamberlain,* Edwin Wallock; *Justice of the Court,* John Cossar; *M. Neufchatel,* Harry L. Van Meter; *Crazy Godule,* Gladys Brockwell; *Marie,* Eulalie Jensen; *Fleur de Lys,* Winifred Bryson; *M. le Torteru,* Nicolai de Ruiz; *Josephus,* William Parke Sr.; *Charmolu's Assistant,* W. Ray Myers; *Charmolu,* Roy Laidlaw; *Hook-hand,* Robert Kortman; *Fat Man,* Harry Holman; *Double for Chaney,* Joe Bonomo; *and* Ethan Laidlaw, Al Ferguson, John George, George MacQuarrie, Albert MacQuarrie, Jay Hunt, Harrison DeVere, Pearl Tupper, Eva Lewis, Jane Sherman, Helen Brunneau, Gladys Johnston, Lydia Yeamans Titus, Alex Manuel, Arthur Hurni, Rene Traveletti.

2

The Bat Thrice Told

Ranking alongside Chaplin and von Stroheim as an individualistic and eccentric actor-producer-writer-director of unusual movies, Roland West made only a dozen features during his 15 years in the film industry.

Numbers 7, 10 and 11 were versions of the old Mary Roberts Rinehart-Avery Hopwood stage play, *The Bat*. The first *Bat*, made in 1926, was a silent picture. The other two were talkies – hence their retitling to *The Bat Whispers* – which were filmed together in 1930, one being shot in the standard 35mm format and the other in a 65mm system called Magnifilm. Although they share a common storyline, differences in the handling of each is considerable.

West, whose real name was Van Ziemer, was born in 1887 in Cleveland, Ohio, the son of noted stage actress Margaret Van Tassel. By age 17 he was playing juveniles in New York and soon began devising crime playlets as vaudeville acts for other performers. In 1915, he formed a partnership with Joseph M. Schenck, then an executive of the Loew's theater chain, to produce movies to be written and directed by West. With a capitalization of

$27,000 they produced *Lost Souls*, which was bought by Fox and released as *A Woman's Honor* (1916). It was amateurish, but their next, *Deluxe Annie* (1918), with Mrs. Schenck – the popular Norma Talmadge – hit the mark. A stage play produced and written by West in 1918, *The Unknown Purple*, proved a popular hit as well. West by this time was wealthy and only made a movie or wrote a play when the fancy struck him.

In 1921 he returned to filmmaking with two crook dramas, *The Silver Lining* and *Nobody*, both with Mrs. West – Jewel Carmen. He really hit his stride with the movie version of *The Unknown Purple* (1923), a fanciful tale of a scientist who discovers the secret of invisibility. In the release prints a purple glow was introduced to indicate the presence of the vengeful scientist.

Both *The Monster* (1925) with Lon Chaney and *The Bat* (1926) were based on stage mystery-farces, which were much in vogue at the time. They are the only West silent films known to have survived. Both have much of the look of the German fantasy films of the period.

The Bat starred Jewel Carmen and was designed by William Cameron Menzies, whose influence upon West was profound. It was photographed by Arthur Edeson, ASC, assisted by a young Gregg Toland (later ASC), and had miniatures and effects by the highly imaginative Ned Herbert Mann.

The picture was among the missing until 1987, when a deteriorating nitrate print of all but the first reel was discovered in a collection donated by

Above: *Emily Fitzroy, Jewel Carmen, Jack Pickford, Louise Fazenda and Eddie Gribbon in* The Bat. *Below: Gustav von Seyffertitz, Chester Morris, Maude Eburne, Charles Dow Clark, Una Merkel, William Bakewell, Spencer Charters and Ben Bard in* The Bat Whispers.

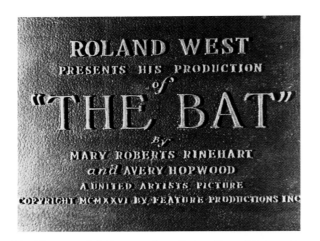

Dr. Raymond J. Bungard to Boise State University. The print was sent to UCLA film archivist Robert Gitt, who was at that time involved with the restoration of both versions of *The Bat Whispers*.

As the print was examined on the bench the ravages of time became all too apparent. Gitt said that if the film had surfaced three months later it might have remained "lost." The ends of most reels, wound tightly on their cores, were crumbling into powder so that sometimes only single frames could be salvaged and "frozen" in the optical printer. Reel nine was the worst, being very splicy and missing perhaps 200 feet. Overall the print was shrunken, brittle and badly buckled. Sprocket holes were worn, cracking and tearing out to the edge. The first test "breathed," weaving in and out of focus so badly that the lab, Film Technology Company, immersed the entire film in redimensioning solution for two weeks. Stability was greatly improved but the film still required step printing with a curved gate to bend the buckled film at a gentle angle.

Meantime, Dr. Bungard and Tom Trusky of the university sifted the minutiae of 20 years seeking clues to the whereabouts of reel one. They succeeded, locating the unique roll of nitrate in May 1988. Save for a handful of deteriorated shots, *The Bat* is now intact.

The rediscovery of a lost film, particularly one that was so well received and so influential in its day, always carries an attendant danger of unfulfilled expectations. The films themselves, of course, don't change; tastes change, circumstances change, and we of the audience change most of all. *The Bat* is not quite the masterpiece one might have expected; indeed it is not as vibrant as certain later examples of the mystery-comedy genre such as *The Cat and the Canary* and *Seven Footprints to Satan*.

Historically, it *is* an important film, being the model for all that followed. It was the long-awaited filming of *the* theatrical smash of its day, akin to the impact *Amadeus* or *A Chorus Line* would have on theatergoers in the 1980s. As a thriller film it is second only to *The Phantom of the Opera* for the nightmares it gave an earlier generation. One mid-western boy named Ray Bradbury recalled *The Bat* with such terror and delight over a quarter century later that he imparted to it some of the life experience of his autobiographical juvenile hero in "Dandelion Wine."

The opening reel is packed with unique imagery. Even the main and credit titles are a surprise, etched in a series of metallic plates. The list of players is presented as a crawl, which is most unusual for the period. "Can you keep a secret?" the picture patron is asked at the start and beseeched not to reveal the villain's identity to future patrons and thereby spoil their pleasure.

The play and novel were heavy on dialogue. For this and other reasons, West rewrote considerably for the screen adaptation:

The Bat, a master criminal, has sent a note to Gideon Bell, millionaire gem collector, daring him to be in his library alone at midnight. Police gather at Bell's skyscraper apartment to protect him. As the clock strikes 12, the Bat lowers himself from the roof, strangles Bell while the police are congratulating themselves in the sitting room, and escapes with valuable jewels. Next night, the Bat is about to lower himself through the skylight of a bank when he spots another looter inside. The rival stuffs $500,000 into a satchel and escapes. The Bat pursues but loses the burglar at the estate of Courtley Flem-

The Bat slides down from a high building to his car.

20

The reclusive millionaire, Bell (Andre de Beranger) in his skyscraper eyrie.

ing, president of the bank. Fleming is supposedly vacationing in Europe and has leased the country mansion to Mrs. Van Gorder, a wealthy recluse. Other residents are her niece, Dale; her addle-brained maid, Lizzie, and an eccentric Japanese caretaker, Billy.

Soon the occupants are disturbed by odd noises and warnings by a disembodied voice. Brook Bailey, a bank cashier under suspicion in the burglary, is engaged to Dale; she persuades her aunt to hire Brook as a gardener so the police will not find him. Having seen the Bat at a window, the occupants feel certain that the money is hidden in the house. Mrs. Van Gorder hires a private detective by telephone. A Dr. Wells arrives to tell Mrs. Van Gorder that he has a cable from Fleming requesting that the place be vacated before Fleming returns from Europe. She refuses to leave.

Dale and Brook search for a reputed secret room, suspecting the bank money may be there. Richard Fleming, the banker's nephew, arrives and finds the blueprint showing the location of the room.

The Bat appears and shoots young Fleming, escaping with the blueprint. Dale retains part of the blueprint she had torn from Richard's hand.

A man arrives and introduces himself as police detective Moletti, on the trail of the Bat. Anderson, the detective hired by Mrs. Van Gorder, also arrives and proves to be an incompetent bump-

Sojin, dwarfed by the Fleming mansion.

21

Ned Mann's establishing shots of the city, a suburban bank, and the country mansion. The full moon and a flying bat are unifying motifs.

kin. Moletti gets the piece of blueprint from Dale. Wells slugs him and locks him in a closet. Meantime, a dazed, bedraggled man wanders in and collapses. Lizzie sets a bear trap in the yard, hoping to catch the Bat.

Dale chances upon an entrance to the hidden room. The door swings shut, trapping her with the Bat. The Bat turns from her as he sees an intruder making off with a satchel containing the money. Dale escapes as the Bat struggles with the man and kills him. Returning, Dale and her friends find the body of the bank president. Moletti comes in, locks Wells up, and goes to investigate the secret room. Mrs. Van Gorder finds the bank funds hidden behind a hamper.

Outside, the garage bursts into flame. The dazed man regains his senses, draws a revolver, and explains that the Bat has set the fire to lure them outside. He bids them to place the loot on a table, turn out the lights, and get back into the shadows. When the Bat enters through a window, the mystery man gets the drop on him. The Bat leaps out the window and almost reaches safety when Lizzie's bear trap closes on his leg. Unmasked, the Bat proves to be the supposed Moletti. The Bat had overcome the real Moletti – the stranger – and taken his place. At the fadeout the exultant Lizzie faints away as the obviously insane Bat tells them he'll be back.

The story is told with a pervading use of monumental shadows and many an expressionistic flourish. In one scene a shadow, thought at first to be that of the Bat, proves to be a moth which has alighted on the headlight of an auto.

The first shot proper fades in with two glowing spots that are slowly revealed as the burning eyes of a stylized, grotesque bat, fangs bared and huge wings spread. We dissolve to a superb Ned Mann miniature of a stylized city at night under the baleful gaze of a full moon. A lone bat hovers, circles the skyscraper, then alights on the rooftop. Inside the penthouse apartment we discover the sinister millionaire Gideon Bell, swathed in black, alone in his palatial chambers. Huge candlesticks flank Bell at his desk, while the moonlit cityscape is seen beyond the multiple glass panes of two dramatic picture windows. As the villian murders Bell and steals the Favre Emeralds, cameraman Arthur Edeson, ASC, imbues the room with a distorted sense of moonlight, invoked again during the Bat's flight across the rooftop as he skirts demonically past a huge frosted glass skylight. The moon is a motif throughout; the subsequent robbery at the Oakdale Bank is presented in another glorious Mann miniature under the same baleful moon.

Edeson's camera is shooting past the silhouette of a scraggly tree as again, a lone bat circles in the sky and descends to the roof of the bank. The supernatural effect is complete as we cut to the real bat at the bank's skylight, delving into a devilish array of tools from his kit to select the precise instruments to accomplish his heist.

The Bat is more literal and hideous than he ever appeared on stage or in subsequent films. On stage his disguise was merely a black handkerchief; here he is outfitted with a literal bat's head with fangs and long upswept ears bristling with fur, and endowed with the unbridled energy of a demon.

Unlike *The Bat Whispers,* there is not a single camera move in the entire film. Some of it becomes stagebound, as is to be expected, but the film's major attributes are masterful art direction and impeccable photography. The Fleming Mansion is mock-Tudor in its exteriors and passionately '20s Art Nouveau in its interiors. The eccentricity of the rooms with their 18-foot-high doors and harsh black pools of shadow take us finally to the genuine "old dark house" realm, as do the back-lit, grime-encrusted window panes of the cobweb-festooned trunk room where the Bat prowls. Edeson maintains throughout the delicate quality of moonlight pouring into the large rooms. The night exteriors of the ominously sculpted gardens of the estate are nightmarish when we catch a glimpse of the Bat lolling on an outstretched tree branch, patiently waiting for a victim to pass beneath.

West's major failing was as a director of actors. His forte was the manipulation of light and shadow. In one shot, the creature's shadow takes on a life of its own and closes a door, pointing the way to West's most distinguished use of shadows in *The Bat Whispers.* Stage space and darkness are used profitably in the sequence where Detective Anderson is attacked by Dr. Wells. West stages this as a single take in long shot with the detective sitting downstage in the study. The angle affords us a view through the doorway into two rooms upstage. Dr. Wells appears on the staircase in the farthest room and upon reaching the landing, snaps off the light. There is a beat or two before he skulks from the blackness and pauses in the second room, again extinguishing the light. A longer pause, then he emerges into the study and switches off that light. Moonlight streams into the room from the tall window, and as the startled Anderson looks about, the Doctor slinks up from behind into the moonbeams and bludgeons the detective. A sequence like this probably would not work in a sound film, but in the dream-like realm of silent film it sums up the basic sensation of a nightmare: something advancing

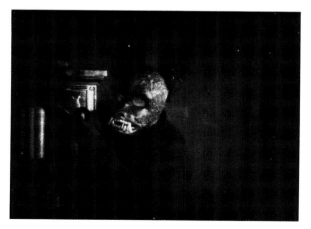

Frames from The Bat *show stylish night lighting by Arthur Edeson.*

23

upon the dreamer, sensed but unseen and moving in darkness to bring him harm.

The performances are a checkerboard, with only Emily Fitzroy as the spinster and Louise Fazenda as the maid really shining with the material. Most unfortunate is the colorless casting of stage singer Tullio Carminati, a Dalmatian count, as the ersatz detective. Perhaps one is spoiled by Chester Morris' crazily overblown portrayal in the 1930 film; his villain seems almost *more* dangerous once unmasked! Carminati is so perfunctory and bland that it is hard to credit his detective with the nerve, agility or wit to pull off the Bat's escapades.

But visually the film is quite fine. It is often strikingly composed and lit, turning to some of the silent medium's most decorative effects for climaxes: the Bat's dialogue gliding down his flashlight beam in an illustrated title card, or red-tinted stock for the

climactic fire (an effect West suggested using again in his screenplay for *The Bat Whispers).* Properly presented as entertainment *The Bat* is tremendous fun.

Similarly Germanic in appearance was West's next (and last) silent film, *The Dove,* (1928) with Norma Talmadge and Noah Beery, for which Menzies won the first Academy Award for art direction (in conjunction with his work in *The Tempest).* Cinematographer Oliver T. Marsh, ASC, provided strikingly mobile camera moves.

Alibi (1929), filmed on the United Artists lot in Hollywood in both sound and silent versions, brought together the team of West, Menzies, Hal C. Kern, an extraordinary film editor with whom West had developed great rapport, Ned Mann, and – for the first time – the cinematographer whose style and imagination best fulfilled West's visions: Ray June, ASC. It also brought into the company the actor who interpreted the hero-villains of West's imagination to perfection, Chester Morris, whose sharp, angular features seemed a part of the world created for *Alibi.*

This police melodrama, which today seems in some moments as old-fashioned as a tintype and in others exceptionally fresh, is filled with oblique compositions, painted shadows, ingenious special effects, and swift, unconventional camera action. The latter was accomplished despite the fact that June and the camera were enclosed in a sound-proof booth throughout. As a breakthrough in the early days of "talkies," *Alibi* is second only to *Bulldog Drummond,* which Samuel Goldwyn produced on the same stages a few months later. But *The Bat Whispers* is the team's *magnum opus* and (arguably) the *meisterwerk* of comedy-mystery movies.

The project was announced in January 1930 under the smokescreen title, *Love in Chicago,* and production began late that summer under the working title of *Whispers.* West denied the rumor that he was remaking *The Bat,* but he obviously was being less than frank about the project. Production proceeded in West's usual secretive manner at the United Artists Studio under sponsorship of his longtime partner, Joseph M. Schenck, then chairman of the board of United Artists.

There were three weeks of tests and rehearsals and seven weeks of shooting. Production wrapped early in October. Three edited negatives resulted: the domestic 35mm edition, a foreign version made up of out-takes, and the Magnifilm version. All have running times of about 85 minutes, and all three are still extant.

Menzies, who had become supervising art director for United Artists, was buried in work.

ROLAND WEST'S
PRODUCTION OF
"THE BAT"

A COMEDY- MYSTERY-DRAMA

The raided bank!

The haunted halls!

The hidden chamber!

The flitting Omen of Ill!

The ghostly shades!

The disguised strangers!

The hysterical maid!

And the stirring tempo of a thousand terrors, gasps and *LAUGHS!*

By MARY ROBERTS RINEHART and AVERY HOPWOOD

From the stage play produced by WAGENHALS and KEMPER

Adapted and directed by ROLAND WEST

West, therefore, obtained Paul Roe Crawley, an art director who had done some excellent designs for silent films such as *Beau Brummel* (1924) and *The Fire Brigade* (1927). He was then working as assistant and chief draughtsman to Menzies and had also been assistant to the great Joseph Urban for two years. He seemed to possess the same kind of flair and imagination as his masters.

For *The Bat Whispers* Crawley designed 110 sets ranging from small modular pieces to the enormous rooms, garden and grounds of a huge country mansion. These were constructed on two adjoining stages where all sequences but one were to be filmed. They were in outsize scale with high walls and massive doors. The garden, where the climax of the film takes place, was lined with box hedges 15 feet high. A bank burglary sequence was filmed at night in a Los Angeles suburban bank, but was lighted and photographed in such a way as to have the same larger-than-life, impressionistic quality as the studio sets.

The visual *motif* of the picture is one of shadows – gigantic, menacing black shapes that

The Bat Whispers: *Morris (right) slaps the cuffs on Von Seyffertitz while Grayce Hampton watches warily.*

dominate almost every shot. Many of these were painted into the sets by an artist named Harvey Myers. Painted shadows were used in the German films as early as 1919 in *The Cabinet of Dr. Caligari*, a film which was deliberately made to resemble the paintings of certain expressionist artists. West had used painted shadows in several of his films, not (as has been said of *Caligari*) because of a shortage of lighting equipment, but to give the cameraman greater latitude in lighting sets and characters.

Ray June began his film career in 1914 at the Wharton Bros. Studios in his home town of Ithaca, New York, starting as a lab man. Before he was 20 he had become a cameraman, specializing in serials. He was also a master of special effects cinematography whose in-camera multiple exposure and matte work was much in demand. *Alibi* was the picture that moved him into the top rank of cinematographers and kept him at United Artists for seven years.

25

June had the sort of resilience that made him an ideal man for a picture like *The Bat Whispers,* which demanded unusual inventiveness.

"One thing I always try to keep in mind: a good cameraman must never let himself become willing to do things always in the same way," June once said. "It's one thing to develop an original style; it's something very different to let yourself fall into a routine and do things in routine fashion, just because it's easier or quicker." He also believed that "adverse conditions are a challenge to any cinematographer. Usually, if he meets the challenge with confidence, he'll come up with far better results than he had imagined. Many of the great achievements in cinematography have come about because of the more-than-usual hurdles that had to be overcome."

Robert L. Planck (later ASC) was brought in as second cameraman, but soon was reassigned as director of photography of the wide film version. He was 27 at the time. June called him "a very excellent man. Uses his head and is on the job all the time. I think he will be one of our outstanding cinematographers in a very few years." Stuart Thompson (later ASC) replaced Planck on the 35mm unit, with Bert Shipman as assistant. Stanley Cortez (later ASC), who had been assisting Hal Mohr at Pathé and Universal, seconded Planck with the Magnifilm camera. June acted as lighting consultant for the wide film unit.

The decision to film *The Bat Whispers* in a wide film version was solely that of West, who personally footed the bill for the extra costs. He purchased the camera, had a 65mm projector built, and installed a 38-foot screen on one of the stages. This screen supplanted its counterpart in the studio projection room, which was not wide enough to permit critical viewing of the 65mm rushes.

"Larger theaters are being built," a press release of September 1930 quoted West during production. Such theaters, West opined, "require larger screens because we have reached the last magnitude of the old 35mm film. If theaters enlarge the narrow film it loses its sharpness. The new 65mm film on a huge screen gives full detail. It also enhances the stereoscopic effect so that there is no distortion of the players to patrons sitting at the extreme side of a theater. The camera has the same range of vision as the human eye."

There is a question as to what wide film camera was used. It was not, as has been claimed, a 70mm Fox Grandeur camera, but a specially made 65mm camera with a 22 x 45mm frame size. Stanley Cortez recalls that it arrived in a large crate from

The Greatest of All Mystery Thrillers!

You'll be pop-eyed with excitement as you watch the greatest of all underworld geniuses on the supreme exploit of his daring career!

JOSEPH M. SCHENCK PRESENTS

ROLAND WEST'S

"THE BAT WHISPERS"

WITH CHESTER MORRIS

Based upon a stage play by Mary Roberts Rinehart and Avery Hopwood which was produced by Wagenhals and Kemper.

UNITED ARTISTS PICTURE

George K. Spoor, Chicago camera manufacturer who had been involved in the development of the 63mm Spoor-Bergren Natural Vision system. Planck devised a special viewfinder and a huge tricycle dolly, electronically controlled, for the camera.

To create the lightning that punctuates many scenes at the Fleming estate, Bill McClellan, chief electrician, invented a new variety of scissors-type lightning machines which were installed in soundproof booths on wheels. These were considerably larger than the machines then in use because of the necessity of throwing bolts across the broader areas of the wide film shots. McClellan also installed lighting dimmer panels equipped with automatic electric stopwatches which were widely imitated at other studios.

For a scene in which the camera races behind Morris as he runs through the garden, the team of June, Planck and studio technician Charles Cline rigged the longest indoor trolley shot that had been made up to that time; the camera runway was 300 feet long and cameras were suspended on steel cables 30 feet in the air. For $400, Cline built a contrivance to *zoom* the camera rapidly from vantage points ranging from eight inches to six feet above the floor. It was mounted on a light truck 24 feet long and was remarkably silent in operation. Cline, incidentally, was one of the finest technicians in the field, credited with the invention of the crab dolly.

The numerous unusual miniature shots that are interspersed throughout were planned by Mann, a former artist and professional auto racer who had entered films as an actor about 1920. He gravitated toward the special effects field, and in 1926 created many of the celebrated fantasy scenes of Douglas Fairbanks' *The Thief of Bagdad*. The miniatures for *The Bat Whispers* were photographed by two specialists often associated with Mann, Edward Colman and Harry Zech (both later ASC). Like most leading effects cinematographers of the time, Colman began his career filming comedies. He had been with United Artists as first "trick cameraman" (the designation of the period for special effects cameraman) since 1927. Zech, who Ray June called "one of the best miniature and trick men in the business, as he proved on *Hell's Angels*," had worked in this field for nearly 20 years and was one of the first specialists in projection process photography.

Virtuoso cinematography, vast sets and fantastic miniature work make *The Bat Whispers* the most spectacular of the many similar comedy thrillers made during the silent and early sound periods. The sets dominate the actors, who (in the standard version) appear often in the lower part of the frame as tiny figures dwarfed by looming shadows. The Bat himself, in flapping black cape and cowl (looking very much like a famed cartoon hero he may

well have inspired) slithers in and out of darkness like a shadow incarnate. Sometimes he is seen in silhouette as he slides down a rope from Mr. Bell's townhouse or is limned by flashes of lightning as he crouches in treetops, leaps upon a victim, or glides toward the house. In one shuddery scene he crawls along the floor and again he is glimpsed crouching over a corpse like some giant, deformed rodent. He is backlighted in the scene in which he shoots young Fleming on the stairs. Often only his shadow is shown – flitting hugely across the facade of the Oakdale Bank, creeping along the walls of the house and bleeding in and out of other shadows.

The Bat's most frightening appearance occurs when Dale is trapped with him in the secret room. His shadow appears on the wall, wings outspread. The wings fold as the shadow shrinks and changes shape until it becomes a black puddle on the floor and lower wall. Then the Bat himself emerges, stalking erratically toward the camera and becoming increasingly larger until his eyes almost fill the frame. The sounds of thunder and the sinister whispering of the Bat add to the genuine terror of the scene.

The miniatures are carefully intercut with full scale action and in some instances linked by

Syd D'Albrook, Wilson Benge and DeWitt Jennings with the murdered millionaire, Richard Tucker.

Bakewell's disguise as an itinerant gardener fools nobody.

Morris shows Clark and Charters where they stand.

camera movements. The opening shot of the film is a clock tower; the camera pulls back to show an expanse of city at night against a turbulent sky. The camera then looks down the front of a towering building and abruptly hurtles towards the street and its moving cars. The camera halts and tilts to a live-action cut of police headquarters with actors and real autos. Later, as the police arrive at the Bell townhouse, the action blends into a miniature shot as the camera wings swiftly up the face of the building and into Bell's open window on the top floor. This cuts almost imperceptibly to a full scale shot in which the camera races across the room to look over Bell's shoulder at the note he is reading at his desk.

There are more striking miniatures: the camera rides atop a model locomotive as it speeds into the outskirts of a miniature city; it follows an auto chase through the woods in which a crook releases a smoke screen to baffle his pursuers; it flies over the grounds of the Fleming estate and into the

Morris and Merkel in a scene typical of the dynamic compositions that abound in The Bat Whispers.

house, moving through the hallways; it watches the burning garage as seen from the main house.

There is little attempt at stark realism in any of this. The lighting is purely dramatic with hardly a thought of the practical. The startling camera moves, the oversized sets and props, and even the stylized acting of the principals, all add up to a picture which creates its own form of reality, much as *Citizen Kane* did a decade later.

Dialogue of the stage original was pared to such a point that when the actors *do* speak, their voices sometimes startle. The chiming of a tower clock accompanies the opening titles and the soundtrack abounds with such unnerving effects as thunder, creaking doors, and a cannonball bouncing down the stairs.

Chester Morris is very much the central figure of the show, giving an effectively overplayed performance. Morris' eyes were damaged permanently by the strong lights used for casting the Bat's shadow. (Incidentally, Morris was never satisfied with his acting in the three pictures he made for West). The picture also owes a great deal to the calm assurance of matronly Grayce Hampton; to the eccentric comedy of Maude Eburne, Spencer Charters and Charles Dow Clark; and to such menaces as Gustav von Seyffertitz, Ben Bard, and Hugh Hunt-

ley. Una Merkel, seen here as an attractive ingenue, was later to prove that her real forte was comedy.

There is almost no music in the film, only a dance tune heard on a radio and a romantic theme for the end titles. However, United Artists' distinguished musical director, composer-violinist Hugo Riesenfeld, lent his expertise to the sound department as a consultant. West was determined that whatever sounds were heard would have meaning and that there would be none of the non-stop dialogue and non-selective noises that were cluttering most sound tracks of the time.

The ending of the picture makes eloquent use of sound: Tied to a tree, the Bat whispers, "Now you think you've got me, eh? There never was a jail built strong enough to hold the Bat. And after I've paid my respects to your cheap lock-up, I shall return, at night. The Bat always flies at night – and always in a straight line." As he laughs insanely, Lizzie faints.

In an epilogue, the Bat slides down a rope onto a stage and emerges from a puff of smoke as

29

Charters and Bakewell have to calm the unnerved Clark.

Chester Morris, who implores the audience not to reveal the Bat's identity. Otherwise, "he's heart-broken...he goes around for days killing people without the slightest enjoyment for his work."

When Gitt decided to restore the picture he located the existing elements of *The Bat Whispers* with The Mary Pickford Company. She had purchased the property in the late 1930s with the intention of remaking it with Lillian Gish and Humphrey Bogart. Examining the holdings, Gitt was faced with a bewildering array of elements.

The camera negative for the 35mm domestic version was not there, having been lost long ago to Astor Pictures, who handled it in reissue in later years. All that remained of this edition was a 1930 lavender print and positive soundtrack. The 1930 equivalent of a fine grain positive, the lavender was grainy and milky with absolutely no sparkle. Fortunately it did not have to be used as the collection also held a 35mm original camera negative compiled of alternate takes for overseas use. Gitt weighed the wisdom of using this negative for the restoration but shot for shot the domestic and overseas versions were almost identical. Gitt opted for maximum pictorial quality. The elements were in remarkably good condition considering their age, although there was some shrinkage and the nitrate sound-track was beginning to turn brown. "We really got to these materials just in time," says Gitt.

YCM Labs of Burbank initially made a wet-gate showprint from the camera negative, and it is of superb quality. But one showprint does not constitute preservation; once the timings were checked by Felipe Herba, YCM then made a wet-gate, fine grain preservation master.

"We also decided to copy the very end of the picture from the American lavender and preserve it separately, as the end titles played differently and had slightly more exit music," says Gitt. "This way, we have it should a historian need to consult it."

Providentially, the holdings included these widescreen elements of *The Bat Whispers:* 65mm camera picture negative; 65mm master positive lavender; 35mm optical sound negative for Magnifilm recorded at 112½ feet-per-minute; 35mm positive optical soundtrack for Magnifilm. Curiously there was also a dubbed down, 35mm positive optical soundtrack for the wide film version running at 90 feet-per-minute and labelled "for reduced picture," suggesting that United Artists seriously considered preparing optically-reduced widescreen prints on standard 35mm film in the manner of MGM's Realife process, which *was* distributed this way. As one Schenck to another, it's conceivable that brother Nicholas of Loews/MGM considered providing Joseph of UA with an outlet for product!

The widescreen soundtracks (both negative and positive) were shrunken and curling. To make a new print from the shrunken negative and then re-record it would induce flutter, so the nitrate positive 112½ feet-per-minute track was played on a

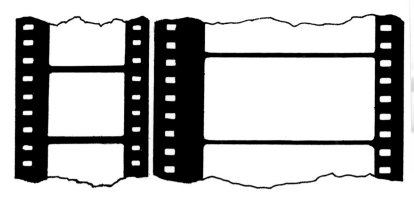

Actual dimensions of 35mm and Magnifilm frames.

sound dummy and transferred to 35mm magnetic stock by Ralph Sargent at Film Technology Company with an optical pick-up that could handle the accelerated speed. Clicks and pops were then carefully scraped from the mag track by hand with a razor blade. The Western Electric variable density track proved to have a very wide dynamic range, with the thunder effects deliberately ear-shattering against low dialogue. The new track was *not* compressed but left full range, with dbx™ noise reduction applied only to sections of absolute silence.

When Don Hagans of YCM Labs first reviewed the camera negative he was encouraged; it corresponded to modern standard 65mm. The archaic shape and sprocket allocations of Grandeur 70mm had forced MoMA to make their preservation masters of *The Big Trail* in 35mm anamorphic. However, Linwood Dunn, ASC, donated to the project a 65mm Bell & Howell printer, allowing Richard Dayton and Pete Comandini to make a direct B&W 65mm fine grain master of *The Bat Whispers* on Kodak 5235 stock. A compressed air system in the printing gate was used to overcome the tendency of the 65mm negative to curl, ensuring film registration. The lab was not able to time the fine grain scene-to-scene, but cinematographers Planck and June had done their job exceedingly well; they had lit their sets so carefully 57 years before that the overall exposures were consistent and yielded an excellent one-light print.

Gitt cherished the idea of presenting *The Bat Whispers* in a 70mm showprint (70mm is the print format for 65mm negative), but 70mm *print* stock is only manufactured now in color. Not only would color print stock compromise the tone of the B&W image, but it is expensive and could only be shown at a handful of institutions equipped for 70mm projection. Gitt elected to make a B&W 35mm reduction dupe anamorphic negative, and a print from that. As the original photography has an aspect ratio of 2:1 versus today's CinemaScope standard of 2.35:1, a black border was left on either side. This way the widescreen version can be presented now by any facility equipped with standard 35mm

Von Seyffertitz and Morris.

31

Actual frames (enlarged one-third) from the Magnifilm version.

projectors and anamorphic lenses, although in the future it will still be possible to strike a direct 70mm print (even if on color stock) from the 65mm B&W safety film fine grain master.

Gitt was surprised to find a slight difference between the 65mm camera negative and the 65mm lavender made in 1930. "They must have changed their minds after the initial previews and recut the ending in the negative, but only after the lavender had been prepared. In the camera negative, Chester Morris delivers his 'mad scene' closing lines in close-up, just as he does in the 35mm version. As he laughs there is a chemical fade out in the negative and we go into the epilogue. When I examinied the lavender I discovered that West had originally kept this scene in long-shot, with the entire cast surrounding Morris. As he delivers his last line, a theater curtain closes over the scene and the camera pulls back to reveal the interior of a theater for the epilogue, as though we've been watching a stage performance! Reasoning that *this* was the way West originally intended to end the film, we went back to the lavender and copied this ending, along with about thirty seconds of additional curtain speech that Morris delivers. Both endings have been preserved, but the 'curtain' ending is the one we kept in the showprint."

The wide screen version plays very much like its junior version, though West uses fewer close-ups, substituting two-shots more suited compositionally to the 2:1 frame. The major disappointment with the widescreen version is that the most spectacular camera moves and effects of the miniature city and railway are rephotographed projected images from the 35mm version. The longer focal length lenses required for 65mm film are probably to blame; a 50mm lens in 35mm photography is roughly equivalent to a 100mm lens for 65mm photography. It must have proven difficult to maintain the proper scale of the miniatures with long lenses while holding any depth-of-field.

Indeed, the picture displays a uniformly shallow depth-of-field attributable to the limitations of the lenses, causing the cameramen to rack focus more often by need than design. The additional tendency of the lenses to induce slight distortion or softness at the edges of the frame can only make one marvel at how smoothly Planck dealt with the limitations of his highly experimental equipment. Where travelling shots *are* employed with miniature sets and photographed in 65mm (such as the emblematic "bat's eye" view of the mansion during a lightning storm) or in the overhead tracking shot pursuing Chester Morris through the garden, they are stunning.

William Bakewell, one of the picture's stars, recalls that "We actors had no idea it was being shot in widescreen – we were confused enough filming all through the night, from 7 p.m. to 7 a.m. – West felt he did his best work during those hours! He was a taciturn, bandy-legged, stocky little guy. He'd call for action, then turn on his heel and walk off into the back of the stage. He'd listen to the dialogue, and call 'cut' at the end of a scene. But he never watched a scene being taken. He was much more concerned with shadows and visual effects than he was with actors."

In 1930 it was believed that widescreen would be the next major, standard industry technology. We forget today that some dozen feature films were made and exhibited in this period in gauges ranging from 56mm to 70mm. Efforts to popularize wide film began in earnest late in 1929 at Fox, MGM, RKO-Radio, Paramount and Warner Brothers. Although some, such as Fox's *The Big Trail* and MGM's *Billy the Kid*, were impressive, boxoffice returns were negligible because fewer than 20 theaters, all in key cities, ran them.

The Bat Whispers is United Artists' only wide film picture of the period and the only one to address a mystery theme prior to the re-emergence of large format presentations in the 1950s. West's ideas were unique among producers who used wide film as a means to glorify the spectacular. He saw instead an opportunity to heighten realism and intimacy.

Theater owners as a rule failed to share West's enthusiasm for a process which would have called for any more expenditure than already had been poured into the conversion to sound. The thought of remodeling and adding special projection equipment was appalling at a time when theaters in alarming numbers were closing. Exhibitor hostility doomed the wide film concept while it was still in a fetal state. The Motion Picture Producers and Distributors of America delivered the *coup de grace* on December 16, 1930 when it forbade the industry "by word or gesture" to cause "the public's curiosity to be aroused about any new invention for at least two years." Until The Museum of Modern Art resurrected *The Big Trail* in 1985 from its Grandeur 70mm negatives, none of these films had been seen in over 50 years.

The cinematographers and most of the technical crew went on to further triumphs in motion pictures. West, who said he had lost interest in making movies, made only one more picture, *Corsair* (1931), with Chester Morris and Thelma Todd. Unfortunately, he is remembered more as a principal figure in the mystery surrounding the death of Miss Todd in 1935 than for his screen contributions. West died in 1952.

—Scott MacQueen, Mike Price and George Turner

The Bat

A Roland West *production; produced by* Feature Production, Inc.; *distributed by* United Artists Corporation; *by* Mary Roberts Rinehart *and* Avery Hopwood, *from the stage play produced by* Wagenhals and Kemper; *adapted and directed by* Roland West; *continuity by* Julien Josephson; *photography by* Arthur Edeson, ASC; *settings by* William Cameron Menzies; *titles by* George Marion Jr.; *assistants on production,* Frank Hall Crane, Thornton Freeland; *film editor,* Hal C. Kern; *technical effects,* Ned Herbert Mann; *production executive,* Joseph M. Schenck; *assistant cameraman,* Gregg Toland, ASC; *production manager,* Fred Stark; *business manager,* A.M. Brentinger; *length 8219 feet; released* March 15, 1926.

Players (as they appear): Gideon Bell, Andre de Beranger; *Man in Black Mask,* Charles Herzinger; *Miss Cornelia Van Gorder,* Emily Fitzroy; *Lizzie Allen,* Louise Fazenda; *Richard Fleming,* Arthur Houseman; *Dr. Wells,* Robert McKim; *Brook,* Jack Pickford; *Dale Ogden,* Jewel Carmen; *Billy,* Sojin Kamiyama; *Moletti,* Tullio Carminati; *Detective Anderson,* Eddie Gribbon; *The Unknown,* Lee Shumway.

The Bat Whispers

A Feature productions-Articinema Associates *production; released through* United Artists; *presented by* Joseph M. Schenck; *produced, directed and dialogued by* Roland West; *based on the stage play, "The Bat," by* Mary Roberts Rinehart *and* Avery Hopwood, *which was produced by* Wagenhals & Kemper; *photographed by* Ray June, ASC; *settings designed and executed by* Paul Roe Crawley; *film editor,* James Smith; *sound technician,* O.E. Lagerstrom; *assistant director,* Roger H. Heman; *dialogue director,* Charles H. Smith; *in charge of sound,* J.T. Reed; *sound and music consultant,* Dr. Hugo Riesenfeld; *production assistant,* Helen Hallett; *makeup artist,* S.E. Jennings; *paintings by* Thomas Lawless; *scenic artist,* Harvey Meyers; *electrical effects,* William McClellan; *special technician,* Charles Cline; *assistant cameramen,* Stuart Thompson, Bert Shipman; *special photography,* Edward Colman, Harry Zech; *running time, 85 minutes; released* November 13, 1930.

Players (in order of appearance): Police Lieutenant, Chance Ward; *Mr. Bell,* Richard Tucker; *The Butler,* Wilson Benge; *Police Captain,* DeWitt Jennings; *Police Sergeant,* Sydney D'Albrook; *Cop,* Charles Hamilton; *Man in Black Mask,* S.E. Jennings; *Cornelia van Gorder,* Grayce Hampton; *Lizzie Allen,* Maude Eburne; *The Caretaker,* Spencer Charters; *Dale van Gorder,* Una Merkel; *Brook,* William Bakewell; *Dr. Venrees,* Gustav Von Seyffertitz; *Detective Anderson,* Chester Morris; *Richard Fleming,* Hugh Huntley; *Detective Jones,* Charles Dow Clark; *The Unkown,* Ben Bard.

Special Credits-Magnifilm

Wide film photography, Robert H. Planck, ASC; *supervisor of photography,* Ray June, ASC; *film editor,* Hal C. Kern; *assistant cameraman,* Stanley Cortez, ASC; *running time, 85 minutes.*

3

The Flight of *Wings*

World War I, like all wars, was a dirty, tragic undertaking. It was also dramatic and colorful, certainly more so than some recent encounters in more enlightened times.

The combat aviators were the nearest thing to the questing knights of old the war offered. The rickety little fighter planes made the same demands on the pilots that a spirited steed demands of a horseman. Combat was close and personal. There was a code of chivalry that governed the gentlemen of the air and a spirit of adventure that was denied the poor blighters on the ground.

A young writer who had flown against the Germans when he was not yet 20, John Monk Saunders, wrote a novel called "Wings" in which he tried to capture the mystique of combat flying. In February 1926 he met with Jesse L. Lasky, who with Adolph Zukor headed what was then the largest American movie company, Paramount Pictures. Saunders expressed his belief that words were not sufficient to tell the story; only the motion picture could do it.

The more Lasky thought about it, the more he liked the idea.

Lasky envisioned a massive production that would become the successor to MGM's *The Big Parade* of 1925. The cost would be heavy; more, probably, than his associates would be willing to invest. *The Big Parade* had been possible due to the

Buddy Rogers finds the body of his pal, Richard Arlen.

cooperation of the Department of Defense; Lasky, therefore, told Saunders to go to Washington and try to get government assistance. Saunders recalled: "In such an event, Mr. Lasky said, he would bring the full resources of the Paramount Famous Lasky Corporation to bear upon the men and material provided." He left for Washington that night.

With moral support from Will H. Hays, head of the Motion Picture Producers and Distributors of America, Saunders interested Major General C. Mck. Saltzman, Chief of the Signal Corps, Major General John L. Hines, Chief of Staff, and Major General Mason M. Patrick, Chief of the Air Corps, in the project. Two weeks after his meeting with Saunders, Lasky was told by Secretary of War Dwight F. Davis that the War Department would cooperate with Paramount under certain conditions. Davis suggested that the military aspects could best be filmed in the San Antonio, Texas, area, home of Kelly Field and Camp Stanley.

The government's conditions were that the picture must be made in such a way that it could be construed as a training program, that the picture could not be released until it received War Department approval, that Paramount would pay for all damages incurred during production, that $10,000 in life insurance must be carried on each man who worked in the picture, and that the government's role in the matter must be kept a secret as long as possible.

Lasky convinced his associates to agree to the terms. In doing so, he went out on a shaky limb, as it was made clear to him that he would be held

Mechanic El Brendel and fresh pilots Arlen and Rogers at the flight line.

he showed promise and had the hard-boiled personality such a project would demand – but mostly because he had been a fighter pilot in the Lafayette Flying Corps during the war. This was a volunteer group of Americans who flew for the French forces before America entered the conflict.

About six months were required to get a script ready, cast the roles and assign the crew. By then preparations were being made in Texas and the Army showed every intention of making *Wings* what it later was called, "the *Big Parade* of the air." Pilots arrived from Crissy Field, California, from Langley Field, Virginia and Selfridge Field, Michigan, and smaller stations. Scott Field, Illinois, supplied balloon officers, crews and materials. Troops, tanks, artillery, explosives and miles of barbed wire arrived from Fort Sam Houston, Texas. All were assembled at Old Camp Stanley and Kelly Field.

Casting of the leading roles was restricted largely to the Paramount contract players. Richard Arlen was a natural choice, as he had been a combat flier in the Canadian RFC. Charles "Buddy" Rogers was young and anxious to learn to fly. Clara Bow, the much-publicized "*It* Girl," was an ideal romantic lead and had a strong audience following. The character parts were assigned to some first-rate actors, including H.B. Walthall, Louise Closser Hale and Richard Tucker.

A lanky contract player from Montana, Gary Cooper, who was doing pretty well in Westerns, was given the small role of a doomed cadet who appears in one sequence. Wellman's friend, director-cameraman Ernest B. Schoedsack, suggested that Cooper should trade roles with one of the leading men. As it turned out, Cooper's few moments on the screen made such an impression that it helped his career enormously.

The screenplay centers upon two small town youths, Jack Powell (Buddy Rogers) and David Armstrong (Richard Arlen), who both love the same girl, Sylvia Lewis (Jobyna Ralston). The rivals join the Army Air Corps after America enters World War I and go through basic training together. After a bitter fight, they become friends. Flying with the Dawn Patrol in France, they bring down a German war plane and as a reward, are given leave in Paris. They encounter Mary Preston (Clara Bow), a tomboyish beauty from their hometown who is now an ambulance driver in the war zone. All leaves are cancelled due to an emergency at the front, but Jack is too drunk to go. Mary sees to it that he gets back, but so compromises her reputation that she is discharged.

David is shot down behind the enemy lines and is presumed dead. Actually, he has fallen into

responsible for the success or failure of the project. There were several men in high places who hoped Lasky *would* fail.

Lasky placed the production in the hands of B.P. Schulberg, head of the Paramount West Coast Studios in Hollywood (much of the Paramount program was still being produced at the Paramount Astoria Studio on Long Island). Lucien Hubbard, a veteran writer, director and production supervisor, was named as line producer. Paramount decided to take a gamble on a young and not very experienced director, William A. Wellman, because

The youthful ace returns from his first kill.

Harry Perry ready to crank the Akeley for Wings.

German hands and is in prison. Jack flies out alone, determined to avenge his friend. Meantime, David escapes and steals a German plane. Jack shoots the plane down and it crashes into a French farm house. Landing, Jack finds that he has killed his best friend. The embittered hero returns home to Mary.

Obviously, the story is a serviceable combination of romance, humor, derring-do and tragedy. It was not sufficient in itself to set the picture apart from the average war melodrama. Nor was it a "star" vehicle, although the lively and youthful leads were popular and dependable. It would be the

airplanes and the skies that would capture the hearts of the audience of a time long before airline travel became commonplace. Only a handful of viewers out of the millions who would see the picture had even been in an airplane or would know what it was like to fly among the clouds instead of seeing them from the ground, or to see the shadow of their plane racing over the undulating earth far below. There had been a few aerial pictures on the screen before, most of them stunt films with ace pilots such as Ormer Locklear, Al Wilson, Dick Grace, Charles Nungesser and others. Nothing approaching the scale of *Wings* had been attempted.

It was evident that such a picture would require highly unusual photographic treatment. Wisely, Hubbard and Wellman agreed upon Harry Perry, ASC, as their director of photography. A

37

veteran cinematographer who had begun his career with Famous Players-Lasky, a parent company of Paramount, Perry was equally at ease with hard-bitten melodramas, Westerns, and the most silken romantic yarns. Of equal importance, he was also a master Akeley cameraman.

The Akeley (popularly called "pancake camera") was invented in 1915 by the great naturalist, Carl E. Akeley, specifically to photograph African wildlife. The cylindrical, all-metal body was mounted on a gyroscopic system so that it could be panned and tilted rapidly and smoothly in all directions. The focal plane shutter with 230° opening was designed to minimize the blurring common to fast panning shots. Framing and focusing of the long-focus lens was done with an identical viewing lens. All of these features were revolutionary at the time and the demand for Akeleys by professional cinematographers outpaced what the manufacturer could produce. Not only was the camera favored for expeditionary and wildlife photography, but it became popular for filming outdoor action scenes in Westerns, war pictures and the increasingly popular airplane melodramas.

"I was engaged for this picture about two months before actual production started because of my experience in aerial photography and so that I could have time to work out the mechanics necessary to get the effects called for in the script," Harry Perry said.

"Many of these at first sight seemed impossible and I spent days figuring out mounts for cameras to be put in every possible and impossible place on an airplane and in making tests and working out electrical devices so that they could be operated by the pilot or actor in the air; also mounts for cameras of several different makes to be used on different types of airplanes by cameramen themselves.

"I also went to Texas twice before the start of production to make tests in the air and help select locations. While on the picture I personally supervised over 200 motor driven cameras on airplanes, working out the exposures and filters used on each shot before it went into the air and, besides this, the other cinematographers and myself had nearly 300 hours of actual work in the air which involved the hardest kind of work and quite a few escapes from serious accidents – which meant no thought for personal safety."

Lt. Cdr. Harry Reynolds and Capt. Bill Taylor assisted Perry in preparing mounts and riggings. Most ingenious was the adaptation of a machine gun ring mount so that it surrounded the cockpit of an aircraft. With the camera mounted on the ring, it was possible to swing it around freely.

Perry assembled as many good cameramen as he could find as they were needed. His key associates were Paul Perry, ASC, his older brother, a long time director of photography and former chief special effects cinematographer at Universal; E. Burton Steene, ASC, a veteran pilot, newsreel cameraman and Akeley specialist; Faxon M. Dean, ASC, who began as a Pathé News cameraman in 1912, was a leading cinematographer at Universal and Paramount, and had survived a plane crash while serving as a combat cameraman during the war; and Alfred "Buddy" Williams, a hard-drinking young action photographer.

A large number of operators and assistant cameramen worked on the picture. Among them were two youngsters who would become famous in coming years: Russell Harlan and L.B. "Bill" Abbott. Several well known first cameramen were pressed into service during production, including Bert Baldridge of Paramount, Herman Schoop, and a prolific photographer of Westerns, Frank Cotner.

An incredible number of cameras were used in the air and on the ground for the re-staging

Clara Bow does her bit for the boys "over there."

of the drive on St. Mihiel. These included studio model Mitchells and Bell & Howells, B & H Eyemo springdriven newsreel cameras, DeVrys, and the hand-cranked Akeleys. Most were specially adapted to be battery powered.

One of the more memorable sequences is one in which Kellerman, the leader of the German squadron, is shot down in flames. The actor in the role has often been mistaken for Jack Holt, star of many Paramount pictures of the Twenties, doing a "cameo" role. Actually, he is Frank Clarke, a famed stunt pilot, who – in helmet, goggles and pencil moustache – is a ringer for Holt. The character has been established as a ruthless killer in earlier scenes, grinning evilly as he guns down the youthful and inexperienced American pilots. His death scene is the most triumphant moment of the film.

In medium close up (as seen from in front of the cockpit), Clarke reacts as though struck by bullets. As smoke pours into the scene as from a flaming engine, blood gushes from Clarke's mouth. From the changing sky behind him it is evident that the plane has gone into a rapidly accelerating spin. This excruciating shot remains on screen for a long time, interacting with aerial shots of the plane spiraling down in flames.

The close shot of the dying pilot was made from a battery driven Mitchell activated by Clarke himself. He also released the gate on a box of lampblack to simulate the wind-blown smoke. The loop-over and tailspin were real, filmed while Clarke put the craft into an out-of-control spin from 6,000 feet. His colleagues were astonished that he was able to play dead while his craft hurtled toward destruction.

The scene could have been done similarly in the studio using one of the composite techniques of the day, such as the Williams or Dunning processes, as was done in some later films. However, the realism of the scene as filmed is beyond question and its impact is still enormous.

The long shots of the hurtling craft were enhanced by the addition of flames touched in directly on the negative by hand, frame by frame. This method was also used on some of the other crash scenes.

Incidentally, Clarke and another equally famed stunt pilot in the *Wings* company were deadly enemies. L.B. Abbott recalled the day he was strolling with Clarke when they noticed the other pilot standing next to the rudder of Clarke's plane. "Frank walked over and said, 'What the hell are you doing to my plane?' (The man) mumbled, 'Aw, just looking around and ambled away. Frank examined the

A beautiful glass shot transforms a Texas road into a French battlefield.

Military police catch Rogers and Bow in an embarassing situation.

wires and said, 'Look what that sonofabitch did!' I could see that he had unscrewed the turnbuckles on the control wires so that they were held by only one or two turns! It would have been suicide to have flown that plane."

Another great stunt pilot who also played a role was Dick Grace. As one of the American fliers, he flinches when a French general decorates him and kisses him on both cheeks. Grace is probably the most famous of the movie fliers because he wrote books and magazine articles about his adventures. One, *The Lost Squadron*, was filmed by RKO-Radio in 1932, with Grace and Clarke doing most of the stunt flying. One of his specialties was deliberately crashing planes without killing himself (one of

The drive on St. Mihiel as it was reenacted in San Antonio.

his books was titled "I'm Still Alive"). In one of the crashes he staged for *Wings,* he was supposed to nose a plane over onto its back. Coming in at too acute an angle, the plane dug in and Grace's neck was broken. He received $500 for the job and was put in a San Antonio hospital, where he was supposed to remain for one year. After six weeks he broke the cast with a hammer, climbed through a window and went to a dance at a downtown hotel.

The aircraft used in *Wings* were not always what they appeared to be. Most of the Spads actually were Thomas-Morse Scouts. The huge German Gotha Bomber was impersonated by a postwar model Martin bomber. Curtiss P-1s doubled as Fokkers. Although a term of the Versailles treaty decreed that all Fokkers would be destroyed, it is believed that Dick Grace crashed a genuine Fokker for one scene.

The ground warfare scenes in the St. Mihiel action are equally impressive. It was staged on a grassy plain of about five square miles on the Camp Stanley army reservation – or, at least, it was that before field guns bombarded it with live ammunition. The trench system of the French battle site was reproduced under the direction of Captain E.P. Ketchum, Second Division Engineers. A telephone network set up by Captain Walter Ellis, of the Second Signal Company, covered the entire area. Captain Robert Mortimer, Second Ordnance Company, planned and supervised the use of all explosives. The men of the Second Division – which had been in the actual St. Mihiel campaign – worked with a

small army of local laborers to prepare the trenches, shell holes, blasted trees and ruins. From the ground or from the air the battlefield was horrifyingly convincing. The cost was about $300,000.

Harry Perry shot some test films from low altitudes to determine how the terrain would register on film. The movement was too rapid to allow the camera to pick up details. High camera angles were a necessity, so a camera tower resembling a giant oil derrick was built. It was 100 feet high with platforms every 25 feet. Cameras were set up on all platforms. Men with Eyemos were concealed in the battlefield behind props and in covered pits. Twenty-one cameramen were utilized to photograph the drive.

Some $16 million in government equipment was deployed for the sequence, consisting of aircraft, tanks, artillery, trucks and field gear. Each day's operations were planned with minute care; to do otherwise would have resulted in chaos and probable casualties. Major A.M. Jones of the Second Division's General Staff directed the tactical operations of the troops. The officers with Wellman and Hubbard worked out details of each day's action with field maps and blueprints and relayed them to sub-officers and squad leaders. The soldiers who were to be "killed" were chosen and "died" according to a timetable.

The army planes were piloted by members of the First Pursuit Group under the supervision of Brigadier General F.P. Lahm, commandant, and Major F.M. Andrews. Real bombs were dropped from low altitudes, usually much lower than would have been the case in actual combat, in order to get the aircraft into the frame with the ground action. About 5,000 men participated in Paramount's version of the drive. The greatest number of fighter craft that can be counted in any one shot is 18, a small fraction of the 1,500 planes that participated in the actual drive, but the impression of a huge air armada is achieved.

E. Burton Steene described his experience while photographing from the bomber in *American Cinematographer,* December, 1926:

"Akeley cameras are always given the most difficult 'setups' when anything big is to be done. Not content with airplanes and balloons being crashed to earth, a whole French village is wiped out by bombs released from a giant Martin bomber, painted and revamped to simulate an enormous Gotha bomber. Chief cinematographer Harry Perry ...assigned me and my Akeley to the bomb compartment containing 12 100-pound bombs of T.N.T. I was hoisted and squeezed in the remaining space in the 'bombay' as the bomb compartment is called. My camera was mounted in such a position that it was shooting straight down... We made several practice flights and dropped dummy bombs over the village to get the range. I soon found that the parachute pack was too cumbersome and interfered with the proper handling of my camera. I then was forced to secure a model of a 'chute that hung on the front, instead of the back; this gave me a trifle more room, as I was shooting from a kneeling position, at an altitude of less than 600 feet.

"In addition to my Akeley, I had three Eyemo automatic cameras shooting down, one operated by Al Lane, an assistant, and the other two by an electrical device... Everything seemed safe and snug perhaps to those on the ground, but [I was crowded in] with 1200 pounds of T.N.T. six inches away in a space so small that I could scarcely move my legs in my kneeling position – suppose something went wrong and we had to make a forced landing or perhaps crash with the 12 100-pound missiles, primed to go off on contact!

"Captain S.R. Stribling was pilot. Twice we circled the village, convoyed to two Fokker ships, while two Martin bombers and three smaller planes were at an altitude of about 1200 feet with cameras mounted on them to show the three invading planes below bombing the village.

"Harry Perry, Faxon Dean and Paul Perry ... covered these shots from the bombers above...

"On the first two trips Captain Stribling dropped a dud to get the range. A thin rope was fastened to my left arm which led to Captain Stribling's cockpit through the interior of the bomber... A signal of two sharp pulls was the word to tell me the bombs would be released within 15 seconds and to start cranking. I could see nothing fore or aft, only a hole in the 'bombay' directly in front of me, two by four feet. I could not see what was coming, hence the signal. Naturally the scene would be a short one as the ship was doing 90 miles and I must get the explosions of all the bombs as they hit the village.

"By this time, I was so interested in making a successful shot that I forgot all about the T.N.T. and everything going on. I had to keep my eye glued to the finder eyepiece – the slightest jar would knock my eye away from it and a foot or two of film lost was not to be considered. Captain Stribling gave the two yanks... Looking through the finder, it was my job to grind and pick up the bombs as they dropped an inch or two from my cranking arm, keep them in the center of the picture until each one exploded. There was dynamite planted in the vil-

lage to augment the explosions. Down they went, all in a row; they slipped out of the compartment like grease for I did not hear or see them until I picked them up in my finder.

"It was a wonderful sight to see these death-dealing messengers speeding down – the terrible explosions took place right on schedule, due to the unerring eye and hand of Captain Stribling.

"I do not know how far the concussion lifted the ship, but for several seconds it shook and trembled with each explosion until I thought it might possibly be out of control, which of course it was not. The sensation of being rocked and thrown about in the air in a giant bomber a scant 600 feet above the ground while dropping 1200 pounds of T.N.T. is a thrill not often given to a man. In my cramped quarters it would have been very difficult if not impossible to get away with my parachute, but my confidence in the pilot kept me in repose.

"The village was totally wrecked by this German invader and the scene was a great success and will be incorporated in the picture... along with the thrilling shots of the three ships, bomber and two escorts, from above... It took about an hour to do the stunt. I had to be lifted out as my legs were totally numb below the knees."

Faxon Dean and "Buddy" Williams had thrills of quite another kind while shooting at 11,000 feet from a bomber piloted by Lieutenant E.H. Robinson. One of the motors quit due to extreme cold, dropping the plane into the heart of a cumulus storm cloud. Buffeted by violent convectional currents, the ship was thrown out of control and the pilot's goggles were covered with ice and frozen fast to his face.

Rogers, backgrounded by cemetery crosses, realizes he has shot down his best friend.

"I knew we were over a mountainous part of the country and that the hilltops would be 1500 feet higher than the field from which we had taken off," Robinson wrote in *American Cinematographer* for January, 1927. "When we had descended 9,000 feet and still I could not see the ground, I called to the cameramen and told them that if ground was not sighted within another 1,000 feet we were going to jump . . . But another 1,000 feet we broke through the clouds and sighted the ground just 800 feet below us. A hurried look served to show me that we had been very fortunate in coming out in the center of a valley, which was entirely surrounded by high hills disappearing into the clouds. In other words, a mile and one-half in any other direction would have unquestionably seen us crashed into a mountain.

"I picked a likely looking field, glided for it – approaching it 'into the wind' – and made a good landing without injuring anything or anybody."

Things did not turn out as well for at least one army pilot. Hubbard and Wellman saw one of the planes crash during the St. Mihiel sequence. The field operations officer told them to think nothing of it, as pilots often were killed during training, and that it would never be heard of. Buddy Rogers has said he believes there were three fatal crashes during production, all involving military pilots.

During the six months of shooting in Texas, Wellman and Hubbard spent much of their time arranging entertainments for the troops to quell their impatience with the vagaries of motion picture staging, settling disputes between the air and ground branches, soothing the outrage of some of the army brass at Paramount's disruption of their routine operations, and trying to cope with government politics.

The company returned to Hollywood to film interiors and began post-production work. Roy Pomeroy, chief of special effects, and Paul Perry took charge of miniatures and composites, which are so well done and smoothly integrated as to be virtually undetectable.

Some of the scenes in which flying was not involved are almost as memorable as the aerial work. Wellman and Perry conceived a shot wherein the camera, on a specially made boom, sweeps through a French night club to "discover" the principals. Wellman disliked the scene because he felt it was "dizzying for the audience" and swore never to do it again. It's really quite a beautiful scene.

Backlighting is used to fine effect in glamorizing the French girls and, especially, in a scene in which Clara Bow emerges from behind a clothesline full of underclothes. Especially memorable is the scene at the crash in which Arlen dies; Rogers alights from his plane backgrounded by rows of white cemetery crosses and framed by the ruins and wreckage in the foreground.

Wellman went to great lengths in behalf of realism in certain parts. Rogers remembers that for the champagne drinking scenes, Wellman made him actually get drunk. The special effects department added hallucinatory bubbles to show what Rogers *thought* he was seeing. Before the fight sequence between Arlen and Rogers, Wellman secretly informed each actor that the other was angry at him and that each had said he was going to "beat the hell" out of the other.

On the other hand, he took no heed of some glaring anachronisms, such as cars, airplanes and fashions that suggest 1926 rather than 1919. As Wellman expected, few patrons noticed.

In the program book for *Wings*, John Monk Saunders, who died by his own hand several years later, wrote:

"A year and a half after the genesis of the piece in the Lasky library, after the books of the production had been closed, after the oil and the high-test gasoline and ordnance had been paid for, after the planes had been reconditioned and the War Department had been indemnified for every bit of government property lost, damaged or destroyed in the filming of the story, *Wings* was completed.

"The result is a slender strip of negative 12,000 feet in length. It can be seen in two hours and a half. But that film will, in the next five years, penetrate the farthest corners of the earth; its subtitles will be translated into 48 languages, it will be viewed by countless numbers of people."

Wings did not reach the general public for a long time. It was premiered first in 14 reels at San Antonio in the Spring of 1927. It put the city in a state of high excitement and its wide acceptance seemed assured. Several months passed while the film was re-edited to 12 reels totalling 12,600 feet, a running time of 140 minutes on the new sound equipment being installed at the larger theaters. J.S. Zamecnik composed a complete musical accompaniment scored for concert orchestra and wrote the then-inevitable "title song" with lyrics by Ballard MacDonald. Release prints were hand colored, so that skies were blue, machine guns spat red and airplanes spiraled toward the ground belching red flames.

When *Wings* finally began its 12-week premiere engagement in New York City's Criterion Theater on August 12, a special projection system called Magnascope was used, reportedly to great effect. The process required a huge screen and an

extra projector equipped with a wide-angle lens which had been invented by Lorenzo del Riccio for projecting giant images outdoors. A Paramount advertising executive, Glendon Allvine, conceived the notion of using Magnascope to enlarge special sequences of big films, and it was introduced at the New York premier of *Old Ironsides* (1926) for the sea battle at Tripoli. The following year it was even more effective when applied to the elephant stampede of *Chang,* which was further enhanced by the booming of two thunder drums from behind the screen. This technique was expanded for *Wings,* in which more than half of the film was shown on the oversized screen (four times normal size) and sound effects recordings played behind the screen provided roars, whines, gunfire, crashes and explosions to accompany the screened images. The movie was shown in two parts, the first running 65 minutes and the second 74 minutes. The Magnascope images commenced with the first dogfight, about 35 minutes after the opening and continued until intermission. The second part opened on the normal-size screen and expanded onto the enlarged screen for the drive on St. Mihiel and the climatic flying scenes.

After several months the picture was shortened to 12,267 feet and an RCA sound track was added, incorporating the score and sound effects but without dialogue. This version and a silent edition at last were put into national release on January 5, 1929, almost two years after the premiere. Despite the "talkie craze" that permeated the movie-going public at the time and doomed most non-dialogue pictures to oblivion, *Wings* was a big hit everywhere.

On May 16, 1929, the Academy of Motion Picture Arts and Sciences held its second anniversary banquet in the Blossom Room of the Hollywood Roosevelt Hotel. At this time the first Academy Awards were given. *Wings* was voted the Best Picture Award for 1927/28, and Roy Pomeroy received the first and only Engineering Effects Award for

Flight commander Richard Tucker tries to console the heartbroken pilot.

Wings, having "rendered the best achievement in producing effects of whatever character obtained by engineering or mechanical means." The category was discontinued after the first year and there were no awards given for special effects until 1938.

It can be added that, after nearly six decades, *Wings* retains its power to captivate an audience.

—George E. Turner

A Paramount picture; Adolph Zukor *and* Jesse L. Lasky *present a* Lucien Hubbard *production; directed by* William A. Wellman; *story by* John Monk Saunders; *adapted by* Hope Loring *and* Louis D. Lighton; *titles by* Julian Johnson; *editor in chief,* E. Lloyd Sheldon; *photographed by* Harry Perry, ASC; *engineering effects,* Roy Pomeroy, ASC; B.P. Schulberg, *associate producer. Unbilled credits: additional photography by* J. Burton Steene, ASC; Paul Perry, ASC; Alfred Williams, Russell Harlan, Bert Baldridge, L.B. Abbott, Cliff Blackston; Faxon M. Dean, ASC; Frank Cotner, Herman Schoop, L. Guy Wilky, Al Lane, Ray Olsen; *photographic effects,* Paul Perry; *assistant director,* Norman Z. McLeod; *flying sequences supervised by* S.C. Campbell, Ted Parson, Carl von Hartmann, James A. Healy, Capt. Bill Taylor, Lt. Cdr. Harry Reynolds; *supervisor of troop maneuvers,* Maj. A.M. Jones; *ordnance supervision,* Capt. Robert Mortimer; *communications officer,* Capt. E.P. Ketchum; *still photography,* Otto Dyer; *musical score by* J.S. Zamecnik; *title song by* Zamecnik *and* Ballard MacDonald; *New York opening August 12, 1927; running time 140 minutes; national release January 5, 1929; running time 136 minutes; sound version recorded by RCA system. Dedication:* To those young warriors of the sky, whose wings are forever folded about them, this picture is reverently dedicated.

Mary Preston, Clara Bow; *Jack Powell,* Charles (Buddy) Rogers; *David Armstrong,* Richard Arlen; *Sylvia Lewis,* Jobyna Ralston; *Cadet White,* Gary Cooper; *Celeste,* Arlette Marchal; *Patrick O'Brien,* El Brendel; *The Sergeant,* Gunboat Smith; *Air Commander,* Richard Tucker; *Mrs. Armstrong,* Julia Swayne Gordon; *Mr. Armstrong,* Henry B. Walthall; *Mr. Powell,* George Irving; *Mrs. Powell,* Hedda Hopper; *French Peasant,* Nigel de Brulier; *Kapitan Kellerman,* Frank Clarke; *Pilots,* Dick Grace, Rod Rogers, Paul Mantz, Hoyt Vandenberg, Frank Andrews, Clarence Irvine, Earl E. Partridge, S.R. Stribling, E.H. Robinson.

4

Derring-do of *Bulldog Drummond*

If any one picture vindicated the talkies – at a stage where the status of the sound-movie idiom teetered between acceptance and denial – it was Samuel Goldwyn's 1929 production of *Bulldog Drummond*.

The self-educated apprentice glove maker from the Warsaw ghetto – his real name was Goldfish – co-founded the Lasky Photoplay Company in 1910 and was instrumental in the merger of Lasky with Famous Players seven years later. This combination led to the establishment of Paramount. With the Selwyn brothers he founded the Goldwyn Pictures Corporation and changed his own name to that of the company (a rival producer suggested that it would have been more appropriate had he used the first syllable of Selwyn and the last syllable of Goldfish instead of vice- versa). In 1924 he sold his share of the company, including a studio in Culver City and a roaring lion trademark, to Metro Pictures and Louis B. Mayer; the result was Metro-Goldwyn-Mayer.

A thoroughgoing perfectionist with a desire for complete autonomy, Goldwyn withdrew from all alliances in 1925 in order to establish his own production company, arranging a releasing agreement with United Artists. In 1927, the owners of UA – Mary Pickford, Norma Talmadge, Charles Chaplin, Gloria Swanson, Douglas Fairbanks, Joseph M. Schenck and D. W. Griffith – elected him as a member-owner of the company. He moved his operations to the United Artists Studio in Hollywood.

At first underestimated as merely a shrewd businessman with a sometimes abrasive personality and a penchant for mangling the English language, Goldwyn proved to have such intangible assets as taste and instinct that make for a great movie producer. He respected and recognized talent, he was not afraid to try new ideas, and he knew how to get the best results from creative people.

William Cameron Menzies, a designer of movie sets since 1917, was supervising art director at United Artists. Like others in his profession he was horrified by the new order of picture making which called for too much dialogue, too-long "takes," static camera angles, limited action and a minimum of sets. When he learned that playwright Sidney Howard was working on the *Bulldog Drummond* script, he approached the writer and suggested a collaboration to break the stultifying trend toward photographed stage plays. Howard cooperated enthusiastically.

As the script evolved, Menzies translated it into hundreds of sketches outlining the action. From these action drawings, he developed 61 sets, all practical for sound and all providing for dramatic camera angles, but some of which could be photographed from only one angle because the perspectives were forced. Menzies said that he included "a suggestion of Edgar Allan Poe" in order "to give a proper air of midnight horror to a story of blackmail, torture, and sudden death." Curiously, the eccentric sets serve equally well to point up the many comedic aspects of the picture.

F. Richard Jones, a veteran director of silent films who began with Mack Sennett in the pre-World War I era, was chosen to direct. Although his

Lilyan Tashman as the svelte Irma looks after the captive Bulldog, Ronald Colman.

specialty was comedy, Jones had directed two pictures during 1928 that demonstrated wider capabilities: the excellent Douglas Fairbanks romantic adventure, *The Gaucho,* and a part-Technicolor Zane Grey Western, *The Water Hole,* in which Jack Holt, Nancy Carroll and John Boles face madness and death in the desert.

Because Jones had never directed a talking picture, Goldwyn hired a director from the legitimate stage, A. Leslie Pierce, to assist in staging the dialogue. This was a common practice with most production companies during the first several years of talking picture production. The cast was rehearsed for two weeks before photography was begun and the actual takes were done quickly with the idea of maintaining spontaneity.

Bulldog Drummond was filmed on a brand-new sound stage at the well-appointed studio in both silent and all-talking versions, the latter recorded with Western Electric equipment supplied by United Artists. The talkie version must be coun-

ted a breakthrough in every department: excellent incorporation of dialogue with script, free and imaginative photography and cutting, a revolutionary approach to scenic design (eventually to be widely accepted), unobtrusive use of sound, and a form of acting perfect for the medium, being neither that of the stage nor of the silent film's pantomimic style. All these innovations were realized despite great difficulties, but – somehow – the picture gives the impression of its having been accomplished without effort.

With the cameras in the hands of the great George Barnes, ASC, and his up-and-coming colleague, Gregg Toland, ASC, the heady atmosphere of the picture was set forth to perfection.

Cinematographers at the time were trying to get rid of the camera booths (which were referred to, grim-humoredly, as "ice boxes") that had become necessary to deaden the noise of the cameras. These were small, sound-proof rooms into which cameramen were locked with their cameras while working. Entrance was through a door at the back; scenes were photographed through a large window of optical glass at the front. Ventilation was nil in the early models and it was not uncommon for a cameraman to collapse during a scene. The glass gave

46

scenes a slightly mushy look that is evident in many early talkies.

Cinematographers at various studios attacked the problem and, by the summer of 1929 had come up with a variety of ways to free themselves and their cameras from the hated booths. John Arnold, ASC, invented the portable camera "bungalow" at MGM. Harold Lloyd's cinematographer, Walter Lundin, ASC, modified a "bungalow." Fox and Pathé muffled their cameras with heavy quilted jackets called "horse blankets." At RKO-Radio, Donald Jahraus, head of the miniature department, created the "blimp camera," a much lighter housing weighing only 30 pounds and made of a yucca wood frame lined with sponge rubber and covered with rubber sheathing.

When *Bulldog Drummond* got under way, booths were still in use at the United Artists Studio. To gain mobility for selected scenes, Barnes and Toland modified the Jahrous "blimp," enlarging it considerably to allow more working space inside. The glass was retained over the lens to avoid mismatching of photographic quality of the shots made from the booths. Access to the camera was through a large door at the back and the left side was removable for loading and other operations. The viewfinder was enclosed in the "blimp" but a large window made viewing possible. Toland invented a device to permit focusing from outside using a dial calibrated for several lenses.

Principal photography of the "all-talking" version was completed in four-and-a-half weeks. An additional two week period was required to produce a shorter silent version of 6,113 feet. The silent edition was released to neighborhood and small town theaters which had not yet installed sound equipment. Little is known of it, but the talkie version unreels in 93 minutes as follows:

After some establishing shots of London in 1925, the camera takes a look from ground level at a towering doorman at an exclusive London club. More low angles show spacious rooms with incredibly high doors and a lot of old gentlemen dozing or reading in plush chairs. The deadly silence is broken suddenly when a waiter drops a spoon. One walrus bellows, "The infernal din in this club is an outrage!" Algy Longworth agrees: "That's the third

Three sketches by William Cameron Menzies: (Top) The Pall Mall Club. (Center) Drummond's library. (Below) Interior of the Green Bay Inn.

47

spoon I've heard drop this month!'' Enter Captain Hugh "Bulldog" Drummond, demobilized war hero, loudly whistling "The Girl I Left Behind Me."

Drummond tells Algy that he is bored – "too rich to work, too intelligent to play" – and he has advertised in the newspapers that he is looking for dangerous adventure. Among many replies he selects one from Phyllis Benton, who is in "hideous danger," and sets out to meet her at the Green Bay Inn. Against his wishes he is followed by Algy and Drummond's servant, Denny. The country inn is angular and labyrinthine, an ideal place for mystery and adventure, and the night appropriately dark and stormy.

Phyllis, who proves to be a beauty, tells Drummond that her wealthy uncle, Hiram Travers, is a prisoner of criminals at Dr. Lakington's Nursing Home. Phyllis is kidnapped by thugs headed by Carl Peterson and his paramour, Erma. The weird Dr. Lakington, wearing cape and monocle and hovering like a ghost outside the window, arrives to warn Drummond to "Stay with the small games, Captain; it's the big ones that spell disaster."

Drummond goes in through the roof of the sanitarium and rescues Phyllis and Travers, who has been tortured and injected with drugs in attempts to make him sign over his fortune. Eventually they all are recaptured and imprisoned at Lakington's place. Lakington lasciviously fondles the unconscious Phyllis while the trussed-up Drummond vows to kill him. Lakington is preparing to give Drummond a fatal injection when Phyllis awakes and frees Drummond, who deliberately strangles Lakington. Peterson and Irma escape by pulling "the old circus gag": their henchmen, impersonating policemen, take them away.

Sidney Howard's witty dialogue received an ideal interpretation from Ronald Colman, whose first talking picture performance it was. Colman was fairly important as a silent star, but Goldwyn was worried because even bigger names were being destroyed by voices unsuited to the talkies. In addition, he was British, and American audiences at the time tended to be intolerant of English accents. Colman's voice proved to be ideal for the sound track; in fact, the added dimension of sound compounded his popularity and assured his stardom of longevity. His Drummond won him an Academy

More Menzies sketches: (Top) The patient in the sanitarium window. (Center) A false perspective skylight. (Below) Dr. Lakington's laboratory.

48

Joan Bennett and Ronald Colman in the hands of Lawrence Grant, Tetsu Komai, Adolph Milar, Lilyan Tashman and Montagu Love.

nomination (he lost to George Arliss) and became the benchmark for future incarnations of the character, but he repeated the role only once, in *Bulldog Drummond Strikes Back* in 1934. Others who have played the role include Kenneth MacKenna, Ralph Richardson, John Lodge, Ray Milland, John Howard, Tom Conway, Ron Randell, Walter Pidgeon and Richard Johnson. None quite recaptured the Colman magic.

The Drummond of fiction – in a series of books and a four-act play by H. C. McNeale, who wrote under the nom-de-plume of "Sapper" – was a hard-boiled vigilante. Square jawed Carlyle Blackwell carried this image into a British silent film version in 1922; Jack Buchanan, of the musical comedy stage, lightened Drummond up a bit in another English-made film in 1925. During the same year the beloved Sir Gerald Du Maurier adapted and starred in the play. Du Maurier successfully transformed Drummond into a breezy, gallant knight-errant, a far more winning hero than McNeale's grim avenger. Colman's characterization is cut from similar cloth.

Another Britisher, Claud Allister, is perfect as Drummond's side-kick, Algy Longworth, the consummate monocled, whiskey-and-soda-drinking, blonde-chasing, idle rich Englishman. Joan Bennett is a lovely but very young leading lady whose considerable acting skills had not yet been brought to the fore. At the time her name was greatly overshadowed by that of her father and sister, Richard and Constance Bennett. Greater fame lay ahead.

The villainy is in the best of hands, with Lawrence Grant being a slimy and genuinely frightening master criminal, a smirking creature so vile that the otherwise pleasantly disposed hero sees fit to kill him in cold blood at the climax. Grant was not only a well-known actor from England but a noted salon photographer as well. Stylish, sophisticated Lilyan Tashman – who had a "look" and a cool

49

manner that suggest the Lauren Bacall of 15 years later – sets forth the villainess with charm and wit. Montagu Love, the bulldog-faced English actor who played with equal ease the most brutal bad men (including Lillian Gish's nemesis in *The Wind*) and heroic figures such as George Washington, is first rate as the tough but romantic and not-100%-despicable Carl Peterson, the most popular of Sapper's many villains.

There are some curiously perverted elements in this mostly good-natured show. In one scene, Peterson and Irma make passionate love while, in the background the tortured Travers writhes in agony. Both Lakington and Markovich, a brute henchman, have turns at taking advantage of the unconscious Phyllis. Lakington delights in making Drummond watch, keeping up a taunting prattle: "I wonder if you know, Captain, how loving my hands can be... And now we are going to amuse ourselves... We're amusing ourselves. And now, Captain, I'm going to put you to sleep. D'you get the idea? You can dream the rest." When Drummond objects, Irma says coolly, "Just an old Spanish custom." Later, when Irma is horrified at Lakington's fate, Drummond tells her, "It's an old Spanish custom."

Bulldog Drummond might almost be a blueprint for Orson Welles' production, *Citizen Kane*, which was photographed by Toland in 1940. Here, more than a decade before Welles' Hollywood debut, are the celebrated deep-focus shots, the exaggerated foreshortening, the ceilinged sets, and the bizarre camera angles that make *Kane* such a visual feast. While the cinematographers and designer of *Drummond* obviously were influenced by the German expressionist films of the 1920s, the introduction of these ideas in a practical way to the production of mainstream talking pictures is a matter of genuine importance.

Moreover, while most of the German classics sacrificed pace for design, the extensive preplanning of *Drummond* resulted in a virtually pre-edited picture that moves so swiftly as to illustrate by contrast just how static most early talkies are.

Although there were several comprehensive sets (the lounge room of the inn, Drummond's apartment, part of Lakington's sanitarium), most of the interiors were partial sets designed to be seen from specific vantage points. Each was simplified to compensate for the overly analytical eye of the camera. Often the camera angles were built into the sets, enabling the cinematographers to place the unwieldy blimped cameras into positions that otherwise would not have been practical. Most shots were made from well above or considerably below eye level to maintain a prevailing effect of angularity. False perspectives, slanted windows, zig-zag stairways, outsized foreground props, leaning walls and painted shadows were utilized.

The purpose of the painted shadows was to provide some of the atmospheric lighting effects in which giant shadows were needed to create a menacing mood, without destroying the the subtle lighting that is necessary to show the actors to best advantage. Real shadows also dominate much of the action, flowing ominously along variously textured walls. Scenes of torture, the crazed doctor administering drugs and molesting the girl, and the killing of Lakington, are enacted as shadowplay.

An architect who visited the stage recorded that "the sets on which Goldwyn's men shot *Bulldog Drummond* resemble the inside of a Coney Island crazy house. Vanishing points are all wrong; windows slant unaccountably; floors slope in several directions at once; there are shadows where no shadows should be and none at all where they might be expected. Walls hang menacingly over furniture which is slightly askew." Miniatures and glass paintings were used to expand the exterior of the Green Bay Inn and the nursing home, the latter being especially huge and forbidding. Rain and lightning add to the baleful atmosphere.

Even today *Bulldog Drummond* holds up remarkably well for a product of its time. Of other 1929 films only *Applause*, directed by Rouben Mamoulian, and *Alibi*, directed by Roland West, made comparable contributions to the technique of the new talkies. There are a few moments wherein the players seem to be (and probably are) hovering close to concealed microphones. Some of the exterior action is speeded up by undercranking, a technique commonly used advantageously in silent pictures and which many directors and cinematographers tried to carry over into the sound film. Somehow the technique became anachronistic in the more down-to-earth ambience of the talkies. But these are minor complaints compared to the agonies that were tormenting most dabblers in the new medium.

Incidentally, *Bulldog Drummond* was F. Richard Jones' first dialogue film and it proved him an ideal director for the talkies. Unfortunately, he died before he could make another.

—Michael H. Price and George E. Turner

50

Bulldog Drummond
(All Talking Version)
Samuel Goldwyn productions *and* Howard Productions, Inc. *presentation; an* F. Richard Jones *production; directed by* F. Richard Jones; *associate director,* A. Leslie Pierce; *based on the international stage success by* "Sapper"; *adapted for the talking screen by* Sidney Howard; *screen play by* Sidney Howard *and* Wallace Smith; *photography,* George Barnes, ASC, Gregg Toland, ASC; *settings by* William Cameron Menzies; *film editors* Viola Lawrence, Frank Lawrence; *assistant director,* Paul Jones; *song,* "(I Said to Myself, says I) She's the One For Me" *by* Jack Yellen *and* Harry Akst; *musical director,* Alfred Newman; *Western Electric sound system; released through* United Artists. *Running time, sound version,* 93 *minutes. Released August 3, 1929.*

Hugh "Bulldog" Drummond, Ronald Colman; *Phyllis Benton,* Joan Bennett; *Erma,* Lilyan Tashman; *Carl Peterson,* Montagu Love; *Dr. Lakington,* Lawrence Grant; *Algy,* Claud Allister; *Danny,* Wilson Benge; *Marcovich,* Adolph Milar; *Hiram J. Travers,* Charles Sellon; *Chong,* Tetsu Komai; *Maid,* Gertrude Short; *Singer,* Donald Novis; *Thug,* Leo Willis.

(Silent Version)
Omit Newman, song and sound credits. Omit Novis from cast. Running time: 68 *minutes.*

Photos by William A. Fraker (Sr.)

Henry King and Lupe Velez on the prow of the Elsie.

5

Hell Harbor — a Sea of Troubles

Inspiration Pictures was formed in 1921 with director Henry King and star Richard Barthelmess as principals, The founders' prestige proved collateral enough to ensure adequate financing and a release agreement with United Artists. Silent successes for Inspiration included *Tol'able David, The Bright Shawl, The Fighting Blade, The White Sister, The Enchanted Cottage, Resurrection, Ramona* and *Stella Dallas.* Its initial talking picture, *She Goes to War,* was released in 1929. King chose next a currently popular novel, "Out of the Night" by Rida Johnson Young, as the basis for the film called *Hell Harbor.* This was an appropriate choice, for the Virginia-bred King was unsurpassed in his depiction of regional themes and picaresque characters.

Inspiration Pictures was headquartered at Tec-Art Studio, a rental lot on Melrose Avenue in Hollywood, near Paramount's main gate. The venerable studio, which was built in 1916 in a lemon orchard, is still in operation as Raleigh Studio, and the Inspiration offices (which have been renovated considerably) are still occupied – by a much younger company. When he set out to make *Hell Habor,* King checked out of the studio and stayed away for some 15 weeks, determined to prove the practicality of making a talking feature in its entirety at a far-off location.

King referred to *Hell Harbor* as "a little tale about five people with as much weight as the plot of *Slightly Dishonorable."* Getting it on film was something else.

The picture was filmed entirely at Rocky Point, the palm-fringed tip of a narrow, rocky peninsula extending two miles into the ocean near Tampa, Florida. King picked the site after a 10,000 mile scouting trip along the Western, Southern and South-eastern coasts. He then sent his art director, Robert Haas, to the point to plan settings.

Haas, an architect from Newark, had joined Famous Players-Lasky in 1920 as art supervisor of their New York studio and later designed sets in Italy and New York for Inspiration. In 1927, he relocated in Hollywood to work for the William Fox Studio. He returned to work with King in 1929, with *She Goes to War.* Although his work in silent films was distinguished by such pictorial classics as *Fury, White Sister* and *Romola,* he is best remembered for the numerous films he designed at Warner Bros. between 1930 and 1950. These include *The Black Legion, Jezebel, The Maltese Falcon, Strawberry Blonde* and *The Glass Menagerie,* to name a few.

Haas's methods were not ordinary. At Rocky Point, he carved a scale-model of the village from soap. Enlisting the aid of Albert S. D'Agostino, then an assistant art director at MGM, but later to become famous for his work at Universal *(Werewolf of London, The Invisible Ray)* and RKO-Radio (all 11 of Val Lewton's celebrated productions, *The Spiral Staircase, Notorious),* he planned a street about two blocks long. All the buildings were erected in September of 1929, utilizing local carpenters and suppliers, at a cost of $130,350. The structures were built solidly, complete with roofs, in anticipation of tropical storms – a wise bit of foresight. Certain key buildings were made complete with interior sets – at no time did King plan to utilize studio interiors.

Newspaper cut from 1930 shows Velez, King, John Fulton and Mack Stengler in the bow of the Elsie. *Inset: John Holland and Velez.*

King gathered some 60 Hollywood performers and crew members. In Key West he advertised for persons to fill bit-player and extra roles and was deluged with applicants. He hired enough locals to populate the village, giving preference to homely and even grotesque individuals. One featured role went to a long-faced young newspaper reporter, Rondo Hatton, once a publicist for Beecroft Studio on nearby Davis Island. Hatton, a victim of a distorting glandular disorder known as acromegaly, much later developed a following as portrayer of monsters in horror pictures.

Musicians were brought in from Cuba and about 40 sailing vessels and small ships were chartered and anchored in the harbor. Largest of the vessels was the *Elsie*, a 140-ton schooner used as the hero's ship. Location photography was scheduled at 10 weeks.

Two directors of photography were assigned. Mack (Macklyn deNelle) Stengler, ASC, had been a first cameraman for 11 years. He had shot Thomas H. Ince dramas for six years as well as many Mack Sennett comedies, but was best known for a number of outstanding Paramount Westerns, including *The Life of Jesse James* and *Kit Carson,* both with Fred Thompson, and *The Border Legion.* Gentle and soft-spoken, Stengler epitomized the artist-craftsmen who had elevated cinematography to new heights during the 1920s and was now coping with the problems talking pictures had brought to filmmaking.

John P. Fulton (later ASC) had become well known at the studios as a special effects cinematographer. His previous work had been mostly with the Frank Williams Process Company, where he specialized in traveling matte photography. At Universal he had created the spectacular forest fire sequence for *The Michigan Kid* in 1928. He earned his designation as a first cameraman (now termed director of photography) the following year when he did both production photography and some remarkable effects work for Inspiration's *She Goes to War.* A tall, sharp-featured Swede, son of the painter, Fitch Fulton, he was a hard-nosed perfectionist and a true genius in his field. He was also, unfortunately, a difficult man to work with.

The genteel Stengler and the mercurial Fulton – it would be difficult to imagine a more ill-matched team. Yet, strangely enough, their collaboration brought forth some of the most beautiful black and white images ever flashed on the screen. Using Dupont's newly improved panchromatric negative and a variety of filter combinations, they captured nuances of sky and sea in compositions that suggested etchings. Only *White Shadows in the*

John Fulton.

54

South Seas, the 1928 expedition film directed by W.S. Van Dyke and photographed by Clyde DeVinna, ASC, was comparable. *Hell Harbor* is the more remarkable in that it was a "talkie," and such pictorial values were rare in the early days of sound films.

Mitchell cameras were used throughout. They were blimped only when close in on dialogue scenes. Fulton equipped his camera with an invention of his own which he later adapted to optical printers. This was a flip-in mirror device which made it possible to view a backlighted previously exposed positive filmclip through the finder so that exposures and filtration could be matched more evenly throughout production. The device was more practical than the primitive extinction exposure meters then in use.

At 11 a.m. on a sunny Saturday, during the fourth week of shooting, an agitated man ran onto the set looking for King, who was putting Jean Hersholt through a scene.

"Tie down everything or take it away!" the man shouted. King halted the scene and asked the

Cinematographer Mack Stengler.

stranger what was the matter. "Tropical hurricane hurrying up the West Coast – better dodge it!" the man replied before explaining that he represented the weather station in Tampa. King ordered the lights pulled and all tarpaulins struck. The Photophone sound equipment was loaded and dispatched to Tampa. Sailboats and schooners were sent to an inlet and moored. Sandbags were stacked about the sets, which stood less than three feet above the waterline.

By 2 o'clock in the afternoon only Haas and a small crew remained to lash down the sets and stow cables. Before dark the storm hit. Gale-velocity winds battered the deserted prop-town all night, but by morning the wind had changed. King and Haas returned after a sleepless night with volunteer workers. Waves beat against the honky-tonk set and some of the houses. The road to Rocky Point soon became submerged and the men were marooned in the turbulent waters. Midnight found the waves ripping away the underpinnings of the crucial set which represented the Morgan house. The men worked in darkness until three a.m. to save the set.

"Some blow," Stengler said later. "But not as bad as we often think."

King agreed. "It wasn't half as bad as we expected it to be. We were back on the set and shooting at eight o'clock Monday morning." The most notable disaster was the *Elsie,* which was fouled and capsized on a reef. Some smaller craft were flung ashore.

In making *Hell Harbor,* King eschewed studio scenes altogether. Even the interiors were done on location – over the objections of many who believed good sound recording would be impossible. RCA Photophone recording was utilized with Dupont's new variable area film. The toughest sound work came in the scenes aboard the *Elsie,* these requiring 17 days' shooting. Cables had to be strung from shore, about a thousand feet distant, and the sound equipment was floated on barges.

Exposed film was shipped to California for processing and the rushes were viewed in a makeshift projection room on location. Photography was completed November 19, 1929, a couple of days over the projected 10-week schedule.

King and film editor Lloyd Nosler remained at Rocky Point for five weeks after the last of the cast and crew returned to California. On their return to Tec-Art they brought an edited film, complete except for art titles, transitional dissolves and chemical fades. It tells its story straightforwardly:

Hell Harbor is a tiny island port and thieves' refuge in the Bahamas. The story opens with the arrival of a sailor called Peg Leg (Harry Allen), who goes by night to the establishment of Joseph Horngold (Jean Hersholt), an unscrupulous trader. Horngold, expecting to profit from the arrival of an American trader named Bob Wade (John Holland), pays Peg Leg £100 for a collection of pearls. Peg Leg happily departs for a dance hall frequented by a tough crowd.

Alone with his acquisition, Horngold begins to have second thoughts. He follows Peg Leg to the dance hall and watches him take out the bundle of banknotes. Abruptly the lights go out, a chandelier crashes to the floor, and the patrons panic.

Gibson Gowland as the menacing stepfather.

56

Art Director Haas·molding the Soap Model Town for HENRY KINGS *production* "HELL HARBOR"

Contemporary newspaper cut showing Robert Haas at work.

When the lights come back on, the body of Peg Leg is found, knifed and robbed, on the floor. Horngold, beaten to his prey, sees a familiar figure flee by a side door. He follows the man and knocks at his house at the end of the village.

Harry Morgan (Gibson Gowland), a notorious highbinder and descendant of the infamous pirate, Sir Henry Morgan, answers the knock. Morgan was a patron of the dance hall at the time of the murder. Horngold covets Morgan's innocent but fiery-tempered step-daughter, Anita (Lupe Velez), and he is blackmailing Morgan for some past indiscretion. Horngold tells Morgan that he must now pay him more than had been agreed upon and is in turn told that he will have to pay more for Anita than he had expected. Morgan is adamant until Horngold tells him of having witnessed the altercation at the dance hall, and of having seen Morgan flee, his pockets stuffed with money. Caught dead to rights, Morgan summons Anita, tells her he has found her a husband, and addresses Horngold as "my son-in-law." Anita refuses angrily, knowing that Horngold is awaiting the arrival of Wade in order to raise the money necessary to buy her.

Imagining Wade to be the enemy – for he holds the key to her situation – Anita asks two friends, a scroungy beachcomber named Blinky (Paul J. Burns) and a youth called Spotty (George Book-Asta), to lure Wade into a trap. Wade's arrival, however, completely disarms Anita; having heard that all Americans were pidgin-speaking aborigines, she is amazed to find him to be a handsome young man. Halting Blinky before he can strike with his garrote, Anita tells Wade of Horngold's shameful bargain and insists that Wade must buy her and take her with him.

Wade laughs off Anita's proposition, but when he finds Morgan and Horngold to be unco-operative, he postpones the deal until evening, arranging a meeting aboard his schooner. Anita hides and observes the bargaining, which ends with Wade's refusal of the deal. Still Wade balks at the idea of taking Anita to Havana, so she steals Horngold's pearls in hope of gaining Bob's favor. Wade, fearing a trap, sends her back with the loot. Meanwhile, Horngold accuses Morgan of the theft. With a knife, he impales Morgan's hand on a table. Morgan wrenches the knife free and hurls it into Horngold's heart.

Returning in the darkness with the jewels, Anita stumbles over the corpse of Horngold. Morgan beats and threatens to kill the girl, whom he has taken to the ruins of an ancient castle. One of the locals friendly to Anita swims to Wade's ship for help. Wade, who has begun to feel love for Anita, comes back and disposes of Morgan. Anita is accused in the theft of the jewels and thrown into prison. Wade establishes her innocence, though, and the two sail away from Hell Harbor.

The labor of love is evident. The enthusiastic commitment to a quality, pioneering product seems almost to have created a competitive spirit among the actors. The villainy of Hersholt and Gowland easily steals the show from the lively and realistic performance of Lupe Velez and the more taciturn Holland. In 1924, on a cracked one-time lake bed in Death Valley, Gowland "killed" Hersholt in Erich von Stroheim's masterwork, *Greed;* the deed is repeated in *Hell Harbor* with equally dramatic effect. Characterization lifts these scoundrels above the typical "bad guy" image; all their actions, however depraved, are made explicable.

Paul J. Burns romances one of the local ladies.

The camera lingers over exquisitely composed seascapes with perfectly rendered cloud compositions and pauses to study the faces of the port's photogenic inhabitants, making for rather a slow-moving film but justifying the pace. The photography is faultless in view of the difficulties of location work. Lighting is realistic and seemingly sunlit, although many of the exteriors were done under tarps using a mixture of carbon and incandescent lighting.

While dialogue is incidental to visuals, some effective things were done with sound. The ominous opening draws upon sounds of the peg-legged man stumping along and of music and laughter from the honky-tonk. The squeaking of Horngold's shoes becomes integral to the character. (This squeaky-shoe gimmick still worked effectively more than 40 years later for Charles Durning's crooked detective in *The Sting.*) There is a theme song, an unfortunate regression to the silent film era, but the on-screen work of The Habanera Sex-

tette, a Cuban musical group, is integrated successfully. Several comedy interludes are effective; others fail.

The picture proved popular with reviewers, most of whom were especially enthusiastic about the photography. The Hollywood Spectator noted that "Some years ago King demonstrated that he had an extraordinary sense of composition, but never before did his cameraman give such gorgeous expression to it...Pictorially, I think it is the finest thing given to us in black and white. Fulton and Stengler have put into their photography a quality that is breathtaking in its beauty."

Unfortunately, Stengler was never teamed with King again, and, like many fine cinematographers of the period, spent the depression years

One of the sets for Hell Harbor. *Film company provided its own fire department.*

58

Harry Allen, the doomed Peg-Leg, gets his tickets punched by a young Rondo Hatton.

working largely for the Poverty Row producers. Fulton, whose relations with the director had become severely strained during the long location work, was director of photography of King's next production, *Eyes of the World*. During location shooting at Santa Barbara, the antipathy between Fulton and King worsened and when the company returned to Hollywood to begin studio work, Fulton was fired. Ray June, ASC, completed the production. Fulton returned to Universal, where he became one of the most celebrated special effects directors.

Hell Harbor was one of the first films to be dubbed into a foreign language version, released in France as *Sous le ciel des Tropiques*. Versions in other languages were issued with subtitles.

Although it seems virtually forgotten today, *Hell Harbor* was popular when first released and remained in circulation for many years via Astor Pictures. It has a secure place in the evolution of motion pictures as a triumph for artistic cinematography, a landmark in effective use of sound, and a picture which – through its vindication of on-location talkie work – proved influential upon other producers.

—Michael H. Price and George E. Turner

Produced by Inspiration Pictures, Inc.; *released by* United Artists; *directed by* Henry King; *based on the novel, "Out of the Night," by* Rida Johnson Young; *adaptation by* Fred de Gresac; *dialogue by* Clarke Silvernail; *continuity by* N. Brewster Morse; *photographed by* John P. Fulton (later ASC) *and* Mack Stengler, ASC; *art director,* Robert M. Haas; *associate art director* Albert S. D'Agostino; *film editor,* Lloyd Nosler; *recording engineer,* Ernest Rovere; *"Caribbean Love Song" by* Clarke Silvernail *and* Eugene Berton, *sung by* Raoul Mondragon; *still photographer,* William Fraker; *RCA Photophone recording; running time, 90 minutes; released March 22, 1930.*

Anita Morgan, Lupe Velez; *Joseph Horngold,* Jean Hersholt; *Bob Wade,* John Holland; *Harry Morgan,* Gibson Gowland; *Bunion,* Al St. John; *Peg Leg,* Harry Allen; *Blinky,* Paul J. Burns; *Spotty,* Paul Book-Asta; *Dance Hall Proprietor,* Rondo Hatton; The Habanera Sextette.

6

All Quiet on the Western Front

All Quiet on the Western Front, produced by Universal Pictures in 1930, is considered today to be a landmark motion picture. It received an Academy Award as the year's best production and ended up on every "10 Best" list that year including that of the National Board of Review. It was a huge critical and financial success.

Two brilliant film craftsmen were largely responsible for the success of *All Quiet*: Lewis Milestone, the director, and Arthur Edeson, ASC, the cinematographer. Edeson freed the camera from the limitations sound had imposed and Milestone brought back the dynamic style of film editing that reached a zenith with silent pictures but had been absent from the early talkies.

The story of how *All Quiet* reached the screen began when Carl Laemmle, the avuncular head of Universal Studios, bought the screen rights to Erich Maria Remarque's anti-war novel in 1929. Many in Hollywood thought that a movie could not be made from the book. It told of a group of youthful German soldiers thrown into the holocaust of World War I trench warfare. One by one they are either maimed or killed or otherwise destroyed by the war. The author had been a teen-age German infantryman. He wrote out of the anguish of his own experiences with an utter frankness and simplicity that was powerful and compelling.

Essentially episodic in content, it had no love interest, no suspense and anything but a glorious conclusion. Moreover, it was controversial. The memory of World War I was still vivid. The rampant anti-Germanism that had followed the entrance of the United States into the war was not easily forgotten.

Published in Germany in 1927 under the title *Im Westen Nichts Neues* (Nothing New in the West), it was an instant success selling over a million copies – no mean feat in a Germany still trying to come to grips with her defeat in 1918. The book was translated into English and published in the United States by Little, Brown and Company and was soon on every best seller list.

Uncle Carl Laemmle, as he liked to be called, was certainly one of the most eccentrically lovable of the early movie pioneers. He had come to the United States as a penniless teen-age immigrant from south Germany. Possessed of natural shrewdness, diligence and thrift, Laemmle had prospered. He got into the motion picture business in 1909 at the age of 39 by opening a nickleodeon in Chicago. By 1912 he had formed Universal Film Manufacturing Company, which grew into Universal Pictures. In 1915, he opened Universal City Studios, described at that time as "the world's largest film manufacturing plant." But by 1929, Universal was in dire financial straits. Several expensive pictures had failed at the box office and the coming of sound had produced more problems. Adding to these woes was Uncle Carl's odd-ball, impulsive way of doing business.

Laemmle's helter-skelter *modus operandi* sometimes resulted in lucky decisions. He elevated his 20-year old private secretary, Irving Grant Thalberg, to head production at Universal City. Young Thalberg brought order out of chaos and produced *The Hunchback of Notre Dame* with Lon Chaney in 1923, an enormous critical and box office success. (Thalberg went on to even greater successes at MGM.)

Convinced that his son, Carl Laemmle, Jr., had the same spark of genius, Uncle Carl appointed him to the same post when he had barely turned 21 – but Junior was no Thalberg. Junior was not a particularly difficult person. He gave people around him considerable freedom to act on their own. Despite his many detractors, Junior deserves credit for the production of *All Quiet*, and especially for his backing of Milestone and Edeson.

Carl Laemmle was certainly aware of the success of such war pictures as *The Big Parade* (MGM), *What Price Glory?* (Fox) and *Wings* (Paramount). With a proven best seller property like *All Quiet* in his hands, he reasoned there was a good chance for success.

The year 1929 was in many ways a transitional period for the motion picture industry. Two years earlier sound pictures had arrived and struck Hollywood with a vengeance. Filmmakers had a new and powerful tool to work with but they were still struggling with ways to use it. Technical problems were legion.

Herbert Brenon, the first choice to direct *All Quiet*, had directed the highly successful *Beau Geste* in 1927. He wanted a fee of $125,000 which the thrifty Laemmle thought was excessive. Whereupon Agent Myron Selznick suggested his client, Lewis Milestone, at a fee of $5,000 per week with a ten week guarantee. It was a shrewd move by Selznick, then just starting a successful career as an agent. It took ten weeks to prepare the script plus 17 weeks to photograph and edit the picture. Milestone's take home pay was $135,000.

Lewis Milestone was born September 30, 1895 in Odessa, the port city on the Black Sea of the Ukraine. His father was a well-to-do manufacturer. Young Milestone received his high school education in Russia but in 1913 was sent to Germany to study mechanical engineering. Long interested in the theater, which was looked down upon by his parents,

he soon lost interest in his studies. At Christmas time the following year, his father sent him money to come home for the holidays. Instead, Milestone decided to make his move. He and two fellow students visited the United States. His money soon ran out, so he wrote his father for more. The elder Milestone answered, "Since you have taken it on yourself to visit the land of opportunity without my permission, suppose you remain and see what opportunity it affords you."

A series of odd jobs followed until he found a job with a theatrical photographer at $7.00 a week. But, for the first time he was interested in what he was doing. He learned developing and printing, helped with the photography and learned to handle film from the standpoint of still photography.

After the United States entered the war against Germany, Milestone enlisted as a private in the Army Signal Corps in September 1917. He was first assigned to the Army's training film unit at Columbia University. After a time there, he was transferred to Washington where he worked in the laboratory and learned to cut film. Victor Fleming, Josef von Sternberg, Ernest Schoedsack, Wesley Ruggles, Richard Wallace and Gordon Hollingshead, all well known for their later work in the motion picture industry, served in the same unit with him.

Following his discharge from the Army in December 1918, Milestone headed for Hollywood to work for Jesse D. Hampton, an independent producer he had met while serving in the Signal Corps. He worked in the cutting room assisting the film editor, splicing film, carrying film cans, sweeping the cutting room floor and running errands. An affable, pleasant young man, he was known to all as "Millie" – an affectionate nickname that stuck with him throughout his career.

He was soon noticed by Henry King, then directing a series of H.B. Warner programmers for Hampton, who made Milestone his general assistant and film cutter. This led to an association of several years with William A. Seiter, a popular director of comedies and family oriented program

pictures. Milestone became his assistant and film editor as well as the scenario writer on several of Seiter's comedies. The two men were fast friends.

The original screen treatment for *All Quiet* was written by C. Gardner Sullivan, the veteran scenarist of many Thomas H. Ince films and the best of William S. Hart's westerns. Sullivan was a highly skilled scenario constructionist. He was especially noted for his skill at planning and laying out shots in advance of shooting. He became the chief scenario editor of *All Quiet*. Milestone brought in Del Andrews, who had worked with him at the Hughes unit, to help on the script. Andrews had been a film editor and was a sort of jack-of-all-trades. This being an early talking picture, it was thought necessary to bring in someone familiar with the spoken word. Hence, the addition of playwright Maxwell Anderson and Broadway producer George Abbott to the writing team. Milestone holed up with his writers in a house on Catalina Island next door to director John Ford and hammered out a shooting script.

Louis Wolheim, who had worked with Milestone in two pictures, was quickly cast as the front-wise veteran Katczinsky or "Kat." A broken nose gotten on the football field gave Wolheim a face that appealed to D.W. Griffith who cast him as the executioner in *Orphans of the Storm* (1921) and as the renegade Captain Hare in *America* (1924). Wolheim next scored in the successful Maxwell Anderson-Laurence Stallings play, *What Price Glory?* This led to a Hollywood contract and his association with Milestone.

George "Slim" Summerville, a much underrated comedian, was given the part of Tjaden. Summerville added some welcome comedy touches to an otherwise grim story. John Wray, a Broadway actor-playwright, became the sadistic drill sergeant, Himmelstoss. The roles of the young school-boy soldiers went to William Bakewell as Albert Kropp; Ben Alexander (later Sgt. Friday's *Dragnet* partner) as Franz Kemmerich; Scott Kolk as Leer; Owen Davis, Jr. as Peter; Russell Gleason (replacing Allan Lane) as Müller; and Walter Browne Rogers as Behm. The latter's brooding face was used on all posters and 24-sheets for *All Quiet*.

The pivotal role of Paul Bäumer presented problems. Milestone knew that a great deal of the success – or failure – of *All Quiet* lay in this role of the chief protagonist. Phillips Holmes, a popular juvenile of the day, was considered, as was John Harron, younger brother of the Griffith star, Robert Harron. Both actors had a certain sensitive quality the part demanded but Milestone kept looking.

German soldiers trudge through a French village which was constructed on the Universal backlot.

Paul Bern recommended a young actor who had played the juvenile in Greta Garbo's *The Kiss*, which he had just produced (incidentally, this was MGM and Garbo's last silent picture). He told Lew Ayres, the young man in question, to call Milestone. But somehow things went wrong and the boy could never get Milestone to either give him an appointment or call him back. Disgusted with his efforts to reach Milestone, Ayres joined the other hopefuls being tested in a scene of the men in a chow-line. Ayres stood out and got the part. His sensitive performance as the doomed young private was to skyrocket him to instant stardom.

In a bit of inspired casting, Milestone persuaded his pal Raymond Griffith to play the part of the French soldier Paul stabs to death in a shell hole and is forced to watch die. Griffith had been an important comedy star known as the "Silk Hat Comedian" in silent pictures. Unfortunately, he had suffered a vocal affliction as a child and spoke only in a hoarse whisper. With the arrival of talking pictures, Griffith turned to production and was already working as a producer at Warner Bros. when Milestone talked him into playing the part. Griffith delivered a poignant, unforgettable performance. He continued his career as a producer and worked in that capacity for many years at 20th Century-Fox where he was one of Darryl Zanuck's closest associates.

63

Zasu Pitts is Lew Ayres' ailing mother in the silent and European versions of All Quiet.

Beryl Mercer is the mother in the talking version. Sequence was re-shot because audiences laughed at Pitts' distinctive voice.

Enter Myron Selznick again with George Cukor in tow. Cukor had been brought from Broadway where he had been successfully directing plays to work for Paramount as a possible director. He knew nothing about filmmaking but a great deal about acting. Selznick persuaded Milestone to take on Cukor to help coach the young actors. He became more than just a dialogue director. His work on *All Quiet* has never received the recognition it deserves. He became one of Milestone's most valuable assistants. He immediately took the young actors in hand and began rehearsing them in their roles.

At the same time, the boys were delivered into the hands of Otto Biber, a former German army drill master. Biber instructed them in the art of the goose-step as well as other military exercises. To insure further accuracy, Hans von Morhart and Wilhelm von Brincken, both former German officers, were hired as technical advisers. Outstanding features of *All Quiet* were the authentic German and French uniforms and props Universal purchasing agents brought back from Europe. For example, in the early training scenes the boys are shown in the old Prussian blue uniforms and then later in field gray. Six complete artillery pieces were secured – not to mention machine guns, rifles and all types of military hardware and accoutrements. Such attention to detail helped establish the proper atmosphere.

Tony Gaudio, ASC was the initial cinematographer considered to handle the cameras on *All Quiet*. Together with Harry Perry, ASC, he had just wrapped up *Hell's Angels* for Howard Hughes. But in Tony's inimical words he'd "had enough of war" so he was not too enthusiastic about doing another war picture. Then Universal executives heard that Arthur Edeson had just finished a Western at Fox Studios and had never gone into a camera booth or "sound house" as they were sometimes called. The picture was *In Old Arizona*, the first of the Cisco Kid stories to reach the screen. It was "all talking" and was one of the first sound pictures to be made outdoors, a feat some of the early sound engineers said was not feasible.

Arthur Edeson is one of the small group of cameramen who founded the American Society of Cinematographers in January of 1919. Over the years he served on the A.S.C. Board of Governors and as president (1949-50). At the time he photographed *All Quiet* he was one of the top rated cinematographers in the motion picture industry. It was a position he consistently maintained until his retirement in the 1950's. A short, handsome man, he was known for his meticulous craftsmanship and his artistic integrity. His sometimes imperious manner earned him the nickname of "Little Napoleon."

In 1968 Edeson described how he got the assignment to photograph *All Quiet.* "I had just finished a picture at Fox for Frank Borzage and they had no assignment for me when I received a call from Roy Hunter, head of Universal's lab.

"'Art, are you available?' he asked me."

"'I'll have to ask Sheehan (Fox production chief) on that.'

"He said, 'We have a picture, *All Quiet on the Western Front,* and they tell me that you never go into a sound house.'

"I said, 'That's true. I have a very, very quiet camera which is my own.' It was a Mitchell (Standard). I didn't tell him what made it quiet. I told him nothing.

"Actually, I had taken the camera over to Gus, the mechanic at Mitchell's, and he put a micarta gear in the rear of the camera. He took some of the metal parts out and that made the camera 50 percent quieter than other cameras. And I also had a big padded bag we called a 'barney' that I put over the camera to quiet it down more. I used this system to photograph *In Old Arizona.* Well, I went over to Universal to see Hunter. Hunter asked me if I would make a test for them. I said, 'Yes, I'll make a test for you – one in the sound house and one outside with my Mitchell camera covered with a barney bag.'

"I went over to Fox and borrowed one of the barneys we had used on the pictures I had worked on there. Then I took all my gear back over to Universal to do the test. The test was the schoolroom scene where the German boys are lectured by their teacher to join the Army. I remembered it well because I picked out the boy (Lew Ayres) who played the lead. I asked Millie if that was the boy and he said 'yes,' and I think he was pleased with that. He was a very nice guy.

Louis Wolheim uses a boot to discourage a hungry rat. Harold Goodwin is in the foreground. In the background from left are Slim Summerville, Scott Kolk, Lew Ayres, Richard Alexander, Ben Alexander, Owen Davis Jr., and in the extreme background, right, Russell Gleason.

Raymond Griffith is the dying French poilu *and Ayres the sorrowing youth who bayoneted him.*

"I shot about 300 feet of film on each take I made both inside and outside the sound house. The little sound man we had there, Bill Hedgecock, never would turn up the gain on his sound panel until the camera got up to speed and the action and dialogue began. He was right alongside me. I told him later, 'you really saved my neck doing what you did.' He said, 'There was no need of going ahead and having the noise of the camera come out. As soon as the dialogue and action started you couldn't hear the camera. It was very, very quiet.' Well, that was real cooperation because a lot of sound mixers wouldn't do that.

"Incidentally, at that time the camera was turned by a flexible shaft connected to a motor that in turn was interlocked with the sound recorder. We were using the Fox Movietone (Western Electric) sound system, which was the best one.

"The next day all the Universal executives were in the big projection room to see the test I had made. The two Laemmles were there, father and son. So was Martin Murphy, the production manager, Henry Henigson, the studio manager, and, of course, Roy Hunter. The room was crowded with people.

"The picture came on – about 300 feet – of the boys in the school room. There were two takes. Hunter had spliced both scenes together and that's it. When it was over, the lights came on and it was quiet for a few moments. Then someone said, 'Now put on the one that was made without going into the sound house.' 'They are spliced together,' Hunter

answered. So they ran it again and when it was over Murphy and Henigson got together with Hunter to talk it over.

"Hunter came over to me and said, 'Arthur, come over to the office with me.' Then he asked me if I'd make the picture and I said 'yes' so we came to an agreement. They paid me $600 a week.

"You couldn't have made a picture like *All Quiet on the Western Front* using those sound houses. I had never gone into one of them. You couldn't get good photography. You couldn't light. Now this picture was at least 50 percent exterior war stuff so my camera could easily handle it. We also shot the battle stuff silent. I often had as many as six cameras turning on those scenes. Sometimes on the interior scenes when the camera moved in close I placed a big piece of plate glass between it and the actors so there were no big problems with camera noise.

"We went on location for about six or eight weeks down in the hills above Laguna Beach. They built roads and a concrete ramp for the big orange-colored camera crane that Hal Mohr had built for them a few months before. It ran alongside the trenches they had dug for the battle stuff. It was really a big show."

Edeson laughingly recalled that after working a number of days in a dugout the Orange County Board of Health inspectors shut them down until it was cleaned up. "It was just like a real war except that part of the day the extras, which they had gotten from an American Legion post in Santa Ana, would change from their German uniforms into French uniforms. They would be fighting themselves. We never had more than a few hundred extras at any one time. Usually, we had about 150 on hand each day.

"I had photographed another war picture for First National, *The Patent Leather Kid*, which Al Santell had directed. It was made at Camp (now Fort) Lewis, Washington a couple of years before *All Quiet on the Western Front*. Without the experience I got on that picture, I don't think I could have done *All Quiet*, which had many of the same problems in the photography of the battle scenes.

"They had gotten some tents from the National Guard for the extras to live in down there on the Irvine Ranch. Except for not using real bullets, we might as well have been in the war. There were some close calls with explosions. Our powderman was working on another picture at night so he didn't get much sleep. He was sometimes a little jittery. Once Millie was hit by some debris from an explosion and was knocked unconscious. He was right by my camera. After that we started wearing those big steel German helmets."

The only fatality was not caused by any of the explosions but took place on the shell torn French village set at Universal City when an extra was thrown off an artillery caisson against the corner of a building.

In addition to the Irvine Ranch and Universal City, other California locations used were: Sherwood Forest and Malibu Lakes in the San Fernando Valley, and the so-called "40 acres" backlot of the RKO Pathé Studio in Culver City (where *Gone With the Wind* Atlanta and Tara exteriors were later made). Captain Charles D. Hall, who had served in the Canadian Army during the war, and William R. Schmitt designed the sets. One of the most interesting was the re-creation of a German Army *kaserne* (barracks), complete with a quadrangle for drill, built on the Universal City back lot. This set was further enhanced by a bird's eye view shot created by special photographic effects cinematographer Frank Booth. Some of his other optical work and matte shots are so well executed they pass by virtually unnoticed.

All Quiet on the Western Front opens with the sub-title (taken almost verbatim from the forepage of the book) that sets the tone for the picture:

> "This picture is to be neither an accusation nor a confession, and least of all an adventure, for death is not an adventure to those who stand face to face with it. It will try simply to tell of a generation of men who, even though they may have escaped its shells, were destroyed by the war."

(Unfortunately, Universal deleted this title after the initial release and substituted instead a list of all the awards, including the Academy Oscar, the picture had won.)

The picture then begins somewhat innocuously. An elderly janitor is preparing to unlock a door while talking to the charwoman scrubbing the floor.

"Thirty thousand," he says to her.

"From the Russians?" ask the woman.

"From the French. We capture that many from the Russians every day," he answers as he opens the door revealing marching spike-helmeted German soldiers in 1914 uniforms. A marching military band seems to catch the nationalistic fervor of the crowd as Edeson's camera cranes upward and pulls back through a window. Inside, an elderly schoolmaster (Arnold Lucy) is exhorting his students to enlist. In a series of sharp vignettes, Mile-

Arthur Edeson, in center on crane, deadened camera noise with heavy blankets, thereby restoring camera mobility. The crane was designed by director Paul Fejos and cinematographer Hal Mohr for the film Broadway *in 1929. Photo was made on the Irvine Ranch.*

stone introduces the young men the picture concentrates on: Kropp, Leer, Kemmerich and the main protagonist, Paul Bäeumer.

We follow the boys through their recruit training and see them suffer at the hands of their sadistic drill sergeant Himmelstoss. His particular pleasure is to march his young charges into a muddy, ploughed field and have them "advance and lie down."

Ordered to the front, they pass through a shell torn French village at the railhead and hear the scream of enemy shells for the first time. Inside a deserted factory, beautifully lit by Edeson in deceptive low-key, the boys meet Tjaden, Westhus (Richard Alexander), Detering (Harold Goodwin) and, somewhat later, the incomparable Kat who arrives with a whole pig they are all soon devouring. That same evening they are ordered front for a wiring fatigue.

They get their first instructions of how to behave under shell-fire from Kat as they pass through a wooded area. Edeson has skillfully lit this sequence day-for-night but it is so convincingly done it seems like actual darkness. His camera trucks along in front of the soldiers, pausing when Kat emphasizes an important point, moving once more when they move. "I'll give you all clean underwear when we get back," Kat tells them.

Edeson lit the scenes of the men putting up barbed wire night-for-night. His lighting of these scenes is very effective. When an enemy bombardment suddenly erupts, the men scatter for cover. In one very effectively lit low-key shot – the light level is *extremely* low but quite visible – a man jumps into a shell hole as an explosion erupts. He screams out in pain, "I'm blind. I can't see," and blindly staggers towards the enemy lines where he is cut down by unseen gunfire. One of the boys runs after him, picks him up and staggers back to cover. Kat severely upbraids him for needlessly exposing himself. "But it's my friend, Behm," the boy says. "It's just a corpse now," Kat admonishes, "no matter who it is." It is a harrowing scene but sets the tone for what is to follow.

Trapped in a dugout for days by the heavy enemy bombardment, the terrified, shell-shocked boys are somehow held together by the iron will of Kat. Edeson has given these scenes in the dugout an especially realistic look. His low-key light level is very effective in catching the claustrophobic effect of the incessant bombardment.

Carl Laemmle, president of Universal, and the author, Erich Maria Remarque, come to terms in 1930.

Suddenly the bombardment lifts and the men run outside to man their positions on the trench fire step. Edeson's camera travels over the trenches, easily picks out Paul (whose helmet spike has been shot away – an effective trick Milestone uses to single out his key character). French shock troops are close to the German barbed wire. Machine guns go into action. Now Milestone and Edeson deliver some of the most effective scenes in the picture. Edeson's camera, mounted on the big crane and swung low to the ground, moves rapidly across and in front of the charging French infantry. Milestone intercuts these shots with short cuts of the machine guns firing. French soldiers are mown down by the terrible machine-gun fire as they race toward the German trenches. The tempo and speed of these shots increases. At one point we see a grenade explode in front of a charging French soldier. When the smoke clears only the hands remain suspended on the barbed wire almost as if in prayer. Paul turns his face in horror against his rifle stock.

The French reach the German trenches and leap onto the defenders. Hand-to-hand combat breaks out. The French are driven out. The Germans counterattack only to be stopped by French machine guns in a series of shots almost identical to what has just transpired. The battle is a stand-off.

This particular sequence has been justly praised for Milestone's mastery of cutting. Trained in the editing tradition of D.W. Griffith and greatly influenced by the so-called "montage" technique of the Soviet directors of the mid-twenties, Milestone and his film cutters (Edgar Adams and Milton Carruth) created some powerful film imagery. And, Edeson's cameras caught every violent moment of combat. Although Edeson photographed virtually all of these scenes silent, the addition of sound is skillfully and realistically applied so that one is never conscious of the deception.

According to Milestone, Junior Laemmle complained about the battle footage he was seeing in the dailies back at Universal City. "All I see is guys running to the left and guys running to the right. Where is the battle stuff?" Milestone told him he'd have to wait. "I'm not going to wait. I'm bringing you back to the studio right now."

Milestone went to work virtually around the clock sleeping in his chauffeur driven car between his home and the studio. Finally, a cut was finished about three o'clock one morning. An exhausted Milestone invited Paul Whiteman, the band leader, working in an adjoining cutting room on his own film, *King of Jazz,* to see what he and his cutter had wrought. There was a bit over a thousand feet of

The charge into the graveyard, filmed at Universal City.

spliced workprint but with no sound. When it was over, Whiteman was overcome. "If the rest of the picture is anything like this, you've go the winner of all time." (From an interview in 1968 with Kevin Brownlow.)

In another powerful sequence, German infantry are attacking through a church cemetery. They are stopped by heavy artillery fire and take cover in some of the graves that have been opened by exploding shells. A coffin, torn out of one of the graves, is flung over Paul who has been slightly wounded. In a panic he jumps into another shell hole. The enemy counterattacks. Paul crouches in the bottom of the hole, draws his trench knife and feigns death. But the counterattack breaks down and the French retreat. Suddenly a French soldier jumps into the shell hole with Paul. In a panic Paul gags the man with one hand and blindly stabs him

in the throat with the other. Unable to leave the shell hole because of heavy fire, Paul is forced to watch the Frenchman die. The ordeal continues through the night. Morning comes. The Frenchman is dead. Paul in remorse begs the dead man's forgiveness. Mercifully, night finally falls and Paul escapes back to his own lines.

Arthur Edeson has treated the passage of day-to-night and from night-back-to-day with a subtle but realistic lighting style. At night flashes of gunfire light up the shell hole. In the morning Edeson's camera catches the dead Frenchman's face in an unforgettable close-up. His dead eyes are open and stare into nothing. A whiff of smoke from the battlefield drifts into the frame. We see Paul's anguished, pleading face. It is a terrible moment put on film with great artistry.

There is a romantic idyll with three French peasant girls. Paul, Albert and Leer steal over the canal that separates their bivouac from the girls. As an inducement, they have brought along food. We hear – but don't see – Paul and one of the French

69

girls make love. The camera moves slowly about the moonlit room. The lighting is soft and in a low key.

Paul and Albert are both wounded and taken to a hospital behind the lines staffed by Catholic nuns. Edeson uses a higher lighting key for these scenes. Albert's shattered leg is amputated, unknown to him. When he comes out of the anesthetic, he complains of pain in his toes and suddenly remembers the complaint was the same he had heard made by another comrade in the same situation. Edeson's camera adroitly captures the pathetic moment when Albert tilts a small hand mirror in such a way that he sees with horror his leg is gone.

For Paul's convalescent homecoming Edeson has lit the scene in a high key. Bright sunlight streams through the front door as Paul enters his parents' home. His sister runs to embrace him. "Paul's home," she tells the mother, who is bedridden. As Paul realizes that he can no longer fit into life on the home front, the mood of the lighting becomes more subdued.

When Paul returns to his comrades at the front he discovers that only Tjaden and Kat are left. All the others have been either killed or wounded. And on the day of his return, Kat is killed.

Then comes the ending that *All Quiet* audiences long remember.

The author gave few clues concerning Paul's death. Milestone thought of several possible endings but rejected them one by one. The date of the world premiere had been set and the picture had to go in for negative conforming. Pressure from the front office was intense. Junior Laemmle threatened to take the whole thing away from Milestone.

Edeson was committed to another picture and had moved on. Milestone now had the services of Karl Freund, ASC, as cinematographer. Freund had just joined the camera staff at Universal City after distinguished work in Berlin's great Ufa Studios. Freund remembered an earlier scene where Paul paused by his butterfly collection when he was home on leave. This gave Freund the idea for the ending that he and Milestone shot that afternoon on the back lot at Universal City.

We see soldiers bailing water from a ruined trench. It is a bright day and is quiet on the front. Only the faint sound of a harmonica can be heard. Paul, on guard, is day dreaming in his trench. Suddenly, he sees a lone butterfly land on a shell casing just outside the parapet. He carefully reaches for it, momentarily forgetting the ever present danger. Cut to a shot of a distant French sniper who suddenly emerges from behind a log with a scope-mounted rifle. Back to Paul as he leans outside the trench reaching for the butterfly. The French sniper draws careful aim on Paul. His hand moves closer to the butterfly when suddenly there is the sharp whine of a shot. Paul's hand (actually Milestone's) jerks back, relaxes in death. The harmonica suddenly stops and there is a cut to sunlight streaming through the trees as the music comes up. It is one of the screen's most powerful, well remembered moments.

With such an unforgettable ending one wonders why someone at Universal decided to go one better. In a tear jerking symbolic epilogue, reminiscent of D.W. Griffith at his worst, we see a ghostly file of all the boys marching obliquely away from the camera and looking back at the audience with a sad, haunting look – the whole scene being superimposed over a sea of white crosses on a shell-torn battlefield. Some of the pacifist advertising appearing in magazines at that time probably influenced the addition of this scene.

When *All Quiet* was sneak previewed it unfortunately followed a comedy in which Zasu Pitts appeared. Miss Pitts, a splendid tragedienne as well as a great comedy actress, played Paul's sick mother. Despite her fine, sensitive performance, audiences snickered. It was the unwanted laugh that every filmmaker fears. Junior Laemmle panicked and despite Milestone's pleas ordered the scenes re-shot with another actress. Beryl Mercer, a plump actress of that period famous for mother roles, appeared in the re-takes. (Zasu Pitts' scenes were left in the silent version which Universal had prepared for theatres not yet wired for sound and also in some of the prints shipped abroad.)

Despite reports to the contrary, *All Quiet* was well received when it opened in Germany in 1930. It was denounced by Hitler, then a rapidly rising leader of the Nazi Party. His SA and SS hooligans released rats, snakes and stink bombs in theaters showing the picture. When Hitler finally came to power in 1933, he banned the picture outright. Remarque, who had already left his native Germany, went on the Gestapo's wanted list.

Over the years, *All Quiet* has been reissued several times. It has suffered the fate of many fine pictures by having many key scenes deleted. The videotape cassettes that are now available appear to have been made from the 1939 re-issue and are complete except for a few scenes that were apparently removed to cut the running time. The mutilated prints that occasionally turn up on commercial TV are a sad parody of the 14-reel version that

stunned audiences in 1930 and generated world wide praise.

All Quiet on the Western Front is still the yardstick by which all great war films are measured.

—George J. Mitchell

A Universal picture; presented by Carl Laemmle; *produced by* Carl Laemmle, Jr.; *directed by* Lewis Milestone; *from the book by* Erich Maria Remarque; *screen play by* George Abbott, Maxwell Anderson, Del Andrews; *story editor*, C. Gardner Sullivan; *director of photography*, Arthur Edeson, ASC; *associate director*, Nate Watt; *supervising editor*, Maurice Pivar; *film editors*, Edgar Adams, Milton Carruth; *recording supervision*, C. Roy Hunter; *art directors*, Charles D. Hall, William R. Schmitt; *dialogue director*, George Cukor; *musical synchronization*, David Broekman; *sound recordist*, William Hedgcock; *photographic effects*, Frank H. Booth; *assistant cameramen*, Allen Jones, Robert J. Bryan; *added photography*, Karl Freund, ASC; *mechanical effects*, Walter Hoffman; *technical advisors*, Hans Von Morhart, Wilhelm Von Brincken; *second assistant director*, Charles Gould; *still photographer*, Roman Freulich; *make-up artists*, Jack P. Pierce; *Movietone sound system; titles for silent version*, Walter Anthony; *narrator, 1939 version*, Graham McNamee. *N.Y. premiere, Central Theatre, April 29, 1930; Released August 24, 1930.*

Running time, 138 minutes (12,423 feet); silent version with synchronized music and sound effects, 15 reels.

Paul Baeumer, Lewis Ayres; *Katczinsky,* Louis Wolheim; *Himmelstoss,* John Wray; *Gerard Duval,* Raymond Griffith; *Tjaden,* George "Slim" Summerville; *Mueller,* Russell Gleason; *Albert,* William Bakewell; *Leer,* Scott Kolk; *Behm,* Walter Browne Rogers; *Kemmerich,* Ben Alexander; *Peter,* Owen Davis, Jr.; *Kantorek,* Arnold Lucy; *Westhus,* Richard Alexander; *Mrs. Baeumer,* Beryl Mercer *(in silent version,* Zasu Pitts); *Mr. Baeumer,* Edwin Maxwell; *Detering,* Harold Goodwin; *Miss Baeumer,* Marion Clayton; *Lt. Bertinck,* George Pat Collins; *Ginger,* Bill Irving; *Ginger's Assistant,* Vince Barnett; *Poster Girl,* Joan Marsh; *Suzanne,* Yola D'Avril; *French Girl,* Poupee Androit; *French Girl,* Renee Damonde; *Herr Meyer,* Edmund Breese; *Hammacher,* Heinie Conklin; *Sister Libertine,* Bertha Mann; *Woman Who Visits Hospital,* Bodil Rosing; *Hospital Orderlies,* Tom London, Ernie Adams; *Young Recruit,* Maurice Murphy. (Fred Zinneman *and* Robert Parrish, *later noted directors, appear as extras).*

Statistics

Production started November 11, 1929 (Armistice Day) and continued for 17 weeks. Total production cost: $1,250,000. Filmed at Universal City Studios, Irvine Ranch (Laguna Beach), RKO-Pathe Studios (Culver City), Malibu Lakes, Sherwood Forest (San Fernando Valley).

7

Two Faces of *Dracula*

On February 14, 1931, New York impresario S. L. Rothafel delivered an unusual Valentine to the patrons of his Roxy Theater. Advertised as "...the story of the strangest passion the world has ever known," *Dracula* corralled the customers in droves. Of greater importance, ultimately, is its trail blazing position as the forerunner of a genre which has ebbed and flowed as a film perennial ever since: the supernatural horror "talkie."

It's true that a number of sound pictures of the spine-chilling variety had preceded *Dracula*, including such popular numbers as *The Terror, Stark Mad, The Cat Creeps, The Bat Whispers,* and *The Gorilla*. Most of these were adapted from Broadway plays in which the scary stuff was intermingled with comedy and anything that appeared paranormal was always revealed as the machinations of malevolent human beings. What made *Dracula* different was that the audience was expected to accept the villain as a *genuine* vampire and not another crook in disguise. There was a strong feeling in the industry that the producers were insane to ask moviegoers, who had just emerged from the Roaring Twenties and stumbled into the morass of the Great Depression, to suspend disbelief in a Medieval superstition.

Above: Frances Dade and Bela Lugosi in the English-speaking Dracula. Below: Carlos Villar and Carmen Guerrero in the Spanish version.

Actually, *Dracula* proved that hard times enhanced the charm of such a picture. The movie companies found in short order that stories which tried to come to grips with the realities already bedeviling the public were not generally popular. After all, the idea of a 500-year old Carpathian nobleman surviving on the blood of lovely young English ladies was only slightly more fantastic than such popular fare as Westerns, murder mysteries, musical comedies, the Marx Brothers, and Hollywood's notions of romance among the millionaires. The allegorical aspects of a tale in which an evil outside force intrudes upon the lives of ordinary people who manage to overcome the menace may have triggered subconscious responses from a populace beleaguered by destructive forces against which it was helpless. The grimness of the theme was alleviated by its abnormality – viewers could forget for a time the realities of the Depression and share vicariously in problems that they knew would never touch their own lives.

It is difficult today to understand why *Dracula* was considered such a gamble in its day, and why, in light of the truly gruesome films that have come in its wake, it was repugnant to many who saw it. Whatever its faults, the picture is done in admirable taste. The only show of blood is a single drop on a man's finger following an accident with a paper clip; even those telltale "two little marks" that are discovered on the necks of the vampire's victims are kept discreetly out of sight of the camera – and there is only one instance of on-screen violence. Yet this picture, now more admired for its atmosphere

73

Renfield's coach arrives at a Transylvanian inn — on the Universal backlot.

and the commanding presence of Bela Lugosi than for any ability to horrify, stirred controversy when it first appeared.

Bram Stoker's book, published in England in 1897, was suggested by Central European vampire legends, which for many years had been utilized by authors of Gothic novels, and the historical accounts of a Wallachian war lord whose cruelty had earned him a reputation of being in league with Satan. From these sources emerged a remarkable work in which the vampire, instead of being a crawling graveyard creature, is a Transylvanian *voyevoda* possessing fantastic strength and the magical ability to transform himself into a wolf or bat or wisp of vapor, to command animals and storms, and to hypnotize humans and animals at a gesture. He can walk only by night, casts no reflection, and is practically immortal so long as he feasts regularly on the blood of the living, stays in his grave during the daylight hours, and doesn't encounter anyone so unkind as to drive a stake through his heart during a nap. He is a withered ancient with white hair and fetid breath, but after feasting he takes on a younger, less forbidding appearance. He fears the Christian Cross and is violently allergic to garlic and wolfbane.

In Germany in 1921, the brilliant F. W. Murnau directed a highly effective unauthorized version titled *Nosferatu*, but released in England as *Dracula*. The vampire – Baron Orlok in Germany, Count Dracula in England – was a rat-like,

74

Part of the country inn. Michael Visaroff (right) is the innkeeper.

Meticulous costuming and details lend conviction to Transylvanian scenes.

ghoulish creature. Stoker sued, but the production company (Prana Film) had gone broke and the plaintiffs had to be content with having prints destroyed. Fortunately, the picture survives as an excellent example of the German Expressionist school.

In 1924 an English provincial play producer and actor, Hamilton Deane, wrote an authorized stage production which proved so popular that he soon had two touring companies on the road. He didn't muster the courage to present it to a London audience until 1927, when he opened it at the Little Theatre on February 14 with Raymond Huntley as Dracula and himself as the vampire's nemesis, Professor Van Helsing. Despite a drubbing from the critics, the play ran for 391 performances. An American producer, Horace Liveright, saw it in March and purchased rights to produce it in the United States. John L. Balderston, London correspondent for the New York *World* and a noted playwright, adapted the show for Broadway. It opened at the Fulton Theater on October 5 to mixed reviews and enthusiastic audience response. The title role was played by a young Hungarian emigre, Bela Lugosi, whose dignified but saturnine appearance and heavily accented delivery created a romantic, urbane image far removed from the repulsive ancients envisioned by Stoker and Murnau. The play ran for 261 performances in New York, then went on the road with great success.

About four months before the Broadway version opened, Universal Pictures considered making a silent screen adaptation. After studying the Stoker book, most of the studio readers conclud-

Carriage from Castle Dracula meets Frye at Borgo Pass.

Through clever lighting in this frame from Dracula Dwight Frye is given the multi-legged appearance of an insect.

Glass shot combining coach at Vasquez Rocks with painting of mountains.

Shadow of the dead captain on the ghost ship Vesta.

ed in their reports of June 15 that as screen material *Dracula* was "...out of the question...it would be an insult to every one of its audience...passes beyond the point of what the average person can stand or cares to stand." A minority opinion averred that "For mystery and blood-curdling horror, I have never read its equal. For sets, impressionistic and weird, it cannot be surpassed. This story contains everything necessary for a weird, unnatural, mysterious picture...It will be a difficult task and one will run up against the censor continually, but I think it can be done. It is daring but if done there can be no doubt as to its making money." In October, following the opening of the New York play, Universal reassessed the work. The majority conclusion was that although it could make "a great picture... from the angle of the pictorial and the dramatic, it is not picture material from the standpoint of the box office nor of ethics of the industry."

In 1929 Universal got a new chief studio executive: Carl Laemmle Jr., five-foot three, 21-year old son of the company's president. Eccentric and hypochondriacal, Junior Laemmle had some ideas that ran contrary to those of many of the studio old-timers. One of them was to put *Dracula* into production on a grand scale. Despite the opposition of his advisors, Laemmle Sr. – with considerable trepidation – okayed the project. Rights to book and play were acquired for $40,000 and in June of 1930 Fritz Stephani completed a 32-page treatment. It was announced that "almost $400,000" would be spent on the production – an impressive sum from a studio in financial trouble.

Other writers – including Louis Stevens, Louis Bromfield and Dudley Murphy, contributed to the evolution of the shooting script, which eventually was completed by Garrett Fort.

The Bromfield screenplay, which was based primarily upon the book, could have been an almost definitive version of the subject, but it was rejected as being vulnerable to censorship as well as difficult to produce as a sound film because of the considerable outdoor action. The final script restricts most exterior photography to the first 25 minutes of the picture, then keeps the action indoors except for a few short scenes.

Tod Browning, a veteran director who specialized in the making of weird and unusual pictures, including some of Lon Chaney's successes at Universal and MGM, was signed for *Dracula*. Browning said that he and Chaney had discussed making the story as a silent film years before, but concluded that it couldn't be done successfully without dialogue. Now the era of talking pictures had arrived, but it was too late to consider Chaney, who was dying of cancer after having completed his first and only talking picture, *The Unholy Three.*

Universal's replacement for Chaney when he moved to MGM had been the German actor, Conrad Veidt, who performed superbly in several Universal silents between 1927 and 1929 – including the marvelous *The Man Who Laughs* and the part-talking *The Last Warning.* Veidt returned to Germany, however, when faced with the prospect of making talkies in English. Laemmle Jr. considered bringing Veidt back for *Dracula.* There is no question but that Veidt would have been ideal for the role, but he was not disposed to leave Europe at the time.

Passing over Lugosi as not being sufficiently well known, the studio considered Fox Film's character star from the stage, Paul Muni; the darkly handsome Ian Keith, a brilliant actor then in disfavor because of a drinking problem; and the distinguished stage actor, William Courtenay. An attempt was made to borrow Chester Morris from producer Roland West. Eventually, Lugosi was brought in for tests. In mid-September he signed a two-picture contract for $500 a week.

Karl Freund, ASC, the most celebrated cinematographer of Germany's "Golden Age" of expressionism, was assigned to *Dracula,* his first American film. His German credits included *Variety, Metropolis, The Last Laugh, The Golem, Symphony of a City,* and other revered classics of imaginative cinema. Born in Bohemia in 1890, he had been a movie technician and cameraman since 1906. He was also an inventor, owned a film lab in Berlin, and was a director and producer for Fox Film in Germany. When he came to America in 1930 to tout a color process in which he had a proprietary interest, William Stull, ASC secretary, informed him that "...at the last meeting of the Board of Governors of the American Society of Cinematographers, you, as Europe's foremost cinematographer, were unanimously elected to Active Membership in that society."

Freund gravitated to Universal, which he had visited in 1924 while *Phantom of the Opera* was being made there. Arthur Edeson, ASC, then Universal's top-ranking cinematographer, championed him as "a great photographer" and "Uncle Carl" Laemmle, who was extremely loyal to his native Germany, welcomed him with open arms. Freund ingratiated himself quickly by suggesting the perfect ending for *All Quiet on the Western Front* that had eluded the writers.

To call the short, rotund Freund "colorful" would be to understate the case. He could be gra-

Lugosi in Carfax Abbey.

cious and charming at one moment, cool and distant in the next. When directing, he proved to be a hard-boiled, Prussian-styled taskmaster in the tradition of his mentor, Fritz Lang. A handful of directorial assignments from 1933 to 1935 *(The Mummy, Moonlight and Pretzels, Uncertain Lady, The Countess of Monte Cristo* and *Mad Love),* all of which were realized with speed and resourcefulness, prove him to have been a brilliant and imaginative director.

Universal's supervising art director, the very British Charles D. Hall, made a number of idea drawings for key sets, including the much imitated cellars of Dracula's London home, with its massed groined arches and monumental stairway. He was assisted by two remarkable artists, Herman Rosse and John Hoffman. Rosse, a noted stage set designer from The Netherlands, had come to Universal for the spectacular *King of Jazz,* which won him an Academy Award for 1929-30. It was Rosse who saved a chunk of the set budget for *Dracula* by designing the spectacular facade of Castle Dracula so it could be pieced together with portions of disassembled Medieval sets from the silent days. Hoffman was one of those brilliant but little known artists who worked behind the scenes at the major studios. He designed sets for several early talkies, but later switched to directing, special effects photography, and, most notably, creating montage sequences.

With a budget of $355,050 and scheduled for 36 working days, principal photography was begun September 29 on the backlot country inn set. It was completed November 15, after 42 working days, at a negative cost of $341,191.20. Added scenes were shot on December 13, and retakes were made on January 2, 1931.

A Spanish language version, utilizing the same sets but with a different cast, producer, director and crew, was begun on the night of October 10, 1930, and completed in 26 working nights on November 11. The negative cost was $69,336. The producer was Paul Kohner, who later founded a leading talent agency but at the time was head of Universal's foreign department. Czechoslovakian-born and Vienna-educated, the tall and personable Kohner had been a production supervisor at Universal for years and was the producer of an excellent silent spectacle, *The Man Who Laughs*. It was because he fell in love with Lupita Tovar, a beautiful actress from Mexico who was playing small parts at Universal, that Kohner talked Carl Laemmle Sr. into letting him make Spanish language productions.

"Lupita told me she couldn't make enough money at Universal and she was going back to Mexico," Kohner said in early 1988. "I lay awake all night trying to figure a way to change her mind. I went to Uncle Carl and told him that I could make Spanish versions of his pictures for about $35,000 each by using the same sets after the regular company had quit for the night. He agreed to give it a try with *The Cat Creeps*. I put Lupita in Helen Twelvetrees' role, the picture was a great success, and she decided to stay in Hollywood." Following a triumphant tour of Mexico, the petite actress was assigned the feminine lead in the Spanish *Dracula*. She also became Mrs. Kohner. The marriage was happy and enduring. Paul Kohner died March 16, 1988, at the age of 85.

George Melford, a veteran director of the hard-boiled school, who was best known for the Rudolph Valentino silent, *The Sheik*, directed. The cinematographer was George Robinson, ASC, undoubtedly one of the many underrated artists in his field. The adaptation was the work of the scholarly Baltazar Fernandez Cue, who did many of the Spanish language screenplays made in Hollywood. In the cast were Carlos Villar as Dracula, Lupita Tovar as Eva (Mina), Barry Norton as Juan, Eduardo Arozamena as Van Helsing, Carmen Guerrero as Lucia, and Pablo Alvarez Rubio as Renfield. Villar somewhat resembled Lugosi and obviously patterned his portrayal after him, only to come out second best. The other players seem not to have been influenced by the first string performers. Tovar and Rubio are very good. Some of the special effects scenes, exteriors and long shots from the first unit production were utilized for the Spanish rendition. At least one glass shot and a fine miniature of Carfax Abbey on a cliff overlooking the sea appear only in the Spanish version.

Both versions of *Dracula* open with a glass shot, which was photographed by Frank Booth, of a horse-drawn coach coming at breakneck speed down a mountain road in the wilds of Transylvania. Swirling mist is superimposed over the scene, which was photographed northeast of Los Angeles at Vasquez Rocks, whose angular hogback formations blend flawlessly into the artist's towering peaks. A young English passenger, Renfield, admonishes the driver to slow down, but is ignored. A local rider explains excitedly, "We must reach the inn before sundown! It is Walpurgis Night, a night of evil. Nosferatu! On this night...the doors, they are barred, and to the Virgin we pray." The coach arrives at the inn, where there is rejoicing that the coach arrived in time. The innkeeper, learning that Renfield plans to continue on to a midnight rendevous with Count Dracula at Borgo Pass, tries to talk him out of it. "We people of the mountains believe that Dracula and his wives are vampires," he explains. "They leave their coffins at night and they feed on the blood of the living." Renfield boards the coach after accepting a crucifix from a peasant lady who admonishes him to "Wear this, for your mother's sake."

The inn, yard, corral and peasant hut were constructed on a backlot hill (now the site of a studio tour rest stop) around a deeply rutted old wagon trail. A large wooden cross, jutting from the brow of the hill, and other Old World props lend versimilitude to the setting. There are other glass shots of the castle and the coach in the mountains and an excellent miniature of Castle Dracula perched atop the crags. The camera roams the ruined cellars, where rats, armadillos and other animals scurry among skeletons and debris. (Some of these shots are different in the Spanish version.) There are several coffins. The lid of one raises slightly and a man's hand snakes forth. The hands of women emerge from three other coffins and a gigantic beetle crawls out of another. Then Dracula and his wives are shown standing majestically beside their coffins. (In the Spanish version a heavy mist spreads from each opened coffin, followed by a pillar of light, then by the standing figure of the vampire).

Subsequent night for night scenes, representing the midnight meeting point in Borgo Pass,

Left: *Van Helsing (Edward van Sloan) and Dracula (Lugosi)*. Right: *Dracula (Villar) and Van Helsing (Eduardo Arozamena)*.

were photographed at a mountainous junction in the west part of the lot. These unreal but eerily effective shots are backlit from below, the light beaming up through the mist, presumably from a town in the valley.

Renfield is all but dumped in the road as the driver hurries away. The closed carriage from the castle awaits. The driver is a silent man in black recognizable as Dracula himself. Renfield boards and is whisked roughly away. He tries to speak to the driver, but the seat is empty. A large bat flaps along between the heads of the horses. Debarking at the castle, Renfield is unable to find the driver. The massive doors of the castle swing open and Renfield enters, appalled to find the great hall in ruins. A voice announces, "I am Dracula," and Renfield looks up the huge stairway to see his smiling host, formally attired, standing in front of a huge spider web. Wolves howl outside. "Listen to them!" says Dracula enthusiastically. "Children of the night. What music they make!" He bids Renfield to follow and the Englishman is startled to discover that Dracula has moved beyond the unbroken web, which spans the width of the staircase. As Renfield hacks through with his cane, Dracula notes, "The spider, spinning his web for the unwary fly. The blood is the life, Mr. Renfield."

Renfield is ushered to a large, cheerful room where a meal awaits him. It is shown that Renfield is a realtor from London who has been asked to come secretly bearing a lease to Carfax Abbey in Whitby. When Renfield accidently cuts his finger on a paper clip, Dracula is transfixed by the sight of blood and approaches menacingly. The crucifix drops out upon Renfield's hand and Dracula steps back, covering his eyes. He then offers Ren-

field a bottle of "very old wine," but doesn't partake with him because, "I never drink – wine." After Dracula departs, Renfield, drugged, stumbles to the terrace window, where he is halted by a large bat that emerges from a wall of fog. As Renfield collapses, Dracula's wives enter and approach wolfishly, but they are driven back by a silent command from Dracula. At the fade, as fog engulfs the room, Dracula bends toward his fallen guest.

The journey to the castle is handsomely photographed, particularly in a stunning pit-shot as the team and carriage hurtle over the camera in a thunderous roar and vanish into the castle grounds. The vaulted hall is introduced in a glass shot that expands the impressive set to enormous proportions. It perfectly conveys decaying grandeur and an atmosphere of dread. A fallen tree thrusts its branches through tall windows, bats flutter and screech beyond breaks in the walls, and the place is littered with fallen stones, decaying tapestries, cobwebs and dust. The deep shadows and some scurrying sounds suggest unseen menace at every hand. The "cheerful" bedroom is also large, with a fireplace of heroic proportions, windows that extend above the frame, ornate pillars and massive furnishings. This room is exploited to better effect in the Spanish film, in which the camera and players move more freely and the flaming fireplace becomes more than a backdrop.

Frye in Carfax Abbey.

In the hold of the sailing bark Vesta, bound for England through a terrible storm, an obviously insane Renfield crouches beside one of three large boxes and hisses, "Master, the sun is gone." He cowers and pleads as Dracula stands over him: "You will keep your promise, master? When we get to England I'll have lives – not human lives, but small ones, with blood in them." One morning, at the dock at Whitby, officials come aboard the derelict vessel which has mysteriously arrived during the night. All the crewmen are dead or missing and the dead captain is lashed to the wheel. Hearing crazed laughter from the hold, they open the hatch and see Renfield staring up at them. A newspaper item tells that the only survivor of the ship, a madman with an insatiable desire to eat flies and insects, has been placed in Dr. Seward's sanitarium at Whitby.

The Vesta is depicted first as a miniature. Full scale shots of the seamen fighting to keep the ship afloat are undercranked, suggesting that they are footage from a silent film. The investigation of the derelict is imaginatively executed, the camera roving over the deck, taking in the details as the voices of the unseen men come over. In Browning's version, the director himself bends into the scene to open the hatch. The scene gunning down at Renfield is quite subtle: the madman's shadow produces an illusion that he has additional arms jutting from

his lower body, lending him an appropriate insect-like appearance.

Dracula next is seen in opera cape and top hat, striding by night through a foggy London street. His eyes fix hypnotically upon a girl selling flowers, then he draws her into a dark corner. Later, he enters a concert hall where a performance of the London Symphony is in progress. Placing a hostess under hypnosis, he sends her to Dr. Seward's box with a message that he is wanted on the telephone. With Seward are his daughter, Mina (Eva), her fiance, John (Juan) and their friend, Lucy (Lucia) Weston. Pretending to have overheard the name of Seward, he introduces himself and explains that he has leased Carfax Abbey, which lies adjacent to the sanitarium. Although it is virtually in ruins, he says he will make few repairs because, "It reminds me of the broken battlements of my own castle in Transylvania." Lucy, who is attracted to him immediately, is reminded of an old toast, "Lofty timbers, the walls around are bare, echoing to our laughter as though the dead were there. Quaff a cup to the dead already, hooray for the next to die!" Dracula, betraying a rapturous longing, cries, "To die – to be really dead! That must be glorious! There are far worse things awaiting man than death."

The interior of Albert Hall, incidentally, is the famed "Phantom" Stage 28, which was built some years earlier for *The Phantom of the Opera*.

Lucy stays the night with the Sewards. Dracula watches her upstairs window as she prepares for bed. Soon a bat appears at the window; a moment later, Dracula approaches her bed. Fade in on an operating room, where Seward and his colleagues are unable to save Lucy from dying of "an unnatural loss of blood which we have been powerless to check. And on the throat of each victim the same two marks."

Crane shots of the sanitarium grounds follow. Screams are heard from an upstairs room and the camera moves up to peer in as Martin, an orderly, confiscates a spider from Renfield and upbraids him for eating flies. "Who wants to eat flies...when I can get nice, fat spiders?" Renfield snarls.

Professor Van Helsing, a wise but unorthodox physician, has been brought from the Netherlands by Seward to investigate the strange deaths. Analyzing blood samples, he announces that "we are dealing with the undead. Yes, nosferatu, the undead – vampires." He suspects that Renfield is the mortal slave of a vampire. To Seward's objections he replies that "the superstition of yesterday can become the scientific reality of today."

Helen Chandler, Lugosi, and Frye on the stairway in Carfax Abbey.

In his moments of sanity, Renfield begs to be sent away because his outbursts might give Mina "bad dreams." A wolfish howling is heard by night; Van Helsing believes it is the vampire communicating with Renfield. Dracula preys upon Mina that night. The next day, Mina tells of her "nightmare." "The room seemed to fill with fog... Then two red eyes... a white, livid face... It came closer, closer; then the lips touched me." Van Helsing discovers the mark of the vampire on Mina's throat. After dinner Dracula comes calling, recognizing Van Helsing as "A most distinguished scientist, whose name we know even in the wilds of Transylvania." Suspicious, Van Helsing tricks Dracula into looking into a concealed mirror. Dracula, livid with rage, makes a hasty apology and leaves through the French windows. A wolf is seen running across the lawn – Dracula, Van Helsing explains. Mina steals outside and is again victimized by Dracula.

A policeman, patrolling near a cemetery, hears a crying child and sees the white-shrouded figure of a woman disappearing into the darkness. Newspapers tell of a mysterious woman in white who attacks children, wounding them in the neck. Mina confesses that she has seen Lucy since her death and that "She looked like a hungry animal – a wolf." Van Helsing promises that he will free Lucy from Dracula's curse. Renfield reveals that Dracula has promised him "rats – thousands, millions of them, all filled with blood" in return for his obedience. Dracula returns and reveals to Van Helsing

81

are better visually, being made up of a greater variety of shots. The sets are decorated more colorfully for the Latin audience, with added frills and filagrees, and the lace negligees worn by Tovar and Guerrero are considerably more eye-catching than the more British nightwear of Helen Chandler and Frances Dade. The one thing lacking is the magical ensemble work that Lugosi, Dwight Frye and Edward van Sloan gave to Browning.

A puzzling sequence in the English version has the silly maid faint when Renfield leers at her. The next shot, made from floor level, has the maid prone in the foreground and Renfield crawling toward her on all fours. The scene fades as he reaches toward her, leaving the viewer to wonder if she was bitten, violated, strangled, or what. The scene plays through in the Spanish film: Renfield grabs a fly that had landed on her dress and eats it!

The climax occurs in Carfax Abbey, a magnificently decadent setting, and in these scenes much of the excitement of the opening reels is regained. Although the elaborate camera moves that were a Freund hallmark are absent in the English version, the lighting of the catacombs and a huge vault with a long, curving, unbalustraded stairway show artistry of a high order. Here again, however, Melford and Robinson take the palm for some stunning camera moves, especially when they utilize the unique "Broadway Crane" to carry the action onto the high stairs.

Renfield escapes from the sanitarium and goes to the abbey, followed by Van Helsing and John. Dracula angrily lifts Renfield by the throat and hurls him down the stair. Escaping his pursuers, Dracula flees to the catacombs below. Finding the coffins at dawn, Van Helsing opens one to reveal the helpless Dracula. The second casket proves to be empty and John goes searching for Mina. When Van Helsing destroys Dracula, Mina feels his death agonies, but as Dracula dies she is freed from his curse. Mina and John ascend the stairs as distant church bells ring.

In the original release prints, the end title was interrupted as Van Helsing stepped in front of the screen to make a brief curtain speech: "Please! One moment before you go. We hope the memories of Dracula won't give you bad dreams, so just a word of assurance. When you go home tonight and lights have been turned out and you're afraid to look behind the curtains and you dread to see a face at the window – why, just pull yourselves together and remember that, after all, *there are such things.*" The speech is taken from the New York play, in which it was spoken by Dracula.

that Mina is lost because "My blood now flows through her veins." He tries to overcome Van Helsing, but is driven away by a crucifix.

Mina tries to attack John, but Van Helsing halts her with the cross. (Eva attacks Juan with considerably more passion). She admits that Dracula made her drink his blood and she is now his slave. Later, as Mina sleeps, Dracula hypnotizes her nurse and causes her to remove the wolfbane that protects Mina. Dracula carries Mina away.

The scenes inside the sanitarium are photographed straightforwardly in rather long takes, showing little of the imagination that distinguishes the Transylvanian action. The action proceeds in the manner of a stage play, with some key material happening off-screen (the werewolf episode, for example). The feeling that great opportunities have been missed is inescapable. It is generally believed that Browning had to hurry through this part of the picture because he had fallen so far behind schedule. The several exterior scenes, however, are fascinating because of excellent night for night lighting and fog effects. The Melford/Robinson sequences

Also from the Spanish version, Rubio and Villar in the "cheerful" part of Castle Dracula.

The picture was photographed in full silent frame aperture for sound on disc presentation and for a subtitled silent version with intercut dialogue titles. When the sound-on-film prints were made (the Vitaphone was rapidly becoming obsolete) the picture area was masked to Western Electric standards to allow for the sound track and some masking at the top and bottom. This operation shifted the optical center and changed the compositions noticeably. The visuals gain considerably when seen at full aperture.

The Spanish *Dracula* was previewed early in January at the studio. The Hollywood Filmograph (January 10) stated that ''If the English version of *Dracula*, directed by Tod Browning, is as good as the Spanish version, why the Big U haven't a thing in the world to worry about...The other evening, before a capacity theatre on the lot, there was screened a preview...which was witnessed by Bela Lugosi...and to use his own words the Spanish picture was 'beautiful, great, splendid.' ''

The English *Dracula* was announced to open at the Roxy on Friday, February 13, and go into national release the next day. Browning, pleading

Actual size of silent aperture (left) and the masking for sound on film presentations.

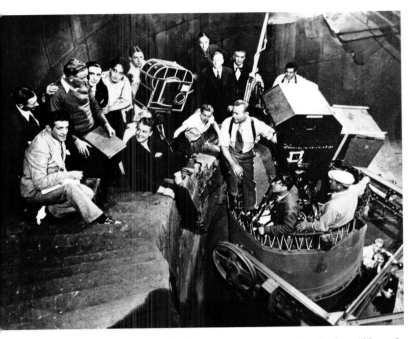

The Spanish Language company in Carfax Abbey. In front of camera from left are visitor Tod Browning, B. Fernandez Cue, George Melford, Carlos Villar and Barry Norton. Riding the Broadway crane are George Robinson and his camera crew. The man wearing the string tie is Eduardo Arozamena.

that he was "born superstitious," telegraphed his objections to the equally impressionable Rothafel, who promptly changed the date to the 14th.

The epilogue, for reasons unknown, was removed when the picture was reissued in 1936. At this time the Production Code Administration, which had become much more strict in the meantime, was unable to find anything visual that was deemed censorable. However, two cuts in the sound track were demanded: Renfield's shrieks when he is being strangled by Dracula, and Dracula's piteous cries (from off screen) while Van Helsing is pounding the stake through his heart.

In 1988 Universal had the English edition restored by YCM Laboratory in Burbank. The original negative was so badly worn as to be useless, according to technician Peter Comandini, but a new neg was struck from a 1930 lavender protection print and the original frame ratio was restored. The censored bits from the sound track were found at the British Film Institute and placed in the new track,

which was improved enormously by use of the Impact Noise Reduction system. The curtain speech was found in fragmentary condition and proved to be unreproducible. Restoration is complicated because the scene was photographed as a fast dolly-in shot.

Although it seems a bit of a museum piece today, *Dracula* has some enduring and endearing qualities. Not the least of these is the performance of Lugosi, whose extravagant acting style and distinctively phrased, heavily accented delivery fit the role to perfection. Similarly, Van Sloan (of the stage play) and Frye are indelibly linked to their roles. David Manners does well by the Juvenile role and Helen Chandler makes a nice transition from ingenue to apprentice vampire. Herbert Bunston – also from the play – is fine as the harried doctor. Freund's photographic style – which achieves a misty poetry at times and set a trend by emphasis upon Lugosi's eyes – still evokes an uncanny atmosphere. The settings could hardly be improved upon.

Its only music is an abridgement of Scene One of Tchaikovski's "Swan Lake" during the titles, and (at the concert) bits of Wagner's "Der Meistersinger" and Schubert's Eighth Symphony. Most present day viewers are critical of the lack of any background music, but audiences in 1931 felt differently. After years of watching silent movies with musical accompaniment, many filmgoers believed that such music was old fashioned and constituted an intrusion upon the natural sounds and dialogue of the new talkies. In this context the long silent sequences which occur through much of the picture are daring and effective.

And what of the Spanish version? An incomplete print exists at the Museum of Modern Art

Villar pays a nocturnal visit to Lupita Tovar.

Frames showing original end title and beginning and end of the lost curtain speech by Edward van Sloan which interrupted it.

in New York. Even with a full reel missing it is considerably longer than the English edition. A complete print in the Cuban Film Archive is listed at 102 minutes – a full 27 minutes longer than the standard version. It's easy to agree with the El Cine Espanol critic Fillipe Veracoechea, who said in 1931 that "Spanish American audiences will receive Dracula as the most fascinating picture made." There was only one squawk from the audiences: the clash of different dialects spoken by actors who hailed variously from Spain, Mexico, and Central and South America.

—George E. Turner

English Language Version

A Universal Picture presented by Carl Laemmle; a Tod Browning production; produced by Carl Laemmle, Jr.; directed by Tod Browning; associate producer, E. M. Asher; by Bram Stoker; from the play adapted by Hamilton Deane and John L. Balderston; play script, Garrett Fort; art director, Charles D. Hall; recording supervision, C. Roy Hunter; cinematographer, Karl Freund, ASC; film editor, Milton Carruth; supervising film editor, Maurice Pivar; continuity, Louis Bromfield; added dialogue, Dudley Murphy; adaptation, Louis Stevens; treatment, Fritz Stephanie; scenario supervision, Charles A. Logue; set designers, Herman Rosse, John Hoffman; photographic effects, Frank J. Booth; musical conductor, Heinz Roemheld; make-up artist, Jack P. Pierce; set decorations, Russell A. Gausman; costumes, Ed Ware, Vera West; miniatures, William Davidson; casting, Phil M. Friedman; research, Nan Grant; art titles, Max Cohen; Western Electric recording. Running time, sound on film and sound on disc versions, 75 minutes; Running time, silent version, 78 minutes. Released February 14, 1931.

Count Dracula, Bela Lugosi; Mina, Helen Chandler; John Harker, David Manners; Renfield, Dwight Frye; Van Helsing, Edward van Sloan; Dr. Seward, Herbert Bunston; Lucy, Frances Dade; Briggs, Joan Standing; Martin, Charles Gerrard; Maid, Moon Carroll; Nurse, Josephine Velez; Innkeeper, Michael Visaroff; English Passenger, Daisy Belmore; Transylvanian Passenger, Nicholas Bela; Girl, Carla Laemmle; Passenger, Donald Murphy; Harbor Master, Tod Browning.

Spanish Language Version

A Universal Picture presented by Carl Laemmle; produced by Carl Laemmle, Jr.; associate producer, Paul Kohner; directed by George Melford; by Bram Stoker from the play adapted by Hamilton Deane and John L. Balderston; screen play by B. Fernandez Cue from a screenplay by Garrett Fort; art director, Charles D. Hall; cinematographer, George Robinson, ASC; editorial supervision, Maurice Pivar; sound supervisor, C. Roy Hunter; film editor, Arturo Tavares; make-up artist, Jack P. Pierce; assistant directors, Jay Marchant, Charles Gould; settings, Herman Rosse, John Hoffman; photographic effects, Frank J. Booth; miniatures, William Davidson; costumes, Ed Ware, Vera West; script continuity, Josephine Llor; title art, Max Cohen; Western Electric recording (film and disc). Running time, 102 minutes. Released January, 1931.

Count Dracula, Carlos Villar; Eva, Lupita Tovar; Juan Harker, Barry Norton; Renfield, Pablo Alvarez Rubio; Professor Van Helsing, Eduardo Arozamena; Lucia, Carmen Guerrero; Dr. Seward, Jose Soriana Viosco; Martin, Manuel Arbo; Marta, Amelia Senisterra.

8

Frankenstein, the Monster Classic

"This is going to be a big year in motion pictures," Carl Laemmle Jr. told the New York *Times* in June 1931. "[A chance for] daring, originality, [to] explore new fields. Yes, sir, explore new fields and I want to do some exploring. There was *Dracula*, which had been on the market for years just waiting to be plucked. That was ideal – good notices and it made money. As as result of the reception given *Dracula*, we're pushing plans for *Frankenstein* and *Murders in the Rue Morgue*. The stories are well under way."

Indeed they were. By mid-March Universal had begun negotiating with Peggy Webling, author of a 1924 British play based on Mary Wollstonecraft Shelley's 1818 novel, "Frankenstein, or the Modern Prometheus," and John L. Balderston, who had written a modern adaptation of the Webling play. In May Universal had agreed to pay $20,000 and one percent of gross earnings to Webling and Balderston. Scenario editor Richard Schayer had already assigned French director-writer Robert Florey to prepare a treatment, develop a screenplay with ace scenarist Garrett Fort, and (presumably) direct.

Laemmle also revealed that the picture would be photographed by Karl Freund, ASC, and that Bela Lugosi would portray the Monster.

Florey and Fort, in accordance with orders from the front office, contemporized the story and strayed far afield of the rambling Shelley saga. Their first draft script contained several ideas that survive in the finished film. One is the idea that Frankenstein accidentally places the brain of a murderer in his Monster's skull. Another is the windmill in which the Monster perishes in a fire. Florey said that the idea came to him because his Hollywood apartment on Ivar Street overlooked one of the delft-blue Van de Kamp bakeries, which were designed as large windmills with wings that turned by mechanical power. Frankenstein's laboratory also was situated in the windmill in the Florey-Fort scenario, but in the final script by Francis Edwards Faragoh it was relocated to an ancient Roman watchtower. A bit from the early concept somehow crept into the finished film: Frankenstein's father asks, "Why does he go messing around in an old ruined windmill when he has a decent house, a bath, good food and drink, and a darned pretty girl to come back to – huh?"

In mid-June, while Florey and Fort were working on the shooting script, Junior Laemmle authorized the making of a test film. After a day of rehearsal the test was made on Stage 12 on June 16-17, with Florey directing and Paul Ivano, ASC, photographing. The cast consisted of Edward van Sloan as Professor Waldman, Dwight Frye as Fritz, two unidentified players as Henry Frankenstein and his friend, Victor, and Lugosi as the Monster. Both Lugosi and Florey were infuriated; they had assumed that Lugosi would play Frankenstein, but Junior Laemmle decreed otherwise, saying that Lugosi was being groomed as the successor to Lon Chaney. It should be noted that neither Lugosi nor Florey ever regarded the Monster as anything more than a semi-mechanical brute which could be portrayed easily by anybody with an imposing physique.

The test, consisting of two full reels (running about 20 minutes), began with Victor calling upon Waldman at the University and being told of Henry's insane ambition to bring the dead to life. Meanwhile, Fritz, Henry's hunchbacked helper, stole a specimen brain of an executed criminal from Waldman's laboratory. Waldman and Victor went to Frankenstein's laboratory in an old windmill and were permitted to watch as Frankenstein endowed his creature with life. The creation sequence utilized the big staircase from *Dracula* with the laboratory arranged before it within a circular room. During the filming Lugosi paced the stage angrily, complaining that he wanted out of the picture. Privately he said he would get a doctor's excuse if necessary. When the rushes were screened, however, Lugosi congratulated Ivano and handed him some expensive cigars.

There is considerable disagreement regarding Lugosi's makeup. Both Florey and Ivano insisted that it was virtually identical to that eventually worn by Karloff. Van Sloan, when interviewed about 30 years later by Forrest J. Ackerman, recalled Lugosi as resembling Paul Wegener as *Der Golem* in the 1920 German film, with oversized head, massive wig and clay-like skin. Jack P. Pierce, who headed Universal's makeup department from 1926 to 1947, stated pointedly that the makeup was mostly of Lugosi's own devising, that it was very hairy and tended to melt and run during the walk from the dressing room to the sound stage, and that Junior Laemmle didn't like it. Whatever is known of the test is hearsay; it disappeared quickly and, though eagerly sought after, has never resurfaced.

As things worked out, Florey didn't get to direct *Frankenstein*. An English director, James Whale, had done so well with Universal's *Waterloo Bridge* that Junior Laemmle felt disposed to offer him any script he fancied. (It was, in fact, an unofficial studio policy to so reward any director who delivered a hit picture.) Whale chose *Frankenstein*. Laemmle assigned the scenario and direction of *Murders in the Rue Morgue* to the unhappy Florey and gave him Lugosi and Freund as well.

Whale had obtained a print of the pioneer German expressionist film, *The Cabinet of Dr. Caligari* (1919), and said he wanted *Frankenstein* to have a somewhat similar look. (So, incidentally, had Florey.) The makers of *Caligari* had made no attempt at realism, instead having the strangely garbed actors

Three of Herman Rosse's conceptual drawings.

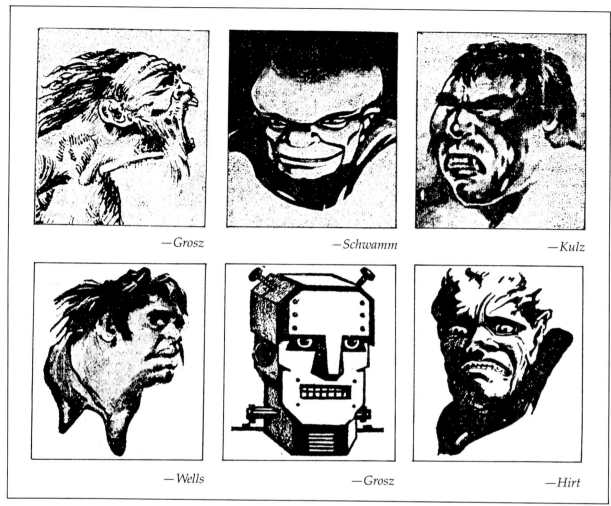

—Grosz   —Schwamm   —Kulz

—Wells   —Grosz   —Hirt

Pre-production concepts of the Monster by Universal artists.

—Rosse

perform in a balletic pantomime amid starkly cubistic canvas sets with painted shadows. The front office, on the other hand, favored a modern, high-tech look.

A brilliant Netherlands-born set designer, Herman Rosse, was given the task of creating the general design of the picture. Rosse came to the studio in 1930 and his work can be seen in such films as *Dracula, Resurrection, Boudoir Diplomat, East is West, Strictly Dishonorable* and *Murders in the Rue Morgue*. The front office wanted an ultra-modern look for *Frankenstein* while Whale was more interested in something part Gothic and part German Expressionist.

Rosse made 32 large ink-and-wash drawings for *Frankenstein*. All are highly imaginative and the influence of several can be seen clearly in the final concept of the film, particularly in the body-snatching scenes at the opening and the torchlit chase sequence. The laboratory design, as requested, is slick and futuristic, entirely unlike the high and angular final concept. Art director Charles D. Hall was in charge during the final pre-production period, and the picture as completed exhibits the imaginative ideas of both men.

Casting went smoothly, although some of Whale's demands were considered excessive by company officials. Junior Laemmle had great faith in Whale's judgment, however. Whale insisted upon sending to England for Colin Clive, who had starred in his stage and screen versions of *Journey's End*, for the central role of Frankenstein. Scion of a military family that included Clive of India, he was a brilliant young actor who seemed to be deliberately trying to drink himself to death. Reluctantly abandoning his intention to cast Leslie Howard in the part, Junior Laemmle acceded. Clive seemed born to the role of the tragically obsessed young scientist, but he was hardly a boxoffice star in America.

John Boles, on the other hand, was a leading romantic singing star with a great fan following – and he was under contract to Universal. Certainly the biggest "name" in the picture, he was cast in the thankless role of Frankenstein's best friend, a handsome fellow kept on the sidelines mostly as someone the leading lady could turn to for solace after Frankenstein's death. He seems uncomfortable in the part and it remains a mystery why the studio assigned him to a supporting role.

Mae Clarke, a pretty blonde from Philadelphia who began as a chorus girl and had become a successful Broadway and Hollywood actress, had given Whale an electrifying performance in *Waterloo Bridge*. He wanted her for the part of Elizabeth and Laemmle Jr. approved. Van Sloan (also under contract) and Frye, both of the *Dracula* cast, were obvious choices for respectively pragmatic and eccentric characters. The elderly Frederick Kerr, one of the great stars of the London stage, was Whale's uncontested choice for crotchety Baron Frankenstein.

A consideration vital to the success of the project lay in developing a concept of Frankenstein's Monster and finding an actor to bring it to life. The makeups used on the stage and in three early silent film versions were too naive for the new talkie era. Nor was Mrs. Shelley's pre-Victorian description of any help:

"It was a dreary night of November, that I beheld the accomplishment of my toils," Frankenstein recounts in the novel. "With an anxiety that almost amounted to agony, I collected the instruments of life around me, that I might infuse a spark of being into the lifeless thing that lay at my feet. It was already one in the morning; the rain pattered dismally against the panes, and my candle was nearly burnt out, when, by the glimmer of the half-extinguished light, I saw the dull yellow eye of the creature open; it breathed hard, and a convulsive motion agitated its limbs.

"How can I describe my emotions at this catastrophe, or how delineate the wretch whom with such infinite pains and care I had endeavoured to form? His limbs were in proportion, and I had selected his features as beautiful. Beautiful! – Great God! His yellow skin scarcely covered the work of muscles and arteries beneath; his hair was of a lustrous black, and flowing; his teeth of a pearly whiteness; but these luxuriances only formed a more horrid contrast with his watery eyes, that seemed almost the same colour as the dun white sockets in which they were set, his shrivelled complexion and straight black lips."

These scant specifications suffice for a written work, in which such adjectives as "frightful" and "ghastly" can be utilized whenever it becomes necessary to remind the reader why everybody is scared green upon seeing Frankenstein's creature. Film is another matter: sooner or later the audience must supply its own response to the Monster's hideousness, and a properly alarmed reaction can hardly be expected from a glimpse of withered complexion, black lips and watery eyes.

In his conceptual art, Rosse had depicted the Monster as a naked and agile but misshapen giant with a tangled mop of hair and a face somewhat resembling that of Lon Chaney in *The Hunchback of Notre Dame*. Junior Laemmle asked the in-house art department, which designed title cards

—Photos by Sherman Clark, Ray Jones, Roman Freulich

Dwight Frye and Colin Clive. "The brain you stole, Fritz."

and advertising materials, to contribute their impressions of the Monster. The resulting sketches included a thick-featured brute by Wells, a Neanderthalish primitive by Kulz, a bulbous-headed alien by Schwamm, a scarred and pain-wracked face by Hirt, and two widely different beings by art director Karoly Grosz – a howling beast-man and a riveted-together metallic man. None of these creatures conveys any suggestion of the grave, but certain details of Gross's robot did survive in the final product: the cubistic head is flat on top and two bolts protrude from the neck.

The responsibility for creating the Monster devolved eventually upon Jack Pierce. A diminuitive, athletic 42-year old Greek immigrant, Pierce was a fiercely independent artist with an encyclopedic knowledge of filmmaking. A jockey and semi-pro baseball shortstop from Chicago, he came to California in 1910 and worked successively as projectionist, theater manager, cameraman, actor, assistant director and makeup artist. Universal hired him after he transformed Jacques Lerner into a chimpanzee for Fox Films' *The Monkey Talks* in 1926. Prior to *Frankenstein* his most conspicuous work at Universal had been Conrad Veidt's makeup for *The Man Who Laughs*. Pierce made hundreds of idea sketches and models of the Monster, including a creature with jagged teeth, an oversized right eye and a scar running down the middle of its face.

"Jack was very fastidious and exacting," makeup artist Harry Thomas, who assisted Pierce on many later projects, recalled to writer Ron Magid. "He was a little cantankerous – didn't like most people. He was secretive; very few people knew that his real name was John Piccolo and that he had been a jockey. He was frugal with materials; if he handed you a box of tissues he wanted you to return the ones you didn't use. He was selfish in the way he worked; he didn't want people to see him do it, unless he had to have somebody help him. Sometimes he'd lock the door and not let anybody in."

Pierce found the solitude he wanted when he was working on any unusual makeup in Dressing Room No. 5, the bungalow where his friend, the secretive Lon Chaney, had retired with a trusted assistant to create his own makeups. He made tests with a number of tall, gaunt-featured actors before Whale introduced him to the man who, Pierce agreed, had the face they needed.

Boris Karloff, then 42, was a lanky Englishman, a veteran of the Canadian provincial stage who had been in pictures since 1919 playing everything from extras to lead heavies. His back was bent

Edward van Sloan, Clive and John Boles. "Now I know what it's like to be God!"

permanently as a result of loading and hauling cement for Eastman Building Supply between acting jobs. The bone structure of his face was sharply defined, his dark eyes were remarkably expressive, and his acting reflected the good influence of his friend and mentor, Lionel Barrymore. While Karloff was playing a gangster role in *Graft* at Universal, Whale had seen him at the studio commissary and invited him to test for the Monster. (Both Lugosi and Whale's best friend, producer David Lewis, said they had suggested Karloff for the role).

For three weeks Pierce and Karloff went each night to No. 5 to experiment with the Monster. Whale added some ideas of his own.

"Jack would say Karloff was a perfect gentleman and the most patient man he ever worked with," Harry Thomas recalled. "Karloff had the face for it – his eyes, his expression, his size, and the fact that he was slender and his face was gaunt. Without that kind of face you can't do the Monster. Each day he'd make a new head and then keep it so he could copy it. It wasn't exactly the same each time because it was custom-made – it wasn't done with prosthetics. He despised prosthetics; he couldn't tolerate any rubber or molds or putting things in an oven and making them like hotcakes."

In 1932, in his article, "Character Makeup" which appeared in the May issue of *American Cinematographer*, Pierce described his approach to the creation of the Monster:

"In creating such a makeup, the makeup artist must first of all know what the story requires. Then he must have time to study the actor in question, and visualize what can be done to make that actor into the desired character. What are the most

91

prominent features of the actor? What does he rely upon most in putting his points over? What should be the most prominent features of this character? Should the actor be concealed by the makeup, or is his normal personality a near enough approximation of the desired character so that the makeup be merely a filling-in of the more sketchy details? And, finally – in such parts as the 'Monster' in *Frankenstein* especially – is every detail technically correct?

"Once this study is completed, and I have, either through imagination or research – or a combination of the two – succeeded in visualizing the character, I prepare sketches of my conception of the character, and submit them to the director. His conception of the part, influenced as it is by consideration not alone of the one part, but of the whole picture, may differ slightly from mine. Either of the two may be the better; sometimes a combination of the two will prove better than either individually; sometimes we have to test both makeups photographically in order to decide. But when this decision is finally made, the rest is purely routine...

"Next to the ability to completely visualize a character makeup, technical research plays the largest part. Sometimes this leads one into strange paths. In *Frankenstein*, for instance, I spent months of study on the anatomical possibilities of the Monster alone. I studied every operation that would be necessary to create such a body from 'spare parts,' as was related in the story. I studied the physical effect of each, and strove to reproduce them in Mr. Karloff's final character. Every line, every scar, every peculiarity of contour had to be just so for medical reasons; the eyes, for instance, were exact duplicates of the dead eyes of a 2800-year old Egyptian corpse!"

Karloff himself suggested one vital touch: heavy eyelids that veiled the eyes, which otherwise appeared too lively for the dead face. Pierce shaded Karloff's cheeks to accentuate their gauntness and Karloff removed a dental bridge to collapse the right cheek. A jutting brow and high, flattened cranium were built up of layers of cheesecloth and greasepaint and embellished with scars, surgical clamps and a wig. A top layer of blue-green greasepaint lent the skin a cold gray look and the fingertips were dipped in shoe polish to suggest the blackening of extremities in death. The face was kept free of anything that might encumber a full play of expressions.

In dramatic contrast to the cadaverous face was the body of a hulking brute, an illusion achieved by dressing the slender actor in a double-quilted suit under the black outer clothing. By shortening the coatsleeves Pierce created an effect of gorilla-like arms. Asphalters' boots weighing 12.5 pounds apiece increased Karloff's height and so weighted his feet as to enable him to lean forward alarmingly as he walked. An iron rod running down his back and metal leg braces helped to create the strange posture of the creature. It is easy to imagine the discomfort of the actor, who had to report to makeup at four o'clock each morning for a three-hour ordeal, then work all day on unventilated stages under hot lights in 48 pounds of costume and makeup from which he had to be dug out after the evening wrap.

The laboratory was quite a different thing from what Rosse had visualized. The high, angular stone walls of the watchtower were filled with eccentric electrical machines created by Kenneth Strickfaden, an energetic little musician from Montana who began his film career in 1921 as an electrician at Metropolitan Studio and later at Paramount.

"I made these things because I didn't know anything and I had fun doing it," Strickfaden said in 1981. "It was just a matter of experimentation. I'd put something together and then sit back and marvel at it. Then I found there was a market for my 'Edison medicine.' The styling all depended upon what kind of junk I had at hand. Some of the pieces were very heavy, being made of the finest china in order to withstand the terrific electricity." Although he often joked about his hobby, Strickfaden took his experiments very seriously. "Electricity is life," he said shortly before his death. "We're just a bunch of sparks with various quantities of air."

Paramount used several Strickfaden machines in *The Return of Sherlock Holmes* in 1929 and Fox showcased the lot the following year in their musical science-fiction extravaganza, *Just Imagine*. Frank Graves, head of Universal's electrical department, put Raymond Lindsay in charge of the weird electrical devices used in *Frankenstein*, which included a lightning bridge, a bariton generator, a nucleus analyzer and a vacuum electrolyzer – to use Strickfaden's names for them. "Ray Lindsay should get the credit," Strickfaden said. "I designed it, he operated it. All I did was make adjustments and replace equipment as it burned up. I lost quite a bit of it, and some of it is in a medical museum in Minneapolis."

Abetting the "Edison medicine" were huge lightning arc machines, which electricians operated above the ceiling opening to provide the blinding flashes of light and showers of sparks that pour down into the lab during the creation scenes.

Principal photography began August 24 on the graveyard set with a 30-day schedule and a budget of $262,007.

Early on an August morning, Jack Pierce leads his creation to Stage 12.

Frankenstein begins with a funeral in a lonely graveyard. This is an expressionistic interior-exterior set backed by a glowering sky cyclorama. Henry Frankenstein (Colin Clive), son of Baron Frankenstein, and Fritz (Dwight Frye), a half-crazed dwarf who assists him, watch from hiding. Whale did something original for this early talkie: He had a mike placed inside the casket, so that when the gravedigger threw the first shovelful of earth into the grave it made a "you are there" *clump*. For today's audiences, who are all too familiar with the effective combining of sound and picture, the effect passes unnoticed, but it had impact in '31. A young director on the lot, William Wyler, was so impressed that he used the same gimmick in his next picture, *A House Divided*. Junior Laemmle told Wyler it was too morbid and made him take it out.

When the cemetery is deserted they dig up the body. Here Whale provides an irreverent touch: Henry throws a shovelful of dirt in the face of a statue of the grim reaper. "He's just resting, waiting for new life to come," Frankenstein says, patting the casket. Later, they steal a body from a gallows. This happens in another expressionistic soundstage set with steeply sloping ground and jagged man-made rocks. "His neck's broken; the brain is useless," Frankenstein laments.

Fritz is next seen at Goldstadt Medical College, peering through a window of the operating theater where Professor Waldman (Edward van Sloan) demonstrates to his students the differences between a brain he has just removed from the corpse of a degenerate murderer and a normal brain. After the group leaves, Fritz enters and steals the normal brain. Jittery after bumping into a skeleton and startled by the closing gong, he drops the jar. Desperately he flees with the criminal brain.

The lecture and other details of this sequence were supervised by Dr. Cecil Miller, a brain specialist who had become famous because of his testimony in the trial of a murderer known as "the Fox." Miller also portrayed Waldman's assistant in scenes that were not retained in the final cut.

Elizabeth (Mae Clarke), Frankenstein's fiancee, and their friend, Victor Moritz (John Boles), are worried about Henry, who for months has been working secretly in an old watchtower. Their meeting is enacted in a large Gothic castle set which includes a great hall built in 1926 for *The Cat and the Canary* and a vaulted sitting room of which upper walls, ceiling and chandelier were added via a glass painting. They go to Waldman, Henry's teacher, who tells them that Henry has left the university because his experiments in chemical galvanism and electro-biology had reached a dangerously advanced stage. He had also complained that the dissecting room cadavers were not perfect enough for his use. "Herr Frankenstein was interested only in human life, first to destroy it, then re-create it. There you have his mad dream." They persuade Waldman to accompany them to the watchtower.

The watchtower, shown on a hill through a rainstorm against a night sky and illuminated by bolts of lightning, is shown in an excellent miniature. The interior is a marvelous, tall set which has been imitated often. Similarities between this tower and one in the 1926 French film, *The Wizard*, have been noted. Henry and Fritz work feverishly with a mass of electrical equipment assembled around a covered body whose blackened, scarred arm protrudes from under the sheet. Calming Fritz's fears, Henry exults, "No blood, no decay. Just a few stitches." He uncovers the misshappen bandaged head. "Here's the final touch: the brain you stole, Fritz. The brain of a dead man waiting to live again in a body I made with my own hands!" They wait anxiously for the storm to reach its peak so they can harness its power. Then the unwelcome guests arrive. When they refuse to leave, Henry swears them to secrecy and takes them up a massive stairway to the laboratory.

"Dr. Waldman," Frankenstein says, "I learned a great deal from you at the university about the violet ray, the ultra-violet ray, which you said is

93

Karloff as the Monster.

the highest color in the spectrum. You were wrong. Here in this machinery I have gone beyond that. I have discovered the great ray that first brought life into the world. At first I experimented only with dead animals, and then a human heart which I kept beating for three weeks. But now I am going to turn that ray on that body and endow it with life!... That body isn't dead, it has never lived. I created it. I made it with my own hands from the bodies I took from graves, from the gallows, anywhere!"

Clive plays these scenes with convincing nervous intensity, not as a madman but as an obsessed scientist whose zeal has driven him to the brink of collapse. Just before he sets the machinery into motion he stands defiantly in front of his creation and cries, "Quite a good scene, isn't it? One man crazy, three very sane spectators!"

The body is sent aloft to a skylight to meet the lightning while the machinery flashes and clatters alarmingly. When the body is brought down its arm, no longer black, moves. Henry is hysterical with excitement.

Some days later in the tower laboratory, Waldman tries to reason with Henry: "Mark my words, he will prove dangerous." Frankenstein's response is beautifully delivered: "Have you never wanted to do anything that was dangerous? Where should we be if nobody tried to find out what lies beyond? Have you never wanted to look beyond the clouds and the stars or to know what causes the trees to bud, and what changes darkness into light? But if you talk like that, people call you crazy. Well, if I could discover just one of these things – what eternity is, for example – I wouldn't care if they did think I was crazy!"

Heavy footsteps are heard in the corridor outside. The lights are snuffed, the door opens and a huge, lumpish figure backs into the room. The Monster (as it will be called) turns around slowly, revealing a placid but monstrous countenance. It obeys a command to sit down. Frankenstein opens the skylight and the creature, who has so far lived in darkness, tries to hold the shaft of light. Unfortunately, Fritz enters, brandishing a torch. The terrified Monster runs amok and is subdued only after a brutal fight.

The Monster is introduced in a series of cuts progressing from a full shot from below eye-level as he enters, to a medium shot as he turns, to a full-face close-up, and to an extreme close-up. Locked up and chained, the Monster howls and rages. Fritz torments him further with fire and the whip. Hearing Fritz's scream, Waldman and Henry rush downstairs to find that the Monster has broken his chains and hanged Fritz's body from a rafter. Barely escaping, they inject the Monster with a powerful drug, but both men are mauled before the Monster loses consciousness. Victor arrives and helps to hide the Monster before Henry's father and Elizabeth arrive. Henry is found in a state of mental and physical exhaustion. Waldman promises that the Monster "will be painlessly destroyed."

In the ensuing days Frankenstein recovers and the village makes ready for his wedding celebration. At the tower, Waldman, finding that the Monster is becoming increasingly resistant to drugs, decides to perform dissection at once. The Monster awakes and strangles Waldman. In the release prints this scene fades while the murder is being committed, but a longer and more brutal version remains in the original theatrical trailer.

On the day set for the wedding, Castle Frankenstein is filled with guests and the villagers dance in the streets. At his home beside a lake, Ludwig tells his little daughter, Maria, that when he returns from checking his traps they will go to the celebration. The Monster comes upon the child and watches as she gathers daisies at the water's edge. Unafraid, she gives him flowers and shows him how they float in the water. The delighted Monster tosses his daisies into the lake. When his hands are empty he puzzles for a moment, then picks up the child and throws her into the water. Maria drowns and the grief-stricken Monster stumbles, weeping, into the woods.

The scenes with Maria, the only off-the-lot location work, were photographed at Lake Sherwood, near Westlake Village, California. They are dramatically powerful in depicting both the childlike innocence of Karloff's reaction to Maria and the violence of his grief. Whale faced down a near-revolt of cast and crew who were opposed to having the girl die. He had his way, saying it was part of "the ritual." Karloff was unable to toss Marilyn Harris as far as Whale wanted, so – egged on by the girl's hovering foster mother – the director had two stagehands throw her in again. Karloff's version was used. It could be argued that the naturalism of the lake setting is at odds with the deliberate unreality of most of the film.

Preparations for the wedding are interrupted when news arrives that Waldman has been killed and the Monster is terrorizing the countryside. The Monster enters Elizabeth's room through a window and tries to seize her.

Elizabeth's screams bring Henry and his friends, who find her unconscious but unharmed as the Monster flees. The street merrymaking ceases as

The Monster—innocent but dangerous.

Ludwig arrives, carrying the body of the drowned child. Search parties are quickly organized and as night falls three torch-bearing groups set out. The village scenes were photographed on an exterior set constructed a few months earlier for *All Quiet on the Western Front*. It was utilized in numerous later films until it was destroyed by fire more than 30 years later. The present European Street was then constructed on the site. The street dances are Laendlers, authentically performed by Austrian musicians and dancers.

Henry leads his men into the mountains, where he becomes separated from them and meets the Monster face to face. Knocking Henry unconscious, the Monster, hotly pursued by a mob and a pack of hounds, carries him into an old windmill. As the mob tries to break down the door, which has been blocked by a fallen rafter, the Monster drags Henry upstairs. Regaining consciousness, Henry flees to a balcony, but before he can climb down he is seized by the Monster, who hurls him at the mob. A windmill blade breaks his fall. The mob sets fire to the mill. A beam falls on the Monster, pinning him down as flames consume the mill. Frankenstein survives to be reunited with his future bride.

Many of the chase scenes were photographed at night in the hills and around Pollard Lake on the backlot. These settings are given an unreal appearance with the massed torches of the villagers and some unusual lighting effects. The mountain scenes were shot on a sound stage among plaster rocks and huge canvas backdrops. The artificiality of the sets irritates some viewers while others admire the film's audacious theatricality.

The exteriors of the wooden windmill are composites of full scale and miniature sets. The lower part was built to a point about 12 feet above the base while the upper two-thirds (including the

Flowers . . .

turning blades) was constructed to scale. John Fulton, ASC, superimposed the actors on the balcony via the Williams Traveling Matte process. The interior is a full scale mechanical set, superbly detailed and aged. The effectiveness of the mill sequence is heightened by the barking and baying of the hounds, which was recognized as innovative in 1931.

Frankenstein finished five days over schedule on October 3 with the filming of added scenes in the laboratory. At $291,129.13 the negative cost was over budget $29,122. In early November a work print was shown to a few trade journalists at a studio screening room. Some doubts were expressed as to its commercial possibilities and Junior Laemmle admitted that Universal wasn't sure how to handle it.

Laemmle Sr., already stung by the extra costs and beset by doubts as to whether the picture was marketable, exploded when he saw the scene wherein Karloff threw Marilyn Harris into the water. "No little girl is going to drown in one of my pictures!" Laemmle raged to his secretary, J. U. Miller, and ordered the scene removed. In the standard release version, as the laughing Monster reaches for the girl there is an abrupt cut to the street dancing in the village. The Monster's abortive en-

A child (Marilyn Harris) . . .

96

counter with Elizabeth follows, after which the bereaved father arrives on the street carrying the dead child, whose short dress and long stockings are disheveled. The unfortunate result is that the crucial theme of the Monster's innocence is abrogated: viewers automatically assume that sexual assault and murder had taken place and that Elizabeth has narrowly escaped such a fate.

Laemmle Sr. was also upset over the original tragic ending, a sentiment echoed by the preview cards when the picture was "sneaked" in Santa Barbara early in November. Colin Clive had debarked for England at the end of October after telling a *New York Times* reporter how pleased he was that *Frankenstein* had "a rather unusual ending for a talking picture" in which "I...am killed by the monster I have created." Meantime, the studio devised a new ending in which Baron Frankenstein emerges from the room in which Henry is recuperating from his ordeal (we catch a glimpse of the bedridden Henry being comforted by Elizabeth) to drink a toast: "Here's to a son to the House of Frankenstein." Also, at the request of Laemmle Sr., a brief pre-title prologue was added in which Edward van Sloan stepped onstage to address the audience:

"How do you do. Mr. Carl Laemmle feels that it would be a little unkind to present this picture without just a word of friendly warning. We are about to unfold the story of Frankenstein, a man of science, who sought to create a man after his own image, without reckoning upon God. It is one of the strangest tales ever told. It deals with the two great mysteries of creation, life and death. I think it will thrill you. It may shock you. It might even *horrify* you. So, then, if you feel that you do not want to subject your nerves to such a strain, now is your chance to – er – well, we've warned you!"

Tragedy...

Remorse.

At least one print was released in America without cuts. Curt Beck, manager of the Majestic in Dallas, threatened to cancel his contract with Universal unless he could exhibit *Frankenstein* complete. The Dallas ads stated that "The RKO Majestic Theater will absolutely show *Frankenstein* without cutting any of the scenes."

With *Frankenstein*, Whale established himself as a highly individualistic filmmaker. Many of his stylistic trademarks can be seen in this early work. There is, for example, a scene in *Waterloo Bridge* in which characters hurry from one room to another and the camera parallels the action, rushing past the wall through an adjoining door. In *Frankenstein* he carried this idea a step further by having both the rambling interiors of the watchtower and the castle designed so that the camera can follow action past the walls or seemingly through them. This technique is even more pervasive in the later *Bride of Frankenstein* and *Remember Last Night?* (both 1935).

Evident, too, is Whale's quirky sense of humor, which was developed with increasing sophistication in several films that followed (*The Old Dark House*, 1932, *The Invisible Man*, 1933, *Bride of Frankenstein*). Here it is restricted to the grumpiness

Villagers search for the killer in expressionistic mountains.

of old Baron Frankenstein and some of the halfwitted antics of the otherwise forbidding Fritz, who mutters to himself and, at one dramatic moment, stops to pull up a grimy stocking.

The cinematography of Arthur Edeson, ASC, is vital to the moods of the show. Most of the picture is photographed from below eye-level, which not only lends the Monster a towering presence but emphasizes the angularity and heroic proportions of the sets. The lighting effects are as varied as the action.

It would be impossible to overstate the importance of Clive and Karloff to the success of

Frankenstein. Clive's intense performance, which may seem somewhat overwrought in light of later styles, is perfectly realized in the context of the period. Eyes blazing, he forces the spectator to accept his genius and the truth of his most fantastic claims.

Karloff, his dialogue restricted to inarticulate, animal-like mutterings and an occasional enraged roar, made the Monster not only frightening but endearing. There is genuine pathos when he tries vainly to clasp a beam of light or wonderingly compares the petals of a flower to the fingers of a child. His terrors, his grief, his pitifully few moments of joy, are conveyed through pantomime as eloquent as that of Chaplin or Chaney.

There were even more walkouts at the preview of *Frankenstein* than at the *Dracula* screening. Studio executives worried as never before. They needn't have: the initial release paid off to the tune of better than $12 million – and that was only the beginning.

Later, because of a European ban on horror pictures, few films in the genre were made during 1936-38. The manager of the Regina Theatre (now Fine Arts), an independent house in Beverly Hills, unable to show first-run pictures because of the dominance of studio-owned theater chains, found some old prints of *Dracula* and *Frankenstein* at a film exchange. Rightly suspecting that the public was starved for some old-fashioned scare shows, he had trailers made up for advance advertising and opened his "Mammoth Horror Show" double bill on August 4, 1937. The theater was packed for four weeks. The Blue Mouse Theater in Seattle picked up the same twin bill and it broke the house record.

Universal finally took note and ordered new prints struck for a national reissue. The master negatives of both films had become somewhat battered and received further damage when they were re-submitted to the Hays Office. The Production Code had become considerably more severe by then and several small but telling cuts were demanded. These included Frankenstein's line, "Oh – in the name of God! Now I know what it feels like to be God," along with the more violent action from the first fight with the Monster, several closeups from the sequence of Fritz tormenting the Monster with a torch, and a closeup of Waldman jabbing the Monster with a hypodermic needle.

The new release prints were made on Eastman's Aquagreen Colortone stock, partly because negative damage is less noticeable in a tinted print, but also in response to the strong impression made by the serial, *Flash Gordon's Trip to Mars*, all 30 reels of which were released March 22 on green stock to lend it a more unearthly quality. The color proved equally appropriate to the 1938 editions of *Dracula* and *Frankenstein*, which were released May 15 and are fondly remembered by many a grandparent after more than a half-century.

The "chill-bill" was a success: All seats were sold by 10 a.m. on opening day at the Victory Theatre in Salt Lake City, and police lines held back a mob of 4,000 which surrounded the place by noon. The boxoffice was crushed and the doors were caved in by the crowd. The manager rented an empty theater across the street and had it filled in 20 minutes, bicycling the reels back and forth. A 3,800-seat house in Waterbury, Connecticut, played to 6,500 admissions on opening day. The Warners in Fresno did the biggest business in its history. Six policemen were necessary to control the crowds at the Fox Uptown in Kansas City. The St. Louis Theatre in St. Louis, Missouri, did double the business of its nearest competitor for a week and the show was held over for another week. On October 17 the program opened on Broadway to huge crowds.

Realizing that the European market was not necessary to make big profits on a good horror show, Universal announced production of *Son of Frankenstein*, which commenced October 24, and immediately sent out new prints of other vintage chillers to fill the void. Other studios followed

One of Charles Hall's designs for the old mill and the actual setting.

quickly with reissues and new product. Ironically, the two pictures that had started the horror cycle in 1931 also launched the second cycle in 1938.

The two chillers are still making money in theaters, television and home video. In the late 1980s Universal had both pictures restored by YCM Laboratories in Burbank to a close approximation of what the Dallas audiences saw in 1931. *Frankenstein* now lacks only the two opening scenes in the graveyard, which vanished in 1935 after they had been lifted for inclusion in the montage sequence at the beginning of *Bride of Frankenstein* (where they can still be glimpsed in abbreviated form), and some flash closeups from the drowning sequence.

Remarkably, in spite of the innumerable sequels, parodies and gags it has inspired over six decades, *Frankenstein* retains its power to chill the spine and command respect for its artistry.

—George E. Turner

Confrontation in the upper floor of the mill. Below, the Monster trapped by flames.

100

Hall's design for the windmill exterior.

A Universal *picture presented by* Carl Laemmle; *produced by* Carl Laemmle Jr.; *directed by* James Whale; *associate producer,* E. M. Asher; *based upon the composition by* John L. Balderston; *from the novel by* Mrs. Percy B. Shelley; *adapted from the play by* Peggy Webling; *screen play by* Garrett Fort, Francis Edwards Faragoh; *scenario editor,* Richard Schayer; *adaptation,* Robert Florey; *continuity,* Tom Reed; *added scenes,* John Russell; *cinematographer,* Arthur Edeson, ASC; *art director,* Charles D. Hall; *film editor,* Clarence Kolster; *supervising film editor,* Maurice Pivar; *recorded by* C. Roy Hunter; *sound technician,* William Hedgcock; *settings by* Herman Rosse; *special effects,* John P. Fulton, ASC; *makeup artist,* Jack P. Pierce; *electrical properties,* Kenneth Strickfaden; *electrical effects,* Frank Graves, Raymond A. Lindsay; *musical director,* David Broekman; *music by* Bernhard Kaun, Guiseppe Becce; *dances arranged by* C. Baier; *assistant directors,* Joseph A. McDonough, Harry Mancke; *technical advisor,* Dr. Cecil Reynolds; *second cameraman,* Allen Jones; *assistant cameramen,* Jack Eagan, George Trafton; *assistant makeup artist,* Tony Mattaracci; *costumes by* Ed Ware, Vera West; *casting,* Phil M. Friedman; *art titles,* Max Cohen; *script clerk,* Helen McCaffrey; *stills by* Sherman Clark, Ray Jones, Roman Freulich; *Western Electric recording. Running time, 71 minutes. Released November 21, 1931.*

Henry Frankenstien, Colin Clive; *Elizabeth,* Mae Clarke; *Victor Moritz,* John Boles; *Monster,* Boris Karloff; *Doctor Waldman,* Edward van Sloan; *Baron Frankenstein,* Frederick Kerr; *Fritz, the Dwarf,* Dwight Frye; *Burgomaster,* Lionel Belmore; *Little Maria,* Marilyn Harris; *Ludwig,* Michael Mark; *Butler,* Joseph North; *Housekeeper,* Maidel Turner; *Villagers,* Francis Ford, Paul Panzer, Ines Palange, Ted Billings, Harry Tenbrook; *Maid,* Cecilia Parker; *Bridesmaids,* Pauline Moore, Arletta Duncan; *Gendarme,* William Yetter; *University Secretary,* Cecil Reynolds *(cut).*

9

Creation, the Lost Epic

In the summer of 1929, from his office at Tec-Art Studio (a leasing lot in Hollywood on Melrose Avenue), Harry O. Hoyt announced that he was writing and would direct a picture called *Creation.* Early the following year he submitted his story outline to William LeBaron, vice-president in charge of production at RKO Radio Pictures, Inc., with these comments:

"Specifically, the story is designed as a basis for a melodramatic picture, utilizing the animals of the saurian and dinosaurian eras...

"Purposely, no attempt is made to paint the picture in pastels. The very size of the animals and the vast cataclysm of nature which we depict call for the brightest of colors and the broadest of brushes.

"On the theory that the average person is not far removed from the elemental, that we are all still children at heart, fascinated by size, by books filled with pictures, by tales of valor, by 'once upon a time' stories, this is offered as an attempt at entertainment on a colossal scale with that modicum of educational value always to be found in pictures of great size possessing replay possibilities and international popularity...

"It is planned to utilize the services of two artists who have constructed and animated these animals in another picture.

Two conceptual drawings for Creation *by Byron Crabbe and Willis O'Brien.*

"Recently developed trick devices made these scenes with the animals very real. In no other branch of the industry has there been greater improvement than in trick work and this, singularly enough, has not been exploited to the extent of its possibilities...

"It should be pointed out here that this picture cannot be compared with any other picture being produced today. It is neither drama nor comedy and yet it contains both of these elements. It is adventure-melodrama of a highly imaginative kind. Only through the medium of the moving picture is it possible to attempt verisimilitude. The stage cannot attempt it – the novel must leave much to the reader's imagination. On the screen we have the perfect illusion – these terrible monsters breathing, fighting and bleeding in mortal combat among themselves and with the people.

"Melodrama is always heightened by sound. It is the thing which we hear, not what we see, in the still of the night, that chills us. Now that we can hear the roar of these beasts in battle in addition to seeing them, we attain perfect realism."

After studying the extremely successful 1925 silent film, *The Lost World,* which Hoyt directed for First National Pictures, LeBaron perceived the merit of making the first talking picture along similar lines. Hoyt assured him that the visual effects genius who made the seemingly alive dinosaurs of *The Lost World* possible, Willis H. O'Brien, would be available to supervise the technical aspects of *Creation.* Hoyt and O'Brien had been preparing a sequel to *The Lost World,* but the project was abandoned after Warner Brothers Pictures acquired First National. Other studios, caught up in the "talkie craze" of the time, expressed no enthusiasm for such fantasy.

RKO Radio, founded late in 1928 as the film production subsidiary of a new holding company established by David Sarnoff, of Radio Corporation of America (RCA), and Joseph P. Kennedy, of the Keith-Albee-Orpheum theatre circuit, was the youngest and most venturesome of the major studios. The parent company was based in New York City. The studio was situated in Hollywood in the former plant of Kennedy's Film Booking Office of America (FBO) company at the corner of Gower and Melrose. Built in 1920 by the British Robertson-Cole Pictures, it was a 13½-acre silent picture facility dwarfed by its next door neighbor to the east, the Paramount Studio. Millions of dollars were spent initially in converting the stages for sound production and installing the first channel of RCA Photophone equipment.

LeBaron, a former playwright and managing editor of Collier's, had been restricted to small budgets and mostly unimpressive pictures as production chief at FBO. Now he was determined to earn for RKO a reputation as a maker of big, extraordinary pictures. He got the studio off to a fair start with *Street Girl* and followed it with the enormously popular musical extravaganza, *Rio Rita*, both in 1929. Ignoring the stock market crash and the impending Depression, he next launched *Cimarron*, one of the most ambitious productions attempted in 1930. LeBaron envisioned *Creation* as a spectacle on a par with *Cimarron* as further evidence of RKO's avowed claim of being "The Most Spectacular Show Machine of All Time."

Hoyt was assigned to develop *Creation* as a screenplay, checking into the lot in April 1930.

Ernie Smythe's diagram showing the 24 camera angles used in the triceratops sequence.

104

Bertram Millhauser, an experienced writer and producer from Pathé, was assigned as supervisor. Millhauser brought in his former collaborator, Beulah Marie Dix, who had written scripts for some of Cecil B. DeMille's spectacular films, to prepare a new adaptation and dialogue. At the same time, early in July, O'Brien was contracted "to render his exclusive services...in connection with the production of the motion picture entitled *Creation...*" Millhauser turned in a budget estimate of $652,242.52 and a 20-week shooting schedule. This was about triple the cost and time allotment of a typical "A" picture of the time.

The studio maintained a strict secrecy as to the nature of the project. Vernon Harbin, later an RKO executive, was a messenger boy at the time. "There was an old wooden building behind the camera department in the southeast corner of the lot, with a sign, 'Authorized Personnel Only'," Harbin remembers. "It was called the *Creation* building. We were all very curious, of course."

The mysterious building, which previously had been the scene of equally secret experiments with a wide-film process called Natural Vision, was O'Brien's domain. There, three fine artists – Mario Larrinaga, Byron L. Crabbe and Ernest Smythe – prepared key illustrations and hundreds of continuity drawings based on O'Brien's sketches. Larrinaga and Crabbe also made oil paintings on 4 x 5-foot foreground glasses and Masonite backings to enhance the effect of depth in miniature settings of a prehistoric jungle. Orville "Goldy" Goldner, a puppeteer, made weird trees of plasticene covered with tissue paper, shellac and paint, and dressed the little sets with real foliage as well as leaves and fronds cut from sheet copper. Carroll Shepphird, an artist and cinematographer, mapped out the perspectives, lenses to be used and other intricacies necessary to the effective matching of the miniature sets with the full scale ones being constructed elsewhere on the lot. The miniatures were scaled at one inch to the foot.

John Cerisoli, an old Italian woodcarver, sculpted prototypes of all the animals described in the script. Technicians from the Mechnical and Miniature Department tooled skeleton-like armatures of these monsters, based upon specifications prepared by O'Brien and his assistant, Marcel Delgado, who had built the 49 dinosaurs of *The Lost World*.

Hoyt stated that "these animals will be from sketches drawn by the celebrated artist, Charles R. Knight, of the American Museum of Natural History, who is a world recognized authority. They

A prehistoric family built by Delgado.

are variously from 15 to 36 inches in length and are built of imported German dental rubber over a brass frame work which is cast in molds. This frame work is hinged with universal friction joints so they are able to move their legs, necks, hands, etc.

"In what is termed the 'close-up' animals, there is a bladder which is pumped up and the air released to give the appearance of breathing. They also have glass eyes which are movable in their sockets and their mouths open and close and have teeth. The background animals have no [air] bladders, their eyes are painted and the only movement is their legs and necks."

Planning included the construction of 17 "close-up" animals, "possibly 20 similar animals for background mass effects," and four aquatic reptiles described as "comparatively inexpensive to make as they have no frame work and are used so little in the picture that detail is unnecessary." The following were made and filmed: three triceratops, two arsinoitheriums (one mechanical and one for animation), two brontosauri (one mechanical and one for animation), a stegosaurus, a pterodactyl, a styracosaurus, and a flock of birds with wooden bodies and copper wings. In addition, a full scale baby triceratops, about the size of a Shetland pony and equipped with walking and breathing devices, and the full size head of an adult triceratops, about six feet in length, were built. Charles Christadoro designed the mechanisms of the full-scale animals.

Karl Brown was director of photography. This remarkable craftsman was trained by D.W. Griffith and ''Billy'' Bitzer before World War I. His versatility may be hinted at by the fact that he had photographed *The Covered Wagon* (1925), directed *Stark Love* (1927), and written *Mississippi Gambler* (1929) – all films of distinction.

Seven months were required for preparation of enough special equipment and properties to begin shooting. Filming of an 1,800-foot sequence was begun in mid-November of 1930 and took 61 working days to complete. It was extremely complex, being chosen specifically as a showcase for the masterful technique developed by O'Brien. In addition to the miniature and full-scale triceratops family and the flying birds, it required two actors, a live

O'Brien's prototype miniature projection device with screen agitator.

ape (the Universal comedy star, Snooky), a jaguar, a kinkajou and a stork. The animals were rented from the Selig Zoo of Los Angeles.

The sequence opens with the triceratops family grazing in the jungle. Snooky, from a limb above, drops a stick on one of the babies, which begins complaining. Ignored by the mother, the baby wanders off. It watches a jaguar stalk and kill a stork and is rebuffed when it noses into a kinkajou's lair. Then the little dinosaur encounters Hallett, the villain of the story, played by a young New York actor, Ralf Harolde. The baby stops and cocks its head. Hallett aims his elephant gun and fires, striking the dinosaur in the eye. The animal stumbles away and collapses. The mother, hearing its cries, charges after Hallett. When Hallett hides, the dinosaur uproots a tree, pinning the man to the ground. Shoving the tree aside, she impales him on her horns and tosses him into the air. The sequence ends with a closeup as she (the full scale version) nudges the body with her nasal horn.

Each shot was planned with mathematical precision. Four detailed illustrations, many continuity drawings and several diagrams of the action were prepared. Shepphird made tracings to separate live, glass and miniature elements. Smythe mapped the action and camera placements over the set. The most time consuming part of actual filming was the animation. To give the animals a semblance of movement, O'Brien had to photograph them in 24 barely perceptible changes of position for each second they would appear on the screen. The maximum amount of animation that could be completed in one day was about 25 feet – 17 seconds of screen time.

Aside from the usual perils of stop-motion work – plants that shrank or bloomed under the hot lights, exploding lamps and unwanted breezes caused by doors being opened by unthinking ''brass,'' etc. – the worst problems were caused by the live animals. Olga Celeste, a noted wild animal trainer, was in charge of the beasts.

The jaguar, when released from its cage, was supposed to run out into a clearing, pounce on the bird, and run out of camera range to another cage. Orville Goldner was called away from his miniature sets and stationed on top of the second cage to close the gate once the cat was safely inside. Jaguars, however, are unpredictable, and this one refused to follow the script. Finally, the cat ran out and seized the chicken (stunt double for the stork) and carried it with him across the set, intent on jumping on top of the cage to have his meal. Terribly vulnerable, Goldner crouched on the cage while the

Baby triceratops in a miniature setting with foreground glass painting and matted-in running water.

beast stared and snarled. At last the jaguar jumped over the top of the cage, brushing past Goldner, then jumped the wire barrier separating the set from the camera and crew. Olga Celeste told everyone to stand still, but many crew members scrambled up ladders. One electrician made it to the highest rafters of the stage before he halted. The beast crouched beside the barrier, gnawing the chicken, until Celeste grabbed him by the loose skin above shoulders and rump and ushered him into the cage.

Goldner also was elected to rig a tree branch which Snooky was supposed to break off and drop on the baby dinosaur. The chimpanzee took a fancy to Goldner and wrestled him affectionately, lavishing wet, whiskery kisses on him while the man tried to stay aloft. Snooky was unable to pull the branch free on the first take, so Goldner climbed up again, struggling in the ape's embraces while he loosened the branch. The second take also failed because the branch was too firmly attached. The disheveled man climbed up a third time and wired the branch so loosely that it would come free at the slightest tug.

This time Snooky gave the branch a hard yank. It came away so easily that he was thrown off balance and almost fell. He was infuriated! There is nothing cute about an angry chimp, which is stronger than any man and can deliver a vicious bite. Snooky leaped through the trees, screeching and snarling in rage. Then he came down to the floor,

107

smashing sets and equipment in his fury. Encountering a tub of plaster of Paris used for mending sets, he thrust his face into the powder, emerging with a mouthful. The trainer was horrified – if the ape swallowed the plaster it could prove fatal. The entire crew began chasing Snooky around the stage, up and down ladders and through the trees so that he would be kept too active to swallow. In good time he was captured and forced to spit out the plaster before it could harden.

The birds which were made to flit among the trees on invisible wires were about one-and-a-half inches in length. Their bodies were carved in wood and the wings were pliable copper. The wires themselves moved, carrying the birds in steps of one-fourth of an inch per exposure while the wings were made to ''flap'' with minute cycles of animation.

"Obie was left handed and worked quickly," Karl Brown recalled. "It was a hell of a thing to watch him work with those little animals, a mother triceratops and two babies. The little ones were only about five inches long."

The sequence is comparable technically to anything of its kind that has been done to date. A flowing river appears in several shots with the animated figures. The birds add another realistic touch. The dinosaurs have personality and are composited with the actors and the live animals flawlessly. Some of the composites were achieved via the Dunning process, a method by which previously photographed elements (the animated figures) could be combined in the camera with newly staged live and full scale action. Surviving frame enlargements, made on the set as tests, show some of the scenes that aren't in the footage now extant.

The mother triceratops charges toward camera.

Triceratops on a rampage. Note falling tree at left.

The expensive *Cimarron* was released early in 1931 to great acclaim and won more awards than any picture of its year. LeBaron decided at that time to make *Creation* even bigger than had been anticipated. The budget was raised to an almost unheard of $1,201,813.53 – only a handful of previous films had cost as much – and the schedule was extended accordingly, with principal photography slated for completion in July. Selection of the cast was begun: Joel McCrea would be the hero, Steve, and Benny Rubin (who was starring in two-reelers at the studio) was to be Bennie, the comedy relief. Locations were set in the Verdugo Hills (near Los Angeles), in the Florida Everglades, at a gravel pit north of Roscoe, California, and along the Kern River of California.

Work on the special effects continued, including experiments with a new technique of miniature projection by which previously photographed live action could be projected into concealed screens and animated a frame at a time with the dinosaurs. O'Brien invented the method and designed special projection equipment which was built in the studio machine shop. The tiny screens were rotated to minimize texture of the translucent rear projection material. The technique was so successful as to be absorbed quickly into studio procedure.

Brown, assisted by Linwood Dunn, ASC, of the special camera effects department, also photographed miniature scenes in which a tornado destroys a Chilean seacoast town and sweeps away a large yacht, a new island rises from the sea, and a submarine is dragged down into a subterranean cavern. The miniatures were built under Don Jahraus' direction. This sequence apparently is lost.

"Most of this work was done entirely under water, in a five-foot glass cube built for the system," Brown said. "For the storm at sea I poured in carbon tetrachloride, which created ripples, waves and so on. We had to show a mountain rising from the sea, along with lava, steam and explosions. The mountain was built in sections and the steam was canned milk.

"When a twister was supposed to come along and destroy everything, we used a canoe paddle to create a vortex in the water and poured negrosin – a black powdered dye soluble only in alcohol – down the funnel. We couldn't make it come forward toward the cameras, so we moved the camera up to to it and got the same thing. Our twister even got the effect of turbulence kicking up around the base, which is present in real tornadoes. Some effects men from Paramount came in and watched us. They tried to do the same thing, but they couldn't make it work because of all the ripples at the top of the water. I had laid a sheet of cellophane across the top and they didn't know that."

Goldner remembered the tank well. "We filled it with water one night so shooting could begin next morning, but the glass broke during the night. It wasn't sufficiently heavy to sustain the weight of the water. We replaced it with heavier glass, but that also burst before morning. The third heavily braced tank with much heavier glass held the water all right but the thicker glass caused the cinematographer to complain because of distortion. The first takes of the headland rising from the water lacked the desired ponderousness, even with heavy overcranking, so they thickened the water with clear gelatin."

Other animation work was done involving the killing of some sailors by an arsinoitherium, a prehistoric mammal with an elephant-like body and huge, paired cranial horns. Another sequence utilized the horned dinosaur, styracosaurus. The animals themselves still exist in private collections.

All of *Creation* that had been shot was without sound, but a musical score was being composed by a young symphonist, Eddison von Ottenfeld.

By May 9, 1931, cost on *Creation* totalled $177,663. About 50 working days of live action remained to be filmed and only a few of the many effects sequences had been done. The Depression had affected attendance and ticket prices to the point where it had become evident that *Cimarron,* however highly acclaimed, was going to lose a great deal of money. RKO's purchase in January of the 40-

Ralf Harolde is pursued by the triceratops in a clever composite shot.

acre lot and other assets of the foundered Pathé Exchange for almost $5,000,000 was yet another financial burden that imperiled the solvency of the young company.

The rocky headland rises from the sea as drawn by Mario Larrinaga.

LeBaron, unwilling to battle such odds further, wanted out. He found a more secure berth at Paramount. His successor, who took the reins as vice president in charge of production at both the Radio and Pathé studios in October, was David O. Selznick, a former "wonder boy" executive at Paramount.

Selznick immediately halted all production. He hired a personal assistant, the colorful Merian C. Cooper, and advanced a young associate producer, Pandro S. Berman, to a second assistant's position. These men were ordered to make a detailed study of all productions contemplated or in work and evaluate them as to viability.

Cooper's assessment of *Creation* was that it was "Just a lot of animals walking around" and lacked the dramatic qualities audiences wanted. O'Brien, learning that Cooper had been frustrated in his attempts to obtain backing for a movie about a gigantic gorilla, suggested to him that such a film could be made in the studio via the techniques used in *Creation*. To back up this claim, O'Brien and Crabbe prepared a large painting showing a wild jungle girl and an explorer being confronted by the colossal ape. Cooper instructed O'Brien to produce

a Dunning process scene of two men fighting a dinosaur and to slow down the actions of the dinosaur by about one-fourth as compared to the animation in *Creation*. Cooper was overjoyed by the results of the test scene.

On December 19, 1931, Cooper wrote a memo to Selznick declaring that "the present story construction and the use of the animals is all wrong." He suggested, however, that things could be put right by using the equipment and personnel assembled and trained for *Creation* to apply to a new story about a "giant terror gorilla." Accordingly, *Creation* itself was abandoned and its costs, assets and technical crew were transferred to Cooper's new project, *The Beast* – the first working title of what eventually would become *King Kong*. Harry Hoyt was terminated at RKO, which refused to relinquish to him the rights to *Creation*.

For several years afterward Hoyt tried to secure backing for a similar scenario, *Lost Atlantis*. He came close in 1938, when Columbia advanced him $20,000 for the making of a two-reel dinosaur sequence in collaboration with Fred Jackman Sr., ASC, who had been director of photographic effects for *The Lost World*. The dinosaurs were built at Jackman's new studio in Burbank and the 20 minute film was delivered. After considerable advance publicity, Columbia decided against completing the picture, however. Another test reel was made later by cartoon producer Walter Lantz and producer-inven-

110

tor James Nasser, but *Lost Atlantis* was never produced and the fate of the three reels of dinosaur footage is not known.

Several of the dinosaurs made for *Creation* appear in *King Kong* and the styracosaurus made a belated debut in the sequel, *The Son of Kong.* Most of the scenes of the attack of the arsinoitherium on the sailors and of Harolde (representing a crew member) being pursued and killed by the triceratops were utilized in the rough cuts of *Kong,* but were discarded later and presumably are lost. Footage of the dinosaurs and Snooky, the baby triceratops's jungle stroll, the live animals, the killing of the baby and what remained of the chase still exists. All of the storm and underwater scenes and the scene of two men fighting a dinosaur apparently are lost.

Several scripts were written during the years *Creation* was in preparation. The version which was storyboarded and spawned the sequences that were actually produced follows:

John Armitage, a hard-boiled American millionaire, undertakes a business trip to Chile in his yacht. Accompanying him are his beautiful but spoiled daughter, Elaine; Billy, his 10-year old son; Ned Hallett, his ruthless foreign manager and fiance of Elaine; Louise Martin, Armitage's widowed sister; Bennie, a valet; and Steve, a young scientist hired as tutor for Billy. Elaine flirts with Steve, who falls for her until he learns her interest in him is merely capricious.

A Chilean submarine surfaces alongside. The captain reports that a tremendous storm is almost upon them. A tornado devastates a coastal town and moves toward the yacht. Everyone crowds aboard the submarine, which dives just as the storm strikes. An undersea upheaval causes a huge promontory to rise from the depths, creating a gigantic cavern in the ocean floor. Millions of tons of water flow into the cavity, drawing the submarine along.

In the morning the passengers see strange monsters in the water as the damaged submarine surfaces in a jungle lake. Everybody gets ashore in a life raft before the craft sinks. They are astonished to discover they are in the crater of a volcano, the floor of which is a tropical jungle. To their horror, they see several brontosauri at the edge of the lake. Bennie is swept off his feet by the tail of one of the beasts. Hallet, who has two hunting rifles, tries to shoot a brontosaur, but Steve halts him, saying the brutes are harmless unless aroused. Following a narrow trail up one of the overhanging walls of the crater, the party finds a ledge that offers a place of comparative safety above the jungle. It is impossible to scale the sheer walls to the summit.

Steve, the submarine captain and the sailors go into the jungle to search for a way out. They are attacked by an arsinoitherium, which kills two of the men. Pterodactyls, great flying reptiles, carry off the bodies. Steve manages to reach a place of safety as the arsinoitherium sends the other men to their death in a chasm. Returning to the ledge, Steve defeats Hallett in a fight and assumes leadership.

Larrinaga drawing of the ledge where the castaways find refuge.

Drawing by Byron Crabbe and O'Brien shows
arsinoitherium attacking sailors.

A menacing styracosaurus.

A month in the lost world regenerates everybody except Hallett, who remains surly and uncooperative. The castaways have built a liveable hut on the ledge. While Steve is away, Hallett shoots a passing diplodocus, which angrily destroys the hut, injuring Armitage. As the dinosaur reaches for Hallett, Elaine thrusts a firebrand into its jaws, driving it away. Armitage and Mrs. Martin denounce Hallett when Steve returns. Although she secretly loves Steve, Elaine loyally sides with Hallett and goes with him when he decides to quit the camp rather than cooperate. In the jungle, Hallett wantonly shoots a baby triceratops. The mother of the slain dinosaur kills Hallett. Elaine is rescued by Steve.

Assisted by Elaine, Steve dives to the submarine and retrieves the wireless. He also sees evidence that the volcano is becoming active. Later, while searching for something from which to construct a leyden jar necessary to repair the radio, Steve, Elaine, Billy and Bennie find the ruins of an ancient burial temple. A pteranodon carries Elaine away. Steve saves her, but now an angry stegosaurus menaces the party. The four flee into the temple, where they encounter a tyrannosaurus, the most dangerous of all dinosaurs. They try to hide in a burial niche, but are driven out by young tyrannosaurs that live in the dark recesses. The stegosaurus enters and is attacked by the tyrannosaurus. Steve leads his friends to safety as the meat eater and its young feed on the vanquished stegosaurus.

The volcano stirs. Lava breaks through the earth and the lake becomes so hot the aquatic creatures are driven ashore. The jungle beasts stampede, fleeing flames and lava. While Steve repairs the radio, Armitage erects an antenna. At last they are able to send out an SOS, but a moment later a dying pterodactyl crashes into the antenna, toppling it from the ledge.

Two Chilean army seaplanes arrive and set down in the steaming lake. The castaways are gathered aboard and the planes take off. A tyran-

The arsinoitherium as constructed by Marcel Delgado, flora by Orville Goldner.

Concept illustration of Steve and a pteranodon at the lost city by Mario Larrinaga and Willis O'Brien.

nosaurus leaps futilely at one of the aircraft. Moments after the planes emerge from the crater a titanic eruption destroys the land of the dinosaurs. In the last scene, Bennie reveals he has enough jewels from the lost temple to make all of them rich.

A short reel of film, a lot of paperwork, several large illustrations, hundreds of continuity sketches, an unfinished musical score (Von Ottenfeld's "Dinosaur Suite" eventually was performed at the Hollywood Bowl), and a scattering of test frames are all that remain of *Creation* itself. It did sire a sturdy offspring, though, because without *Creation* there would have been no *King Kong*.

—George E. Turner

An RKO Radio *picture (unfinished); producer,* William LeBaron; *associate producer,* Bertram Millhauser; *director,* Harry O. Hoyt; *story by* Harry Hoyt; *adaptation and screen play by* Beulah Marie Dix; *chief technician,* Willis H. O'Brien; *director of photography,* Karl Brown; *operative cameramen,* Linwood G. Dunn, Harold E. Wellman; *composites by* Dunning Process Co.; *production artists,* Mario Larrinaga, Byron L. Crabbe, Ernest Smythe; *technical staff,* Marcel Delgado, Carroll Shepphird, Orville Goldner, E.B. Gibson, Charles Christadoro, Fred Reese, John Cerisoli; *set decorations,* Les Millbrook; *assistant director,* Walter Daniels; *continuity,* Elizabeth Hayter; *animal supervision,* Olga Celeste; *music,* Eddison von Ottenfeld. *1930-1932.*

Players: Ned Hallett, Ralf Harolde; *Ape,* Snooky.

10

Tarzan at MGM

There have been many styles of fantasy jungles in books and on the screen. Certainly H. Rider Haggard's concept was not the same as Kipling's or Edgar Rice Burroughs', just as Sol Lesser's *Tarzan* films of the 1940s and 1950s differed considerably from the interpretation presented in Warner Bros.' 1984 production of *Greystoke: The Legend of Tarzan, Lord of the Apes.* This in turn was a major departure from the mythical jungle milieu conjured up by MGM for its six films featuring Johnny Weissmuller and Maureen O'Sullivan during the 1930s and early 1940s. Paradoxically, the MGM *Tarzans* drew little from Burroughs' original concept, but, rather, the impetus stemmed from the studio's 1931 jungle adventure tale, *Trader Horn.*

Although *Trader Horn's* cost eventually reached $1,322,000 (an enormous sum for the early Depression), it did exceptionally good business internationally. And internationally is a key word. The exotic melodrama involving basic, elementary character interworkings and an abundance of action and adventure did not suffer the fate of other genres that may or may not be popular, or indeed, be able to be understood in other countries and cultures.

What production chief Irving Thalberg and supervisor Bernard Hyman needed was a follow-up. Perhaps further adventures of Trader Horn? Well...

Johnny Weissmuller and Maureen O'Sullivan in a scene from Tarzan the Ape Man. *Director W.S. Van Dyke wearing cap and Clyde DeVinna to right of camera.*

But someone at the studio thought of taking the creation of Edgar Rice Burroughs, "Tarzan of the Apes," and devising an original story that might involve Trader Horn with the ape man. Tarzan, in Burroughs' original 1912 story, is brought up by the apes in the jungle and later sees Jane, who is part of a scientific research party, and abducts her. The primitive and the civilized meet in the Garden of Eden. Basic culture clash. In a sense, this was an inversion of the film version of *Trader Horn* wherein Horn and his friend discover a "white goddess" brought up by a tribe in Africa. They rescue her, and she and Horn's friend fall in love. Now the above constitutes only a small portion of *Trader Horn,* the 1927 book, which is essentially a string of reminiscences – at least some of which fall under the category of, shall we say, tall tales. Horn's white goddess had been around for decades in fiction, feature pictures, serials, etc... And, of course, Tarzan was in some way a derivation from the legend of Romulus and Remus, the founders of Rome, who were supposed to have been suckled and raised by a she-wolf. And there was Kipling's Mowgli in *The Jungle Book* – one more variation on the "wolf boy" myths that had fascinated Europe since the Middle Ages.

Negotiations between Burroughs and MGM began in March of 1931, only a few weeks after *Trader Horn* was released. In a memo from MGM story editor Sam Marx to MGM executive Eddie Mannix (April 2, 1931), Marx says "Mr. Thalberg is interested in the title and story *Tarzan of the Apes.*" The actual contract, dated April 15, 1931, specified that "Burroughs grants rights to Metro to

Hippo trouble on lake Sherwood.

write an 'original story,' using character of 'Tarzan,' and any other character used in stories heretofore written by author... Author to point out any material which conflicts or infringes upon any story heretofore written by author... Consideration: $20,000... [and] $1,000 per week for each of five weeks of author's services..." What this last portion meant was that Burroughs would read the scripts to be sure they were not based (in whole or in part) on his own works.

Bernie Hyman was to be the line producer (or supervisor) under Irving Thalberg, and contract writer Cyril Hume was assigned the script. Hume was an obvious choice. He had proved himself after director W.S. Van Dyke and company returned in December, 1929, from filming *Trader Horn* in Africa. Hume was among several writers given the task of providing smoother connective tissue with additional scenes and dialogue to be photographed in the Southern California jungles and the MGM backlot.

Some of the problems encountered in Africa had been brought on by the sound revolution. As director of photography Clyde DeVinna, ASC, recalled in the January, 1930, *American Cinematographer:* "All of a sudden when we were almost half through with the picture, the studio cabled us that as the world was demanding its pictures all-talking, *Trader Horn* would have to talk too, and so a sound crew was on its way to Africa to join us! Well, the sound men reached us all right, and we found that they had brought everything with them but silenced cameras for us to use." The prop man improvised with felt, canvas, and blankets in an attempt to cut down on the inherent noise of the two Bell and Howells and one Akeley that had been transported in the first place. (Later it was discovered that MGM had sent two silent Mitchells, but they never ar-

rived.) When Thalberg and Hyman viewed the film, they knew they had to do some fixing.

Marx suggested to Hyman that Hume (whom Marx had admired for his novels published in the 1920s, and whose option was not being picked up by MGM) be given an opportunity to view the assembled African footage and come up with some constructive ideas. Hume solved some of the problems and then worked closely with Hyman on the additional and revised dialogue. Eventually, the players – Harry Carey, Edwina Booth, Duncan Renaldo, etc. – were recalled and new scenes shot to integrate with the *Trader Horn* African footage.

So, Hume was the logical person for *Tarzan, the Ape Man.* Africa was not contemplated for any of the filming, however. By June 19th, Hume submitted a brief story outline which began with Trader Horn agreeing to lead an expedition to search for a lost tribe. En route they meet Tarzan, who kidnaps one of the party, a woman scientist. She eventually returns to the safari, and later the party is captured by the lost tribe still living under paleolithic conditions. The party is taken to a ruined city replete with moon worship and a religion involving human sacrifices to a sacred gorilla. Tarzan and his friends the elephants arrive in the nick of time and

Van Dyke and O'Sullivan on trading post set from Tarzan, the Ape Man.

the party is rescued. The ape man asks the woman to stay with him in the jungle. She hesitates, then agrees. Horn and the rest of the party return to the trading post.

By September, as the script evolved, Trader Horn was replaced by the fictitious Colonel Parker and the woman scientist was changed to Parker's non-scientific daughter, Jane. The search for the lost tribe and ruined city were modified to the search for the Elephant's Graveyard, where a fortune in ivory would be waiting. This impenetrable spot was bounded on all sides by the Mutia Escarpment, a sacred and forbidden mountain barrier. Other elements in the original outline remained, except that Jane's father dies at the Elephant's Graveyard. (C. Aubrey Smith, who had the small role of Horn's trader friend in *Trader Horn,* was cast in this similar part.)

Burroughs, in his novels and stories, often had Tarzan encountering lost civilizations and barbaric cultures. But he had never used the old African myth (referred to in *Trader Horn,* the book) which says that when they feel death coming upon them, elephants leave the herd and by some mysterious instinct trek to a remote spot in the wilderness where all the elephants go to die – a cemetery of ivory. The Mutia Escarpment (Tarzan's domain) was strictly an MGM concoction having no basis in legend or Burroughs. It was named after Mutia Omoolu, the African portrayer of Horn's gun bearer in *Trader Horn.*

Many were tested for the roles of Tarzan and Jane. As the shooting date approached, Hume saw Johnny Weissmuller swimming at the Hollywood Athletic Club and persuaded Hyman and Van Dyke to interview him. After testing, he was signed by MGM on October 16th, 1931, at $250 a week. Weissmuller had won five Olympic swimming championships in 1924 and 1928, and during his career he won 52 national championships and broke 67 world's records – some of which were not bettered for decades. He had not had any previous acting experience (but had appeared in sports short subjects and a cameo in *Glorifying the American Girl,* a 1929 Paramount feature).

The search for an actress to play Jane continued. Meanwhile, British actor, playwright, screenwriter, composer Ivor Novello was brought in to work on Hume's script. On October 23rd, with filming scheduled to begin in nine days, Novello, Van Dyke, and Hyman were discussing the character of Jane.

The following are abridged excerpts from the transcribed conference in the MGM Collection at the University of Southern California:

O'Sullivan and Neil Hamilton on MGM backlot. Van Dyke in front of camera with Hal Rosson on ladder.

Hyman: I can see her humor as very sophisticated. We don't want her doing anything ingenueish...

Novello: I tell you, Bernie, that her attitude at the beginning is this: She has been living a very sophisticated life in England and has grown very tired of it, that's the reason she's packed up everything and has arrived there [Africa] – as much as to get back to simplicity as anything else. What do you think of that idea, Bernie – of having her come there because she is tired of her own life?

Hyman: I like it, definitely. I think that's the characterization.

Van Dyke: So do I.

Novello: And I think it is the thing that will lead up to the girl's response to Tarzan and the very thing that keeps Holt [Neil Hamilton] and her apart – that he has come out to do this job hating it and longs for the very things that she has chucked up...

Hyman: The girl that was here looked slender enough to be tossed around and had enough strength in her face to be a woman. She'll need help in her diction – unless we suggest he sent her to America for her education... [Note: The actress is not identified, but a strong possibility is Leila Hyams, who, years later, claimed she turned down the role.]

117

Novello: Suppose he had an American wife? Suppose –

Hyman: I think you can be so much more charming with her if she's British.

Novello: There's nothing so silly as an American girl saying conventional English things. It makes her sound affected, where an English girl is perfectly natural saying them...

Van Dyke: I think it would be very nice to establish the sophistication of the girl, with all her sweetness...I don't know, though – this is a kid picture.

Novello: I don't know – I think it's for everybody...

Van Dyke: We should have the flavor of *White Cargo*.

Novello: I think the more light-hearted the expedition is at the start, the more strength there will be when the adventure happens.

On October 30th, 20-year old Maureen O'Sullivan was signed at $300 per week to play Jane. She had been discovered in Ireland by director Frank Borzage while he was there filming some background scenes for *Song O' My Heart* (1930), a screen vehicle for John McCormack, the famous Irish tenor. After appearing in that film, she had featured roles at Fox (*So This Is London, Just Imagine, A Connecticut Yankee*, etc.) for a year or so, but then her option was dropped two weeks before her test at MGM for Jane proved successful.

Tarzan, the Ape Man started filming at the studio on October 31st. Harold Rosson, ASC, and

Hollywood's most popular romantic couple in Tarzan, the Ape Man.

Tree scene is from Tarzan, the Ape Man.

Clyde DeVinna, ASC, shared photographic credit. DeVinna is known for his outstanding work on MGM features made in exotic locations (*White Shadows in the South Seas* (1927), *Trader Horn* (1931), *Eskimo* (1933), etc. – all with Van Dyke. Rosson also had been director of photography on Van Dyke's *The Cuban Love Song* (1931) and was to work with him on many other occasions. In an interview with Leonard Maltin for his book *Behind the Camera: The Cinematographer's Art* (1971), Rosson said that Van Dyke's style "was to emphasize certain things in a picture. In other words, the girl in his picture had to look beautiful. So Van would permit you as a cameraman as much time as needed, within reason, to get a good result of the girl. If I was going to make a photograph of a piece of newspaper that had to be lying on that table, he wanted me to photograph that newspaper in one second, or half a second if possible, but I could take hours with the girl. So I would say that all these stories you heard about Van Dyke as a one-take, hurry-up man – granted he wanted you to hurry up, *on that newspaper,* but he never hurried me up on the girl [were just exaggerations. He often told me] 'Let me know when you're ready.' "

A good deal of material was photographed on the sound stages, the MGM river/lake, and the

Insert: Rod LaRocque, Hamilton, O'Sullivan and Weissmuller in original casting of Tarzan and His Mate. *Full picture shows final choice with Paul Cavanagh replacing LaRocque.*

Mutia Escarpment rocks (a.k.a. the Tarzan rocks). The lake and the rocks were at the west end of Lot 1 at the time. The sequence involving the safari crossing a lake on rafts and being attacked by hippos was photographed at Lake Sherwood. Howard "Dutch" Horton, head of MGM's locations unit for many years, told Tony Scott a few years ago that following the filming of this sequence one of the hippos was reported missing. "He went down in the lake and wouldn't come up. A 'Get the hippo out of the lake' work order came out every day until he turned up in the middle of the road."

Rosson recalled shooting in the area near Lake Sherwood as well (so named after being used in Douglas Fairbanks' 1922 *Robin Hood*). "They had that wonderful trio, The Flying Codonas, and they built trapezes which became part of the set. We did a lot of the flying stuff out near Lake Sherwood." Alfredo Codona was an internationally famous aerialist. He doubled Weissmuller for all the swinging shots, which were used over and over again in subsequent MGM *Tarzans*.

Indian elephants, modified with false ears and extended tusks to make them appear to be African elephants, were selected from circus herds for the climactic stampede into the dwarf village where they crashed into native huts. For five days the elephant stampede was "rehearsed" and then several cameras captured the action from different vantage points (including pit shots). DeVinna and William Snyder, ASC, among others, were placed to record the elephants coming toward the cameras. The elephant stampede and the variations of same in subsequent MGM *Tarzans* were inspired by the prototype sequence in the 1927 expeditionary documentary-melodrama, *Chang,* made by Merian C. Cooper and Ernest B. Schoedsack.

Bert Nelson, animal trainer for the A.G. Barnes circus, was hired in early December to double Weissmuller wrestling a lion supplied by Nelson. Also, four lions were rented from the Goebel Lion Farm in Thousand Oaks (Louis Goebel and Louis Roth were part of the deal, being used as trainers). Emma, the chimp, was the first of several to portray Cheeta (Jiggs, Yama, Skippy, etc. followed). Most of

119

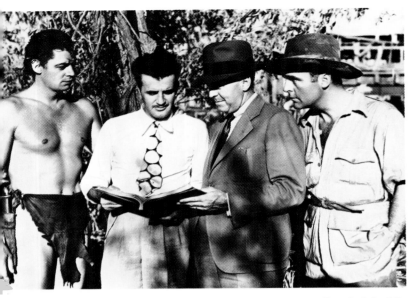

From Tarzan and His Mate, *Weissmuller, Cedric Gibbons, Edgar Rice Burroughs and Hamilton.*

the animals were leased for the occasion by George Emerson, who for several decades held the only job of its kind in Hollywood: full-time studio trainer – exclusively at MGM.

The picture finished shooting in late December, a relatively modest eight week schedule on a film of this nature. The cost listed in the MGM files was $652,675.

The only music used – other than native drums and chants (most, if not all, recorded for *Trader Horn*) – was the unpublished ''Voodoo Dance,'' by George Richelavie, arranged by Fritz Stahlberg and P.A. Marquardt, over the opening titles, and a bit of the love theme from Tchaikovski's ''Overture to Romeo and Juliet'' over the final scene. ''Voodoo Dance'' had been used at least one time previously as the main title music for an MGM ''Dogville Comedy'' short subject of 1931 called ''Trader Hound.''

Early in February *Tarzan, the Ape Man* had an exceptional preview – even more positive than the studio anticipated. Burroughs, contrary to accounts passed down through the years, was extremely enthusiastic. In a congratulatory letter sent to Van Dyke after the preview he rhapsodized that this was ''the greatest Tarzan picture of them all'' and that Weissmuller was ''great'' and Maureen O'Sullivan ''perfect.'' On May 31st he wrote to Bernie Hyman and suggested that Tarzan movies be released as seasonal events, each spring, so that people would look forward to the occasion, much as they did to the circus, ''to which the Tarzan picture is analogous.''

In the MGM version, until Jane taught Tarzan a few monosyllabic words, his primary means of communication was a remarkable, earth-shattering cry/yodel/yell that every boy (and often girl) imitated during the 1930s. There was not even a hint of peerage (he was Lord Greystoke in the novels), nor did Tarzan take on civilized ways in Paris and London. But if there wasn't nobility of blood, there was plenty of nobility of character. The MGM jungle man was simple, straightforward, lovable, strong, and sensitive. It was never explained who his parents were and how he happened to be living in the jungle. In any case, tall, lean and lithe Johnny made a first-rate Tarzan. Indeed, no person before or since has met with the same success. As opposed to some other screen Tarzans, he did not appear muscle-bound, and was able to move about in a loose, cat-like manner. There were other subtle touches of an animal nature – the wariness, the quick turning of the head, and the catching of a scent.

Jane Porter of Baltimore in the novels was changed to Jane Parker of London. Maureen was a lovely Jane, projecting an intriguing blend of inno-

LaRocque and O'Sullivan in scene from aborted version.

cence and sophistication, fine breeding with sensuousness, and fragile femininity with rugged tenacity.

Some of the most effective sequences in the film are those between Tarzan and Jane. Their screen chemistry has a lingering appeal and complete believability, running the gamut from Jane's abject terror at being abducted by the ape man, through her awakening of interest as she realizes Tarzan's tenderness and protective concern, to playful, child-like courting, romantic musing, and finally, physical abandon.

With one of the biggest hits of 1932, MGM immediately thought about a sequel. In April, 1932, Burroughs, for $45,000, granted MGM the right to produce a second Tarzan film and an option to produce two further pictures. Various outlines and treatments were developed from June through January, 1933, by Bud Barsky, collaborators Arthur Hyman and C. Gardner Sullivan, and others. The earliest uncredited "notes" (probably by Barsky) regarding the script for *Tarzan and His Mate,* are from July 8, 1932: "The story should be of a civilized man trying to get a girl, who is now wild, away from a wild man, and her temptation to take him up on it ...[The] safari will have to find Tarzan in order to find the ivory..." It was announced at this time by

the studio that the sequel would be filmed in Africa. These plans were abandoned along the way.

By March of 1933 story conferences were being held with writer Leon Gordon (who wrote the 1923 play, *White Cargo),* Hyman, supervising art director Cedric Gibbons, and production manager J.J. (Joe) Cohn. Among other things, Tarzan's battle with the giant crocodile was discussed and the treatment for a spectacular jungle fire just before the safari reaches the base of the Mutia Escarpment. It was noted that "The fire sequence is one of the biggest in the picture." This was eliminated prior to photography. Then a concern was raised: "Be careful about Jane's costume...She might wear a 'Tondelayo' [*White Cargo*] costume. (If Tarzan were to get Jane cloth from a native trading post, she would probably make it into a dress.) See Amazon woman in *Trader Horn."* Jane's abbreviated outfit evolved into a small halter top and a loin cloth, exposing a good deal of midriff, thighs, and hips.

By May, a dialogue continuity by Howard Emmett Rogers was completed. This, along with all of the earlier script and conference ideas, became the basis for James Kevin McGuinness' various drafts of the screenplay.

During June and July, major special effects decisions were being made. Again, large ears and elongated tusks were built to attach to the several Indian elephants at MGM's zoo in order to simulate African elephants. Indian elephants traditionally had been considered easier to train. Joe Cohn's idea

The tree house on the sound stage.

Josephine McKim, who doubled for O'Sullivan in the crocodile attack.

of making miniature elephants with movable trunks was activated. They would be photographed and projected behind Tarzan, Jane and the real elephants as the herd arrives to protect the Graveyard from the ivory raiders. (Humorist Jules Feiffer refers to the Elephant's Graveyard as "a strip of land so devout in its implications to jungle book fanciers that one could only assume the elephants took instruction in the church before dying.") The safari's climb to the Mutia Escarpment was to be "shot on the lot with [Warren] Newcombe, [Irving] Ries, and [James] Basevi putting in the falling figures... Top of Escarpment on Lot 2 with Newcombe and... Sherwood. Night camp fire scene played on built set on stage... waterfall and burial grounds shot on lot ...River on Lot 2... *Red Dust* [1932] boat... use *Red Dust* house in background..."

At that time, special effects were under Cedric Gibbons and therefore part of the art department. Because of the elaborate physical production being planned, Gibbons assigned A. Arnold "Buddy" Gillespie as the unit art director. Warren Newcombe was in charge of matte paintings (there were many in this and all MGM Tarzans), James Basevi handled miniatures, some mechanical effects, and other trick shots, and Irving G. Ries, ASC, concerned himself with the relatively new area of optical effects, including split screens and soft-edge wipes. Rear projection (then with a glass screen) was rapidly becoming a standard device, and many such shots were designed to be used in *Tarzan and His Mate.*

Since MGM had announced plans in 1928 to film the best-seller *Trader Horn,* many jungle films had appeared – mostly inferior quickies, exploitation films, real or ersatz documentaries, and travelogues. After *Trader Horn* and *Tarzan, the Ape Man,* even more entries in the jungle genre glutted the market – promising (and sometimes delivering) bigger and better thrills. In February of 1933, RKO's sensational *King Kong* broke box office records. Also, Paramount produced and released the excellent *King of the Jungle* in 1933 with Buster Crabbe, another Olympic swimming champ, portraying a Tarzan-like man of the wilderness. Sol Lesser, through a previous arrangement with Burroughs, produced and released a relatively inexpensive combination feature and serial, *Tarzan the Fearless* (1933) with Buster Crabbe. With all this jungle activity, MGM was afraid that by the time *Tarzan & His Mate* was ready for release in 1934 the cycle could be played out. To protect their investment, MGM decided to go all out.

So, the relatively simple bones of a story were fleshed out with every conceivable kind of embellishment. Southern California locations were planned for some sequences (sometimes just one or two shots) to give the film a bigger-than-the-back-lot-look. Sherwood Forest and Lake Sherwood got the most mileage plus Woodland Park near Pico-Rivera in Whittier (swamp), Big Tujunga, and China Flats.

Filming began on August 2nd with Cedric Gibbons directing the first unit. Clyde DeVinna was back, and he and Charles G. Clarke, ASC, shared photographic credit. Weissmuller, O'Sullivan, and Neil Hamilton reprised their roles from the first film. Silent star Rod La Rocque was cast in the important role of Martin Arlington, who – along with Holt (Hamilton) – were the leaders of the safari to get those tusks and Jane away from the Mutia Escarpment. Murray Kinnell and Frank Reicher played the relatively small roles of Pierce and Vanness, rival seekers of the Elephant's Graveyard.

While the first unit concentrated on the dialogue scenes, various other units were filming time consuming and difficult to obtain animal sequences, trick shots, and sundry action material. A 1932 Olympic swimming champion, Josephine McKim, had been signed to a contract in April, primarily as a double for Maureen O'Sullivan in swimming shots. Underwater sequences with Tarzan, Jane, and the giant mechanical crocodile were photographed on the lot in August in what Buddy Gillespie referred to as "The dish-pan tank on Lot 1." Gillespie recalled in an interview with Tim Onosko circa 1978: "We built the crocodile, and he [Weissmuller] was working in around 18 feet of water. He finally maneuvered around with this mechanical beast made out of steel and rubber and started to stab into the throat of the crocodile to kill it. We had planted a bunch of little nigrosine dye sacks in the crocodile's throat. When it came out, it looked like blood."

Josephine McKim appeared in some shots with the mechanical crocodile. She and Weissmuller also were photographed in an extended underwater

"ballet." Weissmuller had on his loin cloth but McKim was nude, to coincide with the requirements of the script. This sequence was no doubt inspired by a similar one in RKO's *Bird of Paradise*, the year before, with Dolores Del Rio and Joel McCrea. When Jane gets out of the water she is hidden by foliage (a la Hedy Lamarr in *Ecstasy* – 1933) until she retrieves her clothes from Cheeta. Edgar Rice Burroughs visited MGM while some of the underwater shots were being made and reported in a letter to his son, Hulbert, on August 14, that the crocodile fight was going to be "very thrilling," but the nude swimming sequence "may get by the censors and may not." On August 16, Burroughs wrote Hulbert: "I am fearful that they are going to spend too much. They are very anxious to make it outshine [Sol] Lesser's picture to such a degree that there will be no comparison."

After approximately three-and-a-half weeks of filming, the first unit shut down for a short period. When shooting resumed in early September, Gibbons was replaced by MGM contract director Jack Conway and Rod La Rocque by Paul Cavanagh. The characters of Pierce and Vanness, who had been played by Kinnell and Reicher in the earlier filming, were now portrayed by William Stack and Desmond Roberts. All of the scenes in which these players and La Rocque appeared were done again. The exact reasons behind the changes never have been made clear, and are not documented in the files. Gibbons never had directed a film previously, nor was he to do another film in that capacity. But, he was very much involved in the planning and coordination of the vast physical as-

Weissmuller really rode the rhino in this scene from Tarzan and His Mate.

pects of the production in addition to continuing his work as supervising art director for all of MGM's productions. Perhaps the day-to-day direction and the elongated schedule plus all of his regular duties proved to be too much. In any case, Conway finished the dialogue portions of the picture while James McKay directed many of the animal scenes and Errol Taggart and Nick Grinde handled other material.

Meanwhile, George Emerson had his hands full augmenting the MGM zoo for the second Tarzan film. Along with the elephants, assorted chimps, zebra, ostriches, etc., Emerson, at the time, was the only animal man to train a rhinoceros (Mary), who had been imported from Germany, to be used in a major sequence in the film. In fact, Emerson doubled Weissmuller for certain shots depicting the jungle man riding the rhino. But Weissmuller rode Mary for some shots and there was a dummy rhino. This material was photographed at the "rhino arena" on Lot 2 with much of the coverage used as back projection with foreground players (including man in ape costume) on stage.

On January 12 Mary caused a near panic at the studio when she charged a heavy cage containing several cameramen on Lot 2 during filming. Shaken up were camera crew members Bob Roberts, Lester White, Ellsworth Fredericks, Ray Ramsey, and William Foxall.

All of the sequences involving effects, animals, rear projection, mattes, and complicated intermixtures of location, backlot, and stage were very carefully broken down shot by shot. For example, there are twelve pages of dictated notes from Gibbons detailing the approach and execution of the complex "lion sequence" – the elongated finish of the film. During this sequence, Bert Nelson once again doubled Weissmuller in a fight with the lioness, Margie, and lion Pasha. Nelson also doubled Paul Cavanagh. There was even a Dunning composite shot used here: The camera is overhead shooting head and shoulders of Arlington on the ledge of a cliff looking down at lions mauling a native. Because of the straight down camera position, rear projection would have been impractical. Although there are many Dunning shots in *Trader Horn* and *Tarzan, the Ape Man*, by 1932-33 rear projection virtually had superseded its need. A few Williams traveling matte shots depicting lions leaping upon and holding onto elephants were contracted. With the exception of the Dunning and Williams shots in the grand finale, all other effects were handled in house.

The Flying Codonas returned for a full aerial act. The group doubled for Tarzan, Jane, and Big Cheeta (man in ape suit). An adagio team stood in for Jane diving from the trees into Tarzan's arms below. The Picchiani troupe, in ape costumes, juggled and lowered by their feet the ailing Tarzan from the treetops to the ground. And one of the Picchianis doubled Weissmuller leaping and jumping from branch to branch and tree to tree.

The picture officially closed March 10th, but retakes, pick-up shots, and additional material involving Jane (doubled by Betty [Mrs. Louis] Roth), Tarzan and the lions were still being done until later in the month. Maureen O'Sullivan was out for 45 days for an appendectomy. Almost eight months had elapsed since the first day of photography. The negative cost on the MGM books was $1,279,142.

Joseph I. Breen of the Production Code Office previewed the picture at MGM on April 5th and rejected it on the grounds that it violated the provision of the Code which stated that complete nudity is never permitted. Louis B. Mayer formally applied for a jury trial to sit in judgment on the verdict. On April 9th, industry figures B.B. Kahane, Carl Laemmle, Jr. and Winfield Sheehan reviewed the picture in an MGM projection room. Also present were Breen, Frederick Beetson, and Geoffrey Shurlock, representing the Production Code Administration, MGM's Bernard Hyman, Eddie Mannix, Irving Thalberg, L.B. Mayer, and Tom Held, the film editor. Breen, on April 10th, wrote to Will Hays, "The jury screened the reel in which the alleged code violation occurred several times, and later viewed six reels of the film of that portion of it which preceded, and a certain portion which immediately followed the offending sequence.

"This offending sequence was an underwater shot of a man and a woman going through a series of movements. The man in the shot wore a loin cloth, but a critical examination of the shot indicated that the woman was stark naked...

"After a rather animated discussion between the jurors, the representatives of Metro and Mr. Breen, the verdict of this office was sustained by the jury. Thereupon, Mr. Mannix, for Metro, suggested some changes in the present sequence:

"(a) To definitely plan at the start of the sequence that the girl wears some clothes.

"(b) That several of the shots, referred to above, be deleted either by cutting, or by darkening the print to cloud and confuse the eye [as in *Bird of Paradise.*] The jury agreed that, in the event these changes were made, to again look at the picture and to pass further judgment upon it.

Famous elephant's graveyard scene from Tarzan and His Mate.

"As the matter stands this morning, Tuesday, April 10th, the picture is rejected. Metro is making certain changes in the picture and will refer it again to the Committee for its verdict..."

From all evidence, *three* versions of the sequence eventually went out to separate territories during the film's initial release. One with Jane clothed in her jungle loin cloth outfit, one with her topless, and one in the nude. The Production Code Office saw and approved the clothed edition but found out later that the variant versions were in circulation – depending upon the different rules and restrictions among certain state and city censors and the noncensorable areas. Clearly this was a code violation. Eventually the studio eliminated the scene in its entirety and had it edited out of the negative.

"Voodoo Dance" once again was the main title music, and a cue by William Axt called "My Tender One," originally used in MGM's *Eskimo* (1933), could be heard at the conclusion. Native drums and chants (some, at least, recorded for *Trader Horn)* made up the source music, and a contemporary tune, "Soldier on the Shelf," by Sher-

man Myers, was the selection played on the portable phonograph in the jungle at night.

Daily Variety and *The Hollywood Reporter* in the April 7th pre-release trade reviews stated in their headlines, respectively, "In its present length [the picture] has a surfeit of excitement which will physically exhaust average audience" and, "New *Tarzan,* packed with showmanship, needs cuts. Plenty of thrills, but shocks in spots...Encouraged by the success of the first [MGM] *Tarzan,* the studio went wild with the second...The film is reels overlong, with several nice stopping places before all the carnage starts." Interestingly, the underwater nude swimming scene was praised as being "beautiful" and "breathtaking."

Between April 9th and April 20th the film was cut from eleven reels to nine (14½ minutes were deleted, to be exact). The trims were made throughout the film – an opening sequence at the trading post, several rather pointed lines of dialogue delivered by Arlington to Jane during the first night at the Escarpment, Tarzan waking up next to Jane in the tree hut, a few gruesome shots, and a long, harrowing scene of carnage involving Arlington, Saidi (number one safari boy portrayed by Nathan Curry), and the killing of lions in the last reels of the film. But another sequence, not photographed until about March 20th and involving Jane, was substituted. During the lion finale, she holds off two lions at the rocks and finally creates a spark out of dry twigs, builds a ring of fire around herself; then Tarzan arrives. The underwater swimming scene, for the time being, remained.

The nine reel version, from all evidence, is the only one that has been exhibited in theaters, 16mm, and on TV since the trade screenings – at least in the U.S.

In late April, 1934, the picture opened in New York to outstanding reviews (many stating that the sequel was better than the original) and no negative criticism. Business was excellent, but not as spectacular domestically as *Trader Horn* and *Tarzan, the Ape Man*. Internationally it was an incredible success.

A protection master positive (fine grain) of the eleven reel version and a nitrate optical negative of the track were discovered in 1987 in the MGM archives – but apparently no negative or other prints of the long version are in any of the MGM vaults. The two-minute underwater sequence included in the master positive is the version in which Jane is completely nude rather than a variant. A second print containing the topless version, reportedly from Canada, has been exhibited recently in Los Angeles theaters.

Metro-Goldwyn-Mayer waited until the latter part of 1934 before deciding definitely to make another in the series – the trouble-plagued *Tarzan Escapes*. But Louis B. Mayer wanted to let newly arrived producer Phil Goldstone handle this one. Goldstone had been identified with many Poverty Row productions before signing with MGM. By the end of January, 1935, cameraman-director-writer Karl Brown had completed a treatment on the tentatively titled *Tarzan Returns*. Then Louis Mosher contributed some material. He was followed by John Farrow (who in 1936 married Maureen O'Sullivan), and then Wyndham Gittens and Otis Garrett. The plot had to do with Jane's cousins (Benita Hume and William Henry) arriving in Africa and engaging Major Fry (John Buckler), a supplier of animals for zoos, to find some trace of their missing cousin. If the cousins can prove that Jane is dead, they will inherit her fortune. At the Mutia Escarpment the party discovers Tarzan and Jane. Jane resents Rita's (her cousin) more than platonic interest in Tarzan and his interest in her. Major Fry, upon seeing Tarzan in action, wants to capture him and bring him back as a circus attraction. After a series of complications, Rita and Fry are killed, Eric returns

home, and Tarzan and Jane are more in love than ever in their Garden of Eden.

Filming began in July, 1935, under the direction of James McKay. McKay had directed some of the animal sequences in the previous MGM *Tarzan* films and *Trader Horn*. During the 95-day shooting schedule, the film had various working titles. In addition to *Tarzan Returns*, it was referred to as *Capture of Tarzan, Tarzan and the Vampires,* and finally, *Tarzan Escapes*. The "vampires" refer to huge vampire bats encountered in a primitive marshland. Two or three units were shooting during the last few weeks of production. At one point William Wellman and George B. Seitz, then under contract, were assigned for a short while.

The film was edited and the main title billing put through. It is not certain if the picture was previewed, but starting November 10 through the end of December many high-level meetings were held to dissect and analyze the (by all evidence) severe problems inherent in the completed film. Apparently Phil Goldstone was not present. Story editor Edwin H. Knopf dictated many notes on December 2nd regarding the reconstruction of the film, including substantial reshooting and many new scenes: "Rita [Jane's cousin] should be a little less 'the spoiled darling' and somewhat more human in every action...I am sure we are all agreed that the less Tarzan talks, the better...A general criticism of the entire film would be that too much of dramatic importance occurs around and about Tarzan without his being an integral part of the action...The vampire [bat] sequence is one of the best in the picture, but somehow the pygmies [in the same sequence] are not as convincing as they might be...The major fault lies in the fact that Tarzan is the rescued, rather than the rescuer...."

On December 26: "...I think we are agreed that the present version as it appears on the screen is entirely devoid of a central plot menace... As Bernie [Hyman] pointed out, almost all of the mystery, the 'Never Never Land' quality which has made Tarzan a thing apart from ordinary people, has been lost; in making him articulate, they have made him common...In all contact with the white people, Jane should act as interpreter and interlocutor; Tarzan's reaction being instinctive and intuitive, rather than an intellectual reaction to dialogue...."

The MGM Tarzan's English vocabulary was up to this film and in the future, limited to such words as: man, hungry, sleep, love, swim, hurt, alone, always, people, us, friend, my, very well, much, thank you, and goodbye. One of his most frequently used "jungle" words was umgawa,

Scene from the unreleased version of Tarzan Escapes, *with Granville Bates and Bill Henry at left, Benita Hume and James McKay (seated), and Leonard Smith (standing behind McKay). Virgil Vogel operates the Mitchell.*

which originally meant get down, but as time went on it became a multi-purpose expression incorporating raise up, let's go, stop, get up, go away, go for help, etc....

Various meetings involved W.S. Van Dyke, staff producer Jack Cummings, James McKay, J.J. Cohn, W. Donn Hayes (the new editor assigned to the film), to say nothing of the top brass: Eddie Mannix, Sam Katz, and Benny Thau. A considerably revised continuity evolved, which was based to a degree on the story and characters from version

one. But there were major modifications. Jane's cousins now only want her to return to England to claim the inheritance and perhaps share it with them, and Rita no longer has designs on Tarzan – nor is there a hint of Tarzan being attracted to her. By the end of March another character had been added to the safari – Rawlins, the comic relief, played by Herbert Mundin. Whole sequences were dropped; new ones written, more stock shots from the previous productions were ordered, and a general reconstruction and modus operandi were evolving. Cyril Hume was assigned to work with Edwin Knopf on the new script in March. And Hyman was officially listed as the producer, although associate producer Sam Zimbalist was the line producer on the new version. Zimbalist, an ex-film editor and assistant to MGM producer Hunt Stromberg, received his first screen credit as associate producer on this film (Hyman's and Knopf's names do not appear on the final "official" credits).

Concept sketch and detail of the full scale engineering drawing of the vampire bat by Harcos, dated 6/18/35. Four bats were used in the unreleased version of Tarzan Escapes.

The first reference to the tree house of Tarzan and Jane occurs in Hume's "outline by sequences" of April 15. Hume referred to it as resembling "a large bird-house, completely encircling the main trunk of a tree, but there are various small annexes among the branches – verandas, a roofed dining platform, a dovecote, and particularly to be noted, a replica in miniature of the whole place, which is Cheeta's quarters. The construction is chiefly of bamboo, though the kitchen oven is made of crude masonry, and the whole place is thatched ...The interior furnishings improvised from the jungle by Jane and Tarzan should parody the 'last word' in modern conveniences.

The *Swiss Family Robinson*-like domicile appeared initially in the revised *Tarzan Escapes;* the earlier version had Tarzan and Jane living in an imaginatively furnished cave. The exterior six-room tree bungalow was constructed on location at Brent's Mountain Crags – specifically Crater Camp – in the Santa Monica Mountains (now Malibu Creek State Park) and duplicated on a stage at MGM. A porch surrounded the tree and an improvised elevator, operated by an elephant, hauled its residents up and down on command. With each new episode in the MGM series artfully contrived accessories were added in and around the perch. The interiors were on another stage.

In mid July, the revised *Tarzan Escapes* went back into production with the same cast and the same director of photography, Leonard Smith, ASC, who had joined MGM in 1928. Smith photographed many of Marie Dressler's films and the interesting *Devil Doll* (1936), among others. Director Richard Thorpe was assigned his first of the four remaining MGM *Tarzan* pictures. Previously active as a director of low budget westerns, comedies, serials, and melodramas, Thorpe was signed by MGM in 1935 and immediately impressed studio personnel with his quietly efficient, well-organized approach to his first two features for the studio: *Last of the Pagans* (1935) – photographed largely in Tahiti – and *The Voice of Bugle Ann* (1935). Thorpe's background was somewhat similar to W.S. "Woody" Van Dyke's. His knowledge of the various areas of filmmaking and ease of manner made him a natural choice for *Tarzan.*

During September the last shots of the revised version were made. In the editing room, footage was incorporated from a variety of sources: Along with the new scenes, artful use was made of some of the material shot for the first version of *Tarzan Escapes.* Bits and pieces photographed around Murchison Falls in Africa for *Trader Horn* were again put to use. The safari's approach to the Mutia Escarpment and the crocodile fight were lifted from *Tarzan and His Mate,* some jungle battles, vine swinging, and elephants stampeding were courtesy of *Tarzan, the Ape Man* – all in all, a skillful mosaic.

Jane's costume reflected the new vigor of the Production Code (in strict effect since July, 1934). Instead of her abbreviated and provocative attire used in *Tarzan and His Mate*, now, and in all subsequent MGM *Tarzans*, she sported variations of a mid-thigh length shift.

Although this entry in the series deliberately avoided or toned down the harsh, raw, Circus Maximus accents so prevalent in *Mate*, a few bits — most conspicuously the attack of the vampire bats in the bog — were eliminated before the release. There is nothing in the Production Code Administration files at the Academy of Motion Picture Arts and Sciences Library or studio records regarding this, so it may have been as a result of adverse comments at previews. MGM always had regarded this sequence as one of the few good aspects of the first version of *Tarzan Escapes*, and it was included in revised scripts — although the swamp sequence had been modified in other respects in the cutting room. As of now, the original unreleased film version of *Tarzan Escapes* cannot be found in the MGM archives.

A curious addition was a large, comical flightless bird, unlike any known to science, which waddles through a sequence to the consternation of Herbert Mundin. How the bird was operated has been a source of mystery for years. Actually the creature was designed around Johnny Eck, a circus performer featured in MGM's *Freaks* in 1932. Eck's body ended just beneath the ribcage and he could walk and run nimbly on his hands. He, alone in the world, was capable of providing animation for MGM's weird bird.

For the revised *Tarzan Escapes*, the studio went back to the main title music used in *Trader Horn* called "Cannibal Carnival." It was written by silent film composer-compiler Sol P. Levy and first published in 1920. (At least one other MGM film, the 1928 *West of Zanzibar*, included the composition in its

The vampire bats attack. They had moving heads, working jaws, and lighted eyes.

Maureen O'Sullivan and Bill Henry rescue Tarzan on the riverboat in the first Tarzan Escapes.

compilation score.) "My Tender One" by Axt was reprised for the close.

On November 6th, 1936, the $1,058,430 production, which presumably includes costs from both versions, was released to very good reviews and business almost a year after its first scheduled release date.

In July, 1938, a three way agreement between MGM, Burroughs, and Sol Lesser called for three additional pictures and an option for two more.

That same month Cyril Hume submitted a fifteen page untitled "suggested treatment" for the first film under the new contract. In this, Jane gives birth to a son in the jungle. Eventually Tarzan, the ninth Lord Greystoke (here was a breakthrough) and his family go to England to assume his vast lands and possessions. There he is "bewildered, wretched, utterly failing to fit in." (At a performance of Verdi's *Aida*, as Aida and Rhadames are about to be buried alive, Tarzan gives his wild cry, calling the elephants instantly out of the wings, and then launches himself to the rescue, via the chandelier, to the stage.) Eventually the family goes back to the jungle, disenchanted with civilization.

130

By August 18th, Hume's new outline treatment has Tarzan and Jane *discover* an infant in the jungle (named "Boy" by Tarzan) – and there is no trip to England. Since the MGM Tarzan and Jane were not legally married, a natural heir would have been difficult to sanction in this "family film" of the time, so the problem of Boy's genesis was solved by having an airplane, with Boy (then a baby) and his British mother and father (Laraine Day and Morton Lowry), who were no relation to Tarzan, crash on the Escarpment. The infant was the only survivor. Incidentally, Tarzan and Jane were married in Burroughs' second Tarzan novel, *The Return of Tarzan* (1915).

By November, the revised continuity outline has Jane die in Tarzan's arms as the result of a Zambeli native spear wound. (The Zambeli tribe was named in honor of Sam Zimbalist, just as the Gibonis were an homage to Cedric Gibbons, the Hymandis a salute to Bernard Hyman, and the Jaconi a whimsical nod to J.J. Cohn, by now a top MGM executive). The decision to eliminate Jane at the end of this film appears to have been the result of several factors: it was becoming increasingly difficult to concoct fresh plot devices for the series and still adhere to the evolving formula that had been so successful. It was felt that by eliminating Jane it would be possible to involve Tarzan in other romantic situations and yet still have another running character in Boy. Also, Maureen O'Sullivan after the first two films often had requested to be relieved of her participation. Needless to say, the productions were for the most part difficult to make and usually involved extended shooting schedules. And Maureen was pregnant with her first child as the *Tarzan* film was being prepared. The contract allowed the studio to kill any character except Tarzan.

Discussing the protracted shooting on *Tarzan and His Mate* during an interview in *Photoplay*, September, 1934, Miss O'Sullivan was quoted as saying: "I never was more consistently sick and miserable in my life. I had one cold after another. . . . I was never without an ache or pain. I was never completely or comfortably warm, and I was never, never without a bite from one of those da – those monkeys. I always had the same average – one fresh bite, one about half-healed, and one scar. . . . And even leaving the monkeys out of it, I wouldn't be a nudist for anything." In the April 14, 1986, *People* magazine she was quoted as saying "I got so sick of those *[Tarzan]* movies."

For the role of Boy, more than 300 candidates were interviewed from which a few were selected to be screen-tested, both with and without Weissmuller. John Sheffield was seven years old at the time of his interview and tests. He recalled in a recent letter:

"I had just finished the play *On Borrowed Time* in New York. My father, Reginald Sheffield [An English actor working in Hollywood], . . . and my mother, Louise, saw and responded to the ad in *The Hollywood Reporter* which asked, 'Do you have a Tarzan Jr. in your backyard?' They did; so father took me over to M.G.M. . . .

"I interviewed with the producers and Mr. Johnny Weissmuller. They liked me and I made some screen tests. . . . I am sure that it was Big John who gave the O.K. on me. (I was later to be known as Little John.)

"I do believe I was out of the running for a while. It was decided that Big John would give me a swimming test. Johnny knew that I didn't swim. That didn't bother Tarzan. So Big John took me over to the Los Angeles Athletic Club pool for the test. [It may have been the Hollywood Athletic Club] Johnny told me not to be afraid. Well if the best swimmer in the world tells you not to be afraid, you are not afraid! He got in the deep end of that great 'tank' and had me jump in. This was before I had learned to swim at the Carl Curtis School. I couldn't swim a stroke at the time I hit the water. Big Johnny saw that I was not afraid and I believe that it was at that moment, when Tarzan took hold of me and put my foot down on his knee, that Boy, son of Tarzan, was born. I passed the test easily.

"Big Johnny had fallen in love with me and I with him and although I was not his real son, I am convinced that I became his motion picture son right there in the deep end of the . . . pool."

Sam Zimbalist, by now a full producer, drew his second *Tarzan* film. Richard Thorpe and Leonard Smith returned as director and first cameraman. (In 1974 Maureen O'Sullivan told Kingsley Canham, "I like working fast. Richard Thorpe. . . . ground them out and brought them in well and ahead of schedule.")

Cedric Gibbons, on December 23rd, 1938, sent out 16 pages of a breakdown indicating in detail where and how each scene was to be photographed. The Buddy Gillespie miniatures and mechanical effects were precisely noted (since 1936 Gillespie had been head of the newly created special effects department), the Newcombe matte shots, painted backings, rear projection, second unit (no director indicated), location material (very little – and almost all second unit). Included were some long shots of the tree house action at Crater Camp, special animal material with Boy at the Goebel Lion Farm, and a few long shots at Lake Sherwood. Obviously, the plan was to do as much of the picture as possible at the studio under controlled conditions. A jungle set and tree house (exterior and interior) were built on the stage. Lot 2 supplied the wrecked plane set, the river, "Tarzan Rocks," an exterior camp set, and the Zambeli village. The miniature plane was photographed on Lot 2 by Max Fabian (he shot most of the MGM miniatures during this period). A "dump tank" on Lot 1 served for a "Newcombe shot of Boy floating toward waterfall, over which pool empties." A third unit planned to photograph "men in ape suits riding elephants." Stock footage (from *Baboona*, 1935) of animals photographed from the air was to be purchased from Mrs.

From the final version of Tarzan Escapes: *O'Sullivan, Hume and Henry in the hands of the Jaconis.*

Tarzan Finds a Son! Weissmuller and Johnny Sheffield at Silver Springs.

Martin Johnson. Other familiar stock shots of crocodiles, hippos, etc. once again were lifted from *Trader Horn.* The attack of the Gibonis on the safari at the base of the Escarpment along with the climb up the Escarpment and the rhino attack (this time Boy is the target) and Tarzan riding the rhino were reprised from *Tarzan and His Mate,* and the vine swinging was once again courtesy of the first *Tarzan.*

On January 6, 1939, three days before filming began, Burroughs wrote Al Lichtman, an MGM vice president, saying that he thought Hume had done his usual "swell job" but he regretted the killing of Jane. "I believe that you will find that it will react badly at the box office, for during twenty-five years' experience with Tarzan fans I have found that Jane is extremely popular and that when I leave her out of the Tarzan books, as I have on several occasions, we receive many letters of complaint. No matter how inartistic a happy ending may be, you are going to discover that the Tarzan fans prefer it."

Filming finished without incident on March 25th, but along with some retakes and pickup shots, a "new alternate ending" script, dated April 19, was scheduled to be done. Instead of Jane dying in Tarzan's arms as a result of the spear wound, she recovers. Presumably both versions were previewed, and after assessing extraordinarily negative reactions to Jane's death, the studio decided to use the happy ending just in time for the June 16th release date. The title *Tarzan Finds A Son!* was not decided on until the last minute. The working titles had been *Tarzan in Exile* and *Son of Tarzan.* The latter could not be used because Burroughs' third Tarzan novel was called *The Son Of Tarzan,* and of course it

was an entirely different story and the son was a natural child.

Yet another relatively late development occurred while the film was in production. All along the intent had been to photograph an underwater swimming scene with Tarzan and Boy in the studio tank, but the reaction around the studio to the filmed material in general was so enthusiastic that approval was granted for a location excursion to Silver Springs, Florida – chosen for its extraordinary water clarity. This was saved until the end of the regular production in California. Because of her pregnancy, Maureen O'Sullivan's scenes had been completed first – and she never left the studio for any shots. For the trip to Ocala, Florida, Weissmuller and Sheffield worked with Baby Bea, a very young elephant trained by George Emerson. The underwater fun and games, photographed from a "photo-sub," were quite extensive and received considerable attention at the time. Contrary to some accounts, only the underwater scenes plus a few surface shots and bits on the bank were photographed in Florida.

"Cannibal Carnival" (with an extension) and "My Tender One" were recorded anew and used, per custom, as the only orchestral music.

Tarzan Finds A Son! completed at a cost of $887,210, was extremely well-received by fans and critics. The original release prints were sepia toned and "platinum" tinted, the latter yielding a soft blue-green hue. In 1937 the MGM laboratory had begun work on a practical way to handle high speed, quantity tinted and toned release printing.

Meanwhile, Cyril Hume already was working on an outline for the next episode in the series. In the beginning of this, Jane and Cheeta are dead;

The Tarzan Family and two of their household pets.

132

In Tarzan Finds a Son! *Tantor and his gang wipe out another native village.*

Tarzan burns the tree house down and he and Boy go off into the jungle and return to the ways Tarzan knew before Jane. Enter ''Sylvia Starke, International Glamour Girl No. 1.... It is her intention to look into this business of big game hunting.'' She eventually meets Tarzan and Boy. A romance develops with Tarzan, and her motherly instincts work well with Boy. After various melodramatic complications ''the early sunlight shines on the three wet, smiling faces as they swim back abreast toward the jungle. Fade out. The End.'' On July 7 this approach was rejected by Bernard Hyman.

     According to MGM producer Lucien Hubbard in a memo dated January 17, 1940, ''Hume.... had been constantly asking to be relieved, so on July

14th [1939], [contract writer] Myles Connolly was engaged. I gave Connolly my short synopsis of July 7th and by July 21st he had expanded it to a twenty-six page story formed on the same basic idea [of Hubbard's] of Boy running away from home.... On July 24th, Mr. Connolly, Mr. Hyman, and I held a conference on this... It was decided to continue along this line with the idea of doing some of the scenes in Africa and bringing natives back to Hollywood.... Various conferences were held.... to which Cyril Hume was sometimes invited by Mr. Hyman. Mr. Hume contributed nothing.... except to say that he did not like the story – reiterating.... that he thought there was only one possible story to be written and that was the one killing Maureen O'Sullivan. Hume begged to be taken off and finally was accommodated on October 24th.''

     However, there are two later 1940 scripts by Hume in the MGM script files and at USC called

Tarzan and America's No. One Glamour Girl, which are based on the earlier outline. From 1938 to 1941 Brenda Frazier reigned as the most prominent debutante ever and was known as "Glamour Girl No. 1," receiving considerable media coverage.

The eventual shooting script of *Tarzan's Secret Treasure,* credited to Myles Connolly and Paul Gangelin, integrated Boy running away from home with members of yet another safari – a scientific expedition, which is diverted to seeking the whereabouts of a gold deposit.

One of the most important of the required formula ingredients of the MGM *Tarzans* was the Escarpment-invading safari, composed of some "good" and some "bad" members. Examples of "good" from various entries in the series: youthful and innocent Eric (William Henry), bumbling and sentimental Rawlins (Herbert Mundin), kindly and paternal Sir Thomas (Henry Stephenson), lovable and quaint O'Doul (Barry Fitzgerald), etc. . . . Examples of "bad": lecherous and urbane Arlington (Paul Cavanagh), grim and humorless Sande (Henry Wilcoxon), wry and weak Medford (Tom Conway), rough-hewn and no-nonsense Buck (Charles Bickford), etc. . . . The ladies on safari were victims of misguided thinking (Benita Hume) or went along with the less than cricket plans of a spouse (Frieda Inescort).

The parties were recurrently looking for tusks, gold, or lions and/or scheming to bring back Tarzan, Jane, or Boy to civilization for selfish and decidedly nefarious reasons.

The erotic element, so prominent in the first two films and to a considerably lesser degree in the third, was totally absent from the last three films in the MGM series. By then the family was thoroughly domesticated.

Comedy antics continued to be provided by Cheeta, the chimp, who was also the bush telegraph; and inevitably, a nearby hostile tribe (they apparently were inexhaustible) captured some combination of Jane, Boy and/or members of the omnipresent safari. Needless to say, the grand finale and major obligatory scene was always Tarzan leading the hustling and trumpeting elephants to the rescue.

Production of *Tarzan's Secret Treasure* began on June 14, 1941, and finished August 18, 1941 at a cost of $978,135. B.P. Fineman produced; Richard Thorpe was by now the automatic choice for director, and Clyde DeVinna ASC, returned for the third time as director of photography. An underwater swimming sequence with Tarzan, Jane (doubled by a Florida resident, according to Richard Thorpe), Boy, Baby Bea the elephant, and a large turtle was photographed at Wakulla Springs, Florida, near Tallahassee.

Lloyd Knechtel ASC, the director of photography on the Florida material, wrote in the August, 1941, issue of *American Cinematographer:* "We did our camerawork from a specially-built underwater camera-bell attached to a barge. Quite properly they called the device 'the hole in the water.' It consisted of a round metal drum, weighted at the bottom with concrete. Steps led down to the floor of the photographing chamber, and the cameras looked out on the underwater scene through a thick optical glass port-hole. . . . The restricted size of the camera port made the camera's actual range of movement very limited. So we finally conceived the idea of panning the entire photographing bell. . . . The camera tube was designed to keep the lens about eight feet below the surface. . . . Wherever possible we saw to it that our sets had a background of clear, white sand. Then, to get the feeling of depth, we 'dressed' the scene with dark, natural objects such as water-plants, weeds, logs, and so on . . .

"Focusing, as is well known, proved a more difficult problem. Fortunately Len Smith, ASC, in filming the previous Tarzan film's underwater scenes, had given us ample data to simplify this problem. . . .

"During most of the actual shooting, director Richard Thorpe and I usually stayed above, leaving operative cinematographer A.L. Lane and assistant cameraman Harold Baldwin more elbow room."

Most of the exterior jungle and above water material was photographed at the new jungle and lake on MGM's Lot 3 and on Lot 2. Earlier thoughts

Jane's death scene in Tarzan Finds a Son! *was removed by audience demand.*

about going to Africa were abandoned as they had been during the preparation of *Tarzan and His Mate.* The rhino attack, crocodile fight, and the climb up the Mutia Escarpment were lifted from *Tarzan and His Mate;* some of Weissmuller's swimming and diving shots were taken from *Tarzan Finds A Son!,* plus, the usual clips from *Trader Horn* and *Tarzan, the Ape Man.*

Once more "Cannibal Carnival" was used for the Main Title, but it was recorded yet again in an extended version, and David Snell's music for the MGM opening trade mark title portion of *Maisie Was a Lady* (1940) was appended. "My Tender One," per custom, was used at the conclusion of the film. The first release prints were processed in Sepia Platinum.

Only four months after the completion of *Tarzan's Secret Treasure* (1941) shooting started on the last film in the series, tentatively called *Tarzan Against the World* but released in July, 1942, as *Tarzan's New York Adventure.*

Finished in six weeks at a cost of $707,166, this episode relied primarily on the novelty of Tarzan and Jane searching for the kidnapped Boy in New York for its interest. Weissmuller (who by now was a far cry from the lean, muscular figure of 1932), was in a double-breasted gabardine suit, swinging from flagpoles and diving from the Brooklyn Bridge. This last shot actually was made by Jack Smith shooting straight down from the top of the scenic tower on Lot 3 at MGM as a dummy plunged into the tank below.

The climax had Boy being rescued by Tarzan and circus elephants. Only a few second unit shots (without cast members) actually were photographed in New York.

Thorpe directed, Sidney Wagner, ASC, (*Northwest Passage,* etc.) was director of photography, and Frederick Stephani (director of the first *Flash Gordon* 1936 serial) produced the William R. Lipman and Myles Connolly screenplay.

In a letter written in 1966, Maureen O'Sullivan agreed that *Tarzan's New York Adventure* was inferior to the preceding five films. "MGM had sold the series to Sol Lesser by then and lost interest." Her opinion of all of the films in retrospect was "mostly very favorable. They were fairy tales – almost Disney-like."

MGM decided definitely to discontinue the series after *Tarzan's New York Adventure,* due in part to the elimination of much of the foreign market brought about by World War II. The great percentage of Tarzan profits traditionally have come from other countries. And the studio felt that the material had been played out.

Matte painting by Newcombe department for scene in which Tarzan crosses a gorge on a fallen tree in Tarzan's Secret Treasure. *Live action appeared in blacked out area at upper right.*

Independent producer Sol Lesser, who now had the *Tarzan* film rights, signed Weissmuller and Sheffield to continue their roles and signed or was close to signing O'Sullivan for at least two pictures (one non-*Tarzan*) as reported in newspapers on February 17 and March 10, 1942. However, shortly afterwards she announced her second pregnancy and was out of *Tarzan Triumphs* (1943), the first Sol Lesser *Tarzan* production for RKO release. Nor was O'Sullivan available for the next, *Tarzan's Desert Mystery* (1943), but on December 3, 1943, Hearst columnist Louella Parsons commented on "Sol Lesser's happiness at getting Maureen O'Sullivan to resume her job as Tarzan's mate. . . . Maureen and John W. will co-star in *Tarzan and the Amazons* (1945) for RKO and Lesser." But again Maureen became pregnant with her first daughter, actress Mia Farrow, and Brenda Joyce was cast as Jane in the next several films (Jane had been "visiting her sick mother in London" in Lesser's first two films and not seen).

In 1959 MGM and producer Al Zimbalist decided to remake in color, *Tarzan, the Ape Man,* the one *Tarzan* property to which that studio still retained all rights. Zimbalist, an economy-minded exploitation impresario, convinced Metro that the project could be brought in on a modest budget by using as much stock footage as possible from MGM's first rate 1950 version of *King Solomon's Mines,* photographed to a large extent in Africa. So, for the new *Tarzan, the Ape Man* (starring Denny Miller in the title role) the lifted material consisted of

Technicolor long shots, originally photographed using Technicolor's Monopack of the *Mines* safari, the animal stampede on the Serengeti, scenes at various native villages, the climb up Mount Kenya, plus assorted atmospheric, action, and animal footage. All of this was spliced in with blue-filtered scenes from the original black and white '32 *Tarzan* showing the ape man swinging through the trees and the elephant stampede in the dwarf village (with red flames superimposed). And that hardy perennial, the crocodile fight from *Tarzan and His Mate* reappeared.

And so it goes. Tarzan continues on and, presumably, on. Recent feature films on the subject are as diverse as yet another version of MGM's *Tarzan, the Ape Man*, made in 1981, starring Bo Derek as Jane, and the opulent, interesting, and back to the source (but only in part), *Greystoke: The Legend of Tarzan, Lord of the Apes*, released by Warner Bros. in 1984.

But the Weissmuller and O'Sullivan *Tarzans* are still with us via television, videocassettes, 35mm and 16mm Classics rentals, and revival houses. The charm of the better entries in the series has not faded; the pictures are timeless, and the romantic myth as interpreted by MGM from Edgar Rice Burroughs' creation continues to capture the imagination and to instill a willing suspension of disbelief for many throughout the world.

—Rudy Behlmer

Produced by Metro-Goldwyn-Mayer; *based on characters created by* Edgar Rice Burroughs; *Western Electric recording.*

1. Tarzan, the Ape Man
A Metro-Goldwyn-Mayer Picture; *Directed by* W.S. Van Dyke; *based on the characters created by* Edgar Rice Burroughs; *adaptation by* Cyril Hume; *dialogue by* Ivor Novello; *directors of photography,* Harold Rosson, ASC, *and* Clyde de Vinna, ASC; *film editors,* Ben Lewis *and* Tom Held; *sound director,* Douglas Shearer; *produced by* Bernard H. Hyman; *production manager,* Joseph J. Cohn; *animal supervision,* George Emerson, Bert Nelson, Louis Roth, Louis Goebel; *photographic effects,* Warren Newcombe; *additional cinematography,* William Snyder, ASC; *music by* George Richelavie, Fritz Stahlberg, P.A. Marquardt; *composite effects by* Dunning Process Company *and* Williams Composite Laboratories: Western Electric *recording; Running time, 99 minutes. Released April 2, 1932.*

Tarzan, Johnny Weissmuller; *Jane Parker,* Maureen O'Sullivan; *Harry Holt,* Neil Hamilton; *James Parker,* C. Aubrey Smith; *Mrs. Cutten,* Doris Lloyd; *Beamish,* Forrester Harvey; *Riano,* Ivory Williams.

2. Tarzan and His Mate
A Metro-Goldwyn Mayer Picture; *Directed by* Cedric Gibbons *(uncredited direction by* Jack Conway*); produced by* Bernard H. Hyman; *based upon the characters created by* Edgar Rice Burroughs; *screen play by* J. Kevin McGuinness; *adaptation* Howard Emmett Rogers, Leon Gordon; *art director,* A. Arnold Gillespie; *directors of photography,* Charles G. Clarke, ASC, *and* Clyde DeVinna, ASC; *film editor,* Tom Held; *production manager,* Jos-

eph J. Cohn; *animal supervision,* George Emerson, Bert Nelson, Louis Roth, Louis Goebel; *second unit directors,* Nick Grinde, Erroll Taggart, James McKay; *special effects director,* James Basevi; *art effects,* Warren Newcombe; *photographic effects,* Irving Ries, ASC; *additional composite effects by* Dunning Process Company *and* Williams Composite Laboratories; *operative cameramen,* Lester White, ASC, Bob Roberts, Ellsworth Fredericks, Ray Ramsey, William Foxall; *sound effects,* T.B. Hoffman, James Graham, Mike Steinore; *music by* George Richelavie, Fritz Stahlberg, P.A. Marquardt, Dr. William Axt; *song, "Soldier on the Shelf," by* Sherman Myers, Erele Reaves; *contributions to screen play,* C. Gardner Sullivan, Arthur Hyman, Leon Gordon, Bud Barsky. Western Electric *recording; Running time, 116 minutes at preview, 105 minutes in general release. Released April 20, 1934.*

Tarzan, Johnny Weissmuller; *Jane Parker,* Maureen O'Sullivan; *Harry Holt,* Neil Hamilton; *Martin Arlington,* Paul Cavanagh; *Beamish,* Forrester Harvey; *Saidi,* Nathan Curry; *Mrs. Cutten,* Doris Lloyd; *Pierce,* William Stack; *Vanness,* Desmond Roberts; *Senor Perron,* Paul Porcasi; *Bearer,* Everett Brown; *Ape,* Ray Corrigan; *swimming double for O'Sullivan,* Josephine McKim; *stunt artists,* Bert Nelson, Louis Roth, Alfred Codona *and* The Flying Codonas, The Picchiani Troupe, Betty Roth, Ray Corrigan.

In aborted version: Pierce, Murray Kinnell; *Vanness,* Frank Reicher; *Arlington,* Rod LaRocque.

3. Tarzan Escapes
(First version; not released)
Directed by James McKay; *produced by* Philip Goldstone; *screen play by* Karl Brown, John Villiers Farrow, Louis Mosher; *(added writing,* Wyndham Gittens, Otis Garrett); *recording director,* Douglas Shearer; *art director,* Cedric Gibbons; *associate,* Elmer Sheeley; *director of photography,* Leonard Smith, ASC; *film editor,* Basil Wrangell; *set decorations,* Edwin B. Willis; *special effects director,* James Basevi; *art effects,* Warren Newcombe; *photographic effects,* Max Fabian, ASC; *operative cameramen,* Virgil Vogel, Walter Strenge; *assistant cameraman,* Albert Scheving, Robert Gough; *sound,* Ralph Sugart, C.E. Wallace, S.J. Lambert, Ralph Pender, R.L. Stirling, Don T. Whitmer, T.B. Hoffman, Michael Steinmore, M.J. McLaughlin. *Completed November, 1935.*

Tarzan, Johnny Weissmuller; *Jane,* Maureen O'Sullivan; *Major Fry,* John Buckler; *Rita,* Benita Hume; *Eric,* William Henry; *Skipper,* Granville Bates; *Bomba,* Everett Brown; *and* Cheeta.

4. Tarzan Escapes
(Released version)
Directed by Richard Thorpe; *(added direction by* James McKay, George B. Seitz, William A. Wellman); *produced by* Bernard H. Hyman; *associate producer,* Sam Zimbalist; *screen play by* Cyril Hume; *(added writing,* Edwin Knopf). *Changes in technical credits: film editor,* W. Donn Hayes; *special effects director,* A. Arnold Gillespie; *photographic effects,* Thomas Tutwiler, ASC; *operative cameraman,* Charles Salerno Jr.; *music,* Sol Paul Levy, Dr. William Axt. *Running time, 95 minutes. Released November 6, 1936.*

Tarzan, Johnny Weissmuller; *Jane,* Maureen O'Sullivan; *Captain Fry,* Hugh Buckler; *Rita,* Benita Hume; *Eric,* William Henry; *Rawlins,* Herbert Mundin; *Masters,* E.E. Clive; *Bomba,* Darby Jones; *Riverboat Captain,* Monte Montague; *Bird,* Johnny Eck; *and* Cheeta.

5. Tarzan Finds a Son!
Directed by Richard Thorpe; *produced by* Sam Zimbalist; *screen play by* Cyril Hume; *recording director,* Douglas Shearer; *art director,* Cedric Gibbons; *associate art director,* Urie McClearie; *director of photography,* Leonard Smith, ASC; *film editors,* Frank

Sullivan, Gene Ruggiero; *underwater scenes photographed at Silver Springs, Florida; special effects by* A. Arnold Gillespie, Warren Newcombe, Max Fabian, ASC; *musical director,* David Snell; *music by* Saul Levy, Dr. William Axt; *animal trainer,* George Emerson; *assistant director,* Dolph Zimmer. *Running time, 90 minutes. Released June 16, 1939, in Sepia Platinum.*

Tarzan, Johnny Weissmuller; *Jane,* Maureen O'Sullivan; *Boy,* Johnny Sheffield; *Austin Lancing,* Ian Hunter; *Sir Thomas Lancing,* Henry Stephenson; *Sande,* Henry Wilcoxon; *Mrs. Austin Lancing,* Frieda Inescort; *Mrs. Richard Lancing,* Laraine Day; *Richard Lancing,* Morton Lowery; *Pilot,* Gavin Muir; *Mooloo,* Uriah Banks; *and Cheeta.*

6. Tarzan's Secret Treasure

Directed by Richard Thorpe; *produced by* B. P. Fineman; *preproduction,* Lucien Hubbard; *screen play by* Myles Connolly, Paul Gangelin; *director of photography,* Clyde DeVinna, ASC; *musical director,* David Snell; *music,* Sol Levy, Dr. William Axt; *recording director,* Douglas Shearer; *art director,* Cedric Gibbons; *associate,* Howard Campbell; *set decorations,* Edwin B. Willis; *special effects,* Warren Newcombe; *film editor,* Gene Ruggiero; *underwater scenes photographed at Wakulla Springs, Florida, by* Lloyd Knechtel, ASC, *assisted by* A.L. Lane, Harold Baldwin; *assistant director,* Gilbert Kurland. *Running time, 81 minutes. Released December, 1941, in Sepia Platinum.*

Tarzan, Johnny Weissmuller; *Jane,* Maureen O'Sullivan; *Boy,* John Sheffield; *Professor Elliott,* Reginald Owen; *O'Doul,* Barry Fitzgerald; *Medford,* Tom Conway; *Vandermeer,* Philip Dorn; *Tumbo,* Cordell Hickman; *Joconi Chief,* Everett Brown; *Headman,* Martin Wilkins; *and Cheeta.*

7. Tarzan's New York Adventure

Directed by Richard Thorpe; *produced by* Frederick Stephani; *screen play by* William R. Lipman, Myles Connolly; *story,* Myles Connolly; *director of photography,* Sidney Wagner, ASC; *musical score,* David Snell; *additional music by* Earl Brent, Daniele Am-

fitheatrof, Herbert Stothart, Sol Levy; *song, "I Must Have You or No One," by* Matty Melnick, Jay Livingston; *recording director,* Douglas Shearer; *art director,* Cedric Gibbons; *associate,* Howard Campbell; *set decorations,* Edwin B. Willis; *special effects,* A. Arnold Gillespie, Warren Newcombe, Jack Smith, ASC; *gowns by* Howard Shoup; *film editor,* Gene Ruggiero. *Running time, 71 minutes. Released May, 1942.*

Tarzan, Johnny Weissmuller; *Jane,* Maureen O'Sullivan; *Boy,* John Sheffield; *Connie Beach,* Virginia Grey; *Buck Rand,* Charles Bickford; *Jimmy Shields,* Paul Kelly; *Manchester Mountford,* Chill Wills; *Colonel Ralph Sargent,* Clyde Kendall; *Judge Abbotson,* Russell Hicks; *Blake Norton,* Howard Hickman; *Gould Beaton,* Charles Lane; *Portmaster,* Miles Mander; *and* Hobard Cavanaugh, Mantan Moreland, Matthew Boulton, Willie Fung, William Forrest, William Tannen, Dick Wessel, Milt Kibbee, Joe Offerman Jr., Eddie Kane, Harry Tenbrook, Harry Semels, George Magrill, Wade Boteler, Eddy Chandler, Frank S. Hagney, Frank O'Connor, Emmett Vogan, Ken Christy, Jack Perrin, Harry Strang, John Dilson, *and Cheeta.*

RESOURCES

Academy of Motion Pictures Arts and Sciences Library (Sam Gill and Bob Cushman); Production Code Administration Files; A. Arnold Gillespie Collection; MGM Art Department Records; *Edgar Rice Burroughs: The Man Who Created Tarzan,* By Irwin Porges, Brigham Young University Press, 1975; MGM/UA (Herbert S. Nusbaum); Turner Entertainment Company (Dick May); UCLA Theatre Arts Library (Audree Malkin); MGM Set Design Collection; USC Doheny Library (Robert Knutson, Ned Comstock); MGM Collection; Hearst Newspaper Collection. And special thanks to Patricia A. Allen, David Chierichetti, Doug Huse, Sam Marx, Clifford McCarty, John Sheffield, Maureen O'Sullivan, and Richard Thorpe.

11

The Monkey's Paw — a Hollywood Jinx

Young David O. Selznick was executive producer at RKO Radio in 1932 when he purchased film rights to a popular story and play, *The Monkey's Paw*. He had fond hopes for the property. His father, Lewis J. Selznick, had released a successful version made in England ten years before and Universal had announced the intention of remaking it as a talkie just before RKO acted.

RKO released its version on January 13, 1933 – an appropriate date, for the picture seemed jinxed from the outset. It was slaughtered by the trade press – an industry paper headlined "Monkey's Paw Worst RKO to Date." Mainstream critics ignored it, exhibitors shunned it and it was virtually unseen by the public.

Like many a commercial failure, it was a fascinating film – a point impossible to prove now because much of the negative has vanished from the studio vault and no full prints are known to exist. It deserves reconsidering if only for the fact that it was directed by Wesley Ruggles and ("now it can be told") an unbilled Ernest B. Schoedsack, and that no less than seven directors of photography worked on it.

That Ruggles, who produced and directed the studio's biggest and most prestigious picture, *Cimarron* (1931), was assigned to a picture with a budget of only $153,574.46 (RKO, at the time, started its "A" product at $200,000) is more explicable than it would seem. Ruggles' popularity at the studio had suffered in the year that had elapsed since William LeBaron vacated the post of chief studio executive in charge of production. Selznick, a

former Paramount executive who had replaced LeBaron at RKO, did not share LeBaron's enthusiasm for Ruggles, either personally or as a director. Ruggles quickly made arrangements to join his old boss at Paramount. *The Monkey's Paw* was his last assignment for RKO to complete his contract.

The picture had an "all-star cast" – Hollywood's way of saying that it had *no* stars. The

IT WILL GET YOU!

If you held in your hand the power of wishing life and death, wealth and love ... would you dare to use it?

Life exacted an awful price from those who knew the secret of

THE MONKEY'S PAW

With C. Aubrey Smith, Ivan Simpson, Betty Lawford, Bramwell Fletcher, Louise Carter

From the story by W. W. Jacobs and the play by Louis N. Parker.

Directed by WESLEY RUGGLES

DATE LINE

An RKO RADIO Picture of course! David O Selznick, Executive Producer

RKO MAYFAIR THEATRE B'WAY & 47th

Leo Tover.

technical crew, on the other hand, was first-rate, being made up of personnel who, like Ruggles, usually were assigned to the higher budget productions.

Leo Tover, ASC, the director of photography, was certainly top drawer. He had been a cameraman since the age of 16, having started at the Norma Talmadge Company in New York in 1918. After coming to California he worked for several of the major studios, moving from Paramount to RKO shortly after the studio was established. He had already shot some of the company's finest, most notably *Symphony of Six Million, State's Attorney, Thirteen Women,* and *The Great Jasper.* Unfortunately, he too was at odds with management and soon decamped for Paramount as well, *The Monkey's Paw* being his last at RKO until many years later. At Paramount, where he remained until 1947 except for a stint with the Army Signal Corps during World War II, Tover specialized in "Lubitsch-style" romantic films. In 1947 he went to Twentieth Century-Fox to photograph the landmark psychological drama, *The Snake Pit.* During the ensuing 12 years at Fox he made more than 30 features. Later, as a freelancer, he worked for most of the major studios until a heart attack claimed him on the last day of 1965, at the age of 62.

140

Shooting began on Friday, August 12, with Alan Mowbray as a one-armed army sergeant spinning tall tales of his adventures to a group of Cockneys in Old Chelsea, London. Although Mowbray, a pal of John Barrymore's, had a habit of secretly tippling between takes, things seemed to be going well enough.

After one day's work, Mowbray had to be replaced due to illness. His replacement was the craggy and beloved C. Aubrey Smith, unofficial leader of the British acting and cricket-playing colony in Hollywood. The company started over on – of course! – the 13th.

One week later, Ruggles requested a camera crane to use in street scenes at Pathé, and was informed that there was none available on the lot. His request that one might be borrowed from another studio was ignored. After the rushes for that day were screened, Ruggles was taken to task by associate producer Pandro S. Berman because the dialogue was deemed "unintelligible." Berman complained formally to Merian Cooper, executive assistant to Selznick at the time, because the day's work was ruined. Ruggles placed the blame on recording engineer Hugh McDowell, Jr., who insisted that he tried to tell Ruggles the dialogue was being played too softly and that the director refused to listen to reason. Berman ended the controversy by blaming *both* men.

Ruggles came under fire again later because he okayed the hiring of a trained monkey called Napoleon to be used in special effects scenes, then decided against using the animal because it didn't appear sufficiently evil. Property chief Thomas Little found a mean-tempered Javanese ape which required three handlers – much to the delight of Ruggles and the chagrin of his bosses. On the following week, the camera effects department head, Lloyd Knechtel, ASC, rehired the ape for a day for some insert shots, further arousing the ire of the men watching the daily accounting reports.

Knechtel's assistant, Vernon Walker, ASC, photographed components of the effects scenes in which the face of the ape is superimposed over various backgrounds. Linwood Dunn, ASC, RKO's chief of optical effects, composited them, dissolving the evil face of the monkey in and out of the hearth fire and, later, into chimney smoke.

The title prop was constructed on a flexible armature by Marcel Delgado, the young Mexican artist who built the monsters of *The Lost World* and *King Kong* for his "discoverer," Willis O'Brien. *Kong* was in active production at the time and O'Brien had assembled a group of remarkable artists and technicians in addition to the regular studio personnel.

The paw was brought to life, so to speak, by another of the *Kong* crew, Orville "Goldy" Goldner, who used stop-motion animation to make the paw move. The task, Goldner recalled, was "comparatively simple because the paw was animated from a fixed axis and didn't shift its weight as those dinosaurs did." (Goldner, who died in February, 1985, was one of those remarkably versatile men whose skills are evident in many early RKO films. He was a sculptor, artist, special effects technician, animator and puppeteer. Later, he headed his own documentary production company and, during World War II, was in charge of all training film production for the U.S. Navy. He was also well known as a magazine editor, educator, and author).

Ruggles completed principal photography of the entire script as written by British author Graham John on August 26, ahead of schedule after only (what else?) 13 working days. With a hasty farewell, he moved to Paramount and a new contract.

Belatedly, the studio bosses learned, to their horror, that the final cut ran just over a half-hour! The picture could hardly be classed as a feature, yet it was too expensive to sell as a short subject. *The Monkey's Paw* went on the shelf along with several other uncompleted projects aborted by the Selznick regime.

This four-reel version, closely adapted from Louis N. Parker's one-act play version of the W. W. Jacobs short-story, opens in Chelsea. Sergeant-Major Morris (C. Aubrey Smith), invalided out of the service after losing an arm in India, has a few drinks at a pub, then departs into a howling snowstorm to the nearby cottage of his old friends, Mr. and Mrs. White (Ivan Simpson and Louise Carter). Living with the elderly couple is their grown son, Herbert (Bramwell Fletcher), who is making ready to go to his night job of tending the flywheels at a power station. Also at the house is Rose Hartigan (Betty Lawford), Herbert's fiancee. Everyone settles down before the fireplace to hear of Morris' latest exploits in India. He tells them of the *fakirs,* saying he has seen great things done by the "dirty holy men of the dark places" and that "the dirtier they are the more startling is their magic." He shows them the mummified paw of a monkey, but refuses to let anybody touch it because "it is deadly." He says, "An old Indian *fakir* with matted 'air and 'arf naked put the spell on it. Fair gave you the creeps, 'e did, rockin' and mumblin' to 'imself outside 'is 'ut in Afghanistan."

A narrated flashback shows the fakir (Nick Shaid), limned in flickering light from an oil-filled human skull. Nearby is perceived the grinning face

Photos by Ollie Sigurdsen

Young, engaged couple played by Betty Lawford and Bramwell Fletcher, make fun of the magical paw. Fletcher's parents, played by Ivan Simpson and Louise Carter, are not amused.

of a dead monkey. Nura (Nena Quartero), a young temple dancer, asks him to put a spell on the man she loves, but is told to go home and await the workings of fate. Accused of being a fraud, he takes a monkey's paw from a boiling cauldron and puts a spell on it. Morris explains, " 'E made it so that three people, if they 'eld the paw in their right 'ands and wished aloud, could each 'ave three wishes, and they'd all be granted. They'd 'appen so natural that you might take them just for coincidence. But 'ere was the catch: although the wishes were granted, those three people would all 'ave cause to wish they 'adn't been." The native girl made three wishes, and the third was for death.

The Sergeant-Major also made three wishes after he was given the paw. Touching the empty sleeve, he says all three were granted – to his regret. White asks for the loan of the paw, thinking to wish for the £200 Rose and Herbert need to set up housekeeping. Morris throws the paw into the fire. White rescues it, but Morris takes it back and puts it into his overcoat pocket. Later, as Morris is leaving, White filches the paw. After Mrs. White has gone to bed, her husband slips down to the sitting room, has a drink, and prepares to test the paw's alleged power. Mrs. White comes down before he can wish, but he jokingly says he will give up the paw after making just one wish. Quickly, he says, ''I wish for 200 pounds.'' The house is rocked by a great gust of wind and the paw clenches into a fist, then opens its fingers. At this moment, Herbert laughingly tells another worker about the paw. Meanwhile, White sees the grinning face of a monkey in the fireplace. He nervously drops the paw and is unable to find it. White falls into his chair, exhausted, and the paw reappears mysteriously on the mantel.

At breakfast, the Whites remain unnerved by the events of the night and wonder secretly if the £200 will appear. The postman brings a letter, but it is only an insurance premium notice. Then a lawyer (Herbert Bunston) arrives. He explains that Herbert has been killed, caught by a flywheel while telling his mates about the paw. He leaves an envelope from the power company. It contains a check for £200.

At the pub, Morris tells his cronies about the paw. He is shocked to learn that Herbert's accident was caused by his carelessness while telling about the paw. White and Rose's father (Winter Hall) go to the mortuary, where they are stunned at the sight of the mutilated corpse. Returning, they argue against the women going to the mortuary. Rose hysterically accuses White of being responsible for the accident.

That night, Mrs. White demands that White make a second wish on the paw. Holding the paw, White says, ''I wish my son alive again.'' There follows a knock on the door – Herbert's special knock. White realizes suddenly what he has done and begins searching frantically for the paw, which again has vanished. Mrs. White struggles with the rusty door latch. At the instant the latch gives way, White finds the paw and silently makes his third wish. Mrs. White swings the door open and cries out in dismay when she sees only an empty street. White throws the paw into the fire. In the smoke rising from the chimney, the expressionless face of a

Simpson and Carter hear their son's familiar knock at the door.

dead monkey appears for a moment. White collapses into his chair.

In the morning, White awakens to the voice of his wife as she complains that Herbert is late getting home. He thinks she has lost her mind. Then Herbert *does* arrive, and as the picture ends, White realizes he dreamed the entire sequence of events that followed his first wish upon the monkey's paw.

In October, John completed an 18-page prologue to *The Monkey's Paw* based on suggestions by Merian C. Cooper, Selznick's executive assistant, who was devoting much of his energy to *King Kong*. The two sequences of which this prologue is comprised are from neither the story nor the play, but they add value by introducing action and adventure into a predominantly stagebound film. More importantly, from a commercial standpoint, they occupy the needed footage. The edited prologue was composed of 74 scenes.

The director of the prologue, retakes and process shots, hand-picked by Merian Cooper, was Ernest Schoedsack, Cooper's partner in Cooper-Schoedsack Productions. Schoedsack was an appropriate choice, inasmuch as the prologue was set in India and he recently had spent several months in that country shooting location scenes for Paramount's *Lives of a Bengal Lancer*.

For the opening sequence, Schoedsack ordered glass paintings by the studio's leading matte artist, Mario Larrinaga, to expand the scope of the Indian street at the RKO Pathé lot in Culver City, set Tom Little's prop men to searching for exotic decorations, and sent out a cast call for Smith and six other featured players, a sword dancer, a juggler, a four-piece Indian orchestra and 49 extras in Hindu costumes and makeup. He hired the voluptuous Ynez Seabury for the role of the tragic dancing girl, but Berman insisted upon using the petite Nena Quartero.

Tover was not available to do the cinematography, so Schoedsack asked for Jack Mackenzie, a 40-year old, hard-working Scotsman from Inverness. A first cameraman for the past 19 years, Mackenzie had recently completed *One Man's Journey*, directed by John S. Robertson and starring Lionel Barrymore, which was highly praised for its photographic subtlety.

The street scenes were completed in one very long day's work on October 7. The second sequence, a battle in the Khyber Pass, was staged in Bronson Canyon, a rock quarry a few miles north of RKO's Hollywood studio. Nine actors were cast as British "sappers" and 30 extras were garbed as hill tribesmen. This action was filmed in one night, finishing at 5 a.m. on October 19.

Home life in Chelsea: Fletcher and Simpson.

Schoedsack, who seldom admitted any fondness for his studio productions because he preferred the rigors of expeditionary work to those of the board room, termed the sequence "very good." He recalled that "Harry Redmond, the powder man, placed charges in several spots and had push-button controls to detonate them. The last was a bomb that exploded right in front of the camera. One thing I like to get into action scenes like that is plenty of dust to add to the movement."

Later, Schoedsack directed close-ups and voice-overs of C. Aubrey Smith while the actor was between calls on a picture at Universal, as well as some process shots involving Nena Quartero's death scenes. These were made on Stage 3 at the Hollywood facility, where the *Kong* crew was working on miniature sets. Another of the *Kong* cameramen, J. O. Taylor, ASC, made the rear projection shots of Quartero using a revolutionary new process screen invented by Sidney Saunders, of the studio paint department.

The Saunders screen, which measured 16 X 20 feet, was made of cellulose stretched on a frame and spray-painted on one side. Previous process screens, which were made of sand-blasted glass, were necessarily small and produced a middle-grey projected image with no white highlights or rich blacks. The images were dulled further because filters had to be used to control hot-spot and fall-off problems. They were fragile, non-insurable and hard to replace. Breakage of glass screens already had caused serious injuries to personnel at two studios. The Saunders screen increased image brilliancy by 20% while reducing hot-spots by about half. It was first used for the sequence in *Kong* in which Fay Wray watches the battle between the giant ape and a *Tyrannosaurus rex*. The success of these scenes earned Saunders an Academy Award for his part in "the development and effective use of the translucent cellulose screen in composite photography." (The award was shared by Fox Film Co. and Fred Jackman, ASC, of Warner Bros.)

The close-ups were photographed by Edward Cronjager, ASC, one of the studio's leading cinematographers (*Cimarron, Seven Keys to Baldpate* and *The Lost Squadron* were among his more notable films of the period). Schoedsack was able to get Cronjager because he had a few days off between pictures.

Just before Leo Tover left RKO, Schoedsack acquired him to do retakes of some of his work for Ruggles. This was necessary for matching of the brief flashback scenes of the original footage to scenes in the prologue.

The final negative cost was $158,584.82—a matter of only $5,010.36 over budget.

The prologue opens in a village in India, where Morris and Corporal O'Leary (J.M. Kerrigan) watch an old *fakir* perform his magic. A boy is placed in a basket, which the *fakir* pierces with a sword; the boy emerges unharmed. O'Leary scoffs, insisting he can duplicate the gag. When he attempts to do so, the holy man gestures and O'Leary is paralyzed. Once freed from the spell, O'Leary continues walking with Morris. Nura is thrown into the street by her lover (Lal Chand Mehra), who is wrestled to the ground by O'Leary. When Morris offers to help the girl, whom he has known since her childhood, she draws away and hands him the monkey's paw. Morris comments that a *fakir* gave Nura the paw in his presence, telling her it will grant her three wishes. He tries to return the paw, but Nura tells him, "I have wish my last wish, the one wish of my heart; I have wish that I may die." As she flees down a narrow lane, a runaway army wagon hurtles past the soldiers and into the lane, crushing Nura under the wheels.

Later, Morris and O'Leary are on the Northwest Frontier with a handful of men, fighting off a nocturnal attack by a horde of zealots. A runner arrives with word that reinforcements armed with trench mortars are on their way. O'Leary falls wounded, and when Morris fumbles in his haversack for medical supplies he encounters the paw. It is still in his right hand when the tribesmen charge. Morris says to a soldier, "I wish those trench mortars would open fire." An instant later, the mortar shells begin bursting among them, falling short of the enemy because they were fired too soon. A bomb explodes next to Morris. (The scene fades and Ruggles' film begins).

The press preview was disastrous. The short running time, the lack of boxoffice cast names, the "unintelligible English accents," and the "morbidity" of a story "dealing with dismemberment" brought almost universal condemnation from the

C. *Aubrey Smith tells his friends how he lost his arm.*

trade papers. Cooper voiced a feeble word of encouragement by reporting to the board of directors that the English distributors liked the picture. *American Cinematographer,* which was highly critical of some photographic trends at the time, commended it as "another example of artistic effect-photography in a mystery/horror film. A time-honored British story, played by a British cast, this film might, except for Tover's cinematography, have been made in deah old Lunnon. But I have yet to see the British film that is so excellently and tastefully photographed as is this American-made 'quota film.'"

The short, very British-oriented picture was anything but a viable commercial venture of its time. Bookings were almost non-existent and it was little seen and soon forgotten.

Actually, *The Monkey's Paw* was a fascinating picture. Ruggles, Tover and Ullman did a commendable job of recreating the milieu of a London working-class neighborhood, both in the busy pub and the cozy cottage where most of the action occurs.

Schoedsack and his men did equally well by the exotic scenes (they did not receive screen credit). The principals—notably Smith, Carter, Simpson, Kerrigan and DeBrulier—did fine professional work, even though their names meant nothing to the public. Tover's photography could hardly be bettered (camera crane or no!), being especially inventive in the handling of firelight effects in the cottage and depicting the awful emptiness of the wintry street. Jack Mackenzie's night-for-night scenes at Bronson Canyon are memorable for their simulation of moonlight punctuated by flashes of gunfire. Taylor's projection shots are superior to most similar efforts of the time and Larrinaga's glass shots are flawless. The several montage sequences, which were composited on a shop-made optical printer that would be considered primitive today, typify the skillful multi-image work which was fast becoming a virtual trademark for RKO.

Max Steiner provided strong, atmospheric "exotic India" music for the titles and a street sequence, as well as utilizing J. S. Zamecnik's composition, "Oriental Atmosphere." Steiner conducted a 29 piece orchestra which was recorded by music supervisor Murray Spivack, who also provided the sound effects. Additional music was performed by an Indian orchestra led by C. Monsoor.

The dream ending is unfortunate from a dramatic standpoint, perhaps, but it can be argued that the story would be unbearably tragic without it. A picture of the size and theme of *The Monkey's Paw* would be a "natural" as a television feature on a series such as *Twilight Zone* or *Thriller* but in 1933 it was only a maverick that could not be merchandised. The studio regarded it as an embarrassment and were more than willing to let it sink into an obscurity from which it never has emerged.

—George E. Turner

A 1985 photo of the site of the battle scene in Bronson Canyon.

Executive producer, Merian C. Cooper; *directed by* Wesley Ruggles; *additional scenes directed by* Ernest B. Schoedsack; *associate producer,* Pandro S. Berman; *screenplay by* Graham John; *from the play by* Louis N. Parker *and the story by* W. W. Jacobs; *photographed by* Leo Tover, ASC; *additional photography by* Jack MacKenzie, ASC, Edward Cronjager, ASC, J. O. Taylor, ASC, Harold Wellman, ASC; *art director,* Carroll Clark; *unit art director,* Syd Ullman; *musical director,* Max Steiner; *assistant director,* Doran Cox; *set decorations,* Thomas Little, G. Rossi; *photographic effects,* Lloyd Knechtel, ASC, Vernon L. Walker, ASC, Linwood Dunn, ASC; *effects technicians,* Harry Redmond Jr., Marcel Delgado, Orville Goldner; *film editor,* Charles L. Kimball; *recorded by* Hugh McDowell Jr.; *music and effects recording,* Murray Spivack; *unit manager,* Fred Fleck; *second assistant directors,* Fred Spencer, Hal Walker; *Makeup artists,* Sam Kaufman, Paul Stanhope, Mae Mark, J. Baker; *hairdresser,* Alma Hendrickson; *gaffer,* J. Almond; *stills,* Ollie Sigurdsen; *titles,* Consolidated Film Industries; RCA Photophone *sound. Running time, 58 minutes. Released January 13, 1933, an RKO Radio picture.*

Mr. White, Ivan Simpson; *Mrs. White,* Louise Carter; *Sergeant-major Morris,* C. Aubrey Smith; *Herbert,* Bramwell Fletcher; *Rose,* Betty Lawford; *Mr. Hartigan,* Winter Hall; *Sampson,* Herbert Bunston; *Nura,* Nena Quartero; *Afghan,* Leroy Mason; *Hindu Fakir,* Nick Shaid; *Police Sergeant,* Col. Gordon McGee; *Electrician,* Scott McKee; *Corporal O'Leary,* J. M. Kerrigan; *Lance Corporal,* Leo Britt; *Hindu Lover,* Lal Chand Mehra; *Hindu Fakir in Prologue,* Nigel DeBrulier; *Sergeants,* Harry Strang, Angus Darrock, Harold Hughes; *Juggler,* George Edwards; *Soldier,* Gordon Jones; *Flute Player,* James Bell; *Pensioner,* Sidney Bracy; *Barmaid,* Aggie Steele; *Commissioner,* Harry Allen; *Bookmaker,* Will Stanton; *Mule Driver,* Ed Miller; *Hindu,* John George; *Merchant,* Joey Ray; *Orchestra Leader,* C. Monsoor.

12

The Black Art of *White Zombie*

The word *zombie* was introduced to the American reading public in 1929 in ''The Magic Island,'' a credulous but fascinating book about Haitian Voodoo by William B. Seabrook. Playwright Kenneth Webb brought zombies to the drama in his play, ''Zombie,'' which opened in New York City in February of 1932. In March of that year Webb brought suit against movie producers Edward R. and Victor Hugo Halperin, who had announced their intent to make a movie called *White Zombie* from an original script by Garnett Weston.

Webb, who had been negotiating movie rights to his play, felt (understandably) that his territory was being infringed upon. The defendants demurred, saying the play, having closed after 21 performances, could not have been affected adversely by their plans for a film along admittedly similar lines and that the word *zombie* was in the public domain.

The Halperin brothers won the case and completed their movie for summer release, thereby introducing the zombie to motion pictures. Their film had a boxoffice star, Bela Lugosi, fresh from his successes at Universal in *Dracula* and *Murders in the Rue Morgue,* and the prestige of a United Artists release – quite an honor for an outside producer in those days. United Artists was a company of enor-

Madge Bellamy, the white zombie, with Brandon Hurst, Bela Lugosi and Robert Frazer.

mous prestige which was owned by and released the product of a select group of top independent producers, such as Samuel Goldwyn, Douglas Fairbanks and Mary Pickford, Joseph M. Schenck, Howard Hughes, Charles Chaplin, Lewis Milestone and Henry King.

Although the Halperins had been associated with major studios during the silent era, they were on their own in the tough world of the talkies and in the depths of the Great Depression, occupying an office at RKO-Pathé Studio in Culver City. They now found it necessary to operate within the financially structured parameters of ''Poverty Row.'' No one in the industry would have mentioned the Halperins in the same breath with Goldwyn or Chaplin.

White Zombie was bankrolled by Amusement Securities Corporation, a New York firm specializing in motion picture financing. The capital involved fell far short of the needs of a United Artists sort of project, putting the producers in a caste with the likes of Allied, Invincible-Chesterfield, Majestic, Monogram and Tiffany.

A typical independent operation of the era obtained financing, arranged for deferment of lab costs, rented studio space by the day or week as needed, and avoided retakes. Special effects other than art titles and optical transitions were generally not considered cost viable. Schedules were grueling and budgets were tight, features often being brought in for as little as $8,000 to $10,000 with from four to 10 days of shooting. Two weeks and $75,000 constituted a super-production well beyond

Burial in the roadway was shot night-for-night on the Universal backlot.

the grasp of most Poverty Row impresarios. The working hours for cast and crew were long and the pay was scale or less (the actual compensation often being less than what was reported officially). Film editors crammed six-reel features onto five reels because sound tracks were taxed by the reel – $500 per.

Low budget Westerns for the rural and Saturday matinee audiences dominated the independent output. The non-Western features were designed chiefly as the "exciting co-hits" at the bottom of double-feature programs. Sometimes they were awful, sometimes they helped, and – occasionally – they saved the bill by providing the entertainment an audience failed to find in the bill topper.

With a rumored $50,000 in hand the Halperins were able to produce their film with amazing speed and economy, yet achieve spectacular production values through proper utilization of settings, photographic technique and special effects. Strong pre-production planning was the key. The cinematography, which is of major studio quality throughout, is by Arthur Martinelli, ASC.

The Halperins – Victor always directed and Edward was the line producer – came to Hollywood from Chicago in the early 1920s as a producing team. Victor, born in 1895 and an alumnus of the

University of Wisconsin and the University of Chicago, had been a stage actor and director. Edward, born in 1908, was a Northwestern University graduate. Both men were athletic and poured enormous energy into their work. They produced about 20 silent pictures, some for their company and others for First National, Inspiration-United Artists, Vitagraph and others. Most were romantic melodramas about life in the big city, as typified by the successful *Dance Magic* (1927), with Pauline Starke and Ben Lyon. None of their earlier works bear any thematic resemblance to *White Zombie* except in the persistence of an almost Victorian romanticism.

The brothers were continually theorizing and experimenting to find a scientific approach to movie-making. They made graphs analyzing successful films in an effort to establish foolproof structural formulae. By the time they embarked upon *White Zombie* they had made about 30 pictures. Their analyses of hit pictures brought their attention to the successes scored by a number of horror pictures, notably Universal's *Dracula* and *Frankenstein* and Paramount's *Dr. Jekyll and Mr. Hyde*. Hav-

148

ing thoroughly studied the available talking pictures, they reached the accurate conclusion that most contained too much talk and not enough action. They decided to hold dialogue to 15 per cent of the action, limiting it to whatever was necessary to advance the story. Just as a good artist will follow through with a planned design with as little deviation as possible, the Halperins stuck with their decision and came close to achieving their goal, even though it meant pruning pages from the script. The result is a rapid, smooth continuity, a simple and direct rendering of a fairy tale theme:

Along a desolate road in the Haitian mountains, a carriage bearing Neil Parker (John Harron) and Madeline Short (Madge Bellamy) encounters a funeral in which the body is being interred in the roadway. Their driver (Clarence Muse) explains that such practice is widespread in Haiti – it protects the body from theft by ghouls. Further down the road the coach stops again at sight of a man of satanic appearance, later to be identified as a man called Murder (Bela Lugosi). Six human shapes step forth. The coachman cries, "Zombies!" and whips the horses on at breakneck speed as the stranger pulls a scarf from about Madeline's neck. We might have been killed!" Neil admonishes. "Worse than that, *Monsieur*, we might have been caught!" is the reply. The zombies, the driver explains, were resurrected from death through witchcraft and made to work by night in the fields and mills.

Dr. Bruner (Joseph Cawthorn) has been called to the Beaumont mansion to marry Neil and Madeline. Neil, a bank employee in Port au Prince, has brought his fiancee from America. She met the wealthy Charles Beaumont (Robert Frazer) aboard ship. Beaumont has insisted that the wedding take place on his plantation. Bruner is uneasy about Beaumont's penchant for debauchery, but he cannot voice his suspicions because of the hovering presence of Beaumont's loyal servant, Silver (Brandon Hurst).

In a coach driven by one of Murder's creatures, Beaumont is taken to a huge sugar mill where numerous zombies labor. One of them stumbles and topples into a cane chopping machine and is ground to bits by his heedless fellows. Beaumont is brought to the office of Murder, who still carries Madeline's scarf. Beaumont has tried to hire Murder to kidnap Madeline, but the zombie master maintains such action will not bring about the desired result. He suggests the only way to win her is to make a zombie of her. Beaumont is horrified, but Murder insists: "There is no other way." He instructs Beaumont to put the merest pinpoint of a potion on a flower or in a glass of wine.

Beaumont pleads with Madeline, but she refuses to reconsider her plans. He gives her a rose. The wedding takes place and a banquet follows. Meantime, Murder appears outside the house and takes a candle from a lamp. This he carves into the shape of a woman and wraps it in Madeline's scarf. As Madeline looks into her wine glass she sees the face of Murder. "I see – I see death," she says, and as Murder melts the effigy in the flame of another lamp, she crumples to the floor. She is pronounced dead by the doctor.

Neil's mind almost snaps. He becomes a

Photos courtesy of Enzo Martinelli

Enzo Martinelli in his days as an assistant cameraman. *Arthur Martinelli at work.*

The Legendre Sugar Mill, where workers ''aren't afraid of long hours.''

drunken derelict, seeing his wife's pale form in every shadow. He stumbles down a road, calling her name, in the black of night. Murder and Beaumont, accompanied by the six zombie bodyguards, disinter the body of Madeline. Neil finds the crypt empty. Later, he and Dr. Bruner set out into the jungle to seek the lair of Murder.

At Murder's clifftop castle. Beaumont realizes his rash action has made of Madeline a mechanical, soulless creature. He pleads with Murder that ''She must be gay and happy again,'' but Murder poisons him with a drug that will slowly turn him into a zombie. The bodyguards throw Silver to his doom in an underground torrent.

Neil and Bruner see the castle; vultures hover and screech. Leaving the feverish Neil below, Bruner goes to reconnoiter the castle. By some mystic reaction to the nearness of her lover, Madeline goes out onto a balcony. Neil is drawn to the castle, where he wanders aimlessly until he collapses at the top of a staircase. Murder sends Madeline with a knife and telepathically orders her to kill Neil, but, because of opposition from Beaumont's waning mind, he must summon all his willpower to make her strike. Her hand is stayed by the interference of Bruner. She runs to a veranda and is about to leap to her death, but Neil recovers and stops her. Murder's zombies crowd Neil to the edge of the cliff. Neil empties his revolver into the creatures, but bullets have no effect. Bruner fells Murder as Neil flings himself to the floor and the zombies shamble mind-

lessly over the edge. Madeline recovers her mind for a moment, but lapses into a coma when Murder awakes.

Seeking to escape, Murder hurls a gas grenade; the gas, combined with his magic, could make living corpses of his enemies. Beaumont, half paralyzed, appears on the parapet and grapples with Murder. Both men fall to their deaths. Madeline wakes and says, ''Neil, I – I dreamed.''

White Zombie opened on Broadway at the Rivoli Theatre. No movie ever received a more thorough critical scourge, although the public loved it and it brought in a great deal of money. In recent years it has gained notice as an outstanding film of its time. This belated acknowledgement is hardly as paradoxical as it seems, for it was the fashion among critics to take a condescending view toward genre films, especially horror pictures, Westerns and gangster yarns. They had been kind to *Dracula,* *Frankenstein* and *Dr. Jekyll and Mr. Hyde* a few months earlier, but once a ''fad'' was established the honeymoon was over.

White Zombie suffered even more than others of its ilk because of an embarrassingly outmoded, silent-movie style of acting – a fault of Victor Halperin, who nearly a decade later still insisted upon heavy, pantomimic performances from his players. While such a style suited the unreality of the Lugosi character, it was almost fatal to the credibility of some of the other actors. Madge Bellamy was handicapped further by a makeup – including painted Cupid's-bow mouth – that suggests 1926 more than 1932.

Frazer deigns to accept Lugosi's proffered hand as monstrous Frederick Peters stands by.

150

Such failings were duly remarked by the press, but critics failed to note *any* of the elements that raise this remarkable film above such handicaps. If the Halperins were unable to adjust to the talkies' new acting techniques, they certainly were ahead of their contemporaries in mastering sound as a dramatic device at at time when many directors were unable to reconcile the possibilities of a mix of sight and sound without sacrificing one to the other. There's a prefiguration of techniques that Orson Welles, Val Lewton and others brought to fruition on the screen much later in this flawed – but perennially fascinating – curio.

Principal photography was completed in two weeks on the stages and backlot of Universal City. The Howard Anderson Company, an independent photographic effects studio in Hollywood, produced glass shots and optical photography. Arthur Martinelli, ASC, was director of photography.

Martinelli was one of the many cinematographers scrambling for work as the Depression threatened the very existence of the movie companies. He was a veteran of the movies, having started as a lab technician at American Biograph in Hoboken, New Jersey, when the industry was in its infancy. Following World War I he spent 16 months in Germany as head of the camera department at First National Studio in Berlin. During the 1920s he had photographed many pictures for the major studios, including a string of slick romantic pictures with Bert Lytell for Metro and First National's "epic drama" of the war, *The Greater Glory.* Like most of the other top cinematographers, Martinelli became "affordable" on Poverty Row as the Depression ground into its third year.

J. Arthur (Jockey) Feindel (later ASC), a former illustrator and designer from New York, was second cameraman (operator), and Charles Bohny was first assistant. The sole surviving member of the camera crew is Enzo Martinelli, ASC, nephew of Arthur, who was second assistant. Now retired, he remembers the circumstances of that early job well:

"'It was just two weeks' work, a short budget picture – after all, we were on Poverty Row. I was lucky to get on the show; I think it was my only picture that year! I really needed that $30 or $40 a week; needed it bad.

"We never went off the Universal lot," Enzo recalled, "Even the night exteriors on the backwoods roads were shot there. All the night shots were night for night. My uncle always made sure it was possible to recognize the source of the light in those scenes. In so many shows today they just ignore the light source. When working on the

Lugosi limned by candlelight.

indoor sets he always gave them a little scope, a little depth. He kept the actors well *into* the set, not back against the walls. The sets were nicely lit for depth and mood."

In a picture notable for its sparseness of dialogue, there is one curious scene in which a great deal of explanatory talk is disposed of in one take lasting an actual five minutes. This is where Dr. Bruner tells Neil about voodoo and zombies, incorporating a recital of Article 249 of the Haitian Penal Code: "Also shall be qualified as attempted murder the employment of drugs, hypnosis or any other occult practice which produces lethargic coma, or lifeless sleep, and if the person has been buried it shall be considered murder no matter what result follows." It is somewhat prescient of the method used by Alfred Hitchcock in the 1948 *Rope,* which consisted entirely of eight- or nine-minute takes with a constantly mobile camera; endings and sub-

Bellamy is sent on an errand of murder while Frazer is helpless to interfere.

sequent beginnings of reels were bridged by bringing people or objects close to the lens to cause a momentary blackout. Here the opening dialogue is heard over a black screen (Neil's back is close to the lens), then the camera moves to cover the speeches and, as the scene ends, returns to the original position while the closing lines come over the darkness. There is an improvisational quality to this dialogue in contrast to the measured delivery of lines characteristic of the other scenes.

A dominating image of *White Zombie* is that of Lugosi's supposedly hypnotic eyes in extreme closeup. In other scenes in which the actor is exerting his will over others his eyes are emphasized by the lighting. "I learned how that was done on the first day," Enzo Martinelli said. "Arthur just took a cardboard and cut two holes in it about as wide apart as Lugosi's eyes, placed it in front of Lugosi's face and put a light through it. It put two little spots right on his eyeballs when he started to become dangerous.

"Lugosi wasn't really a friendly type," Martinelli recollected. "In those days, of course, most of the stars were a little aloof in order to preserve their mystique. Only a few would fraternize much with the help or be chummy with the guy who fixed the coffee. I thought he looked ill, as though he was in pain. Later, I learned that he *was* ill during the whole production!"

152

Lugosi played his role in the grand manner – restraint wasn't his forte – and it's exactly what the character demands. Murder is a man who not only possesses extraordinary powers but is completely evil without mitigation. His satanic qualities are underlined by a makeup consisting of widow's peak, downturned moustache, forked beard, and hawklike eyebrows. The superb makeups of Lugosi and his zombies were the work of Jack Pierce, borrowed from Universal, for which he had created Boris Karloff's celebrated monster makeup of *Frankenstein* the previous year, and the veteran Carl Axcelle. The rich delivery and timing of his sardonic lines by Lugosi must be heard to be appreciated; they are beyond description.

Scarcity makes dialogue all the more striking. Lugosi has the best lines, delivering them with demonic intensity. He tells Frazer he cannot hope to win the girl: "Not in a month, nor even a year. She *is* deep in love – but not with you." After the girl has been made a zombie, he hears Frazer despairingly tell her that he must take her back. He interrupts with a smirking, "Back to the grave, *Monsieur?*"

When Frazer realizes he is being made into a zombie, Lugosi seems evil incarnate as he explains, "I have taken a fancy to you," then offers a toast: "To the future, *Monsieur.*" Harron, trapped by the zombies at the frantic climax, asks Lugosi who they are. He is told, "For you, my friend, they are the angels of death."

Lugosi said that the producers offered him only $500 for a week's work on the picture. He did the job, he stated, for $800 or $900, and was amazed when the picture proved a huge financial success. According to Dr. Clarence Muse, the composer and

Zombies, from left, are John T. Printz, Claude Morgan, Frederick Peters, John Fergusson, unidentified, and George Burr McAnnan.

The main hall of the castle was assembled, appropriately, from parts of the set of Dracula. *Glass painting extended the set to cavernous proportions.*

actor who portrayed the coachman, Lugosi rewrote some scenes and even directed some retakes. Muse's scenes are among them; a different actor appears in all but the close-ups and dialogue scenes. The first player was hired because he could drive a team, but it was found that his dialogue delivery was unconvincing. Muse had difficulty trying to drive the coach down a winding mountain road at night but his voice was excellent, so the two performances were intercut.

Beautiful, blonde Madge Bellamy, a star of silent pictures who had been out of pictures for two years while studying stage technique, took the title role with the intention of re-establishing herself in cinema. A unique beauty with eyes that could express things beyond the reach of dialogue, she was excellent in pantomime. Her voice, however, did not register well in some scenes, and it is probable that the picture did her career more harm than good despite its success.

John Harron, a popular leading man of the silents (and brother of the D.W. Griffith star, Robert Harron), also seemed unable to adapt to the talkies successfully. Robert Frazer, however, was ideal for the Byronic role of an unprincipled roue who eventually is perceived as a sympathetic character. Veteran actor Joe Cawthorn, utilizing a comic German accent that he had developed for a vaudeville act years before, provided with skill both the pragmatic occultist necessary to such a show and some equally imperative comedy relief. Muse, Brandon Hurst and Dan Crimmins did well.

The most impressive of the convincingly cadaverous zombies is Chauvin, as played by six-foot-six, 250 pound Frederick Peters, who had been in films since 1916 specializing at portraying Goliath and other giant warriors in Biblical epics. Murder's description of his six bodyguards is worth noting:

"In life they were my enemies. Latour, the witch doctor, once my master. The secrets I tortured out of him. Von Gelder, the swine, swollen with riches; he fought against my spell even to the last... Victor Trisher, Minister of the Interior; Scarpia, the brigand chief; Marquis, captain of the gendarmerie; and this – this is Chauvin, the high executioner, who almost executed *me!*" He has a simple sales pitch for his creatures: "They work faithfully; they're not afraid of long hours."

Much of the credit for the expensive look of the picture is attributable to Ralph Berger, who designed the settings, and to one of the great matte and glass painters, Conrad Tritschler. Berger was an expert at adapting existing sets so that they seem to have been built entirely for the project at hand, an art he utilized often in making of serials. The gigantic main hall of Murder's castle was created by rearranging the Castle Dracula hall, which was further expanded and disguised for the long shots

153

John Harron is surrounded by zombies.

the Castle Dracula staircase. He placed great hovering shadows in many scenes.

There are a surprising number of optical effects, including the main titles in which the credits appear over the opening scene of the roadway funeral – an unusual touch at that time. A moment later, as the carriage comes toward camera, Lugosi's eyes are superimposed over the scene, at first filling the screen, then growing smaller until they vanish into Lugosi's silhouetted figure. An unusual optical is a diagonally split screen showing the mesmerized girl in the castle and her distraught lover, both parts being superimposed over the glass shot of the castle. There is some noticeable shakiness in the compositing of this scene.

The soundtrack makes fine use of long silences punctuated with unexpected noises – the screeching of vultures, the scraping of a coffin being slid into a crypt, the creaking and groaning of the mill, etc. – and occasional bursts of music. Musical arrangements were handled by Abe Meyer, a silent picture maestro who, unable to get a musical directorship with any of the major studios after theater orchestras became obsolete, undertook to supply scores for the independents through his company, Meyer Synchronizing Service. The native drumming and chants were specially composed by Guy Bevier Williams, an expert in ethnic music then employed at Universal. Also commissioned for the film was a Spanish *jota* by Xavier Cugat; this work is properly unnerving in sequences where Harron pursues the vision of his lost bride. An unusually weird effect is produced by the tragic spiritual, "Listen to the Lamb," as hummed by alternating male and female choruses. Some of the other action is scored by appropriate agitatos from Meyer's silent film music library.

Amusement Securities Corporation retrieved the distribution rights to the picture and kept it in reissue for many years – which led to an interesting sequel. In 1936 the Halperins, then proprietors of a small producing company called Academy Pictures at Tec-Art Studios (now Raleigh Studio), produced *Revolt of the Zombies,* an unsuccessful attempt to repeat their 1932 success. Although the theme, subject matter, locale and other particulars differed widely from the first picture, Amusement Securities brought an injunction suit against Academy for "Unfair Competition By Use of Name 'Zombie' in Title." The producers were enjoined from using the word in a title and from using any advertising or materials tending to identify the picture with *White Zombie.* Damages and an ac-

by glass paintings. The expansive veranda of the castle contains a wide stairway from the *Dracula* set and pillars and properties from *The Hunchback of Notre Dame* and other Universal epics of the past. Tritschler added more castle details, mountains and sky, and Anderson matted in the sea. The wine cellar from *Frankenstein* and an old dungeon set, which were being flooded by Universal for their Tom Mix picture, *My Pal, the King,* were utilized – torrent and all – for the cavernous corridors where the characters must walk along narrow pathways to avoid being swept away. The hanging balcony on which Madge Bellamy is seen is from *The Hunchback,* some of the rooms of the Beaumont mansion were made up of walls from the Seward home in *Dracula.* The sugar mill is a dizzying mass of girders, catwalks and huge windlasses. Scenes in which Neil and Bruner look up at the mountaintop castle from the beach are composed of an actual bit of coastline and a glass painting. Some marvelous props, such as the monumental chairs from *The Cat and the Canary,* are artfully deployed.

Martinelli made the most of the settings, many scenes of strong depth being framed through trees and such architectural details as quatrefoils on

A posed gathering of the principals on the veranda set. On screen the upper castle, mountains, skies and the sea were matted in for larger views.

Released by United Artists, *a* Halperin *production; produced by* Edward Halperin; *directed by* Victor Halperin; *story and dialogue by* Garnett Weston; *director of photography,* Arthur Martinelli, ASC; *assistant director,* William Cody; *editor,* Harold MacLernon; RCA Photophone *recording by* Clarco; *sound engineer,* L.E. (Pete) Clark; *settings by* Ralph Berger; *art effects,* Conrad Tritschler; *special effects by* Howard Anderson; *makeup artists,* Jack P. Pierce, Carl Axcelle; *second assistant director,* Herbert Glazer; *dialogue director,* Herbert Farjeon; *assistant to producer,* Sidney Marcus; *musical director,* Abe Meyer; *original music,* Guy Bevier Williams, Xavier Cugat; *additional music,* Nathaniel Dett, Gaston Borch, Hugo Riesenfeld, Leo Kempenski, Hen Herkan, H. Maurice Jacquet; *operative cameraman,* J. Arthur Feindel; *assistant cameramen,* Charles Bohny, Enzo Martinelli; *photographed at* Universal Studio; *running time, 69 minutes; released July 28, 1932.*

Murder, Bela Lugosi; *Madeline Short,* Madge Bellamy; *Dr. Bruner,* Joseph Cawthorn; *Neil Parker,* John Harron; *Charles Beaumont,* Robert Frazer; *Driver,* Clarence Muse; *Silver,* Brandon Hurst; *Pierre,* Dan Crimmins; *Chauvin,* Frederick Peters; *Von Gelder,* George Burr McAnnan; *Latour,* John Printz; *Zombies,* Claude Morgan, John Fergusson; *Maids,* Annette Stone, Velma Gresham.

counting of profits also were ordered. The court, after a 14-day trial, decided that the word had acquired a secondary meaning suggestive of the earlier picture and that the title *Revolt of the Zombies* constituted unfair competition. The Halperins, therefore, had to retitle their picture *Revolt of the Demons,* although sanity prevailed eventually and they were able to again use the word they had made famous.

Wild, different and sometimes overdone, *White Zombie* has earned a loyal following and at least as many detractors. It creates and sustains a Gothic mood as few other pictures have, provides some diabolical chills (the sight of a bullet thudding into the bare chest of the giant Chauvin without halting his advance or drawing blood is as frightening a moment as any film can offer), gave the underrated Lugosi his finest role, and remains one of the most haunting and interesting films of its time.

—Michael H. Price and George E. Turner

155

13

Man, *The Most Dangerous Game*

An enormous Gothic door fills the opening frames of *The Most Dangerous Game.* The call of a distant hunting horn is heard as the camera moves in to examine the massive door knocker. It is fashioned as a centaur, its brute face twisted in agony, a metal arrow protruding from its breast. In hinged arms the creature holds the body of a girl whose torso forms the hammer. A man's hand reaches into the frame, takes hold of the girl's waist, and lets the hammer fall. Music builds as the main title dissolves in: *Radio Pictures Presents A Cooper & Schoedsack Production*... Here was good news for the many 1932 movie goers who were bored with the overly talky talkies then dominating the screen. It meant that two men who always made *moving* pictures were back.

Merian Coldwell Cooper left his Jacksonville, Florida home as a youth and became, in rapid succession, a newspaperman, an Annapolis midshipman (who didn't graduate because he went "over the hill" to see a girl), a trooper chasing Pancho Villa along the Texas-Mexico border, and a much-decorated combat pilot of World War I. He refused the Distinguished Service Award because he didn't want to be singled out from his buddies. He became chief of the Polish Air Force during the Russo-Polish War, and his escape from a Russian prison after being shot down by Budenny's Cossacks made international headlines. He continued to attract attention as author, explorer, movie producer and airline executive.

Ernest Beaumont Schoedsack ran away from his Iowa home when he was 14. Within a few years he was F. Richard Jones' top cameraman at the Mack Sennett Studio, then a combat photographer for the Army Signal Corps. Later he led rescue missions while cranking a camera for the Red Cross during the Russo-Polish and Greco-Turkish conflicts. He met Cooper in Vienna in 1918 and again in Singapore in 1922. During an African expedition they formed the film making partnership that took them into the Bakhtiari Mountains of Persia, where they filmed the celebrated "natural drama," *Grass* (1925). They made *Chang* (1927) in the jungles of Laos and shot part of *The Four Feathers* (1929) in East Africa. On his own, Schoedsack photographed *Rango* (1930) in the Sumatran wilderness. Each of these films was made under incredibly difficult, dangerous conditions.

The stocky, hard-nosed Cooper became executive assistant to RKO-Radio's new vice-president in charge of production, David O. Selznick, late in 1931. There was an understanding that Cooper would also be permitted to develop productions on his own. The company owned the former FBO Studio in Hollywood, which they renamed The Radio Studio, and the old Pathé lot in Culver City. Founded in 1929 on the eve of the Depression, the brave new company was in financial straits almost from the start.

Schoedsack returned to Hollywood in January 1932, after several months' location work in India for Paramount's *The Lives of a Bengal Lancer.* Exasperated by a long wait for studio chiefs to approve a final script for the project (eventually to be directed by Henry Hathaway in 1935!), he asked

Photos by Felix Schoedsack, Seymour Stern

to be released from his contract. Immediately he joined Cooper at RKO and began pre-production work on what was to be the first all-talking Cooper-Schoedsack collaboration, an adaptation of Richard Connell's O. Henry Award winning story, "The Most Dangerous Game."

Schoedsack, standing a lean six-foot-six, was Cooper's physical opposite. The partners were equally dissimilar in personality, Schoedsack epitomizing the "loner" who shrinks from publicity, while Cooper was contrastingly flamboyant and loquacious. Both men possessed a love of adventure – the more dangerous the better – and an appreciation of the artistic, the dramatic and the spectacular. They divided their work according to individual abilities and preferences, their differences contributing as strongly as their similarities to their excellence as a team.

Connell's 1924 short-story tells of General Zaroff, late of the Czar's army, who has only one passion: the hunt. The hunting of brute animals no longer offers the challenge he wants, however, so he decides to *create* a game worthy of his mettle. Retiring with a trusted Cossack servant to a small Caribbean island, he stocks his game preserve with human beings, the survivors of shipwrecks Zaroff arranges by tampering with the light buoys that

Noble Johnson, Leslie Banks, Dutch Hendrian and Steve Clemento as Zaroff and his hunters.

mark a channel between treacherous reefs. When famed hunter Sanger Rainsford falls overboard from a pleasure yacht and is cast upon Zaroff's shore, the madman conceives his greatest hunt. Rainsford wins the game, kills Zaroff in a duel of swords, and succeeds him as keeper of the preserve.

This masterful tale has all the elements of a first-rate film thriller save one: there is no "love interest." To compensate for the loss of the purely masculine concept and the caustic ending of the original, Zaroff was made even more horrid. "He cannot love until he has known the thrill of the hunt with a human being as his prey," Cooper explained. "Such an atavistic creature is the man who by his savage instincts dominates the most dangerous game." As for casting a woman into the lupine hunt, Cooper had no qualms. "Woman has retained, fortunately, the fighting, dominant blood of the savage," he said. "She would have perished as a distinctive individual long ago had it not been for her savage strain which has always given her the impe-

158

tus of fighting for her own rights. This quality can be found in the most fragile of women. For a long time I always thought that 'the most dangerous' game naturally would be one in which a woman was involved."

James Creelman, a noted writer of adventure yarns, succeeded remarkably well in delineating this complex, highly original monster.

Another story change demanded by the producers was to make Rainsford the victim of a planned shipwreck rather than a man overboard. This situation, like many in even the most fantastic of their films, was suggested by personal experience. They were members of the ship's company of the Wisdom II ten years before, when Arab wreckers decoyed the ship onto a reef by disabling a lighthouse.

The New York office put a damper on the producers' plans to make a spectacular production when it decreed a budget of only $202,662 and a three-week shooting schedule. In an attempt to stay within this inadequate figure, Cooper and Schoedsack pored over the script, seeking ways to eliminate expensive details in order to apply the money where it would show best on the screen. An example is reworking a shipwreck sequence, which would have cost a great deal more had it been staged as originally planned. Schoedsack wrote this note to manager Val Paul on May 4, 1932:

Mr. Cooper and I have discussed and approved a change in the yacht sequence which should result in considerable economy, while improving and adding realism to the wreck with a more modern and convincing method...

At the instant that the ship scrapes bottom, we leave the interior of the dining salon as the sets rocks over, but before the water enters. We cut to the flash on the bridge as the officer discovers the water has reached the boilers. We cut to a miniature explosion of flash powder on our miniature hull and instantly dissolve to a series of overlapping and rapidly dissolving flashes such as falling wreckage (all in closeups), a man being washed along a deck, falling spars and gear, drowning sailors, hissing steam, etc., accompanied by screams, crashes and the roaring of water. Over all will be exposed flashes of foaming and churning water, and the last flash might be the last of the masthead disappearing under the water. Inasmuch as these scenes are fast and impressionistic, I think they could be very cheaply made, or perhaps a great many found in stock. At the end of the series, we dissolve to the scene of the boy in the water, as in the present version.

As you will see, this lineup eliminates the following items:

1. *Building salon set in tank, with water dumps.*
2. *Possibly eliminate rockers on both bridge and salon.*
3. *Eliminates deck set in tank entirely.*
4. *Simplifies miniature yacht work to some extent.*
5. *Eliminates costume changes for extras in cabin.*

Later, Schoedsack eliminated nine actors from the already small cast. Dropped from the passenger list of the doomed yacht were veterans Walter McGrail, Cornelius Keefe, Creighton Hale, Theodore Von Eltz, Christian Rub and Alfred Codman, plus three young hopefuls – Leon Waycoff (later Ames), Creighton Chaney and Ray Milland.

Hoping to get the role, Bruce Cabot submitted portraits of himself made up as Zaroff is described in the story. Advertising department used Cabot instead of Banks in this ad.

159

Glass shot by Mario Larrinaga; the water is real, the night sky is painted, and the buoy lights shine through places where paint has been removed.

Shooting began May 16, 1932, on the jungle set, and ended June 17. Final cost was about $16,000 over the original budget. Two Russian language advisors helped Creelman write the dialogue and another stayed on the set to see to the accuracy of Zaroff's frequent lapses into Russian dialogue.

Henry Gerrard, ASC, was in charge of the studio photography, seconded by Robert DeGrasse, ASC. Gerrard, a Canadian war hero then 38 years old, had been a leading cinematographer at Paramount and was on his first assignment for RKO. *Phantom of Crestwood, Blind Adventure, Little Women* and *Of Human Bondage* were among his later RKO credits before his death in 1934. DeGrasse hailed from New Jersey and had began as an assistant cameraman at Universal in 1916. He had been a director of photography since 1921, but with the coming of sound in 1928, he asked to be demoted to operator status because he felt intimidated by the new techniques. Resuming as director of photography in 1935, he photographed most of Ginger Rogers' RKO pictures, two Val Lewton classics, *The Window, Miracle of the Bells,* and nearly 80 others. He died in 1971 at the age of 70.

Nicholas Musuraca, ASC, then an all-purpose cinematographer at RKO, photographed the location scenes, including some glass shots and process plates. Musuraca, who died in 1975, had been a cinematographer since 1913. During the late 1940s he became the most celebrated "mood and atmosphere" expert at the studio and today is widely regarded as a father of the *film noir* style.

"Our jungle set was all on Stage 12 at Pathé," Schoedsack recalled. "We moved the plants around different ways and used glass shots to get different views."

The swamp was built in a tank 60 feet long, 35 feet wide and 15 inches deep, with the slopes built up on ramps. The rest of the jungle included a trail with a Malay deadfall, a cave, a crevasse bridged by a huge log, cliffs and ledges of artificial rock, and a portion of the chateau of Zaroff built at the edge of the undergrowth. The waterfall and rapids sets, composited by glass art and the Dunning travelling matte process with both real and miniature cataracts, was built on Pathé Stage 14. Byron Crabbe's glass paintings of the chateau were matted in with live player action and seascapes via the Dunning process. Kenneth Peach, ASC, was process cinematographer. Optical effects were added in post-production by Linwood Dunn, ASC.

Exteriors of the chateau and its courtyard, yacht interiors and the miniature and process shots were created on Radio stages 1, 3 and 9. Scenes of the men in the water following the shipwreck were shot in a tank at Pathé, where stuntman Gil Perkins and a law student from Hawaii, Buster Crabbe (no relation to Byron), executed the stunt falls. Crabbe, who received $5 for his day's work, won the Olym-

Banks and "Shorty" Schoedsack on the set.

pic Free Style Swimming competition the following
year and embarked on a long acting career.

Location work was minimal but took advantage of nearby California coastline. Stuntman
Wes Hopper, doubling as Rainsford, swam ashore
on a rocky beach near San Pedro. Glass paintings by
Mario Larrinaga gave the scenes an ominous night
sky and supplied buoy lights. Views of the cove from
a chateau window were made from cliffs near the
former site of Marineland of the Pacific. Other clifftop scenes by the sea were filmed at Redondo.

Cooper was delighted with the jungle set
because it fit into his plans for what was to be the
next Cooper-Schoedsack venture, *King Kong.* On the
strength of illustrations made by Larrinaga and
Crabbe under the supervision of technical expert
Willis O'Brien, he had convinced the studio heads to
allow him to produce a test reel of *Kong.* Cooper
became a frequent visitor to the set, bringing with
him writer Creelman, a camera crew, some tough-
looking stunt extras and a young and untried contract player named Jacques de Bujac (soon to be
renamed Bruce Cabot). Whenever possible he borrowed Fay Wray and Robert Armstrong, put them in
soiled costumes, covered the actress' brown hair
with a blond wig, and put them to work in scenes
improvised by Creelman and himself. Schoedsack
became irritated at his partner's interruptions. Cabot
said the two "argued all the time on that set." Film
editor Archie Marshek remembers that Schoedsack
sometimes hid in the editing room when he saw
Cooper approaching. The use of these sets in both
pictures combine with similarities of directorial and
technical style to create a close kinship between the
two films.

Joel McCrea, who was being groomed for
stardom by RKO, was only 26 when he was assigned
to the Rainsford role. Arrangements were made to
borrow Margaret Perry from MGM. When, however, she proved unavailable at production time, the
producers seized the opportunity to hire their
friend, Fay Wray, who had worked for them in *The
Four Feathers.* The lovely Canadian-born actress
proved an ideal leading lady for such a tale of terror.

Robert Armstrong, a stage and screen veteran, began in this picture a long personal and
professional association with Cooper and Schoedsack. Noble Johnson, the distinguished black actor,
was another alumnus of *The Four Feathers.* Evil-
visaged Steve Clemento was a professional knife
thrower described by Schoedsack as "the sweetest
little Yaqui Indian in the world." Brawny Dutch
Hendrian was a football star.

*Robert Armstrong enjoys the Count's vodka and
emperor-size cigarettes while Banks plans his next hunt.*

An English stage star who had never before
appeared in a film, Leslie Banks, was chosen for the
difficult role of Zaroff. He was, according to Schoedsack, "great fun to work with, a fine actor and a
great guy with a real sense of humor. His face was
badly injured during the war – the left side was
paralyzed – which made him interesting to photograph." Though he was no stranger to heavy drama, having appeared in scores of plays since 1914,
Banks was most noted for drawing room comedy. He
was starring in "Springtime for Henry" on Broadway when RKO signed him. He subsequently returned to England, where he appeared in numerous
films, but he never made another picture in
America.

"When I read the script I felt that nobody
would believe it," Schoedsack said. "I decided the
main thing was to keep it moving so they wouldn't
have time to think it over. I didn't know a damned
thing about stage direction, but I tried one thing that
worked: I brought a stopwatch to the stage and
sometimes I'd say, 'That scene took 30 seconds; I
think we could do it just as well in 20,' and we'd
speed it up that way. The front office was afraid I

Joel McCrea and Fay Wray in the Pathé jungle.

Twenty Great Danes, five of which were specially trained by the Hollywood Dog Training School to enact the chase, were then cast. "Some of them belonged to Harold Lloyd, and he didn't appreciate our blacking them up to make them look fiercer. Once, when we were working on the Fog Hollow set, Leslie came bounding out of the fog, clutching his rear end, and told us, "I say, one of those dogs bit me!' The lady from the training school said, 'Oh, no, it's impossible! None of those dogs would do that!' Leslie said, 'Well, perhaps it was a cameraman, but *something* bit me in the ass.' He was bleeding and had to have first aid and stitches."

In the opening scene, Bill Woodman's (Hale Hamilton) yacht *Sylph* approaches notorious Baranka Island, off the African coast. The captain suspects that light buoys indicating a clear channel between the island and the mainland are not positioned correctly. He asks Woodman for permission to take a long route because "there are no more coral-reefed, shark-infested waters in the whole world." The guests, including a noted hunter and author, Bob Rainsford (Joel McCrea), are in favor of following the captain's suggestion, but Woodman refuses.

As the group studies photos of their recent hunting trip, Doc (Landers Stevens) comments:

Henry Gerrard on the set.

couldn't handle dialogue so they sent Irving Pichel over and he just stood behind me and watched.

"I went to a morgue to find out how to pickle human heads. The deadfall came from my experience in Siam and Sumatra. We cheated – we had the tree up on chains, and when we dropped it, we thought the whole stage was going to come down."

Although the film follows Creelman's script cloesly, some of its best moments were improvised. The design of the door knocker and the corresponding motif of a large tapestry were devised during production, as were many striking details of the chase. Schoedsack liked the lines in which Creelman poked fun at his old adversaries, the Russians, such as Zaroff's comment that "Russians aren't the best mechanics." On the other hand, he found the writer somewhat impractical.

"He could concoct some wild ideas," Schoedsack said. "He decided it would be more scary if Zaroff used hunting *leopards* instead of dogs. I reluctantly hired a leopard and its trainer from the Selig Zoo, and the cat immediately ran away on the jungle set. People were climbing to the rafters and we spent hours rounding him up."

162

"The beast, killing just for his existence, is called savage. The man, killing just for sport, is called civilized. Bit contradictory, isn't it?"

Rainsford argues that hunting is as much a sport for the animal. "Now take that fellow right there," he says, indicating a tiger he bagged. "There never was a time when he couldn't have got away. He didn't want to. He got interested in hunting *me*. He didn't hate me for stalking him any more than I hated him for trying to charge me. As a matter of fact, we *admired* each other." Doc demands to know if there would be as much sport in the game if Rainsford were the tiger instead of the hunter. Bob replies, "This world's divided into two kinds of people, the hunters and the hunted. Luckily, I'm a hunter. Nothing can ever change that, can it?"

The ship strikes a reef. Water rushes into the engine room, causing an explosion that hurls everybody into the sea. Rainsford finds the captain and another survivor clinging to wreckage, but both men are dragged under by sharks. Rainsford swims desperately through the darkness toward a distant light.

Rainsford collapses on a beach, lying unconscious until the sound of dogs barking and the cry of an unidentifiable animal arouse him. He walks towards the sounds and sees, on a cliff overlooking a lagoon, an imposing chateau. He finds a ponderous door, which is adorned with the bronze knocker seen in the opening title. When Rainsford knocks, the door swings open. He enters and finds a giant Cossack (Noble Johnson) who only glares menacingly.

"Ivan does not speak any language," interrupts a man (Leslie Banks) dressed in formal attire. "He has the misfortune to be dumb... Welcome to my poor fortress." He explains that his chateau was "built by the Portuguese centuries ago. I have had the ruins restored to make my home here. I am Count Zaroff..."

Rainsford says he is the only survivor of the wreck. Zaroff responds that "We have several survivors from the last wreck still in the house. It would seem that this island were cursed." A huge wall tapestry above the stairway, Rainsford notes, repeats the centaur-woman motif.

The other guests are the beautiful Eve Trowbridge (Fay Wray) and her brother Martin (Robert Armstrong). The latter is drinking heavily, to Zaroff's annoyance. Eve explains that only she, Martin and two sailors survived a recent shipwreck. Zaroff announces proudly that Rainsford is a great hunter.

McCrea and Wray try to avoid a crocodile in fog hollow.

"Only in your books have I found a sane point of view," Zaroff tells Rainsford. "We are kindred spirits."

Martin avers that Zaroff "sleeps all day and hunts all night, and what's more, he'll have you doing the same thing... he's had our sailors so busy chasing around the woods for flora and fauna that we haven't seen them for three days." Eve seems disturbed. Rainsford asks Zaroff what he hunts.

"I'll tell you," is the reply. "You will be amused, I know... I have created a new sensation ... God made some men poets, some He made kings, some beggars. Me, He made a hunter. My hand was made for the trigger, my father told me. My father was a very rich man, with a quarter of a million acres in the Crimea, and an ardent sportsman... My life has been one glorious hunt. It would be impossible for me to tell you how many animals I have killed... It was here in Africa that the cape buffalo gave me this." He indicates a deep scar in his forehead. "It still bothers me sometimes.

"One night, as I lay in my tent with this — this head of mine, a terrible thought crept like a snake into my brain. Hunting was beginning to bore me! When I lost my love for hunting, I lost my love of life, of love. I even tried to sink myself to the level of the savage. I made myself perfect in the use

Clemento and Johnson restrain McCrea as Banks invites him to a nocturnal hunt.

of the Tartar war bow . . . but, alas! . . . What I needed was not a new weapon but a new animal . . . Yes, here on my island I hunt the most dangerous game." Zaroff smiles at Rainsford's suggestion of tigers. "The tiger has nothing but his claws and his fangs." Zaroff calls the trophy room "My one secret. I keep it as a surprise for my guests against the rainy day of boredom."

Martin suggests a hunt. "We're pals. We'll have a big party, get cockeyed, and go hunting . . ."

"A charming simplicity," Zaroff says aside to Rainsford. "He talks of wine and women as a *prelude* to the hunt. We barbarians know that it is after the chase, and then only, that man revels. You know the saying of the Ogandi chieftains: 'Hunt first the enemy, then the woman.' . . . It is the natural instinct. What is woman, even such a woman as this, until the blood is quickened by the kill? One passion builds upon another. Kill, then love! When you have known that, you have known ecstasy!"

While Zaroff plays the piano, Eve guardedly tells Rainsford that Zaroff has kept her and Martin on the island by pretending his motor launch is out of repair. All windows are barred and huge hunting dogs guard the chateau. Further, "One night after dinner, the Count took one of our sailors down to see the trophy room . . . Two nights later he took the other there. Neither has been seen since. He says they've gone hunting."

Later, Zaroff sends Eve and Rainsford to their rooms, but delays Martin with conversation. "Don't worry, Sis, the Count will take care of me," Martin calls.

"Indeed, I shall," Zaroff adds.

Sometime before dawn, Eve comes to Rainsford's room to say Martin has disappeared. Rainsford goes with her to the trophy room where they find mummified heads of men mounted as trophies. Another head floats in a jar of embalming fluid. Eve and Rainsford hide as Zaroff and his men – Ivan, a Tartar (Steve Clemento) and a scarfaced Cossack (Dutch Hendrian) – return bearing the body of Martin. Eve lashes out at Zaroff, who orders her carried to her room. The servants overcome Rainsford and chain him to a wall.

"Come, come, my dear Rainsford, I don't want to treat you like my other guests," Zaroff says. ". . . I know what you think, but you are wrong. He was sober enough and fit for sport when I sent him out . . . You see, when I first began stocking my island, many of my guests thought I was joking, so I established this place. I always bring them here before the hunt. An hour with my trophies and they usually do their best to keep away from me."

He explains that he is able to get a supply of game because "providence provided this island with dangerous reefs" and he moves the buoys that mark a safe channel. He gives his guests "every consideration: good food, exercise – everything possible to get them in splendid shape . . . I give them hunting clothes, a woodsman's knife and a full day's start. Why, I even wait until midnight, to give them the full advantage of the dark. And when one eludes me, only till sunrise . . . he wins the game." He indicates some medieval torture devices. "If a chosen one refuses to be hunted, Ivan is such an artist with these that invariably they choose to hunt . . . To date I have not lost. Oh, Rainsford, you'll find this game worth playing! When the next ship arrives we'll have gorgeous sport together!"

Rainsford refuses angrily: "You murdering rat, I'm a hunter, not an assassin! What do you think I am?"

"One, I fear, who dares not follow his own convictions to their logical conclusion. I'm afraid, in this instance, you may *have* to follow them. I shall not wait for the next ship. Four o'clock . . . the sun is just rising. Come, Mr. Rainsford, let's not waste time!" He frees Rainsford and gives him a knife. "Your fangs and claws." Eve elects to accompany Rainsford. Zaroff consents because, "One does not kill the female animal."

Rainsford is surprised to find the island is "no larger than a deer park." It is composed of dense jungle, a swamp, and rocky high ground. He sets about building a Malay deadfall, a heavy tree prepared so it will fall on anyone who touches a vine hidden in the path. The couple has only time to hide in a shallow cave before Zaroff approaches.

Zaroff's foot almost touches the trigger, but he halts, sizes up the situation, and sends an arrow into the vine. After the tree falls, he shoots an arrow into the cave. He tries to taunt Rainsford into coming out. "But surely you don't think that anyone who has hunted leopards would follow you into that ambush? Very well, if you choose to play the leopard, I shall hunt you like a leopard." He returns to his fortress.

"You've heard him say he'd hunt us as you'd hunt a leopard," Bob says, "That means he's gone for his high-powered rifle." Eve runs in terror. Rainsford halts her at the edge of Fox Hollow. "We've got two hours until dawn," he explains. "We've got to use our heads instead of our legs." On higher ground he finds a deep, narrow crevasse, which he bridges with thin branches, leaves and grass.

A sudden uprising of frightened birds announces Zaroff's return. Eve and Rainsford lure Zaroff to the trap. He almost falls, but regains his footing. "Very good, Rainsford," he calls, "but you have not won yet." With a half-hour left till sunup, Rainsford leads Eve into Fog Hollow. They hear Zaroff's voice: "As you are doubtless saying, the odds are against me. You have made my rifle useless in the fog. You cannot blame me if I overcome that obstacle." He sounds his horn, which is echoed by an answering horn and the baying of dogs. Ivan and the Tartar emerge from the chateau grounds with several hunting dogs on leash.

Rainsford plants a bamboo spear in the foggy path. The hounds drag Ivan onto the spear, killing him. The dogs race free, followed by Zaroff and the Mongol. Eluding a crocodile, Eve and Rainsford emerge from the swamp. Crossing a gorge via a log, they climb a tree. From a limb, they reach some high rocks. Rainsford decoys one dog into a roaring stream. Backed to the edge of a cliff next to a waterfall, he kills two more with his knife. Another dog leaps upon him, and as man and beast struggle, Zaroff fires. Rainsford and the dog fall into the river far below. Zaroff has won with three minutes to spare.

In his drawing room, Zaroff plays his demoniacal waltz as the Mongol goes upstairs to bring Eve. Zaroff turns to find Rainsford standing in the doorway. "My dear Rainsford, I congratulate you. You have beaten me!"

"You hit the dog, not me. I took a chance and went over with him."

Zaroff tosses Rainsford the key to the boat-

Banks, Clemento, and three of Harold Lloyd's dogs.

house, then draws a pistol from a cabinet. Rainsford tackles Zaroff. The Cossack servant attacks, but after a vicious fight Rainsford breaks the man's spine. Zaroff reaches for his warbow, but Rainsford wrests it from him and plunges the arrow into Zaroff's back.

The Tartar appears with Eve on the stairway. He throws a knife, but Rainsford dodges aside and grabs the Count's pisol. Killing the Tartar, he leads Eve to the motor launch. Zaroff drags himself to a window and watches as the boat comes out of the boathouse. Fitting an arrow to the bow he takes aim. "Impossible!" he gasps, unable to draw the bow. He falls from the window into the courtyard – and the jaws of the blood-mad hounds. The motor launch races toward the horizon at the fade-out.

Several scenes which were cut from the trophy room sequence before release possessed a certain grim charm. In one, Zaroff indicates a row of human heads. "Stupid sailors – a thoroughbred dog is worth the lot of them!" he snorts. He shows Rainsford a mounted group consisting of a downed man, full figure and badly mauled, and two hounds. Zaroff refers fondly to the central subject at "a fine specimen" who "killed my two best dogs – in fact, the ones you see here with him. That's why I rarely use the brutes. Wound a man and they'll pull him down before you've a chance to make the kill

This is from a scene cut after the preview. Banks displays his prize trophy, which is dedicated "To a game loser."

again allowed a moment to catch its breath before the violent climax.

The shipwreck sequence is a striking example of film construction, especially for a product of the early talkie era, when montage most often was determined by the demands of the sound track rather than visual considerations. The sequence is composed of 25 shots ranging from one foot (running about three-quarters of a second) to 11 feet (about seven-and-a-half seconds). The assemblage totals only 70 seconds.

Photographically, the film is a *tour de force*. The most striking visuals are in the chase through the jungle and swamp. The camera is spectacularly mobile at times, keeping pace with the hunted in their flight. Intercut are artistically composed static shots from an astonishing variety of angles. At one point hunters and dogs rush over the camera, appearing as giants looming through the fog. Extensive use of glass art adds to the scope and detail of the sound stage jungle. There is even a scene of model birds rising from the jungle, animated by Orville Goldner of the *King Kong* crew.

Banks easily steals the show from his colleagues. He appears initially as a mincing aristocrat, but when he begins his dissertation on hunting, it becomes disturbingly evident that there is much more to the man than genteel manners and musical ability. Entirely credible is his umbrage at the girl because she considers her brother's life more important than the hunt, and he is the epitome of savagery as he joyously summons the hounds to the kill.

McCrea appears somewhat more boyish than might be expected of a famed big-game hunter, but his lean physique and natural acting style suit the action. Fay Wray is, as always, the quintessential lady in distress. Armstrong is amusingly irritating, and Johnson and Clemento supply impressive presences.

RKO's overworked musical director, Max Steiner, commissioned W. Franke Harling to compose the score. Harling's music, fully orchestrated, was delivered in August. An excellent score, it was never used, because Cooper felt it failed to capture the spirit of outdoor adventure and action. "It was like music for a Broadway show," Cooper remarked. Rather than adapt the existing music, Steiner – himself an operetta and show composer-conductor – worked day and night to produce one of the most exciting of his scores. Based upon a three-note figure heard initially as a hunting call, the music builds to an ominous theme titled "The Iron Door." This is developed through numerous variations, including Zaroff's lilting, yet threatening, waltz. The

yourself. Even Ivan wouldn't be safe if they smelled his blood." When Rainsford remarks at the scope of the tableau, Zaroff explains sincerely, "Well, he deserved the honor. Like you, Rainsford, I never fail to bestow credit where credit is due. Look there, you can see I borrowed an inscription from your own collection." The plaque reads, "To a Game Loser."

"Oh, you mustn't think I feel that way about most of them," he adds. "An inferior lot, usually, I regret to say. This chap here – all skin and bones, isn't he?" The emaciated figure is pinned to a post by an arrow. "The foolish fellow tried to run through the swamps of Fog Hollow. We preserved him just as he died, as an object lesson, you might say."

The film is fabricated in a manner typical of Cooper and Schoedsack. It begins leisurely, building to the sudden and shocking shipwreck, then settles down again to set the stage for the next shocker, the revelations of the trophy room. By this time, there has been an almost clinical elucidation of Zaroff's possibly unique form of madness as presented from his own point of view. All of this is splendidly dialogued, but once the chase begins there is a minimum of talk and a wealth of action. There is no pause in the suspense and excitement of this magnificently staged and edited sequence. After Rainsford's supposed death, the audience is

166

The prize of the game.

piano version was performed by Norma Drury, wife of director Richard Boleslawski. Steiner, like Zaroff, saved his real passion for the chase. Here is music to make the heart beat faster as it races along with the feverish action on the screen and underscores each sinister nuance. The climactic scenes are played with musical accompaniment, but without speech other than Zaroff's barely audible dying word, "Impossible!"

"I knew the picture was going to be a classic as soon as I'd seen a few of the dailies," editor Archie Marshek recalled. "I took special pains with the cutting. At the preview there were two places where a lot of people walked out. One was when they saw a head floating in a jar, and the other was when McCrea broke a man's back. I put that sound in myself, by snapping a dry stick."

Schoedsack, who devoted much of his life to the study of music, said he made a conscious effort to compose this film as though it were a symphony. He succeeded admirably. One critic called it, "sixty of the most exciting minutes of your life."

—George E. Turner

An RKO-Radio *Picture; A* Cooper & Schoedsack *production; executive producer* David O. Selznick; *directed by* Ernest B. Schoedsack *and* Irving Pichel; *associate producer,* Merian C. Cooper; *screenplay by* James Ashmore Creelman; *from the story by* Richard Connell; *photographed by* Henry Gerrard, ASC; *music by* Max Steiner; *settings by* Carroll Clark; *sound recording by* Clem Portman; *film editor,* Archie S. Marshek; *camera effects by* Lloyd Knechtel, ASC, Vernon L. Walker, ASC, Linwood Dunn, ASC, Kenneth Peach, ASC; *production effects,* Harry Redmond, Jr.; *miniatures by* Don Jahrous; *animation,* Orville Goldner; *special properties,* Marcel Delgado, John Cerisoli; *technical artists,* Mario Larrinaga *and* Byron L. Crabbe; *second camera,* Robert DeGrasse, ASC; *location camera,* Nick Musuraca, ASC; *production supervisor,* Val Paul; *production managers,* Walter Daniels, James Crone; *makeup,* Wally Westmore; *added dialogue,* Edward Eliscu, Owen Francis; *assistant directors,* Percy Ikerd, Edward Killy, Hal Walker; *continuity,* Marie Branham; *technical advisors,* Nick Koblinsky, Professor Markover, Alexis Davidoff; *set decorations,* Thomas Little; *pianist,* Norma Drury; *sound effects,* Murray Spivack; *process supervision,* Dodge Dunning; *song, "A Moment in the Dark," by* Carmen Lombardo, Arthur Freed; *cutters,* Del Andrews, Tom Scott; *stills,* G. F. Schoedsack, Seymour Stern; *RCA sound system; running time, 63 minutes, released September 9, 1932.*

Zaroff, Leslie Banks; *Bob Rainsford,* Joel McCrea; *Eve Trowbridge,* Fay Wray; *Martin Trowbridge,* Robert Armstrong; *Woodman,* Hale Hamilton; *Ivan,* Noble Johnson; *Tartar,* Steve Clemento; *Russian Servant,* Dutch Hendrian; *Captain,* William B. Davidson; *Doc,* Landers Stevens; *First Mate,* James Flavin; *Guest at Radio,* Arnold Grey; *Guest at Table,* Phil Tead; *Steward,* Clem Beauchamp; *Cook,* Martin Turner; *Helmsman,* Charles Hall; *Stunt Artists,* Gil Perkins, Buster Crabbe, Wesley Hopper.

167

14

Desert Madness of *The Lost Patrol* and *Bad Lands*

Merian C. Cooper – war hero, soldier of fortune and producer of extravagant adventure films like *Chang* and *King Kong* – became vice president in charge of production at RKO Radio Pictures when David O. Selznick vacated the job early in 1933. Although he was instrumental in the making of many successful pictures in a genteel vein, such as *Little Women* and *Top Hat,* Cooper's real interest was in picturizing stories of courage and high adventure.

One such yarn which Cooper hoped to produce as a vehicle for Richard Dix, the studio's leading action star, was Philip MacDonald's novel, *Patrol,* which had been the basis for a 1929 silent film made in England. Cooper's bosses in New York read the story treatment and were horrified at the prospects. It called for an all-male cast of tough character actors and not even a glimpse of a woman's face, the story was unrelentingly grim, and the earlier version had failed miserably at the box office. But Cooper persisted and at last was given permission to acquire the property, which required payment of £350 to the original producers, British Instructional Pictures, and $7,000 to MacDonald.

Although he had never met John Ford, Cooper admired his penchant for directing he-man pictures at Fox and wanted him for *Patrol.* The Irish-born Ford was equally anxious to direct a heavy drama of the Black and Tan Rebellion, Liam O'Flaherty's *The Informer,* for which the boxoffice potential appeared dim. A deal was struck: Cooper would let Ford make *The Informer* if he would first direct *Patrol.* These negotiations mark the begin-ning of a 23-year producer-director partnership that gave the industry some of it's more memorable works. This first Ford-Cooper production, which was released as *The Lost Patrol,* earned critical ac-claim and, through periodic reissues over a period of many years, repaid its modest cost many times over, despite the fears of the company executives.

Production was slated to begin on August 31, 1933 in the sand dunes near Yuma, Arizona. Cooper's enthusiasm was dampened when he was given a total budget of only $227,703.22 for a picture which would require a difficult location shoot and a strong cast. In an attempt to meet the budget, Cooper allotted only 21 days for principal photogra-phy, including two days of travel time and one holiday (Labor Day).

Ford found the early drafts of the screen-play unacceptable and, just 10 days before the start-ing date, he asked his sometime collaborator at Fox, Dudley Nichols, to lend a hand. Obtaining leave from Fox, Nichols worked for eight days and nights, often with Ford present, writing an entirely new adaptation of the novel. Jamiel Hasson, an actor-director from Damascus, worked with them for three days providing technical advice regarding Arab customs. Advice on British military life was provided by Ford's long-time associate, Major Frank Baker, a hard-bitten Australian. The final script was ready on August 28. In brief:

Somewhere in the Mesopotamian Desert during World War I, a 12-man British cavalry de-tachment loses its only officer to an Arab sniper's bullet. The Sergeant (Victor McLaglen) takes

charge, confiding in Corporal Bell (Brandon Hurst) that the dead man kept their secret orders in his head. They are isolated, they have no idea where they are, and their food and water supplies are low. Sanders (Boris Karloff), a religious zealot, is on the verge of insanity. As the end seems near, they find an oasis with a water hole, date trees and a ruined mosque. Pearson (Douglas Walton), just 19, had run away from home to be with the heroes he read about in Kipling. He is stabbed to death that night while on watch. All the horses have been stolen and Bell has been wounded.

Abelson (Sammy Stein), dazed by the sun, staggers out to attack the unseen enemy. Morelli (Wallace Ford), an ex-vaudeville comic, brings him back, dead. Hale (Billy Bevan), a lovable Cockney, climbs a palm tree to look for the hidden Arabs, only to topple down, a bullet hole through his head. Veteran sappers Mackay and Cook (Paul Hanson and Alan Hale) team up to steal away and seek help. They return in death, strapped to their horses. Brown (Reginald Denny), a gentleman, slips out to fight alone. Quincannon (J. M. Kerrigan), 30 years a soldier, rushes out after revenge. Bell, delirious, dies as he totters out to fight. Now only the Sergeant,

Morelli and the increasingly demented Sanders remain alive.

The young pilot (Howard Wilson) of a British warplane spots the survivors and comes in for a landing. The survivors try vainly to warn him, but an Arab bullet ends his life as he steps from the plane. At this Sanders goes berserk and the Sergeant and Morelli have to tie him down. Because neither man can pilot a plane, the Sergeant sets fire to it after removing the machine gun. Morelli fears he will be the last man alive; the Sergeant now thinks only of revenge. Sanders works his way free and, clothed in rags like a Biblical prophet, strides out across the dunes in an exaltation of religious fervor. Morelli runs out to bring him back, only to see him die. Morelli is killed as he tries to return.

The Sergeant digs himself a shallow grave next to those of his comrades. After a long silence a handful of Arabs slink into the oasis. The Sergeant, screaming his fury, rises from his grave and cuts them down with the machine gun, continuing to fire until the gun is empty. Another Arab appears, fires at him and misses. The Sergeant grabs a rifle and kills him. A moment later a cavalry unit arrives to find the Sergeant standing shirtless, disheveled and alone. "Speak up, man – where's your section?" the officer demands. The lone avenger of the lost patrol turns to stare blankly at the row of swords that mark the graves.

Dix had been slated for the central role of the Sergeant, with Boris Karloff (at liberty because of a salary dispute with Universal) as a religious fanatic and Victor McLaglen as a former prizefighter. On August 29 – one day before the company was scheduled to depart for Yuma – Cooper jettisoned his most expensive actor, Dix, and moved McLaglen into the leading role. Curiously, McLaglen's look-alike brother, Cyril, had played the part for BIP. An ex-pugilist turned small-parts actor, Sammy Stein, was given the role previously intended for McLaglen. McLaglen and Karloff received $5,000 and $4,000 per week, respectively, while Stein's salary was minimal.

Cast and crew departed by train on the morning of August 30 and were checked into a Yuma hotel that evening. Next morning at 6:30 they were at the location ready to film the opening scenes of the cavalry column in the dunes.

The site was on government land consisting of a high range of sand hills near a state highway maintenance camp. A studio construction gang under supervision of unit art director Sidney Ullman had already graded a road to the site, created an artificial oasis with a desert pool and fifty artificial date palms, and built a plaster replica of a ruined Arabian mosque approximately the size of a five-room house. The location company dubbed the setting Abdullah Abbey.

Actors at the scene were McLaglen, Karloff, Stein, Reginald Denny, Wallace Ford, Douglas Walton, Billy Bevan, Alan Hale, Brandon Hurst, J. M. Kerrigan, Paul Hanson and Nowille Clarke. Key personnel on location included chief recordist Clem Portman, production manager Wallace Fox, assistant director Argyle Nelson, film editor Paul Weatherwax and recording supervisor Clem Portman.

Denny, Karloff, Bevan, Sammy Stein, Hale, Hanson, Wallace Ford, McLaglen and Kerrigan.

McLaglen tries to buck up the crazed Karloff and youthful Walton.

Harold Wenstrom, ASC, was director of photography. His crew included operative cameramen Russell Metty, ASC, and Edward Henderson, assistant cameramen Bill Reinhold and Charles Burke, and head gaffer James Almond. Wenstrom wasn't one of the "star" cinematographers at RKO, usually being relegated to the less important productions. *The Lost Patrol* was his only opportunity to photograph a classic film.

Cliff Reid, a veteran filmmaker and valued confrere of Cooper, was listed as associate producer but actually functioned as line producer. Reid arrived by plane after production began. After a rocky beginning, he soon learned to admire Ford's tough but effective methods of getting a movie in the can in the face of formidable complications. Ford, who generally was noted for his cavalier treatment of studio supervisors, found Reid to be a valuable ally in this and later projects at RKO.

Life at Ford's oasis lacked many of the comforts of home. The sun was blinding, the heat oppressive and the frequent sandstorms were vicious. The generator for the sound equipment broke down on the first morning and a second one was trucked out from Hollywood. The new generator wasn't sufficiently strong to carry the necessary load. The temperature quickly rose to 110 degrees Fahrenheit in the shade. When the sun was high the light was too flat for effective photography and the glare made long shots impossible. A few scenes were shot MOS in the morning hours and again at mid-afternoon. Only the opening scene of Clarke

172

getting shot from the saddle – which was without dialogue – proved usable. So went the first day's work, which proved a baleful preview of things to come.

By the second day a third generator had arrived and sound recording was begun. Eight scenes of the script were filmed plus seven more which Ford improvised at the site. Several were day for night shots. At mid-morning a windstorm arose, assailing the company with sand that stabbed like needles. More importantly (by industry standards of the time), the cameras were suffering, the storm was too noisy to permit sound recording, and the palm trees were being toppled like tenpins. Production was halted while the cameras were rushed into the mosque for cleaning and inspection. The storm subsided sufficiently by 3:45 p.m. to allow photography to resume. By 5:30 the light had become so low and yellow that work was halted.

Clarke was the first actor to be sent home. Because all but one of the players appearing in the opening scenes are killed in the course of the story, the cast dwindled accordingly, each actor decamping after his "death." The third day was even more disastrous. Work began at 6:30 and ended at 9:45, when another sandstorm hit. The company stood by until 11:30 a.m., broke up, and returned in the afternoon, but the storm did not subside. Next day it was still storming, so some of the interior scenes in the mosque were made. Wallace Ford fell ill and it became necessary to shoot around him.

Hit by a sniper, Bevan falls from a tree.

The fifth day, Monday, was Labor Day. The company, which already had agreed to work Sundays, also ignored the holiday to make up for lost time. That day there was no wind, but the heat became intolerable, by noon rising to 118 in the shade. After four of the crew members who were laying dolly tracks collapsed with heat prostration, work was postponed until 3 p.m. At that time the sequence depicting the burial of the lieutenant was completed in five shots.

The temperature hit 119 on Tuesday. Reid and Stein joined Wally Ford and five others on the sick list. Several scenes, including a rigged stunt fall with a horse, were photographed. Ford and Stein returned Wednesday, at which time scenes at the waterhole were made. That night, Wally Fox sent a triumphant telegram to the studio:

SHOT OVER SEVEN MINUTES YESTERDAY STARTED SIX FORTY FIVE TODAY WALLACE FORD AND SAM STEIN RETURNED TO WORK TODAY SEVEN MEN ILL AT HOTEL PROGRESSING NICELY PART WILL RETURN TO WORK TOMORROW HAVE NEVER RECEIVED SECOND DAYS RUSHES...

The worst sandstorm yet hit at 11 a.m. on the eighth day and raged until evening. A few silent pickup shots were made in the dunes. Day nine proceeded fairly well, with occasional delays for windstorms. The 10th day brought a large storm which lasted four-and-a-half hours and cost a half day of work. Douglas Walton's post-mortem scene was completed and he departed happily for Hollywood. The 11th day was the most successful thus far: there was no wind and the temperature topped at only 108 in the shade. A large number of exteriors at the oasis were completed.

Heat, sand, wind and frustration were eroding the nerves of a mostly good-natured group of men. Arguments and fights became everyday occurrences. Wallace Ford pummeled a cook who had refused to serve a black laborer. McLaglen's sometimes nasty practical jokes soon ceased to be amusing. Some of the actors were behaving very much like the characters they were portraying, a situation the director used to advantage.

The 12th day started promisingly with a good morning's work. Heavy clouds moved in and made work impossible in the afternoon. The next five days yielded good weather and the company worked rapidly, shooting 18 to 22 setups per day. Ford helped matters along by slashing scenes from the script. Bevan finished his role and returned home on the 14th day. Hale, Hurst and Hanson finished two days later. Stein finished on the 18th

A Mirage of Women on the Blazing Sands as On They Trudged Toward Love or Death!

JOHN FORD'S PRODUCTION

"In an atmosphere electric with mystery... emotion stirring romance of men who live to die!"
—Motion Picture Herald

These men actually lived their roles in the sweltering heat of the desert. Touchingly simple, astoundingly real, it blasts the bedrock of the human heart!

with

VICTOR McLAGLEN
BORIS KARLOFF
WALLACE FORD
REGINALD DENNY

J. M. Kerrigan, Billy Bevan, Alan Hale, Brandon Hurst, Douglas Walton, Sammy Stein, Howard Wilson, Paul Hanson

RKO RADIO Picture

RADIO CITY MUSIC HALL
SHOWPLACE OF THE NATION

from the novel, "Patrol" by Philip MacDonald
MERIAN C. COOPER executive producer

morning, when oasis exteriors were being done, but cloudy skies followed by a sandstorm drove the company inside the mosque at 10:30 a.m. More clouds next morning kept them working inside for a time, but later the sky cleared and more exteriors were shot. Denny and Kerrigan finished their chores and checked out.

Good weather blessed the 20th day and ten retakes were made. Karloff's death scene was one of them, and he headed for home. Wallace Ford finally escaped the following morning after the scenes with the airplane were done. A World War I Sopwith Camel biplane, piloted by Garland Lincoln, was utilized. Aerial shots of the oasis were photographed from a Stearman camera plane. A full-scale dummy plane, built at the studio and shipped to the location, was substituted for the scenes in which the warplane burns to the ground. Twenty-two setups were made during the morning. The rest of the day was ruined by windstorms.

Of the principal actors, only McLaglen remained on September 21, the 22nd day at the oasis. Major Baker, who had been on hand throughout as technical advisor, was pressed into service to portray the leader of the Arabs gunned down by McLaglen. McLaglen at the time was gloriously drunk, which was exactly the way Ford wanted him, the better to convey the Sergeant's maniacal jubilation at his one moment of triumph. Baker was horrified when real bullets began kicking up the sand around him. The live ammunition was being fired by an expert marksman stationed off-scene while the McLaglen, bellowing and staggering, was firing blanks. Baker then changed costume to play the officer leading the detachment that arrives in the closing scenes.

Ford and a skeleton crew remained the next day to make 17 pickup shots and close down Abdullah Abbey. Their 23 days in the desert had yielded a virtually complete feature, lacking only in the niceties that would be provided in post production.

Six days later, on RKO Stage 3, Vernon Walker, ASC, staged some rear projection shots needed to complete the aircraft sequence. Weatherwax made the final cut in eight reels – 6693 feet with a running time of 74 minutes, 22 seconds. A matte painting provided the night sky and full moon needed for one scene. Titles were made at Consolidated Film Industries, musical director Max Steiner supplied some opening and closing music, and the picture was submitted to the censorship board of the Motion Picture Producers and Distributors of America.

The censors demanded the deletion of much earthy dialogue: "Bloody stinker...That praying louse... Filthy sow...Slimy, festering,

The last survivors — Karloff, McLaglen and Ford — see an airplane circling their oasis.

Karloff, completely insane, attacks McLaglen.

butchering swine...Stinking trap...Rot my bleeding eyes!...God blister their stinking souls..." Most of these lines were cut, but the MPPDA was cajoled into relaxing their rulings regarding McLaglen's reference to "them stinkin' Arabs," Denny's "the...joy of killing Arabs," Bevan's innocent prattle about his two month old son (he hasn't seen his wife in years) and his response to Denny's refusal to tell details of a shipboard orgy with naked Polynesian women ("...you didn't ought to leave us 'igh and dry like that.")

The opinion at the studio was that Ford and Cooper had brought in a picture that the public would hate.

Cooper, too, realized that the picture lacked something: the implied malevolence of the invisible enemy could not really be felt by an audience. He conferred with Max Steiner about composing a complete score, underlining every scene. As Steiner said, "He wanted me to *paint in* those Arabs with music." A prodigious worker, Steiner put in impossibly long hours on a score as elaborate as that of an opera, lavishing the same kind of detail he had applied earlier to *King Kong* and *Bird of Paradise*. Bernhard Kaun headed the team of arrangers and orchestrators needed to meet a seemingly impossible deadline. The result is a prime example of a type of film scoring that is no longer done; its detractors call it "Mickey Mousing," because it is so closely synchronized to the visuals. It's true that music of this type will not work with most pictures, but just as it had brought a greater semblance of life to the animated prehistoric animals of *King Kong*, for *The Lost Patrol* it makes the omnipresence of the enemy more palpable and renders the rough comradeship of the soldiers more touching. The augmented scoring added $10,730 overage to the cost of the picture – arguably, money well spent.

The titles are accompanied by a wild, barbaric theme which Steiner re-used a decade later for the opening of *Casablanca*. The threat of the watching Arabs is suggested by low, sinister rumblings that contrast with sprightly military themes and sentimental echoes of English songs. The howling of wind is given weird overtones by dirge-like choral music performed by thirty singers conducted by Dudley Chambers. Even dialogue is enhanced by underscoring, the most remarkable example being the rollicking tunes that accompany Reginald Denny's beautifully phrased reply to Karloff's demand to know what he believes in (Writer Nichols' lyrics aren't bad either):

"A good horse; steak and kidney pudding; a fellow named George Brown; the asinine futility of this war; being frightened; being drunk enough to be brave – and being brave enough to be drunk; the feel of the sea when you swim; the taste and strength of wine; the loveliness of women; the splendid, unspeakable joy of killing Arabs; the smell of incense – and bacon; the weight of a fist; an old pair of shoes; toothache; triumph..."

It is not surprising that several scenes of *The Lost Patrol* betray signs of haste and a paucity of cover shots. The climactic gunfight, for example, seems perfunctory, although McLaglen (inebriated or not) gives it strength. On the other hand, the scenes of the desert by day and night, with long and ominous shadows moving across the convoluted sands, are eerily dramatic. There are many admirable directorial touches, such as the cut from the opening long shot of the young officer falling from the saddle to a close shot of his horse calmly turning his head to look back.

The acting is first rate, top to bottom, with McLaglen projecting toughness and tenderness to dominate a strong cast. Karloff's portrayal still arouses controversy; he had wanted to underplay the role but Ford insisted upon a flamboyant approach to contrast Sanders' madness with the stolidity of the other soldiers. Depending upon the spectator's response, his is either the best or the worst acting in the show. There is no question about the work of Denny or Ford: both are magnificent. Billy Bevan, the Australian actor who starred in Mack Sennett silent comedies for 10 years, deserves special mention for his touching performance.

The Lost Patrol speaks eloquently of many things – of loyalty, the glory of comrades, the futili-

McLaglen, the last man, defies the enemy to come and get him.

ty of war, loneliness, intolerance, the love of home and the longing for women. Over everything hovers the spectre of fear. In the beginning it is the fear of death, but gradually the fear of being the last man alive becomes an even more terrifying burden. At the last there is vengeance, without which the picture would be intolerable. Revenge may be the most tawdry of motives in real life, but – as Shakespeare demonstrated so well – it can be devilishly satisfying in storytelling.

The advertising department, baffled at having to ballyhoo a picture with no "love interest," did its damnedest to cover the oversight. One ad shows A MIRAGE OF WOMEN ON THE BLAZING SANDS AS ON THEY TRUDGED TOWARD LOVE OR DEATH! Another pictures a beautiful blonde on the horizon with the heading, HEARTS THAT BURN FOR WOMEN ON THE BURNING SANDS OF HELL!

In spite of everything the picture was an all-around success and it continues to be shown. The currently available version is about seven minutes shorter than the original release.

Just over five years after *The Lost Patrol* RKO produced a virtual remake called *Bad Lands*.

175

BAD LANDS

WITH

ROBERT BARRAT ★ DOUGLAS WALTON
ROBERT COOTE ★ NOAH BEERY JR.
GUINN WILLIAMS ★ ANDY CLYDE ★ ADDISON
RICHARDS ★ PAUL HURST ★ FRANCIS FORD
FRANCIS McDONALD ★ DIRECTED BY LEW LANDERS
PRODUCED BY ROBERT SISK
STORY and SCREEN PLAY BY CLARENCE UPSON YOUNG

RKO RADIO PICTURE

This time there was a major change of time and place, from the Mesopotamia of 1917 to the equally hostile Arizona Territory of 1875, which was depicted correctly for once as an unknown and very savage land. In short, the 1939 version was a Western. The critics, of course, were horrified – but *Bad Lands* has strong characterizations and a rough sort of dignity lacking in many more pretentious pictures.

While Clarence Upson Young's script repeats the general outline and certain incidents of *The Lost Patrol*, the dialogue and some details are different. The patrol of sappers has become a hurriedly recruited posse riding into an Apache hideaway in search of a murderer. Apache snipers, as unseen as the Arabs that beleaguered the Britishers, are the implacable foe. The possemen are not too different an assortment than the original group, but for the inclusion of one who proves cowardly and villainous. Going into production as *The Great Seizer* –

purely a working title – and emerging as *Bad Lands,* was this new version of the *Patrol* theme.

That this film wasn't designed for the Gene Autry fans is evident in the grim theme and the casting. Again, there isn't a woman in sight, and the hero is of a rugged, mature sort rarely seen in leading roles since the days of William S. Hart. The story is one of murder, implied rape, insanity and suspense, with all but one of the mostly likable principals dying violently:

Ten men ride out into the Arizona desert in pursuit of Apache Jack (Jack Payne), a renegade half-breed who killed a Mexican girl on the eve of her marriage to Manuel Lopez (Francis MacDonald). Sheriff Bill Cummings (Robert Barrat), stern and more experienced than the others, leads the posse. The other members are the grief-crazed Lopez; Bob Mulford (Doug Walton), a young Easterner who ran away from domineering parents; Eaton (Robert Coote), a courageous rancher from England; John

176

Rayburn (Addison Richards), a world-weary cynic who came along for the excitement and seems to have a fatalistic wish to die; Henry Cluff and Charlie Garth (Andy Clyde and Francis Ford), crusty old prospectors; Billy Sweet (Guinn Williams), a good-natured cowboy; Chick Lyman (Noah Beery Jr.), a young braggart; and Curly Tom Kier (Paul Hurst), a hard-drinking frontiersman.

Jack heads into the Dragoon Mountains and some of the men are reluctant to follow because, as Lyman says, "That's where Geraldine hangs out." Garth adds that Geraldine is "sort of a pet name for Geronimo, the fightin'est Indian chief this side of Hades." The party finds the body of a murdered army scout. Their water supply is low and Cummings explains they are too far past the last waterhole to turn back. He rides ahead and finds a spring-fed pool surrounded by towering rocks. The group makes camp before nightfall. In the morning they awake to find all their horses missing, as is Eaton, who was standing watch.

Cluff and Garth find a silver cache and mine nearby. Their joyous dancing halts as a bullet, seemingly from nowhere, kills Cluff. The men commence shooting back, but Cummings stops them. Why waste bullets shooting at something you can't see? Skeletons found with the silver indicate that others have blundered into the same trap. Smoke signals above the cliffs reveal that the Apaches are plotting their doom.

At nightfall, Cummings plans to send two men to try to reach a cavalry post some 25 miles to the north. He puts Mulford on guard duty, considering him too "green" to send out. As the men play cards to determine who will go, hoofbeats are heard. One of the missing horses returns to the camp carrying Eaton's body, mutilated by torture and tied in the saddle. Garth and Sweet, "winners" of the game, steal away.

Bad Lands: *a sheriff's posse heads into danger.*

Lopez wanders into the rocks in search of his dead bride. Curly Tom tries to stop him and is seriously wounded by Lopez' knife. Lopez falls prey to sniper bullets. Rayburn brings him back to be buried with the others. At daybreak, the bodies of Garth and Sweet are found propped up in the rocks. The survivors spend the day watching in vain for a sign of the enemy. That night, while Mulford is standing guard, Lyman knocks him unconscious and steals the only horse. Curly Tom tries to stop Lyman but the effort kills him. The Apaches shoot Lyman from the saddle.

Rayburn and Cummings, their nerves worn raw, tangle in a fist fight with Rayburn getting the worst of it. Morning finds Rayburn climbing among the high rocks, determined to kill a few Apaches before he dies. He fires several rounds and shouts to Cummings that he has succeeded. A moment later, his bullet riddled body plummets down. A cavalry detachment on the desert hears the distant gunfire and sets out to investigate. Cummings and Mulford add more crosses to the graveyard and hide in a rocky buttress.

There is a stirring among the rocks as Apache Jack and a small band of Indians come forth to investigate the camp. As they prowl through the row of crosses, Cummings and Mulford gun down Jack and his friends. A wounded Apache kills Mulford before he dies. After Cummings buries his friend, his nerves finally snap. He is shouting his defiance to the watchers in the cliffs, daring them to come down and face him, when the cavalry party rides in. "Where are your men?" the leader asks.

The crazed sheriff gestures towards the graves. "There, and there – and thousands of dollars in silver!"

The main location for *Bad Lands*, representing the foothills of the Dragoons, was an outcropping of huge sandstone rocks at the edge of the Mojave Desert just north of Victorville. Early scenes of the trek across the desert were made nearby. Principal photography began under a blistering sun

Francis Ford shows gold ore to Guinn Williams, Andy Clyde and Noah Beery Jr.

on May 15 under the direction of action specialist Lew Landers, who was known as Louis Friedlander in 1935, when he directed *The Raven* at Universal. Cinematography was in the experienced hands of Frank Redman, ASC, who photographed many of the Pathé serials of the 1920s and had worked since on many RKO melodramas.

Fifty-three actors went on location: ten principals, whose salaries ranged from $500 to $1500 per week; three bit players, two stuntmen, four standins, 16 Indian extras, and 18 riding extras (soldiers).

A construction crew under unit art director Field Grey's supervision graded a road, dynamited a clearing in the rocks and created necessary paths. A 5,000 gallon cement water tank was built to become the desert pool and the water was hauled from a nearby ranch. Desert bushes and grasses were transplanted around the tank and small animals and birds soon made themselves at home there. One unwelcome denizen, a four-foot rattlesnake, almost made history. Williams shot the coiled snake at Landers' feet as he was stepping down from a rock. Location work was rigorous, but there were no serious injuries or illnesses.

Landers had a budget of $116,466. To the delight of producer Robert Sisk, he finished the film on June 8 for considerably less. The savings made practical the addition of an unusually detailed score. A famed Broadway arranger-composer, Robert Russell Bennett, was slated to write the music, but the prolific Roy Webb asked for and got the assignment. A studio official complained that Webb was holding up production when he asked for more time to polish the scoring, but Sisk intervened and the composer was allowed to devote an additional five days to the picture, including synchronizing sessions with a 28-piece orchestra. This exciting 50 minutes of music adds a great deal of dramatic emphasis and production value to the film.

Hawk-faced Robert Barrat – replacing the more popular Harry Carey, who was held up on another picture – does a fine piece of work as the hard-bitten but understanding sheriff. Addison Richards projects an appropriately enigmatic quality in the role (corresponding to that formerly portrayed by Reginald Denny) of an apparent gentleman with a mysterious past and a wish for a meaningful end to his existence. Richards was a last-minute substitute for Stanley Ridges, who had to finish a behind-schedule picture. Douglas Walton, the sensitive and idealistic youth of *The Lost Patrol*, practically repeats his role with added elements from the earlier Wallace Ford portrayal.

The underrated "Big Boy" Williams is convincing as a good-hearted cowboy. Robert Coote, most often cast as a "silly ass" Englishman, is fine as an heroic character. Andy Clyde, the beloved star of innumerable two-reel comedies, and Francis Ford, older brother of John Ford, team up well for brief comedy relief. Veterans Paul Hurst and Francis MacDonald could hardly be bettered in their characterizations. An unusual piece of casting is that of Noah Beery Jr. – whose likable features and manner bring to mind the young Will Rogers – as the one unsympathetic member of the posse.

A particularly touching moment has Barrat, while on night watch, reciting the Lord's Prayer to himself as his eyes carefully scan the cliffs. His voice is tranquil, but he chokes on the words, "Thy will be done." This eloquent scene was deleted by the English censors.

Also memorable is the last scene of the film. As the sheriff and the cavalrymen ride away,

178

the camera pans over the graves, which are marked by stick crosses bearing the gunbelts of the dead men. The camera pauses at each gunbelt just long enough for an action vignette of the owner to dissolve in and out of the scene.

A tight directorial job maintains strong suspense and gives the proper play to occasional comic notes which somewhat relieve the tragic overtones of the tale. The sun-baked, heavily textured settings, beautifully photographed, provide an ideally harsh ambience. Most shots benefit from the long shadows of early morning and late afternoon. The nocturnal scenes, done with both day-for-night and night-for-night techniques, are convincing.

Once again the advertising department, in trying to sell a picture without stars or a leading lady, spotlighted a pretty girl in some of the ads. In this instance she was Lilly Ann Starr, who agreed to let her "poses, acts, plays and appearances" before the still camera be used for the sum of $11. The trailer doesn't have a girl, but it opens with shots of the hard-riding posse, over which these lines are superimposed: THESE MEN ARE RIDING... ACROSS A FAR-FLUNG EMPIRE OF DEATH... FOR A WOMAN THEY'VE NEVER SEEN!

—George E. Turner

The Lost Patrol

An RKO Radio Picture; a John Ford production; executive producer, Merian C. Cooper; *directed by* John Ford; *associate producer,* Cliff Reid; *screen play by* Dudley Nichols; *adaptation by* Garrett Fort; *from the story "Patrol" by* Philip MacDonald; *music by* Max Steiner; *music recorded by* Murray Spivack; *photographed by* Harold Wenstrom, ASC; *art directors,* Van Nest Polglase, Sidney Ullman; *sound recording,* Clem Portman; *film editor,* Paul Weatherwax; *process photography,* Vernon L. Walker, ASC; *assistant director,* Argyle Nelson; *unit managers,* Wallace Fox, John E. Burch; *operative cameramen,* Russell Metty, Edward Henderson; *assistant cameramen,* William Reinhold, Charles Burke; *recordists,* Bailey Fesler, Dave Ridgeway, James G. Stewart; *gaffer,* James Almond; *head grip,* L. F. Anderson; *grips,* Sam Bell, C. F. Mallory, Mike Graves, R. J. Clement; *properties,*

George Gabe, Nate Berrager, R. Hoffman; *makeup artist,* Carl Axcelle; *production effects,* Harry Redmond Jr.; *wardrobe,* Sandeen; *technical advisors,* Major Frank Baker, Jamiel Hasson; *choral director,* Dudley Chambers; *musical arrangements,* Bernhard Kaun, *with* Leonid Raab, Max Rapp, Fritz Rosler, Joseph Mueller, John Britz, Andre Dore, P. F. Goldenson; *pilot,* Garland Lincoln; RCA *recording; Running time, 74 minutes. Released February 16, 1934.*

Sergeant, Victor McLaglen; *Sanders,* Boris Karloff; *Morelli,* Wallace Ford; *Brown,* Reginald Denny; *Quincannon,* J. M. Kerrigan; *Hale,* Billy Bevan; *Cook,* Alan Hale; *Bell,* Brandon Hurst; *Pearson,* Douglas Walton; *Abelson,* Sammy Stein; *Mackay,* Paul Hanson; *Aviator,* Howard Wilson; *Lt. Hawkins,* Nowille Clarke; *Officer, Arab,* Major Frank Baker.

Foreword: Mesopotamia – 1917. While the World War raged in Europe, British troops were fighting in a far corner of the world. Small solitary patrols moved over the vast Mesopotamian desert, that seemed on fire with the sun. The molten sky gloated over them. The endless desert wore the blank look of death. Yet these men marched on without a murmur, fighting an unseen Arab enemy who always struck in the dark – like a relentless ghost.

Bad Lands

An RKO Radio picture; produced by Robert Sisk; *directed by* Lew Landers; *executive producer,* Lee Marcus; *story and screen play by* Clarence Upson Young; *director of photography,* Frank Redman, ASC; *music by* Roy Webb; *art director,* Van Nest Polglase; *associate art director,* Field Gray; *film editor,* George Hively; *sound recording,* Earl A. Wolcott; *assistant director,* Sam Ruman; *continuity writer,* John Twist; *special effects,* Manion Zamora; *properties,* Greg McGonigal, Max Henry; *operative cameraman,* Charles Burke; *assistant cameramen,* Ledge Haddow, Jack Kenny; *makeup artist,* Dan Burns; *still photographer,* Oliver Sigurdson; RCA *recording; running time, 70 minutes. Released August 11, 1939.*

Sheriff Bill Cummings, Robert Barrat; *Mulford,* Douglas Walton; *Eaton,* Robert Coote; *Sweet,* Guinn "Big Boy" Williams; *Cluff,* Andy Clyde; *Lyman,* Noah Beery Jr.; *Rayburn,* Addison Richards; *Curly Tom,* Paul Hurst; *Garth,* Francis Ford; *Lopez,* Francis MacDonald; *Apache Jack,* Jack Payne; *Lieutenant,* Carlyle Moore; *Sergeant,* Walter Miller; *Indians,* Frank Little Pine, William Wilkerson; *Stunts,* Lee Allen, Doc Van Horn; *Standins,* John Huettner, John Campbell, Max Rose, Ivan Deputy.

Foreword: Arizona – 1875. As civilization moved westward, motley bands of horsemen sometimes rode across the Bad Lands of Arizona bent upon a dangerous business... Manhunters... recruited hastily in the cause of frontier justice.

Doug Walton and Robert Barrat are the last men alive in Bad Lands.

15

Enigma of *The Black Cat*

"Even the phone is dead." – Hjalmar Poelzig

It's been said that nobody ever made films better or faster for less money than Edgar G. Ulmer. The visual schemes he wrenched out of small sums and a few sets are remarkable, and *The Black Cat* (1934) is a testament to his modus operandi. Shot in 19 days at a cost of $95,745 (which included overhead and retakes), Ulmer churned out one of the most disturbing films of the decade.

In its twisted sexual relationships that shrewdly circumvented the Production Code, in its arch teaming of Boris Karloff and Bela Lugosi, and its obsession with set design and classical music, *The Black Cat* maintains its own following, and its patina resists critical erosion. Few Thirties films could boast a more diabolical fusion of sight and sound than Karloff as Hjalmar Poelzig entering a doorway with a fully-orchestrated blast of Liszt's *Piano Sonata in B Minor*, despite the genre's preoccupation with vampires and monsters. Unique was Ulmer's oddball marriage of German expressionism and Ibsenesque tragedy, a style almost telegraphing that of Ingmar Bergman.

Of the 13 horror films made at Universal in the Thirties only *The Black Cat* has remained enigmatic, its true meaning elusive. The storyline is confusing, and although written in haste, much of its haziness stemmed from a frantic recutting period and the addition of unscripted scenes required to preserve continuity. It is no wonder, then, why historians have been bewildered by it, while others seeking to wrest logic from its plot flounder in its dark corners.

The film is steeped in trauma and incongruity – a Bauhaus mansion towering over a nameless graveyard, a psychiatrist with "an all-consuming horror of cats," a basement of crystal coffins in which young blonde women hang by their hair. The aberrations woven into the story read like a Krafft-Ebbing menu: incest (sort of), necrophilia, pedophilia, sadism, murder, and Satanism to boot. Consider the difficulties in 1934 in bringing to the screen an offbeat (and ultimately sick) tale of an Austrian general who leaves his best friend to die during a bloody siege, abducts the friend's wife and daughter, murders/embalms the wife and marries the daughter, reigns over a devil cult in his basement, kills the daughter, and gets skinned alive by his adversary before being dynamited to death.

This was pretty wild stuff for the Thirties! That the film contains personal information about its director seems even more disturbing, and it is, in an odd way, autobiographical. Specific images are keyed not only to European films whose styles Ulmer revered and claimed to have worked on, but to his morbid fantasies and troubled childhood.

Stripped of its "supernatural baloney," *The Black Cat* is really a macabre study of sexual repression and Ulmer's personal equation of fear with religion. It *was* the first American psychological horror film. So dark are its Freudian twists, the director seemed uncomfortable about it later in life. When asked in 1965 of his views on eroticism in

181

"'...An intense and all-consuming horror of cats." —Bela Lugosi as Werdegast.

fantastic films, he replied furtively: "It's perhaps the hardest thing to handle because one can easily fall into sexual aberrations. I am a little afraid to go in that direction because it can easily become vulgar."

Typically, *The Black Cat* had it share of shelved treatments. Poe's original horror tale was sitting on story editor Richard Schayer's desk early in 1932 for consideration. Schayer named the anonymous first-person narrator "Edgar Doe" as a vehicle for Boris Karloff. But the story of an alcoholic brute walling his wife and cat up in a cellar seemed too trite and unsavory for a feature. On December 19, 1932 – three days before the release of *The Mummy* – Stanley Bergerman, an in-law of production head Carl "Junior" Laemmle, submitted an eleven-page treatment called *The Brain Never Dies* which he wrote with Jack Cunningham. The concoction had a mad scientist performing brain transplants in the House of Usher, a banal fusion of Poe and Frankenstein. As the old house crumbles to ruins, the surgeon's cat (whose skull houses half a human brain) pushes him into the falling debris. The brain may never die, but Bergerman's story did. Quickly.

With the coming of the new year, *The Black Cat* clawed its way out of the dead file. On January 19, 1933, contract writer Tom Kilpatrick joined forces with producer-writer Dale Van Every (the team responsible for *Dr. Cyclops* at Paramount) and contrived a new version, melding the sadism of Poe with elements derived from *Dracula, The Old Dark House,* even *The Mummy* to some extent. Working from Van Every's 28-page original, Kilpatrick completed a first draft of 68 pages on February 15, 1933. Set in the Carpathian Mountains, the story concerned an unctuous count named Brandos and his lecherous son Fejos living in a decadent, cat-strewn castle, and the entrapment of a young couple. The

girl is an ailurophobe (fear of cats), whom Brandos tries to drive insane by inflicting upon her gruesome nocturnal tortures. Herein lies the harebrained plot – Fejos is insane, and to perpetuate the family, Brandos must mate his son with an insane woman. In a *Pit and the Pendulum*-type ending, the boyfriend is shackled to a "torture rack" above a fiery pit. Brandos is devoured by snarling canines and Fejos falls into the inferno. Delirious and parched, the couple escapes.

Again, the project was to star Karloff, and German director E.A. Dupont was tentatively scheduled to direct after his two Karloff specials, *Bluebeard* and *The Wizard,* fell by the wayside. Then, financially troubled, Universal ordered a shutdown until April 1, 1933, and Karloff flew to England on loan to make *The Ghoul.* Consequently, Kilpatrick's draft was never scripted, and *The Black Cat* remained on a slab in the Universal morgue.

Enter Edgar Ulmer. "He had a dark side to his character that was unbelievable," revealed his widow, Shirley Ulmer. "It took me a year or two to dig under and find out the 'why' of it. You couldn't use the word 'crazy' in his presence; it would petrify him. Like Kafka, he always worked in shadows."

A designer for Max Reinhardt at age 19, a set builder on scores of German films in the Twenties and many at Universal (including *The Phantom of the Opera*), and an assistant art director on all of Murnau's American films, Ulmer was awarded his first writing job by Junior Laemmle in December 1933 – *Love Life of a Crooner,* with Edward Buzzell set to direct. It wasn't his cup of tea, but he started on the scenerio. When *Crooner* evaporated, Ulmer began building the sets for Frank Borzage's *Little Man, What Now?*

Festering in his mind, however, was a yen to design and direct a horror film in the style of *Caligari,* which would pair Karloff and Lugosi for the first time. The notion of teaming them was not new – Universal had toyed with it in 1931 (for *The Suicide Club*) and in 1933 (for *The Return of Frankenstein*). Ulmer's idea fired Junior's enthusiasm. Produced quickly, it could have a significant effect on the studio's second quarter. Ulmer figured on a mere $9000 for his exotic set plans, which he worked out with chief art director Danny Hall, and a cast tab of $17,350 (which included fees for Karloff and Lugosi). Studio manager Martin Murphy approved an estimated picture cost of $91,125. Amazed, Junior gave Ulmer free rein to proceed with his own scenario, on the condition that he retain Poe's title for commercial reasons. That suited Edgar Ulmer just fine. He had his own ideas.

The seed of Ulmer's *The Black Cat* actually germinated during his apprenticeship on *The Golem* in 1920, based on a grisly anecdote told to him by *Golem* author Gustav Meyerinck, about the French fortress Doumont which had been shelled by the Germans, and a sinister commander who returned to the scene of his crime. In the film, Doumont became Fort Marmaros, and the commander became Hjalmar Poelzig, warlock and master builder. The surname, that of *The Golem's* designer Hans Poelzig, denoted either an artistic nod or a black memory. "Hjalmar," clearly Scandinavian and used by Ibsen in *The Wild Duck,* probably pointed to playwright Hjalmar Bergman, who, like Ulmer, snubbed Christian orthodoxy. The idea of Satanism was ostensibly inspired by the furor in 1933 over occultist Alesteir Crowley. The character also personified Ulmer's hostility toward Fritz Lang, whom he often referred to as a sadist. Poelzig's adversary, Vitus Werdegast, a psychiatrist with hysterical cat phobia, was the director's sly poke at *Caligari,* the title character being the head of an insane asylum who is put away in a straight jacket. And, in the relationship between Werdegast and Poelzig, there seems to be a covert translation of the fatality of Faust's submission to Mephistopheles. Ulmer finished his draft of *The Black Cat* on February 6, 1934.

For his scriptwriter, he chose Peter Ruric. "He was a very young man who had come out of New York when I met him," said Ulmer. "A very intelligent boy who should have been a great playwright but got lost." Ruric in truth was a rather obscure literary figure with no known ties to playwriting or theater. Under the pseudonym of "Paul Cain," he wrote mystery stories for *Black Mask* magazine in the Thirties and was more of a prefiguration of Mickey Spillane than a budding Arthur Miller. In 1933, he mulled around Hollywood and landed a writing job for Paramount's *The Gambling Ship,* which The New York *Times* called "a stale and profitless narrative."

Ruric's influence on Ulmer's story is an unknown quantity. Being a mystery writer, he may have brought in more of the occult. Basically what he did was flesh out Ulmer's undetailed passages and string along dialogue derived from the narrative. He must be credited, though, with whipping up a complete script of 333 scenes on a two-week deadline, which he handed in on February 19, 1934.

Edgar Ulmer and Lugosi during the production of The Black Cat

(The two mysteries mentioned in the final scene – *The 69th Crime* and *The Purple Spot* – may have been actual titles penned by Ruric. It is no coincidence that the husband in the film is named Peter, who at one point describes himself as "one of the greatest writers of unimportant books.")

Ulmer's only demand of Junior Laemmle was that Karloff play Poelzig. Casting Karloff in another horror film took a bit of persuasion, though, as he was determined to play no more monsters, but he was intrigued by the wardrobe Ulmer had designed for him and felt he could project an "out of this world appearance."

His makeup in *The Black Cat,* however subtle, is quite odd. Jack Pierce created a headpiece featuring deep V-shaped sidewalls and a triangular widow's peak blending him into the geometric atmosphere. White pancake and lip rouge finished the effect. It could be that Ulmer patterned the Poelzig head after a self portrait of German expressionist painter Max Beckmann, who fit into Ulmer's stable of pop-culture influences. The canvas *(Self Portrait in a Red Scarf)* shows Beckmann with an alarming resemblance to Karloff as Poelzig. The end result of Pierce's labors suggests a translation of the Beckmann head into something totally evil – still human, but teetering on the zoomorphic.

For Lugosi, the transition to straighter roles was rough. His mere presence smacked of Dracula, an image he found inescapable. While he was boning up for a Broadway play, Universal allegedly offered him a three-picture deal, to be kicked off by *The Black Cat.*

Once again Lugosi shifted gears. After appearing at the Hungarian Actors Ball in New York on February 10, he returned to his old haunt where

Boris Karloff as Poelzig with Lucille Lund as Karen in a scene indicative of the sensual texture of the film.

the Transylvanian setpieces were still standing. Lugosi, as he later said in an interview, persuaded Ulmer that he could play "a romantic or at least a benign role." Though far from romantic and not exactly benign, "Vitus Werdegast" became the finest excuse for his shortlived reputation as the male Garbo. He drenched the role with passion, while Karloff merely walked through the film. That Lugosi had to accept the part for a weekly paycheck of $1000 against Karloff's flat rate of $7500 must have irked him no end.

To play the female parts, the studio picked two "WAMPAS Baby Stars" of 1934. This was a title given to promising starlets by the Western Association of Motion Picture Advertisers from 1922-34. Jacqueline Wells was chosen to play Joan, named after Ulmer's first wife Joan Warner. She had just played the sister in Paramount's *Alice in Wonderland* and shuttled over to Universal as a freelancer. Lucille Lund, whom Ulmer trussed up in a blonde Rapunzel wig, had already appeared in two Universal releases, *Saturdays Millions* and *Pirate Treasure*. On hand was stock hero David Manners. Harry Cording, Werdegast's deadpan manservant, was spotted by Ulmer in *The Patriot* with Emil Jannings.

Ulmer's desire to form a stock company of European emigrés, *a la* Ingmar Bergman, as backup talent for pictures went unrealized. But as a result, several class names popped up in *The Black Cat* in the most peculiar roles. Egon Brecher, the Czech actor hailed throughout Europe for his performances in *The Master Builder* under Eva Le Galliene, became Poelzig's majordomo. Anna Duncan, the stepdaughter of Isadora Duncan and an acclaimed dancer whom The New York *Times* called "the very embodiment of grace," played the sinister servant. And Herman Bing, Murnau's assistant director on *Sunrise,* was cast as a maitre d' only to become a casualty of the cutting room.

The final script was bound on February 27, 1934. Shooting began the next day! Earlier, Ruric had scripted an opulent Viennese cathedral wedding for Peter and Joan, based on a prologue in Ulmer's draft. Shots suggesting Joan's virginity ("camera tilts up to face of Madonna, dissolve to face of Joan") lead to hurried farewells as they board the train, and the kiss of a "heavily upholstered aunt" was to dissolve to the first puff of steam. Ulmer discarded the sequence, paring the script down to 320 scenes. Tom Kilpatrick wrote the continuity sheets, and assistant script girl Shirley Kassel tried to keep things in line. A year later, she and Ulmer were married.

That *The Black Cat* was made at all was a fluke. Carl Laemmle Sr., who would never have allowed the making of a film as offbeat as this, flew to Germany on an extended vacation. On February 15, Junior Laemmle left for New York, having been blasted in court on charges of salary gouging, leaving E.M. Asher as "production supervisor." That meant no supervision at all. For this, Asher pulled in $2000, while Ulmer plugged away for $150 a week.

The cinematography was the work of John Mescall, ASC, a brilliant artist whose career was ultimately defeated by alcoholism. Mescall's work give *The Black Cat* much of its unique imagery, notably in the play of lights and effective shifts of focus.

The film opens with the *Orient Express* chugging into a Budapest depot. On board are newlyweds Joan and Peter Alison, bound for a honeymoon resort near Vizhegrad. They exchange endearments and muse over the wedding luncheon.

Even before this happens, the negative was cut severely, though to no ill effect. The film actually began at the Czech border enroute to Bratislava. Excised were 23 scenes of the maitre d' (Bing) trying to overwhelm the Alisons with his charm and his Chateaubriand. Oddly, the first scenes in the release print – bakers loading bread into the dining car in Budapest – were not scripted, even though the depot set had been built specifically for *The Black Cat.*

Lugosi makes an impressive entrance, the result of a mixup in the seating arrangement. As Werdegast, he is svelte and aristocratic. Ulmer described him as "a man with an abstract tenderness and an infinitely wistful smile." Yet he is ominous, and he ushers in an air of doom. He tells the couple that he had been in a Russian prison camp, that he has come to visit "an old friend." Then his face grows taut and his eyes glaze. "After 15 years – *I* have returned." Ulmer wanted him to punctuate this line by the crash of his fist on the window sill, but Lugosi's delivery was so intense, the director threw the idea out. By the time the night rain pelts the window, Werdegast has become the incarnation of a dark memory, and the train itself has taken a sinister quality.

The scene initiates the film's leaning on sexually repressed situations. Werdegast stares at Joan, who reminds him of his lost wife. He touches her hair while she sleeps, and the husband is both annoyed and mesmerized by the triangle. The honeymoon is never consummated. By the middle of the film, Joan has become the sexual apex for three men, each of whom is forced to repress his desires. And though the film's development of this is *itself* repressed, the undercurrent of sexuality is always there.

When they leave the train, Werdegast's servant, played by Cording, joins them ("Thamal," wrote Ulmer, "is an enormous Tibetan, slant-eyed, with the cold, impassive face of an evil Buddha") and they all enter a rickety bus. Werdegast instructs the driver to take him to "Engineer Poelzig's house" and to continue on with the Alisons. After the driver (whom Ulmer made up to resemble Emil Jannings in *The Last Laugh)* exults over "Marmaros, the greatest graveyard in the world," where Poelzig has built his mansion, the bus skids into a ravine. The driver

Lugosi, Karloff, and Lund in the chart room.

is killed, and the girl is rendered unconscious. When Werdegast commands Thamal to pick up Joan, the idea penned by Ulmer that he carry her as though she were a ''sacrificial offering to a savage god'' does not quite click, but the intention here was to foreshadow just that – her deliverance to Satan in the person of Poelzig. Through the rain can be seen the house, an unsettling apparition.

The first glimpse of the living room, a sweeping panning shot as the house lights snap on in sympathy with the camera movement, is visually poetic. This seems strange from a director who claimed so much allegiance to Caligarism, for these sets are the very antithesis of *Caligari*. Bright, geometric and clean, the set is surprisingly simple – a backlit cyclorama, a large framework of Bauhaus squares, and a curved staircase – Ulmer's $3,700 marvel. From here on, composition is obsessive. The dramatic emphasis on design is too alien to induce feelings of comfort in ''normal'' people, and everything seems anachronistic. ''When one sees *The Black Cat* today,'' Ulmer reflected, ''one realizes that the sets could have been conceived by Poelzig twenty years after the film was made.'' Digital clocks, glass tables, and breuer chairs dot the futuristic fort. As Werdegast describes it, ''The masterpiece of construction, built upon the ruins of the masterpiece of destruction.''

Even in the simple montage that precedes Karloff's first entrance, Ulmer and Mescall demonstrate an unusual sense of buildup with camera angles and daring transitions. Cinematically, they broke the rules. In low angle shots of the guest bedroom, a partial ceiling built in perspective caps the frame oppressively, dissolves are made from extreme closeups to three-shots without denoting any passage of time, and the lovers are modeled in such a way as to detach them from the menace lurking in the hallway. Finally, when a harp glissando rips through the quietude and the camera dollies in on Karloff's ghostly face, the effect is startling.

Ironically, the only surviving sequence that tries to put *The Black Cat's* supernaturalism on film becomes muddled. While making small talk in the atelier, Poelzig turns on an art deco radio which sneaks Schubert's *Unfinished Symphony* onto the soundtrack. The cat comes by, Werdegast shrinks back, mortified, throws a knife and kills it. Suddenly Joan enters the frame and slinks toward her husband with feline seductiveness. Werdegast writes it off as an effect of the narcotic he had administered, suggesting that she has become ''mediumistic, a vehicle for all the intangible forces around her.'' ''Sounds like a lot of supernatural baloney to me,'' says the husband. To which Lugosi counters with sinister precision: ''Supernatural, perhaps. *Baloney*, perhaps not. There are many things under the sun.''

Abstract undertones made for complications. When Ulmer first conceived this episode, he wrote: ''The seed and spirit of all evil, symbolized by the Black Cat, passes from the cat to her, and she in turn becomes the living incarnation of evil itself.'' The idea was further translated into the script, but inhibited staging and lack of close-ups (perhaps resulting from the rushed shooting schedule) failed to capture it: ''The body of the cat is suggested on the floor. Joan appears above it, as though she had materialized out of thin air. She will not be dissolved in; rather her appearance will be accomplished with lighting to suggest materialization. Her eyes close and a faint tremor disturbs her body, growing to a violent shudder as the music reaches its apex. By means of makeup and lighting, her chaste beauty takes on a sensual, faintly animalistic contour.'' (Eight years later, this subtle lighting effect *was* achieved in *The Cat People*, when Simone Simon proceeds to attack her psychiatrist.)

Beneath the clarity of Poelzig's house lies its demonic inversion – a dark cellar, vestiges of an artillery complex, and a gallery of embalmed women mounted upright in crystal coffins, the most prominent corpse being that of Werdegast's wife! Here in this Stygian netherworld he prowls at night, a black cat cradled under his arm, casing his radiant mummies one by one.

(Remarkably, this haunting interlude wasn't even scripted. It was filmed during the retake period. The virgin footage consisted of Karloff's feet pacing the hallway, which dissolved to

After the bus wreck, Werdegast and Peter Alison (David Manners) decide to take the unconscious Joan (Jacqueline Wells) to Poelzig's mansion.

a clock near the husband's bed. For the new scene, a match dissolve was made from his feet in the hallway to his feet traversing the basement, and six girls wearing blonde wigs were paid $12 each to stand motionless in glass booths.)

This is Hjalmar Poelzig's poisoned universe. As Ulmer wrote, "The idea, to be conveyed as abstractly as possible, is that Poelzig, as the earthly incarnation of Satan, takes, at the climax of the ritual, the sacrificial virgin as his bride" – meaning, morbidly, that he rapes and murders them at the altar, while others look on.

The film's finest moments occur when Poelzig leads Werdegast into the basement, a grand tour of what both men once knew as Fort Marmarmos. A bleak piece of dialogue that Ulmer wrote on the set ("I can still sense death in the air") defines the atmosphere, and John Mescall's buoyant camera glides through the gun turrets like a phantom eye.

Even in this mordant milieu, Ulmer's set design is as powerful and surreal as a Magritte canvas. An illuminated panel of frosted glass (used for wartime trajectory equations) looms over Lugosi like a large sheet of graph paper, while Karloff, at screen right, flicks on a light switch revealing the body of Karen Werdegast. The staging here is shrewd and deliberate – Werdegast is manipulated against the graph, as though his movements had been calculated by Poelzig along its coordinates.

"You see, Vitus? I have cared for her tenderly and well. You will find her almost as beautiful as when you last saw her." Werdegast gapes in horror at the mounted corpse. Poelzig says that she died after the war, "of pneumonia," but a feline blink signals his deception. "And the child?" asks Werdegast. "Dead!" Then, looking at his masterwork, Poelzig's eyes mist. "Is she not beautiful? I wanted to have her beauty – always." Grief turns to fury and the doctor draws a Luger. As originally written he cries out: "Lies. You killed her *to save her youth and beauty for your own monstrous end!* You killed her as I'm about to kill you!" The black cat jumps in and Werdegast collapses against the glass.

Their retreat from the basement is a masterwork of camera movement and shadow. With the creak of a door, Lugosi's underlit face slowly pans to the hand of the dead woman, which dissolves to the subjective camera as the two ascend a spiral staircase. In a poignant monologue tying these shots together, Karloff speaks of them as being living ghosts of the war, then returns to his bed where the young Karen Werdegast lies. He tells her that she is the core and meaning of his life, and reads a book describing *The Rites of Lucifer* by moonlight. Origi-

Thamal (Harry Cording) looms in the background as Peter and Werdegast attend to Joan upon their arrival at the mansion.

nally the book was to have been Ibsen's play *When We Dead Awaken,* the story of a sculptor who made a marble statue in the image of his lover, which Ulmer had planned to use as a metaphor for the two Karens. The poetic idea was changed during the filming.

Unfortunately, the maturity of these moments is undermined by the confusion of the remaining reels. Poelzig decides to use Joan as a sacrifice in the "Black Mass" and challenges Werdegast to a chess match over her destiny. Thamal draws a knife, but Werdegast instructs him to "obey Poelzig" until he is told otherwise. Sensing danger, the husband tells Poelzig that he and Joan want to leave, but "the car is out of commission" and "even the phone is dead." Werdegast is checkmated, and Peter during an escape attempt is throttled and battered by Thamal, who deposits him in the cellar and carries the fainted Joan to her room. Triumphant, Poelzig strides over to a terrace organ and vents his emotions by playing a Bach toccata.

Werdegast warns Joan that she is supposed to play "an important part" in the ritual. When he leaves her room, Poelzig is waiting at the bottom of the staircase and takes the key from Werdegast. Then Poelzig goes upstairs and discovers that, despite his order for her to stay secluded, Karen has entered Joan's room through the connecting door. With murderous eyes, he corners Karen off camera and murders her. Joan faints, and Poelzig stares madly at "the dark of the moon" while his servants "prepare things" for the cultists.

All enter the basement chapel. Werdegast is there, too, because Poelzig has suggested that "the ceremony will interest him." Joan is abducted and lashed to an inverted cross. When the organist stops, Poelzig chants a Latin litany over her body.

Suddenly, a female cultist screams and faints, interrupting the ceremony. Werdegast seizes his advantage, and he and Thamal release Joan. When Werdegast tries to drag Joan to an exit, she reveals that his daughter is still alive and has in fact become Poelzig's wife. Horrified, he runs into the fort's control chamber (now the "embalming room") and screams as he sees Karen lying dead under a sheet.

Poelzig pounces on Werdegast, but Thamal (mortally wounded by the majordomo) overpowers him and ties him down to an embalming rack. With eyes glazed, Werdegast selects a knife, rips off Poelzig's shirt, and rants the following (cited here the way Ulmer wrote it): "Did you ever see an animal skinned, Hjalmar? That's what I'm going to do to you – tear the *stinking, putrid skin* from your body, slowly – bit by bit!"

Meanwhile the husband has escaped, and when he thinks that Werdegast is hurting Joan, he shoots him through the door's grille. Dying, Werdegast tells them to go, and pulls "the red switch" which ignites the fort's old dynamite traps. As the place explodes, the couple escapes – a finale that James Whale would lift one year later for *The Bride of Frankenstein*.

Why, then, is the best half of *The Black Cat* so confusing? So many story points seem to make little or no sense. Why does Poelzig murder Karen if she is "the core and meaning of his life?" Why does Werdegast's servant practically crush the husband's skull in, an act too brutal to fit in with the charade of his instructed allegiance to Poelzig? And why is Poelzig not surprised in the least when this happens?

Most of this was due to the change made in Werdegast *after* the fifteen-day shoot was com-

pleted. Throughout the film, Lugosi plays an embittered soul bent on retribution, with only a protective interest in Joan. But, as *originally conceived*, Werdegast's retreat from the basement triggers his own malignancy. Traumatized by the sight of his dead wife, and contaminated by the "intangible forces" he described earlier, he undergoes a transformation (an increase in libido and moral decay), paving the way for his eventual madness.

The Black Cat's script shaped Werdegast in this manner, and the film was actually shot according to plan! In the original footage, he was no longer the brooding altruist – his only goal was the calculated murder of Poelzig and the abduction of Joan for himself. Werdegast's presence at the ceremony was not merely as a casual observer – he had been playing host to the cultists arriving in the living room.

By the time editor Ray Curtiss assembled the rough cut, drastic changes were afoot. Some of it was prompted by the discontent on the part of Lugosi, who had been promised a "benign" role. But most of the heat came from the front office. The last three reels were saturated with highly suggestive leers ping-ponged by Karloff and Lugosi over the girl. When more erotic ideas were conveyed with shadows, the shots seemed uninterpretable. As far as the 1934 Production Code was concerned, the film was flirting with death.

Moreover, no mention had been made of the still-operative dynamite charges, throwing the finale into a quandary. Scenes of Karen raving demonically were jarring and obtrusive, and those of the arriving cultists were labored and unnecessary. The pivotal chess game carried no apparent significance. And with no music score, most of Karloff's entrances seemed incoherent.

The main problem, though, was Werdegast. Two lunatics in one film were hard to take, and the lack of a sympathetic character alienated the audience. The decision was made to pull *all* scenes depicting Werdegast's lechery and shoot new ones, reshaping him as a "good guy." After Karloff and Lugosi leave the basement together, we are really dealing with two versions of the same film!

Another $6,500 was allocated for retakes and added scenes. Cast and crew gathered for two days and two nights, starting on Sunday, March 25

Egon Brecher as the majordomo and Wells as Joan.

and ending March 28. Lugosi and Lund remained for three and one-half days, Wells and Cording for two and one-half days, David Manners stayed on for two, and Egon Brecher for one. The additional actors' fees only amounted to $1400, and Karloff appeared gratis for the revised chess game and the prowl in the morgue, since he had already agreed to a flat rate. Ulmer took no extra salary. (Though it is unlikely that the virgin footage of *The Black Cat* still exists, a fairly accurate reconstruction can be made by comparing the final script with the retake schedule, the release print, and production stills which show the staging mentioned in the script.)

The first added scene was that of Werdegast instructing Thamal to obey Poelzig. In the original scheme, Werdegast used his servant to counter interference with his plan to possess Joan. That meant the husband. In the "new" version, he wants the newlyweds released. In order to justify a salvaged scene in which Thamal thwarts Peter's escape attempt by knocking him unconscious, a token scene was devised which "absolved" Werdegast of his iniquity. "Not yet, Thamal," he says. "Put that (knife) away. We will bide our time; other lives are at stake. And this place is so undermined with dynamite, the slightest mistake would cause the destruction of all. Until I tell you otherwise, you are *his* servant, not mine."

Unfortunately the patchwork does not sit well with Thamal's brutality, who (as scripted) "very deliberatly lifts one great fist and smashes it down with pile driver force on Peter's head," throwing the new slant on Werdegast's benevolence out of whack. Nor does it explain Poelzig's nonchalance to this maneuver – all of which was in keeping with the original conspiracy against the Alisons!

Other sequences merely required the pruning away of Lugosi leering at Joan and retaining a closeup of Karloff doing the same. The scene of Werdegast changing Joan's dressing in her bedroom had the two men ogling over her body, and an entire breakfast scene had to be deleted when, in a flurry of rapidfire cuts, even the majordomo threw a Machiavellian smirk her way.

In the orginal footage, the chess match started casually. "We imply that Joan's fate does *not* revolve upon the chess game," wrote Ulmer. "Rather, that it is a symbol of a deeper game – the game of life and death." Little of this, however, came across on film. The game extended into the evening and ended in a stalemate. "We are evenly matched, Vitus. The advantage moves back and forth like a pendulum!" At that point, Poelzig strode to the terrace and stared at the moon, a moody process

shot that was later transposed to bridge Karen's murder with the assemblage of the cultists.

To spike the chess game with conflict, and to spell out Werdegast's "new" intentions, a clever chunk of dialogue was contrived for Karloff and Lugosi, in an added scene that turned the tide of the film and saved it from total confusion:

WERDEGAST: Don't pretend, Hjalmar. There was nothing spiritual in your eyes when you looked at that girl. You plan to keep her here!
POELZIG: Perhaps. (fondling the Queen's breasts)
WERDEGAST: I intend to let her go!
POELZIG: Is that a challenge, Vitus?
WERDEGAST: Yes, if you dare fight it out alone!
POELZIG: Do you dare play chess with me for her?
WERDEGAST: Yes, I will even play you chess for her – provided if I win, they are free to go.
POELZIG: You won't win, Vitus.

He doesn't. The checkmate is strategically sutured in just before the escaping husband gets throttled by Thamal. Lugosi no longer "smiles obliquely" when this happens. In his retakes, he looks mournful.

The bedroom scene in which Werdegast warns Joan that "We're all in danger" had to be pruned and parts reshot. Originally, Joan was standing with her back against the wall when he entered. "We don't see Joan at first," wrote Ulmer. "The camera sweeps to a square blank of wall beyond the bed. There she stands, the back of her hand to her mouth. She is the *bas-relief* of fear." Lugosi was diabolical:

189

WERDEGAST: You are very beautiful!

JOAN: (Darting backward) Where is Peter? What have they done to him?

WERDEGAST: That is hard to say! Herr Poelzig has strange and effective ways of disposing of people who get in his way!

JOAN: Your servant struck him down. You are his accomplice!

At that point, he starts making a weird sexual advance. "Werdegast sinks to one knee, the shadow of his body falls over her, and his hand flattens against the wall above her shoulder. His dark mass moves across the lens. But as the organ music crashes to a halt, Werdegast's body moves out swiftly." The scene was clipped and replaced with Lugosi telling her to "be brave, it's your only chance."

To further convey the supernatural, Ulmer conceived Karen at first as zoomorphic, a product of Poelzig's satanic power of mutation. According to Shirley Ulmer, "Edgar was going to have Lucille Lund made up to look like a beautiful Siamese cat. He wanted to demonstrate the feline qualities she was supposed to suggest. She was no longer 'a human being.' This would have upset Lugosi quite a bit! But it was an abnormality that couldn't be shown; it was to have been something that Karloff imposed on her along the lines of *Rosemary's Baby*. He had to throw the idea out."

Ulmer and Ruric took Karen further into the demonic when she meets Joan in the adjoining bedroom. Her severed lines appear in italics.

KAREN: *You are new here, aren't you?*

JOAN: *What do you mean?*

KAREN: *I have not been out of this house since I was brought here nine years ago. In that time, many women, young and beautiful like you, have come.*

JOAN: Who are you?

KAREN: I am Karen – Madame Poelzig.

JOAN: And he married you? You are his wife? (Sound of door chimes downstairs) *What's that?*

KAREN: (An evil look takes hold of her, she laughs suddenly) *Your wedding bells, my dear!* (Camera moves to closeup) *Another bride for the devil! Another offering to the gods for my master!* (Hysterically) *Prepare!*

The scene was clipped before the doorbell rang and new dialogue was written for Wells and Lund, recalling the *angst* of an old horror story with which Ulmer had taunted his infant sister Elly –

Werdegast and Poelzig engage in a chess game to decide Joan's fate.

that Karen's father "has come for her," that "He's here in this very house!" Then Poelzig enters, corners Karen with a cat under his arm, and somehow murders her.

Why does this happen? There is no answer – the character and the act are illogical. Only a brief passage in Ulmer's draft tried to explain it, in the scene where Karen and Poelzig lie in bed: "In his face is the passionate adoration he feels for her – an adoration so macabre, so intense, as to suggest the *sadism* it will grow into under pressure."

Odder still was Ulmer's scripted concept of the cultists. In the deleted footage, Lugosi hosted their entrance while Karloff donned his ceremonial robe. With the exception of a dwarf, there was nothing aberrant about their appearance. But as Ulmer envisioned them, "They are to be as aberrant as possible. A stable of misfits, members of the decadent aristocracy of the countryside." The director based the idea on the woodcuts of Aubrey Beardsley, whose style melded the macabre and the erotic. He further wrote, "They are all dressed in keeping with their twisted natures, and give the impression they have been made of old pieces of celluloid, wire, *papier maché*, flesh and red plush." Only one character from Ulmer's draft was not written into the script – *Frau Goering*, "to be played by a man, the dark fuzz on her lip suggesting Hitler's moustache."

Neatly edited down to 3½ minutes, what remains of the ceremony is haunting. Mock-religious images and the inversion of natural order taint the subterranean landscape. Poelzig ascends the altar, his face buried in his robe, hands crossed. On

190

cue, women remove their cowls and the *men* follow suit, an impudent poke at religious orthodoxy. Only here does the film afford cameraman John Mescall the sweeping pans, high angle shots, and sharp cuts written in the script. The altar is a case of geometry gone haywire, the painted pentagram on the floor recalls the hand-rendered splashes of light in *Caligari*, and the gathering around the Mystic is staged something like the worker's revolt in *Metropolis*. Poelzig's Latin chant, a hodgepodge of fragmented homilies, was written during the shoot. Relying on his ability to emote in any situation, Karloff's biting delivery made the nonsense sound genuinely spiritual. The translation bears repeating:

> With a grain of salt,
> > The brave may fall but cannot yield,
> Judge a tree but not of leaves,
> > The wolf changes his skin but not its mind.
> Great is the truth and it shall prevail,
> > That which I admit I do not know I cannot lose,
> The loss that is lost is not lost at all,
> > Every madman thinks everyone is crazy,
> He who repents is almost innocent.

The ritual was to have reached orgiastic proportions. The plan called for Poelzig to sway in unison with his minions in a "mechanized ballet" until he violates Joan at the altar, at which point one of the women watching this experiences an orgasm! Only a hint of the idea remains, when a girl turns to look. Ulmer wrote, "She goes into hysterical paroxysms, her whole body shaking voilently. She shakes the men off, head thrown back, her sustained scream sensually keyed." In the film, she turns, screams, and faints.

When Werdegast releases Joan from the cross, his original intention was to drag the girl up to

Poelzig descends the stairs to lead his guests to the basement chapel for the Satanic ritual.

her room and rape her! "A very hot scene," wrote the director, "as Joan comes to and Werdegast goes into the big rape motif, climaxed by Joan playing her ace, telling him that his daughter did not die, that she is married to Poelzig." Werdegast runs to find her. But unlike the film, Ulmer described a more gruesome discovery. "Werdegast turns and stares at the corpse of Karen as it *hangs on a rack* in readiness for Poelzig's mummification process. We see stark madness take possession of him."

The skinning scene in the *The Black Cat* was ostensibly inspired by Irvin Willat's 1919 wartime vengeance film *Behind the Door*, in which a German U-boat commander usurps a taxidermist's wife and gets skinned alive as he hangs from a shower stall. A lover of *grande guignol*, Ulmer wanted to take the idea into forbidden waters. Fired up by Gustave Dore's illustrations of *Dante's Inferno*, with its graphic depictions of hell, chests being splayed open, etc., he took a batch of them to Junior Laemmle and said he wanted to do the scene that way. Amused by his audacity (but probably figuring it to be "good horror stuff"), Laemmle said okay, and Ulmer wrote it accordingly.

In the film, the scene is done as stark, Kafkaesque shadow play. Karloff remains rigid while Lugosi appears to be giving him a barbershop shave – a scene which *Variety* nevertheless saw as "a truly horrible and nauseating piece of sadism." Only his manacled hands twist in agony, but there is a hellish quality to it, particularly in a singular canine yelp during the shadow scene, suggesting some synthesis of man and animal.

191

The Black Mass.

The script had a different ring to it. As Ulmer saw it, "The shadow describes an effect as if Werdegast was splitting the scalp slowly, pulling the sheath of skin over Poelzig's head and shoulders." Then, after Werdegast is shot, "Poelzig, *sans skin*, struggles on the rack. By superhuman effort, he frees himself and falls to the floor." Lugosi was then to have raised himself on one elbow, stared at Karloff, and laughed hysterically as he would later do in *The Raven*.

The idea was dragged out ad nauseam. Wrote Ulmer, "As Joan feverishly tries to pry the exit key out of Thamal's dead hand, Poelzig, *still living* as a hideous pulp of blood, raises his putrid body with eyes focused on Joan. He comes closer. With redoubled strength, she gets the key and runs to the door." Then, as the doctor pulls the red switch, Poelzig was to "turn with the last vestige of his strength and crawl on his belly toward Werdegast!"

The film ends on a light note, but the ultimate in-joke never made the release print. When the Alisons hail a passing bus, the driver was scripted as being none other than Edgar Ulmer, disguised in white beard and goggles. Speaking in Austrian, he eyeballs the couple and shakes his head contemptuously. "Will you take us to Vizhegrad?" asks Peter. "I'm not going to

Vizhegrad," replies Ulmer. "I'm going to a sanitarium to rest up after making *The Black Cat* in fourteen days! However, it will be a long walk. For *you*, I shall make an exception."

Whether or not Ulmer actually got into costume and wound up on celluloid is lost to history.

The Black Cat is a grand summation of the decade of cinema that preceded it. Woven into it are the echoes of Murnau, of Robert Wiene, of Wegener, and the pioneers of the Bauhaus. In his overall appearance, for example, Karloff was meant to resemble Cesare the Somnambulist in *Caligari*. In his opening bedroom scene, Ulmer described him as "a dead white face moving through the darkness, wearing black glove-silk pajamas to give the effect of tights," and his rising motion mimicked the awakening of the vampire in Murnau's *Nosferatu* ("the upper part of his body rises slowly, as if being pulled by wires").

Thamal, the stone-faced hulk, was Ulmer's nod to *The Golem*. For that reason the character was

192

kept silent, and the scene of Harry Cording carrying Jacqueline Wells "like a savage god" was staged to dredge up dormant memories of Paul Wegener as the clay giant cradling Lyla Salmonova. Ulmer went so far as to write, "No flicker of expression will disturb his face during the entire picture. This is to be insured by plaster of Paris makeup, if necessary." To make his silence logical, he thought of conveying the impression that Thamal is deaf and dumb. "We shall learn later that he is not," Ulmer wrote in his draft, "when we use his last despairing cry for a climactic effect." Curiously, Ruric dropped this idea in the script, and Thamal remains silent, even as he dies.

Doppelgangers (counterparts of living beings) were used by Ulmer in the tradition of Hitchcock and Lang. In the prologue, Joan sleeps upright on the train, her head tilted downward in cameo style, while Lugosi speaks of her resemblance to his wife. Later, the dead Karen Werdegast is framed almost identically. The other cadavers are blonde clones. And Egon Brecher as the majordomo wears a black hairpiece to vaguely resemble Lugosi, the idea being that Poelzig not only exerts control over his servant, but also over an exterior character who now becomes part of Poelzig's world.

Discounting the process backgrounds by John Fulton, ASC, for the train compartment, only two special effects shots were squeezed from the budget. In Ulmer's $250 bus wreck, we never see the collision. Instead, a tree stump in silhouette, printed over a falling miniature tree, is suspended over a dissolve to the overturned bus. As the fog clears, the stump fades away — a fleeting shadow of death, the ephemeral imprint of blight. The long shot of Poelzig's house, seen through the rain, was patterned by Ulmer after the Bauhaus school at Dessau, but it more closely resembles something by Le Corbusier or Frank Lloyd Wright with its jutting, linear terraces. The image was a glass painting rendered by matte artist Russ Lawson, backed by rear-projected clouds, and photographed by Jack Cosgrove, ASC. The tab for this effect? $175, yet for all its economy, the sight of the machine-like mansion looming over the gothic graveyard is alarming.

One magnificent shot went unfilmed. When Karloff reads *The Rites of Lucifer* in bed, the book was to have fallen softly to the floor. The camera was supposed to crane up, move out the window, creep up the side of the house, and catch the rays of the rising sun.

Other ideas fell out in the wash, particularly those depicting the Black Cat as a supernatural image. How much of this was shot is

Lugosi and Cording.

unknown. According to the script, Joan lies unconscious in the ravine. A shadow envelopes her face, "the camera shooting up at an enormous silhouette of the black cat etched against the sky. The only points of light are its smouldering eyes (a $90 electrical prop). The cat licks a trickle of blood from her shoulder. Werdegast stares at the cat in terror, grabs it by the throat, flings it against a rock, and buries his face in his hands." A return shot shows that the cat "is no longer there." Ulmer may have scratched this from the script to avoid repetition when Lugosi kills the cat later on. Or perhaps it was shot but cut from the negative as being too harrowing.

A note on the music: With the exception of *Fantasia, 2001,* and *A Clockwork Orange,* no other sound film embraced the classics from head to tail. Music was Ulmer's passion. Fortuitously, he connected with Heinz Roemheld, who orchestrated for *The Black Cat* a variety of sonatas, preludes and piano works. Roemheld was discovered by Carl Laemmle in 1929. After writing the score for *The White Hell of Pitz Palu* – part of which was sutured into *The Mummy* – he became Universal's music director, a post he held for a year. He returned as a freelancer to score *The Invisible Man* and met Ulmer shortly thereafter.

Originally Ulmer planned only five passages, some rather tritely. A Palestrina wedding hymn was keyed to the discarded cathedral opening, a Schubert love song to scenes on the train (changed in the film to *Jazz Caricatures),* Dukas' *The*

Sorcerer's Apprentice to Lugosi and the cat murder, Beethoven's *Fifth Symphony* to the unfilmed crane shot in the bedroom, and Bach's *Toccata and Fugue in D Minor* to the Black Mass. Eventually Ulmer realized that music was necessary to carry the film throughout. Ulmer and Roemheld chose sixteen pieces as character motifs and mood statements. Twenty-eight musicians performed during a nine-hour session, and an organist had his own eight-hour session.

The result was practically a case of Lisztomania. The opening allegro of Liszt's *Piano Sonata in B Minor* was hammered into a satanic musical portrait for Karloff with strings and brass. Ulmer and Roemheld called it "The Devil's Sonata." Their leaning on Liszt was deliberate – not only because of the Hungarian flavor, but because Liszt's interest in the devil was intensely personal. Much of his music exploited what were regarded as infernal regions. Some musicologists contend that the *Sonata* was another of the many forays Liszt made into illustrating scenes from Goethe's *Faust*.

Lugosi's dark motif was Liszt's *Tasso*, which Roemheld often dovetailed with the *Piano Sonata*. He also transformed the *Sonata* into something he called "Morgue," a metronomic lullaby written in 5/4 time for Karloff's prowl in the basement. Other Liszt passages underscored the Budapest depot *(Hungarian Rhapsody No. 1)*, the retreat from the ravine *(Les Preludes)*, and the exterior of Poelzig's home *(The Rakoczy March)*. Roemheld clowned up the march for an unnecessary scene of two gendarmes, calling it "Hungarian Burlesque," and orchestrated the allegro energico of the *Piano Sonata* into a frenzied, savage rhythm for the climactic fight, which extended into the skinning scene.

For the love theme, he encroached on Tchaikovski and called it *Cat Love*, a composite of two motifs. Joan's theme was based on *Romeo and Juliet* and Peter's theme was a variation of *The Pathetique*, and although lushly played, it became ubiquitous and diabetic. Part of the *The Pathetique* was also bastardized into an agitato passage when Peter tries to escape. Karen's theme was Brahms' *Sapphic Ode*, a German song played on a muted violin to suggest her frailty.

Darker themes for *The Black Cat* are more memorable. A mordant cello arrangement of Chopin's *Piano Prelude No. 2* underscored the entrance into Poelzig's house. For the queasy survey of the gun turrets, Roemheld took Schumann's *Piano Quintet in E Flat* and used it as a dirge for cellos and violas. (He also varied a violin passage from the *Quintet* for the scene of Poelzig leering at Joan in her

room. The haunting allegretto from Beethoven's *Seventh Symphony* underscored the subjective camera's retreat from the basement and Karloff's disembodied monologue. In its wailing melody is suggested resignation, futility, and the resurrection of dreary wartime memories.

For the cat murder, Schubert's *Unfinished Symphony* was modulated to choreograph the action. The whole sequence seems to glide along with a kind of lyrical ballet rhythm, and the footage was edited to correspond with the crescendos and diminuendos. The "climax" – Poelzig's spasmodic gripping of a nude statuette as Joan and Peter embrace – is the film's most blatant statement of sexual repression.

The Black Cat was the first talkie to use Bach's *D Minor* organ fugue as a devoted statement to dark forces, now a horror film cliché. The more funereal Bach work, the adagio from the *Toccata and Fugue in C Major,* imbued the ceremony with a woeful passion no other composition could match. The last classical piece, Brahms' *Piano Rhapsody in B Flat, No. 1,* was vigorously orchestrated for Joan's escape from the altar.

"The idea of using classical music as a full score was unheard of in 1934," Shirley Ulmer recalled. "When Old Man Laemmle came back from Germany, he nearly had a heart attack! He raised holy hell with Junior, because he had allowed Edgar to make this picture and use that music. He didn't want to *hear* of scored classical music; he felt it wasn't commercial. But Junior stood up for Edgar and said 'It's going to go just as it is.' This was just prior to its release."

Ulmer loved working with Karloff, who never took himself seriously and often broke up the set by turning a corner and muttering "Here comes the heavy." With Lugosi, it was a different situation. "Lugosi believed he was Dracula. I was always obliged to say '*Please* don't overact. Diminish it by 50%. You can do this in the theater, but not here!'" *The Black Cat's* script contains amusing notations to that end. For the scene where the bus driver rants about the countryside, the marginal comment reads: "We know – God, Thespis, and Mr. Lugosi willing – that he was there."

Shirley Ulmer harbors a grislier memory. "Lugosi lived the part of the guilt-ridden hangman. He told us he *was* a hangman. Whether that was one of his wicked jokes is beyond me. He even spoke nostalgically about the thrill he got out of being one, and how guilty he felt about it later on! His wife had to serve him and genuflect. With huge dogs all over

194

On the set. Ulmer can be seen in the midst of the crew, cinematographer John Mescall is to right of camera, and ladies at left are Anna Duncan and Shirley Ulmer.

the place and the decor of the house, I felt I *was* in a horror film."

Of the 35 pictures Universal released in 1934, *The Black Cat* was the top grosser, yielding a $140,000 profit during its first run. Remarkable for a film hatched virtually overnight. Ulmer proved that it took little money to make profitable pictures.

Ironically, it was his last film for a major Hollywood studio. Shirley was married to Max Alexander, Uncle Carl's favorite nephew. Ulmer's ability to lure her away so infuriated Laemmle, he banished him from Universal. For the next three decades until his death in 1972, the director toiled in the hellholes of Gower Gulch and for the independents, grinding out incredible little pictures (in any sense of the word) on shoestring budgets. The spectre of *The Black Cat* haunted many of them – the subterranean landscape, the tragic hero, and the dark power figure crept into such peculiar efforts as *Bluebeard*, *The Amazing Transparent Man* and *Journey Beneath the Desert (L'Atlantide)*.

The Black Cat was Edgar Ulmer's most personal work, and in some ways his best. Certainly it was his most memorable, despite the critical triumphs of *Detour*, *Ruthless*, and *The Naked Dawn*. In the final analysis, it is an art film. In its constant distortion of human relationships, in its deliberate positioning of characters and objects within the frame and the consideration given to their relative size, shape and texture, in its triangular configurations, both human and geometric, and in its narcotic images of evil, *The Black Cat* infused an eerie com-

bination of Caligarism and Futurism into formula-film melodrama. To paraphrase Werdegast: "It is indeed hard to describe. As hard to describe as life – or death."

—Paul Mandell

A Universal *picture; presented by* Carl Laemmle; *directed by* Edgar G. Ulmer; *produced by* Carl Laemmle Jr.; *"based on the immortal classic by* Edgar Allen Poe;" *story by* Edgar Ulmer; *screenplay by* Peter Ruric; *cinematographer*, John Mescall, ASC; *art director*, Charles D. Hall; *musical director*, Heinz Roemheld; *special effects*, John P. Fulton, ASC; *film editor*, Ray Curtiss; *make-up artist*, Jack P. Pierce; *matte artists*, Russell Lawson, ASC, Jack Cosgrove, ASC; *assistant directors*, William Reiger, Sam Weisenthal; *script clerk*, Moree Herring; *continuity*, Shirley Kassel; Western Electric *sound. Running time, 65 minutes. Released May 7, 1934.*

Hjalmar Poelzig, Boris Karloff; *Vitus Werdegast*, Bela Lugosi; *Peter Alison*, David Manners; *Joan Alison*, Jacqueline Wells; *Karen*, Lucille Lund; *Thamal*, Harry Cording; *Major-domo*, Egon Brecher; *Lieutenant*, Albert Conti; *Sergeant*, Henry Armetta; *Border Patrolman*, Tony Marlow; *Conductor*, Andre Cheron; *Station Master*, Paul Weigel; *Bus Driver*, George Davis; *Maid*, Anna Duncan; *Stewardess*, Leonore Kingston; *Organist*, John Peter Richmond (John Carradine); *Cultists*, King Baggott, Virginia Ainsworth, Duskal Blaine, Symonia Boniface, John George, Lois January; Michael Mark, Peggy Terry, Harry Walker, Paul Panzer, *The following were cut from final version: Porter*, Alphonse Martel; *Maitre d'hotel*, Herman Bing; *Steward*, Luis Alberni; *Waiter*, Albert Poulet; *Passenger*, Andy Devine; *Brakeman*, Rodney Hildebrandt; *Stewardess*, Lenore Kingston.

16

Ironic Justice of *Crime Without Passion*

The curiously productive misadventures of its filming, a distinctive avoidance of formula in its telling, and a wealth of visual sweep and musical exploration combine to make *Crime Without Passion* more than an entertainment to cherish. Richly imaginative throughout and laced with an irony only life can approximate, the film attests to the brilliance of its sires and acknowledged makers, Ben Hecht and Charles MacArthur. The two had become preeminent in journalism, popular literature, and scripting for stage and screen.

Its under-credited artistry-by-committee, however, involving the often overwhelming contributions of such professionals as Lee Garmes, ASC, Slavko Vorkapich, and Leo Lippe, ASC, is a testament to a manipulative gift at which the producers excelled. Like cartoonist Walt Disney, performing artists Count Basie and Bob Wills, and the ambitious Howard Hughes, Hecht and MacArthur possessed a motivational *chutzpah* with which to rally exceptionally creative types and provoke from them superior efforts.

Next to Laurel and Hardy, the funniest team in pictures was that of Hecht and MacArthur. Having decided to produce and direct their own movies after a long string of successes, they set up shop in the summer of 1934 at I.S.S.I.-Eastern Service Studio (the former Paramount Eastern Studio at

Gentry (Claude Rains) needs an alibi in a hurry after a violent argument with Carmen (Margo).

Astoria, Long Island, and today site of the new Kaufman Astoria Studios Center) and struck an independent production deal with Paramount Pictures. Their first and best effort, *Crime Without Passion,* was no great success with the public but instantly built an enormous critical reputation for artistry. Then *The Scoundrel* (1935) starred Noel Coward in another critics' darling which was also cold-shouldered at the boxoffice. *Once in a Blue Moon* (1936) sank with hardly a ripple, and *Soak the Rich* (1936) was no money maker. A fifth script, *The Monster,* was shelved until 1940, when Paramount filmed it as *The Mad Doctor* (with Basil Rathbone in a role written for Noel Coward) – but without screen credit to Hecht and MacArthur.

"The secret of good film production," Hecht remarked when *Crime Without Passion* went into production, "is that pictures should first of all amuse their own brainparents. What makes so many important-looking productions so heavy, stodgy and mechanical is the fact that the cast and technical staff worked like dogs in making them. People don't want to feel an atmosphere of tension when they go to the theater, they want to play. Well, we're going to play with them."

Claude Rains was a veteran stage actor who had just achieved screen stardom in his first picture, *The Invisible Man* (1933). Hecht and MacArthur saw Rains portraying a criminal lawyer in the Broadway play, *They Shall Not Die.* Inviting Rains to the home of MacArthur, which was made especially pleasant by the presence of Mrs. MacArthur, the distinguished actress Helen Hayes, the

197

team read him their script. They asked him to play Lee Gentry – the self-styled "champion of the damned," a defense attorney who has saved 30 murderers from the electric chair only to put his own neck in the noose.

"It's beautifully written," Rains replied, "and it has everything an actor could ask for." He accepted the role in spite of a pinch-penny salary, so pleasing the authors that they beefed up the role with more dialogue and business. Many years later, toward the end of a distinguished career, Rains chose Gentry for his segment in the "The Role I Liked Best" series in the *Saturday Evening Post*.

Money could not buy a better interpretation than Rains visited upon Gentry. "The only crime punishable by law is stupidity," he snaps upon having saved another killer from execution. Privately involved with two women who represent an intractable conflict – Whitney Bourne as a gorgeous blonde socialite and the seductive Margo as cabaret dancer Carmen Browne – Gentry fends off a jealous attack by the jilted Carmen, striking her an evidently fatal blow. Subduing his panic, Gentry undertakes to cinch an alibi. His alibi is undermined by a former lover, played by Greta Grand-

stedt, whose escort, Stanley Ridges, is killed by Gentry before a club packed with witnesses. No sooner have the police arrived to take Gentry away, than he sees Carmen – whom his blow had only stunned – walk onto the dance floor. Humiliated by publicity, Gentry attempts suicide but is stopped, left to fall prey to his own definition of "the only crime punishable by law."

The madcap authors of this compelling scenario recruited Lee Garmes, the genial young cinematographer who had most recently gained praise for *Shanghai Express* and *Zoo in Budapest*, on the strength of the argument that even though shooting their picture would mean a substantial drop in salary, it would enhance his prestige. They even offered him a co-director credit if he would accept a further salary cut, but here he refused.

"Nothing I ever encountered in the movies was as uniquely talented as the eyes of Lee Garmes," Hecht said many years later.

"We had a wonderful partnership," Garmes recalled less than a year before his death

(1978). ''Financially, it hurt me, but professionally, it helped me.'' The partnership was continued through *The Scoundrel* and *Once in a Blue Moon*. After MacArthur's death, Garmes and Hecht co-directed and co-produced three artistic but unpopular pictures: *Angels Over Broadway* (1940), *Spectre of the Rose* (1946) and *Actors and Sin* (1952).

Albert R. Johnson, a top Broadway stage designer, was hired to do the sets. Unfamiliar with the needs of the cinema, in which only those elements of a scene that fall within the angle viewed by the lens are considered, Johnson built each set to fill a stage, with high ceilings and vast floor space – ''The bedroom was 40 feet wide,'' Garmes chuckled. Garmes and a carpenter hastily rebuilt the sets, mostly in small, portable sections much as William Cameron Menzies had done in 1929 for the pacesetting *Bulldog Drummond*.

The courtroom was done in this way, with all the elements mounted on wheels. Although this meant dispensing with the usual establishing long shot of the room, it proved a highly practical, money-saving approach. The judge's bench, the jury box, the witness stand, a piece of wall, a window, and the attorneys' tables were used in turn. As the scenes using each portion were finished, the section was wheeled out of the way, the next section was rolled into place and the lighting was adjusted.

Garmes had studied the lighting of Rembrandt paintings in his earliest days as a cinematographer, striving to duplicate the distinctive north light effects of the great painter. Instead of utilizing the backlighted effects favored by most cameramen when working in black and white, he strove to maintain a consistent north light effect in which significant details are highlighted while other details are minimized. This effect is particularly successful in the courtroom scenes, lending verisimilitude to the sections to make them seem parts of the whole.

The company soon ran short of money and one of the more important sets had not been budgeted. Garmes and the carpenter spent $20 on draperies and cellophane and built a small stage, moved in some tables and chairs, utilized shadows and smoke and a handful of players. Somehow, in Garmes' shots, these odds and ends appear to be a convincing typical New York night spot.

Key personnel confer between takes at Astoria: Arthur Ellis, cutter; Lee Garmes, Ben Hecht, Charles MacArthur.

The producers came to depend more and more upon Garmes' expertise, having him direct more than half the scenes. Sometimes either or both directors were on the set, quietly observing or even indulging in a game of cards. Usually, they told the actors in advance how they wanted the dialogue played, then wandered away and left the actual direction up to Garmes. Although the crew was on stage each morning at nine, the producer-director team never started work before 11:30. They often communicated by means of large signs stuck on the walls of their office. A typical sign from MacArthur to Hecht: ''What was the audience doing ALL that time?'' This meant that yesterday's scene was dull and should be redone differently.

Even though Garmes had refused the salary cut requisite to receiving a co-director credit, the producers gave him a full frame credit that was unique at the time: Associate Director and Photographer.

Frank Tours, a Broadway composer-conductor (son of Berthold Tours, the Rotterdam composer and music educator, and grandson of Barthelmy Tours of the conservatories of Leipzig and Brussels), had charge of the score. It was a pleasingly strident work whose strategic use of orchestral dissonance and the flatted thirds and sevenths of jazz – chiefly to depict the conflict between libertine abandon and the mounting hysteria of

guilt – anticipates the much later scoring styles of Bernard Herrmann, Henry Mancini, Pete Rugolo and Lalo Schifrin. The jazz influence may be attributable to Oscar Levant, the age's principal interpreter of Gershwin's music, who was brought in to compose part of the score – and to his surprise received neither pay nor screen credit!

Some of the most unusual visuals result from the fascination Slavko Vorkapich inspired in the producers. The Yugoslavian-born "Vorky" already had distinguished himself as a portrait photographer, writer, commercial artist, dance director, set designer (for Rex Ingram's *Scaramouche* and *Prisoner of Zenda*), director-photographer of short films, second unit director, and co-director of RKO's recent *The Past of Mary Holmes*. He had become a specialist in creating montage sequences for RKO, Paramount and MGM, adding spice to the likes of *Viva Villa*, *Dancing Lady* and *Manhattan Melodrama*. Later he would become a leader in the field of education, lecturing often at the Museum of Modern Art and serving as head of the film department at USC 1952-56. Although he died in 1976, his writings and theories are still widely studied and used.

Vorkapich was hired initially to make atmospheric shots and handle special effects. So impressed were Hecht and MacArthur with his ideas that they soon let him build up a second unit comprising a dozen players, a camera crew, a stunt pilot, soundmen, stage hands and stunt artists. Vorkapich's contributions are enormous, changing what would have been a gripping but stage-bound murder yarn into a piece of cinematic virtuosity. As director of photography he acquired Leo Lippe, ASC, a New York-based special effects cameraman.

Most noteworthy is the opening sequence, a pre-title prologue which Vorkapich described as "The Furies rising from the blood of victims of passion and flying over New York, laughing at the lovers." A close-up of a woman's eye dissolves to a matching gun muzzle. Flash cuts show the eye twitching, the gun firing, the eye blinking in pain, the victim's POV (out of focus) of the smoking gun in the killer's hand, a woman falling (slow motion), and an extreme closeup of a drop of blood splatting to the floor. One by one the three Furies of Greek legend – diaphanously gowned, voluptuous women with hideously evil faces – fly up from the blood and into the spaces above New York City. They plunge and swoop among the man-made canyons, each in turn diving down to witness a different scene of guilty passion. Sometimes they seem to fly into the camera's lens. Laughing fiendishly, they smash windows and skylights. The falling shards of glass, through adroit stop-frame work, fall to the

200

Selected frames from the Furies prologue designed by Vorkapich and photographed by Lippe. Certain images, such as the laughing skull, are intercut in segments ranging from two to five frames in length.

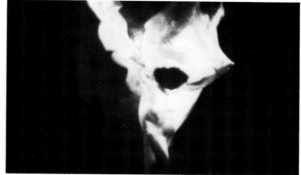

floor and form the letters of the main title! (The credit titles appear at the end of the picture. Although pre-title prologues and end credits titles are common today, they were highly unusual at the time.)

The Furies were portrayed by three beautiful professional dancers – Betty Sundmark, Fraye Gilbert and Dorothy Bradshaw – whose faces were painted garishly. They performed on a platform covered with black velvet. A wind machine whipped their hair and the filmy gowns which somewhat concealed their bodies. To make them rise from the blood, the camera moved down past them from a 45° angle as they rose from a crouching position and the shot was superimposed over the drop of blood. The "flying" scenes were made with the players strapped into concealed leather corsets attached to piano wires. Suspended high in the air in front of black velvet backdrops, the players were buffeted by a wind propeller to keep their hair and

201

gowns flapping. These shots later were superimposed over moving and stationary shots of New York City buildings. Some background shots were made from an airplane piloted by a young woman stunt flier, Swanee Taylor.

The more spectacular diving scenes for all three Furies were made by a pretty circus aerialist, Mickey King. These leaps – 45 feet into a net – were all done in one day. Remarkably, the artist had just emerged from the hospital where she had been for

Garmes explains camera mechanism to Alice Jefferson, a dancer in the film.

nine weeks after a rigging collapsed during a stage show. She had fallen to the stage, suffering a brain concussion and fractures of the skull, back and shoulder.

Vorkapich and Lippe took a crew to shoot some exteriors of the J. P. Morgan Building at 23 Wall Street as part of their montage. They arrived before dawn on a Sunday morning in order to avoid crowds, and found the streets deserted, as they had hoped. A night watchman, seeing them unpack their equipment, decided he was about to be burglarized. As dawn broke and Lippe was preparing to shoot, the company was besieged by the police.

Lippe was a little-known but highly qualified cinematographer who usually worked anonymously behind the scenes in the days when only department heads occasionally received billing for special effects. Born in Brooklyn in 1899, he had been in the business for about 15 years at the time of *Crime Without Passion.* He was assistant to Roy Pomeroy, ASC, special effects chief at Paramount's Hollywood studios, until 1928, when he was put in charge of the effects department at Paramount-Astoria. There he worked on *Nothing But the Truth, Cocoanuts, The Hole in the Wall, Jealousy, Applause, The Return of Sherlock Holmes, Roadhouse Nights,* and others until the studio closed in 1930. He then shot 16 travelogs for Cinelog and 13 Musical Moods shorts for ERPI, as well as other short films made in New York, before joining the Vorkapich unit. Later, he became a designer and manufacturer of motion picture cameras and equipment and vice-president of Cineflex Corporation. During World War II he made a bomb-spotting 35mm movie camera for the Air Force. He moved to San Antonio after retiring and died there in 1969.

Vorkapich also directed several straight dramatic scenes, and brought the Furies back to laugh viciously at Gentry's plight at the finale. Lippe made a number of highly original – and much imitated – scenes in which Rains was able to express his thoughts: a ghostly double exposure of the actor prompts, chides and advises the flesh-and-blood Rains as he plunges into his "perfect" crime. This technique is a marked improvement over the stage's cliche of asides to the audience, which was tried (disastrously) by MGM in their version of Eugene O'Neill's play, *Strange Interlude* (1932). Garmes also photographed that one, which he called "very dull."

Most of the players, including Rains, were new to the screen. In his only previous screen venture, he portrayed *The Invisible Man,* whose face wasn't seen until the last shot in the picture, after the character's death. His third picture bore the appropriate title, *The Man Who Reclaimed His Head* (1934). Margo – Marie Castillo y O'Donnell, and later Mrs. Eddie Albert – was a 17-year-old Mexican-born nightclub dancer who had never acted professionally. Mrs. Albert, a strong civic leader in Los Angeles, died July 17, 1985.

Whitney Bourne was just what she played in the picture – a New York socialite with some minor stage experience. Stanley Ridges – excellent in his talkie debut as the man who goads Rains into a blood rage – was a Theatre Guild actor who had previously appeared in only one film. Leslie Adams, Paula Trueman, Greta Grandstedt, Fuller Mellish, Esther Dale, Ralph Riggs, Lionel Pape, and Charles Kennedy were stage actors, several of whom had some screen experience. The other cast members consisted of dancers, models, singers, and even circus performers. Twelve members of the Bobby Duncan Dance Troupe and 16 dancers from the New York Hollywood Restaurant floor show appear in dressing room and dance floor scenes.

The cast was bolstered with celebrity bit players such as Helen Hayes and Fannie Brice. Hecht and MacArthur cast themselves fairly prominently as a pair of obnoxious, pushy reporters.

"New players are the only ones who are really natural, except for the really great screen players," MacArthur explained. "Besides, how many geniuses have we in America? Don't answer – you might not include me."

The only casualties among the players were severe cases of motion sickness suffered by all three "Furies" and a bruised cheek for Rains. The latter was the result of being slapped 19 times in the course of rehearsals and takes for the scene in which Ridges goads Rains in the night club. The directors called for several takes on each of three setups – long shot, medium shot and closeup – while insisting that Ridges make each blow "more realistic." Ridges, apologizing after each take, was unnerved by the experience.

Except for the screeching Furies, the actors perform in a subdued manner considering the period and the subject. Rehearsals, Garmes recalled, were conducted "almost in whispers," with the voices "raised only a trifle" when the actual takes began. "The reason for this restraint is that intense emotion doesn't have to be stressed," Hecht said.

Despite the strangeness of its production methods, the picture was finished in only 28 days, a benchmark of inventiveness and the effective blending of many artistic visions. Aside from its unusual photographic treatment, *Crime Without Passion* is memorable chiefly for Rains. He incurs audience dislike with his arrogance and yet makes one hope he will not get caught. He appears in almost every scene, always photographed in a manner that at once emphasizes his diminuitive stature and conveys his naturally commanding presence. His dissolution from confidence, to mere bravado, to cowering fear, and the camera's pitiless depiction thereof, propel the story to an inevitable climax.

—Michael H. Price and George E. Turner

A Hecht-MacArthur *production; produced at I.S.S.I. Studios, Long Island; Western Electric sound system; written, directed and produced by* Ben Hecht *and* Charles MacArthur; *associate director and photographer,* Lee Garmes, ASC; *special effects by* Slavko Vorkapich; *musical score composed and arranged by* Frank Tours; *general manager,* Arthur Rosson; *scenery,* Albert Johnson; *film editor,* Arthur Ellis; *recorded by* Joseph Kane; *photographic effects,* Leo Lippe, ASC; *assistant to Vorkapich,* Leslie Bain; *effects cutter,* Elvira Trabert; *stunt supervisor,* Swanee Taylor; *additional music,* Oscar Levant. *Running time, 80 minutes. Released August 24, 1934, by Paramount Pictures, Inc.*

Lee Gentry, Claude Rains; *Carmen Browne,* Margo; *Katy Costello,* Whitney Bourne; *Eddie White,* Stanley Ridges; *Buster Malloy,* Paula Trueman; *State's Attorney O'Brien,* Leslie Adams; *Della,* Greta Grandstedt; *Miss Keely,* Esther Dale; *Lieutenant Norton,* Charles Kennedy; *Judge,* Fuller Mellish; *Foreman,* Lionel Pape; *The Furies,* Betty Sundmark, Fraye Gilbert, Dorothy Bradshaw; *Acrobat,* Mickey King; *Model,* Ethelyne Holt; *Man,* Ralph Riggs; *Dancers,* Alice Jefferson, Alice Anthon; *Reporters,* Ben Hecht, Charles MacArthur; *Women in Lobby,* Helen Hayes, Fannie Brice; *Dance Troupes,* the Bobby Duncan Dancers, the New York Hollywood Restaurant Dancers.

17

Flash Gordon, an Interplanetary Gothic

Universal Studio in 1935 teetered precariously on the edge of bankruptcy. Each year since the advent of the Great Depression the company had temporarily suspended all contracts and shut down operations for several weeks in order to save enough money to resume production.

An old Carl Laemmle colleague and sometime studio manager, Henry MacRae, was in charge of producing all Universal serials, which were issued at the rate of four per year. A dapper Scotsman from Canada, MacRae was able to work very much as he pleased as long as he kept his serials within time limits of six to eight weeks and brought them in on budgets ranging from $175,000 to $250,000. These were fairly substantial feature allotments for that time, but since serials were actually 12 to 15 two-reel chapters totalling four or five hours of running time, it meant long hours and hard work for cast and crew and the necessity of making as many as 80 camera setups per day.

Universal had been making serials since 1914. They were regarded as surefire money makers which were booked year-round by more than 4,000 theaters in the United States alone. The foreign market was extremely rich as well. Inexplicably, the chapter plays were accorded a stepchild status in the industry and they had to be made under abysmal conditions with a minimum of departmental cooperation.

The Laemmles knew that MacRae could deliver the goods and they kept the lesser management out of his hair. For example, liquor was forbidden on all sets, yet MacRae openly kept his actors

and crewmen high on "jungle juice" to help them get through the arduous days and nights. He mixed the concoction (which included gin and fruit juices) in a large barrel and every half hour or so he would call a halt and serve everybody a drink. Hourly he served caviar or sandwiches.

The first serial to be based on a newspaper cartoon was *Tailspin Tommy,* produced by Universal in 1934. A sequel followed. The success of these pictures set the studio heads to looking at other adventure strips with the idea of making serials which were pre-sold to millions of readers. *Flash Gordon,* drawn for King Features Syndicate by the young and brilliant Alex Raymond, was optioned by Universal for $10,000. Science-fiction elements had often been used in serials before, but *Flash Gordon* was an interplanetary yarn necessitating fantastic sets, bizarre characters, a great variety of costumes, and a mind-boggling number of special effects shots. Four writers – Frederick Stephani, George Plympton, Basil Dickey and Ella O'Neill – put the screenplay together in 13 episodes. The cartoon version was followed as closely as any literary adaptation. Stephani had written romantic dramas at Paramount; Plympton and Dickey were veteran serial specialists; O'Neill was MacRae's assistant.

In casting the serial, MacRae selected Jean Rogers and Priscilla Lawson, who were Dale Arden and Princess Aura, respectively, from the studio contract list. He borrowed a reluctant Paramount contract actor, Larry "Buster" Crabbe, for the starring role after he saw Crabbe watching other athletic actors being interviewed for the role. "I thought the

idea was crazy and that nobody would buy it," Crabbe said. "When MacRae talked to my bosses at Paramount, I had no choice in the matter." It became his most famous role.

Born in California and raised in Hawaii, Crabbe was freestyle swimming champion of the 1932 Olympics. While studying law, he was "discovered" by Paramount scouts who dubbed him "the world's most perfectly developed male" and starred him in an excellent melodrama, *King of the Jungle,* in 1933. Muscular, but lean and graceful, he looked like Flash Gordon come to life, except that Flash was blond. Having his hair bleached proved to be an ordeal. The first treatment turned his brown hair a bright red. The second covered his scalp with a mass of sores. The final one made him so "pretty" that he wore a hat pulled down to his ears wherever he went. "I was getting wolf whistles from *guys,*" Crabbe said.

"We were in makeup at 7 o'clock every morning and on the set by eight," Crabbe recalled. "There were breaks for lunch and dinner – 30 to 45 minutes – and then we were back at work until 10:30."

Denied by both priority and budget the services of the studio's famed special effects department headed by John Fulton, ASC, MacRae created his own department by obtaining contract cinematographer Jerome Ash, ASC, as co-director of photography. A heavy-set, personable ex-actor, Ash had been an Akeley cameraman as well as a special effects cinematographer. Some of his best visual

effects are in *The Cat and the Canary* (1927), *The Man Who Laughs* (1928), and *King of Jazz* (1930). In an unused barn-like structure on the backlot, Ash set up equipment for filming the miniatures for the picture. It came naturally to him because he was an illusionist by avocation, having learned the art as assistant to a famed conjuror, Ching Ling Foo.

Most of the "straight" photography is the work of English-born Richard Fryer, ASC, who had been a director of photography for 18 years. At the time he was specializing in serial work, having done the 1933 *Perils of Pauline* and *Pirate Treasure* (1934). The picture for which he was to receive his greatest acclaim was the artistic *Voice in the Wind* (1944).

The miniatures were built by Elmer R. Johnson, Swedish-born head of the studio wood and plaster shops. They include the graceful rockets of Ming's war fleet, the hydrocycle submarine of the Shark Men, the flying disc ships of the Lion Men, the floating sky city of the Hawkmen (supposedly borne aloft by beams of radioactive light), the undersea city of the Shark Men, Ming's turreted city, and the craggy desert landscape of Mongo. Dr. Zarkov's rocket ship was originally designed for the Fox musical extravanganza, *Just Imagine* (1930). The flying craft were operated on wires and while they are

Frames from Flash Gordon. *Ape man at lower right is Constantine Romanoff.*

laughable today in light of what is known about rocketry and spacecraft, they were enchanting to the audiences of 1936. Curiously, they have retained a primitive charm comparable to that exercised by the fanciful scenes of *The Wizard of Oz* (1938). George Lucas has acknowledged his debt to *Flash Gordon* in the creation of his *Star Wars* saga.

Large sets, such as palace interiors, were built on sound stages using enormous draperies to conceal the stage walls and decorated with oversize vases and other exotic-looking props. Some were revamped from standing sets built for other pictures. Ming's laboratory, for example, is the planetarium set from *The Invisible Ray* (1936), produced a

short time earlier. The interior of the watch tower from *Bride of Frankenstein* (1935) was incorporated into Ming's castle. The desert scenes were photographed on the southernmost part of the backlot, at a man-made canyon constructed of hydrocal. The Tunnel of Terror was a tunnel in Brush Quarry in Hollywood's Bronson Canyon. The quarry was created about 1907 when stone was needed for street construction in downtown Los Angeles, and has been used in hundreds of films. A natural false perspective in one area of the tunnel was cleverly utilized by the cinematographers to make the Gocko appear gigantic alongside Flash, who was impersonated by a little person.

The Gocko, an impressive monster, was portrayed by a man in a suit, aided by wire riggings. The suit was redesigned as the Fire Dragon for later episodes. The actor inside was Glenn Strange, a tall

207

Texas cowboy who specialized in playing Western heavies. Much later, he portrayed the Frankenstein Monster in three films and, still later, was Sam, the bartender on the long-running "Gunsmoke" television show.

The Dragons of Death were real, living reptiles – iguanas, etc. – heavily made up with horns, dorsal plates and spines and photographed at 72 fps. Stationary mattes were used to put actors in scenes with the dragons. Ursol, King Vultan's striped bear, was a real bear in makeup. The sacred Tigron was a trained tiger. The Octosak was a rubber monster constructed four years earlier for an uncompleted picture, *Black Pearl*, making a belated debut intercut with scenes of a real octopus.

The fantastic electrical machinery, which performs impressively in the laboratory scenes, was created by Kenneth Strickfaden, an electrical genius whose creations appeared in all of Universal's *Frankenstein* films, *Just Imagine*, *The Mask of Fu Manchu* (1932), *The Invisible Ray* and many others.

Some familiar props appear, among them the statue of Amon-Ra from *The Mummy* (1933), the moon ray from *Werewolf of London* (1935), and the telescope and ray machines from *The Invisible Ray*.

The Oracle of Tao, a gigantic multiarmed idol which rolls its eyes and leers at scantily clad dancing girls writhing in its moving hands, is lifted from *Just Imagine*. When Ming watches a weirdly costumed rebellion on his television screen, he is really seeing back-projected ballet scenes from Universal's 1927 spectacle, *The Midnight Sun*. Another prominent piece of stock footage is the fight between a Sharkon and an Octosak from a nature documentary by Stacy Woodard.

After Flash has defeated three ape men and the royal guard, Princess Aura (Lawson) leaps to his defense.

The soldier costumes which, true to the cartoon strip, derive from Roman and Greek armour designs, were made of light materials such as aluminum, leather and rubber so they would not impede the swift action demanded of serials.

Even with all the corner-cutting involved, *Flash Gordon* was clearly not a picture that could be brought in within the standard serial budget. Costs rose to a reported $350,000 – an "A" budget at the time. Serial veteran Ray Taylor was brought in to direct several episodes to help meet the deadline. Crabbe said that he considered Taylor a better serial director than Stephani. When shooting finished late in February, 1936, Carl Laemmle reported that "Financially it is the biggest serial investment ever made."

Charles Middleton, who was the perfect choice for Emperor Ming; Richard Alexander, ordinarily a Western heavy, who played his one sympathetic role as Prince Barin; Frank Shannon, an Irish stage actor who (Dublin accent and all) became permanently identified as the enigmatic Dr. Alexis Zarkov; and most of the other players were from the freelance ranks. Many of the bit actors were Western players, whose drawling voices sound somewhat out of place on Mongo.

Flash hints to King Vultan (John Lipson) that he shouldn't molest Dale further.

Frederick Stephani, the director, was a young man who had been a revolutionary in Hungary. He worked in classical drama on the stage and with the advent of talking pictures became a well-known scenarist. *Flash Gordon* was his first directorial effort in films. Afterward he returned to writing, eventually becoming a producer at MGM.

The screen adaptation follows the cartoon story with remarkable fidelity, considering the far-out nature of the strip. It begins with earth being menaced by a supposed comet which enters the universe, causing panic and natural disasters. Astronomer/Professor Gordon receives a telegram from his son, Flash, who "has given up his polo game to be with us at the end." The Ford Trimotor airliner carrying Flash is struck by a meteor shower and, grabbing up a pretty girl named Dale Arden, he bails out. They land near a rocket ship with which crazed Dr. Zarkov plans to fly to the intruding planet and try to halt its progress toward the earth. With earth's destruction imminent, Flash and Dale go along as his assistants.

Landing near a turreted city, the travelers disembark but are menaced by huge dragon lizards. They are rescued by an unfriendly group of soldiers who take them in a rocket ship to the palace of Emperor Ming. Ming controls the planet, called Mongo, and plans to conquer the earth. He demands Dale for his harem, orders Zarkov to be put to work in his experimental laboratory, and has Flash thrown into an arena with three ape-like men. Flash defeats the ape-men and is regarded passionately by Ming's beautiful but dangerous daughter, Princess Aura. Escaping a dragon pit with Aura's aid, Flash becomes allied with the Lion Men's leader, Prince Thun, and the deposed ruler of Mongo, Prince Barin.

Further adventures take Flash and his friends into the undersea city of the Shark Men, where Flash defeats King Kala and a sea monster called the Octosak. After that they spend a harrowing time in King Vultan's sky city. Eventually they befriend Vultan, who initially is perceived as being as cruel and lecherous as Ming. Among other menaces overcome during the 13 chapters are the Gocko, a giant dragon with lobster-like claws; a fire-breathing dragon; the sacred Tigron; the Orangopoid, a horned ape-like monster; and hordes of Ming's minions. At last Ming is defeated by the Lion Men and flees into the flaming abode of the God Tao, "from which no man ever returns."

The actors lend a great deal of charm to the picture. Crabbe, a better actor than he ever was given credit for, was as perfect a Flash Gordon as

Crabbe, Rogers and Frederick Stephani on the backlot during Chapter One.

could be imagined. Jean Rogers has the innocent beauty and sex appeal with which Raymond invested the cartoon version, although she is blonde whereas the cartoon Dale is a brunette. Middleton's Ming is superbly evil in a Fu Manchu sort of characterization. Priscilla Lawson adds a dimension seldom encountered in movie serials by investing Aura with more than a suggestion of nymphomania. In one memorable scene in the Tunnel of Terror, as she and Flash flatten against a wall while Ming's soldiers march past, she stares at Flash with undisguised carnality and runs her hands over his chest.

Because of the rapid changes of setup, the actors found it impossible to memorize all their lines. When an actor flubbed a line during a key shot, the bad portion was redone in closeup and cut in or occasionally redubbed. Often the voice heard was that of supervising editor Saul Goodkind. Ad libs were frequent, even encouraged. In the second Flash serial, Crabbe yells to Frank Shannon, who is piloting their rocket ship, "Head for the hills, Doc!"

209

Flash is tortured by the Hawkmen in Flash Gordon.

Crabbe said, "I must have thought I was in another western."

The serial is richly scored throughout. Clifford Vaughan, organist and composer of a large body of symphonic works and religious music, wrote original compositions for the main and end titles and chapter prologues. These are exotic and romantic, setting the mood to excellent effect. The trumpet fanfares heard in the various palaces of Mongo are the work of staff composer David Klatzkin. The balance of the score was arranged from music composed originally for other pictures. Most of this is by Heinz Roemheld, American-born and German-trained composer of the Romantic school, and is taken mainly from *Bombay Mail, The Invisible Man, The Black Cat* and *White Hell of Pitz Palu.* Hungarian composer Karl Hajos's memorable score from *Werewolf of London* and L. Franke Harling's ethereal music from *Destination Unknown* also were woven into the fabric. Ironically, these borrowings have become more popularly associated with *Flash Gordon* than with the pictures for which they were created.

MacRae ordered a feature version to be edited from the serial. Running 72 minutes, it is understandably chaotic. The sound track of the feature utilizes much of Franz Waxman's superb music from *Bride of Frankenstein.*

In March, 1936, Carl Laemmle, through a fluke, sold Universal to a group of investors for $5,500,000. The new regime, under control of the Bank of America, included Charles R. Rogers as executive vice president and William Koenig as general production manager. On April third – three days before *Flash Gordon* went into release – the new owners officially took over the studio. There was an immediate purge of all known members of the Laemmle and Stern families (the latter being Mrs. Laemmle's relatives) on the studio payroll. Director Edward Laemmle was fired and replaced on the ninth day of shooting *Crash Donovan.* Carl Jr. was allowed to finish his production of *Showboat* before leaving the studio.

The main titles of unreleased pictures were re-shot to replace the traditional "Carl Laemmle presents" with "Universal presents." The beloved old airplane circling the earth motif gave way to a sparkling, modernistic glass globe surrounded by spinning stars and accompanied by sprightly Jimmy McHugh music. Boris Karloff was quickly dethroned as the studio's top star, to be replaced by a youthful light-opera soprano, Deanna Durbin. The New Universal (as it was styled in all advertising for the next several years) had no sympathy for the Gothic tastes of the Laemmles, embarking instead upon the establishment of a new, slicker image more in the mold of Rogers' former studio, Paramount.

Despite their lack of enthusiasm for such demeaning fare, the studio chiefs retained the serial program, which provided a dependable source of profit that helped cover losses suffered by some of the ambitious feature product.

MacRae remained on the payroll despite his close association with the Laemmles, partly because *Flash Gordon* was the studio's second-largest grosser of 1936. He was called on the carpet several months later to explain why his serials cost more to produce than those being made by the new Republic Studio, which was turning out highly successful serials for $100,000 (more or less). Ben Koenig, the younger brother of the general manager, was of the opinion that he could make serials for considerably less money than MacRae.

MacRae was reduced to making only two serials per year, the other two to be produced by Koenig and Barney Sarecky, formerly of Mascot and Republic's serial programs. The first Koenig-

210

Sarecky effort, *Ace Drummond,* which was highly successful, was brought in for about $125,000. Budgets were cut accordingly as the bitter rivalry between the two serial units continued over the next several years.

In 1938, to MacRae's chagrin, *Flash Gordon's Trip to Mars* was given to his competition, a deliberate move in view of the cost of the original. The budget for the second set of 15 episodes was expanded to $175,000, considerably less than was spent on the 1936 serial but more than most serials were allotted. Jerry Ash, Ken Strickfaden, Elmer Johnson and others of the original crew were brought back. Art director Ralph DeLacy designed some dazzling new sets, including an ultra-modern palace with strangely designed doors and windows, a forest of misshapen trees which covered an entire stage, full scale interiors and exteriors of the stratosleds used by the Martian airmen, the underground lair of a race of Clay Men, a Martian airdrome, and a number of laboratories. Some of the old sets and props were adapted into the new decor.

Ford Beebe, veteran writer-director, and Robert S. Hill, who had been with Universal in the silent era, directed. Both men had the know-how to work fast and economically, having specialized in serials and action pictures. Hill also had a pronounced artistic bent, having worked on four productions with the celebrated German expressionist director, Paul Leni.

Queen Azura (Beatrice Roberts) and her ally, Ming, in Flash Gordon's Trip to Mars.

Flash Gordon's Trip to Mars: *Flash and Dale at the mercy of the Clay King (C. Montague Shaw).*

The new screenplay by Wyndham Gittens, Norman S. Hall, Ray Trampe and Herbert Dalmas bears less resemblance to the cartoon feature, although it utilizes some of the characters as played by the same artists – Flash, Dale, Ming, Zarkov and Barin – plus the "Witch Queen" Azura, who for a time replaced Princess Aura as Dale's rival in the

Ming, in his laboratory on Mars.

Flash shows the magic sapphire to Azura.

cartoon. Jean Rogers, whose hair had gone back to its normal brown, more closely resembled the Dale of the comics page than before. A comedy-relief newspaper reporter, Hapgood (Donald Kerr) joined the adventurers. The new costumes worn by Flash and Ming were consistent with the changes made by Raymond during the first four years of the cartoon.

The key role of Azura was played by Beatrice Roberts, who had been an extra and bit player for years. Universal gave the attractive, aristocratic-looking actress a buildup as a dramatic "find," giving her first the Azura role, then the lead opposite Victor McLaglen in *The Devil's Party*. Neither role seemed to help her career, although she was very good in both, and she soon returned to small parts.

Hapgood was also a highlight in the career of Kerr, a little comedian with a fine vaudeville voice. He had been fairly well known on Broadway, having appeared in the Ziegfeld and Music Box shows, but never gained much prominence in the movies. There are noteworthy contributions from Kane Richmond (himself a serial star almost the equal of Crabbe) and such old-timers as Wheeler Oakman, Warner Richmond, Anthony Warde, Jack Mulhall, Lane Chandler, Ray Turner, and Reed Howes. The stunt artists included Eddie Parker, Tom Steele and George de Normand, all of whom also appear among the heavies and spear-carriers.

The story begins with the return of the Zarkov expedition from Mongo. Sometime later, the earth is plagued by a continuing series of earthquakes, floods, hurricanes and other disasters. Scientists are baffled. The cause is a ray from a powerful nitron lamp on the planet Mars, which is drawing the element nitron from earth. Azura, Queen of Magic and ruler of Mars, under the influence of Emperor Ming, who has been exiled from his own planet, uses the nitron in her war against the Clay People. The men of clay, reduced to a living death by Azura's magic, hide in caves in the Valley of Desolation.

Zarkov, Flash and Dale believe Ming to be the source of the deadly ray and set out for Mongo, accompanied by a comical stowaway, reporter Happy Hapgood. Caught in Ming's magnetic ray, their rocket is drawn to the red planet, where it crashes near the Clay Men's domain. They fall into the hands of the Clay People, eventually earning their friendship.

The earthmen fight the barbaric Forest People, allies of Azura, and aided by Prince Barin of Mongo, obtain the two magical sapphires that give Azura her power. Azura falls in love with Flash, but

The earthlings and Prince Barin in the Forest Kingdom of Mars.

is killed by one of her own stratosled bombers at Ming's orders. Ming, seemingly insane, tries to devastate the earth by running the nitron ray at full power and further threatens to destroy Mars. His former ally, a Martian scientist named Tarnak, forces Ming into the disintegration room where he apparently is destroyed.

Although only two years separated the two serials, *Mars* has a much more modern look than the

Hapgood (Donald Kerr), Flash, Barin and Zarkov escape in Azura's stratosled.

original. The chapter synopses written by Herbert Dalmas appear in the form of a cartoon strip viewed by a Martian on a futuristic television set! The sets are unusual and dramatic. The picture also uses rear projection and optical effects which were denied its predecessor. Glass shots are used to stunning advantage, both in the interior of Azura's palace and in the expansive outdoor setting of the airdrome and the nitron lamp. The stratosled bomber craft used by the Martians are represented as both miniatures and exterior-interior practical sets. Dr. Zarkov inexplicably travels to Mars in one of Ming's rocket ships instead of his own craft.

Particularly effective is Ash's depiction of the Clay Men seeming to emerge from the walls of the caves. The illusion was achieved with careful dissolves done in camera.

Some of the best visual gags are the work of Eddie Keys, a resourceful property and mechanical effects man. A small idol sacred to the Forest People is destroyed by Azura's magic in Chapter Seven, crumbling to dust without dissolves or other optical effects. The effect is repeated later when Ming demonstrates his new disintegrating ray by aiming it at a bust sculpted of "the hardest metal on Mars." Keys made forms of the sculpted images and cast them in

Flash turns the trick on two Martian guards played by stuntmen George DeNormand and Tom Steele.

powdered steel, which was magnetized into an apparent solid stage. When the magnetic field was broken, the images disintegrated. Keys also constructed an impressive "death ray" machine which fired a harmless stream of lethal-looking sparks.

Strickfaden's electrical gadgets, including some not seen in the previous serial, again are much in evidence. The miniature of Ming's city on Mongo, somewhat embellished, reappears on Mars as his stronghold in the heart of Azura's kingdom. Another pleasantly familiar artifact is Zita Johann's Egyptian princess costume from *The Mummy,* which looks even better on Jean Rogers, despite the addition of some cover-up material demanded by the more vigilant censors of 1938. Ming ecstatically watches earth's agonies through Karloff's telescope from *The Invisible Ray.* The Amon-Ra statue, redecorated and with the head replaced by that of some grinning beast, has become Kalu, god of the Forest People. Queen Azura wears the crown which formerly adorned the head of Princess Aura. The nitron ray lamp is the *outside* of the tank in which Flash fought the Octosak. There is also a flashback sequence from *Flash Gordon* and stock shots showing the destruction caused by Ming's attacks against earth which combine disaster footage from the Universal Newsreel files with earthquake scenes from *The Shock* (1923) and *Looking for Trouble* (1935).

These eclectic touches, probably included solely as economy measures, prove an asset to the picture by providing a certain kinship to its predecessor without distracting from the more sophisticated look of the new sets and costumes.

The musical score derives entirely from library sources. The title music is from *The Black Cat,* the chapter prologue music from *The Invisible Man,* and the body of the score is composed of most of the music used in *Flash Gordon,* plus heroic excerpts from Waxman's *Bride of Frankenstein* and *Sutter's Gold,* Alexandre Iljinsky's "Orgy of the Spirits," Roemheld's *Dracula's Daughter* music, and other bits and pieces. It has often been said that Queen Azura's theme is from Tchaikovski's "Romeo and Juliet Fantasia Overture," but it is actually Roemheld's Tchaikovski-inspired composition, "Cat Love," from *The Black Cat.* Somehow, this melange of symphonic melodrama backs up the visuals very well.

The original release prints were made on green stock, which lent an eerie, otherworldly aura to the visuals and suggested that each two-reel episode, surrounded by the predominantly black and white features and short subjects of the theater programs of the time, was something special. The fans loved it.

A 67½ minute feature version, originally titled *Rocket Ship*, was edited from the serial. On the night of October 30, 1938, the CBS Radio Network aired Orson Welles' radio dramatization of H.G. Welles' "War of the Worlds," which created headlines by provoking widespread panic among listeners who thought Martians really were invading earth. Universal quickly retitled the feature *Mars Attacks the World*, retitled the first *Flash Gordon* feature *Rocket Ship* for use as a running mate in double-bill areas, and rushed the prints into release on November 18, in time to profit from the free publicity.

Universal soon made a deal with the John F. Dille newspaper syndicate to produce two serials based on a rival science-fiction cartoon strip, *Buck Rogers*. A 12 chapter serial of that name starring Buster Crabbe was released in 1939. Although the production is comparable to *Flash Gordon's Trip to Mars* and was made by virtually the same production team, the public was adamant in its wish for Buster Crabbe to return to his Flash Gordon role. The planned sequel, therefore, was aborted and arrangements were made for the production of two more Flash Gordon serials. Only one was filmed.

A studio shakeup resulted in the exit of Charles Rogers. The new studio head, Clifford Work, restored Henry MacRae to his old position

Flash Gordon Conquers the Universe: *A war conference with Ronal (Donald Curtis), Zarkov, Dale (now Carol Hughes), Flash, Queen Fria (Luli Deste), Count Korro (Sigurd Nilssen), Barin (now Roland Drew), and Aura (now Shirley Deane).*

as sole producer of all serials. MacRae teamed Ford Beebe and Ray Taylor to direct *Flash Gordon Conquers the Universe* from a script by George Plympton, Basil Dickey and Barry Shipman. Jerry Ash concentrated on the effects photography this time while most of the main unit work was photographed by William Sickner, ASC.

Sickner, who was born in Rochester, NY in 1894, free-lanced as an Akeley cameraman for years. After working in this capacity for Daniel B. Clark, ASC, on the excellent Tom Mix pictures at Universal in the early Thirties, he joined the serial unit. Among the many Universal serials he photographed were *Jungle Mystery, Heroes of the West, Pirate Treasure, Gordon of Ghost City, The Vanishing Shadow* and *Call of the Savage*. He and Beebe worked well together and were teamed often after Beebe became a producer-director at various studios. While Sickner specialized in serial and Western action, he also built a reputation for his handling of mystery atmosphere in such subjects as *The Mum-*

215

Even with Carmen D'Antonio at his beck, Ming lusts after Dale Arden.

my's Ghost (1944) and television episodes of "The Whistler" and "Alfred Hitchcock Presents."

Flash Gordon Conquers the Universe was made during November and December, 1939, and released the following year. The Raymond cartoons had changed dramatically by then, becoming more sophisticated in both art and story. Larger panels, costumes less derivative of the classical mode of the early strips, and a change from a cartoon style to something closely akin to slick magazine illustration gave the feature a definite new look. Even as burlesque queens were performing in costumes borrowed from Raymond's drawings of the 1934-37 period, top fashion designers were borrowing Dale Arden's "wedgie" shoes, Queen Aura's bare-midriff evening gown and the gorgeous coiffures worn by all the Mongo ladies. *Flash Gordon* had become the most beautiful cartoon feature ever seen. This status was not gained without cost, however; much of the youthful enthusiasm and reckless adventure of the earlier material inevitably was sacrificed.

This mixture of fantasy-melodrama, glamour and sophistication was heady stuff for a serial, but MacRae, Beebe and Taylor did their best to capture it. The result is a picture less satisfying in certain important respects than either of its predecessors, but which must be regarded as the most

elegant of all serials. It is filled with handsome, athletic men – Crabbe, Lee Powell, Roland Drew, Donald Curtis – and beautiful women – Carol Hughes, Luli Deste, Shirley Deane, Anne Gwynne, Carmen D'Antonio, Jeanne Kelly (later Jean Brooks) – and decorative sets. The costuming is opulent enough to do justice to a DeMille epic. Flash no longer has to battle his way through a dozen episodes in the same clothes, but dons a Robin Hood sort of costume when in the Forest Kingdom, furs while in the icy mountains of Frigia, and a military dress uniform while associating with royalty. Dale changes gowns as often as a Philip Barry heroine. Even Emperor Ming is dashingly clad in a bejeweled military ensemble instead of his old robe.

Crabbe, Middleton and Shannon appear in their customary roles, in which they are as effective as ever. Carol Hughes, a big-eyed brunette beauty who had played in numerous Warner Bros. and RKO pictures, is a Dale true to the Raymond drawings. (Jean Rogers, who was then under contract to Twentieth Century-Fox, was not available.) Roland Drew, usually cast as a society smoothie, is a streamlined Prince Barin more in the Raymond tradition than the likeable tough-guy projected by Richard Alexander. Two Raymond secondary heroes, Roka, Barin's aide from the Forest Kingdom, and Captain Ronal, of Frigia, are depicted faithfully by Lee Powell (star of Republic's popular *The Lone Ranger* serial) and Donald Curtis. A popular Raymond

D'Antonio dances for her emperor.

216

glamour girl, Queen Fria of Frigia, is played in blonde wig by the Viennese actress, Luli Deste, whose name does not appear in the credits. Queen Aura, now blonde and virtuous, is the sweet-faced Shirley Deane, of Fox's *Jones Family* series.

There are welcome appearances by beloved character actors, whose seamed countenances offer welcome contrast to the youth and beauty of the principals. Byron Foulger, William Royle, Chief Yowlatchie, Jack Roper, Earl Dwire, Harry C. Bradley, Michael Mark, Ernie Adams, Frank Hagney, Roy Barcroft, John Hamilton, Herbert Rawlinson and Ben Taggart are among them.

In addition to the new settings, there is considerable location work at Red Rock Canyon in the Mojave Desert, here standing in for the land of the Rock Men. The superb set built for James Whale's *Green Hell*, representing a lost underground temple with a towering idol and the enthroned mummies of ancient kings, was appropriated by the MacRae unit at almost the instant Whale's company vacated it. The castle and grounds for the just-completed *Tower of London* also were utilized.

Stock shots from the previous *Flash Gordon* serials and *Buck Rogers* were used, as well as much mountain climbing and avalanche footage from the 1930 German film, *White Hell of Pitz Palu*. Matching shots of the principals were made on the backlot's man-made cliffs, which were painted silver for the occasion. The idol and dancing girls from *Just Imagine* are back for Ming's entertainment, but this time he has more to leer at because Carmen D'Antonio, then a popular Hollywood night club entertainer, is

A remote controlled robot attacks Flash and Dale.

out front executing a censored version of her celebrated "Hot Voodoo" act.

Jerry Ash's visual effects are abundant. Miniatures of Ming's resplendent new palace, assorted desert vistas and mountaintops, and a slightly different collection of rocket ships are in almost as many shots as the actors. Ming's rockets are similar in design to the originals but are somewhat heavier and the fire from the jets is considerably improved. There are a number of process shots in which foreground elements, such as architectural details, are composited with rocket action. Death rays are superimposed in a process superior to that used earlier. Ming's murderous robots were photographed in a time-lapse style so that their movements are quick, erratic and unreal. Excellent glass shots lend the establishing shots of Ming's throne room vast proportions.

The theme music is from Liszt's tone poem, "Les Preludes." The rest of the score includes much of the music heard in the first two serials, excerpts of the Frank Skinner – Ralph Freed music for *Son of Frankenstein* and *Tower of London*, and quasi-Oriental music by Sam A. Perry. All of this was newly orchestrated and played at a faster tempo than before.

The chapter prologues are presented in a manner familiar to followers of the *Star Wars* saga;

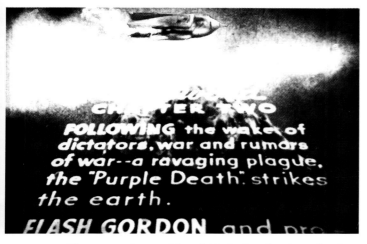
Chapter prologue title which looks ahead to the Star Wars *saga.*

Minions of Ming: Sonja (Anne Gwynne), Thong (Victor Zimmerman), Torch (Don Rowan), and soldiers Roy Barcroft and Lane Chandler.

the lettering moves toward a vanishing point in the distance and is superimposed over a scene of a rocket ship circling above a mountain top. (Actually, the style was initiated in *Buck Rogers*).

Chapter one begins with earth in the thrall of a mysterious plague known as the "purple death." Zarkov and Flash find evidence that "death dust" from the plant Mongo has been introduced into the atmosphere to cause the phenomenon. Returning to Mongo in Zarkov's rocket ship (a redesigned version of the original), Flash, Zarkov and Dale join forces with Barin and Aura, now rulers of Arboria, the forest kingdom, who reveal that Ming is responsible. They go to the frozen kingdom of Frigia, ruled by Beautiful Queen Fria, to seek the antidote for "death dust." There they are bedeviled by Ming's army, headed by Captain Torch, and a troop of exploding robots. They unknowingly have a traitor in their midst, the beautiful Sonja, who reports their activities to Ming.

Flash and his friends also venture into Ming's palace during much of the action and into the Desert of Death. They are captured by the hostile rock men, who disguise themselves as rocks to escape being eaten by the dragons that infest the region. Flash rescues the Rock Prince, thus gaining the alliance of the grotesque cave dwellers.

At last Ming is destroyed when Flash crashes a rocket ship loaded with explosives into the turret of the palace.

The third serial, despite its visual attractiveness, never attained the popularity of its predecessors. Much of the fault lay in its slower pacing and less vigorous action.

The character was reprised in a German-made television series in the Fifties, which proved a dismal failure. A Saturday morning cartoon series and a feature version produced by Filmation Studio appeared in the Eighties.

Flash Gordon returned to the big screen in 1980 in a very expensive, handsomely staged version produced by Dino de Laurentiis. It is colorful and exciting, but somehow it couldn't capture the imagination as well as those crudely exhilarating old serials. For this viewer, at least, the feature got off track when Flash was introduced as a football jock instead of a polo champ.

—George E. Turner

218

Flash Gordon
(1936)

A Universal *picture; producer,* Henry MacRae; *directed by* Frederick Stephani; *second unit director,* Ray Taylor; *screenplay by* Frederick Stephani, George Plympton, Basil Dickey, Ella O'Neill; *art director,* Ralph Berger; *directors of photography,* Jerome H. Ash, ASC *and* Richard Fryer, ASC; *electrical effects,* Norman Dewes; *special properties,* Elmer R. Johnson; *edited by* Saul A. Goodkind, Edward Todd, Alvin Todd, Louis Sackin; *original music by* Clifford Vaughan *and* David Klatzkin; *electrical properties,* Kenneth Strickfaden *and* Raymond Lindsay; RCA Photophone *recording. In 13 chapters. Total running time, 256 minutes. Released April 6, 1936.*

Flash Gordon, Larry "Buster" Crabbe; *Dale Arden,* Jean Rogers; *Emperor Ming,* Charles Middleton; *Princess Aura,* Priscilla Lawson; *Doctor Zarkov,* Frank Shannon; *Prince Barin,* Richard Alexander; *King Vultan,* John Lipson; *High Priest,* Theodore Lorch (*and* Lon Poff); *Prince Thun,* James Pierce; *Officer Torch,* Earl Askam; *King Kala,* Guy York Jr.; *Zona,* Muriel Goodspeed; *Gordon Sr.,* Richard Tucker; *Professor Hensley,* George Cleveland; *and* Loren Dowell, Carroll Borland, Lynton Brent, Don Brodie, Bull Montana, Constantine Romanoff, Sana Rayya, House Peters Jr., Jim Corey, Ray Corrigan, Glenn Strange, Lane Chandler, Fred Kohler Jr., Al Ferguson, Charles Whitaker, Bunny Waters, Fred Sommers, Monte Montague, Howard Christie, Fred Scott, Jerry Frank, Bob Kortman.

Chapter titles: 1, The Planet of Peril; 2, The Tunnel of Terror; 3, Captured by Shark Men; 4, Battling the Sea Beast; 5, The Destroying Ray; 6, Flaming Torture; 7, Shattering Doom; 8, Tournament of Death; 9, Fighting the Fire Dragon; 10, The Unseen Peril; 11, In the Claws of the Tigron; 12, Trapped in the Turret; 13, Rocketing to Earth.

Flash Gordon's Trip to Mars
(1938)

A Universal *picture; directed by* Ford Beebe *and* Robert S. Hill; *associate producer,* Barney Sarecky; *original story and screenplay by* Windham Gittens, Norman S. Hall, Ray Trampe, Herbert Dalmas; *director of photography,* Jerome Ash, ASC; *art director,* Ralph M. DeLacy; *supervising editor,* Saul A. Goodkind; *dialogue director,* Sarah C. Haney; *edited by* Alvin Todd, Louis Sackin, Joe Gluck; *mechanical effects,* Eddie Keys; *electrical properties,* Kenneth Strickfaden; Western Electric *recording. In 15 chapters. Total running time, 316 minutes. Released March 22, 1938.*

Flash Gordon, Larry "Buster" Crabbe; *Dale Arden,* Jean Rogers; *Emperor Ming,* Charles Middleton; *Queen Azura,* Beatrice Roberts; *Dr. Zarkov,* Frank Shannon; *Happy Hapgood,* Donald Kerr; *Clay King,* C. Montague Shaw; *Prince Barin,* Richard Alexander; *Tarnak,* Wheeler Oakman; *Pilot Captain,* Kane Richmond; *Airdrome Captain,* Kenneth Duncan; *Zandar,* Warner Richmond; *Flight Commander,* Jack Mulhall; *Mighty Toran,* Anthony Warde; *Pilot,* Ben Lewis; *and* Stanley Price, Earl Douglas, Charles Bud Wolfe, Edwin Stanley, Lou Merrill, James C. Eagles, Hooper Atchley, James G. Blaine, Wheaton Chambers, Ray Turner, Edwin Parker, Jerry Frank, Herb Holcombe, Lane Chandler, Reed Howes, Jerry Gardner, Tom Steele, George DeNormand.

Chapter titles: 1, New Worlds to Conquer; 2, The Living Dead; 3, Queen of Magic; 4, Ancient Enemies; 5, The Boomerang; 6, Tree Men of Mars; 7, The Prisoners of Mongo; 8, The Black Sapphire of Kalu; 9, Symbol of Death; 10, Incense of Forgetfulness; 11, Human Bait; 12, Ming, the Merciless; 13, The Miracle of Magic; 14, A Beast at Bay; 15, An Eye For an Eye.

Rocket Ship
Running time, 72 minutes. Released November 18, 1938.

Mars Attacks the World
Running time, 67½ minutes. Released November 18, 1938.

Flash Gordon Conquers the Universe
(1940)

A Universal *picture; directed by* Ford Beebe *and* Ray Taylor; *associate producer,* Henry MacRae; *written by* George Plympton, Basil Dickey, Barry Shipman; *directors of photography,* Jerome H. Ash, ASC *and* William Sickner, ASC; *art director,* Harold H. MacArthur; *dialogue director,* Jacques Jaccard; *film editors,* Alvin Todd, Louis Sackin, Joseph Glick; *supervising film editor,* Saul A. Goodkind; *electrical properties,* Kenneth Strickfaden; *assistant directors,* Edward Tyler *and* Charles Gould; RCA *recording. In 12 chapters. Total running time, 258 minutes. Released April 9, 1940.*

Flash Gordon, Buster Crabbe; *Dale Arden,* Carol Hughes; *Emperor Ming,* Charles Middleton; *Sonja,* Anne Gwynne; *Dr. Zarkov,* Frank Shannon; *Roka,* Lee Powell; *King Barin,* Roland Drew; *Queen Aura,* Shirley Deane; *Captain Ronal,* Donald Curtis; *Captain Torch,* Don Rowan; *Count Korro,* Sigurd Nilssen; *Karm,* Michael Mark; *Captain Sudin,* William Royle; *Thong,* Victor Zimmerman; *Turan,* Edgar Edwards; *Arden,* Tom Chatterton; *Keedish,* Harry C. Bradley; *Verna,* Mimi Taylor; *Drulk,* Byron Foulger; *General Lupi,* Benjamin Taggart; *Zandar,* Earl Dwire; *Queen Fria,* Luli Deste; *Giant,* Jack Roper; *and* Charles Sherlock, Paul Reed, Harold Daniels, Edward Payson, Reed Howes, Clarice Sherry, Jack Gardner, Joey Ray, Paul Douglas, Ernie Adams, Edward Mortimer, Robert Blair, Bill Hunter, Charles Waldron Jr., Pat Gleason, Frank Hagney, Ray Mala, Chief Yowlatchie, John Hamilton, Herbert Rawlinson, Jeanne Kelly (Jean Brooks), Allan Cavan, John Elliott, Roy Barcroft, Carmen D'Antonio.

Chapter titles: 1, The Purple Death; 2, Freezing Torture; 3, Walking Bombs; 4, The Destroying Ray; 5, The Palace of Terror; 6, Flaming Death; 7, The Land of the Dead; 8, The Fiery Abyss; 9, The Pool of Peril; 10, The Death Mist; 11, Stark Treachery; 12, Doom of the Dictator.

18

The Mighty Spectacle of *Gunga Din*

*T*hrills *for a thousand movies plundered for one mighty show!*

This phrase from one of the newspaper ads for *Gunga Din* offers a fair assessment of the picture – allowing, of course, for some traditional Hollywood exaggeration. Make that a *dozen* ordinary movies and it's no exaggeration at all.

Gunga Din was produced during the latter half of 1938 and the first two months of 1939. It was one of a mere handful of pictures made during the Thirties that cost close to $2,000,000 – an amount exceeded only by *Hell's Angels* (1930), *Gone With The Wind* (1939) and maybe one or two others. In those days of 25¢ bargain matinees (10¢ for kids), Bank Night, double features and free dishes, such a show hadn't a chance to make a profit. Fortunately, *Gunga Din* proved popular enough to be reincarnated often as a reissue, and eventually it brought in a lot of money.

The picture was inspired by an 1892 poem by Rudyard Kipling, a young Englishman who was born in Bombay and had spent much of his life in India. Written when Kipling was 27, it was a tribute to the regimental *bhisti* (appropriately pronounced "beastie"), the native water carriers who accompanied the British soldiers and irregular troops during their campaigns against the tribes of the northern boundary. In the rough lingo of an infantry private, it tells of a lowly *bhisti* who loses his life while trying to help the wounded. The soldier declares that

Tho I've belted you and flayed you,
By the living Gawd that made you,
You're a better man than I am, Gunga Din.

Kipling died in January, 1936. Two months later, rights to the title, *Gunga Din*, were purchased from Kipling's widow by Edward Small and Harry Goetz for their independent company, Reliance Pictures, which headquartered at RKO Pathé. William Faulkner was assigned to develop a scenario suggested by the poem. The novelist produced treatments and a partial script. In June, Reliance was liquidated and Small joined RKO as a producer. As a part of the deal, the studio inherited the screen rights to *Gunga Din,* for which Small had paid $5,000. Lester Cohen and, later, John Colton, prepared treatments for a version proposed as a King Vidor production.

Howard Hawks joined RKO in September and, ignoring the existing adaptations, began work in New York City on a new version with the madcap writing team of Ben Hecht and Charles MacArthur. By the end of the year the trio had written a story which closely resembles the movie as we know it. It was envisioned as a spectacular production with top-line players. Among those considered for leading roles were Ronald Colman, Victor McLaglen, Madeleine Carroll, Robert Montgomery, Robert Donat, Roger Livesey, Clark Gable, Spencer Tracy, Franchot Tone and Jack Oakie.

Hawks and Dudley Nichols continued to polish the *Gunga Din* script and Hawks produced the Cary Grant-Katharine Hepburn comedy, *Bring-*

Art director Perry Ferguson shows his sketch of the proposed hidden temple to director George Stevens.

ing Up Baby, which went well beyond the budget and schedule. Soon Hawks was at loggerheads with the vice-president in charge of production, Sam Briskin, and his long-term contract was terminated in 1937 by mutual consent. Before the end of the year Briskin also left the financially troubled studio to be replaced by young Pandro S. Berman, a strong producer who had learned the business under David O. Selznick and Merian C. Cooper.

Berman considered bringing Hawks back to make *Gunga Din,* but felt he was too reckless with time and money to entrust with a project which, at best, was certain to strain the company's resources. George Stevens, who was under contract to RKO, seemed a less risky choice.

Stevens had been a cinematographer, most notably for Hal Roach comedies and Westerns, during the late Twenties and Thirties. He began directing Bert Wheeler and Robert Woolsey's popular comedy films for RKO in 1932 and soon graduated to the likes of *Annie Oakley* (1935), with Barbara Stanwyck, *Alice Adams* (1935), with Katharine Hepburn and *Vivacious Lady* (1938), with Ginger Rogers and James Stewart. He was noted for working with quiet, easy efficiency and hewing close to RKO's often stringent budgets.

The Hecht-MacArthur yarn had plenty of action and some great individual gags, but lacked cohesion and overall suspense. As the starting date (late in June) neared, Stevens and two writers, Fred Guiol and Joel W. Sayre, retreated to Arrowhead Springs, a mountain resort area, to complete the script. Guiol was a comedy writer-director who had

worked with Stevens at the Roach Studio and had succeeded him as director of the Wheeler and Woolsey features. Sayre was a former newspaperman and novelist *(Rackety Rax)* who had written scripts for *Annie Oakley* (1935), *The Road To Glory* (1936) and others.

Guiol's research turned up what Stevens felt was "an essential thing necessary to glue this whole thing together" – an article about the Thuggee cult. This was a secret society dedicated to the worship of Kali, a four-armed Hindu goddess who, the Thuggees believed, demanded human sacrifice. The Thugs (the name has remained in the language to denote any violent criminal) killed more than a million persons in India before they were put down by Lord William Bentinck, governor-general of India from 1827 to 1835. They had their own language and all carried "strangling cloths" with which to kill their victims (it was forbidden to spill blood) and small pickaxes with which they were obliged to dig the graves of chosen victims in advance. Bentinck imprisoned 1,562 Thugs, hanged 382 and exiled 986. These mysterious assassins were far more dramatic and frightening than the bandits envisioned by Hecht and MacArthur.

Several weeks before the official shooting script was written, Stevens and the unit art director, Perry Ferguson, flew to the little desert highway town of Lone Pine, California, in the foothills of the High Sierras. Stevens knew the place well, having photographed Westerns in the vicinity, and realized it strongly resembled the northwest region of India. Locations were selected in the Alabama Hills, a stretch of weirdly eroded rock formations towering over desert terrain and backgrounded by Mount Whitney and several smaller snow-capped peaks. Ferguson made his preliminary set designs at the sites where they were to be constructed. The first was the frontier village of Tantrapur, which covered about eight acres, and included a business section, European quarters and the native quarter. Six miles away the military cantonment and parade ground was planned. Two miles nearer the base of Mount Whitney, in a natural valley surrounded by towering rocks, was the site of the hidden temple, headquarters of the neo-Thuggees.

All of these settings were built more solidly than most because they had to stand up under the vagaries of desert weather and because a great deal of stunt action was planned on the rooftops and stairways of both the native village and the temple. About 200 men worked for four weeks setting up tent quarters and galleys for the cast and crew. Once the quarters were established, a procession of studio vehicles arrived consisting of 16 cars, 12 trucks, ten 30-passenger buses and a large trailer housing a film laboratory. More than 500 technicians settled into the tent city to prepare the sets.

The story occurs during Victoria's reign, some 50 years after the last known Thuggee activity. A rollicking trio of sergeants, MacChesney, Cutter and Ballantine, are sent to investigate a village whose entire population has vanished. Attacked by a large force of fanatics, they hold off the enemy by throwing dynamite and return with evidence that

The finished set of the Thuggee temple.

Fairbanks in the thick of the fighting at Tantrapur.

the villagers were destroyed by Thugs. Eventually a treasure hunt leads them to a secret temple in the mountains which proves to be the stronghold of the Thugs. The soldiers capture the Guru who is the spiritual leader of the Thugs, but he sacrifices himself by leaping into a pit of snakes so his followers will not be deterred from carrying out his plan to ambush a detachment of English troops. Through the bravery of the sergeants and the regimental *bhisti*, Din, the regiment is saved and the Thuggees are defeated in a terrific battle.

Through this narrative runs a romantic sub-plot involving Ballantine's engagement to the beautiful but clinging Emmy Stebbins. The general tenor of the show is one of fun and escapade, but the major set-piece which everyone remembers most vividly – the weird adventures in the hidden temple and the suspense as the regiment marches toward certain doom – is tautly dramatic. The painful climb of the wounded Din to the pinnacle of the temple to sound his bugle and warn the regiment in the nick of time, is nerve-wracking, and Din's fall to his death is an unforgettably tragic moment.

The leading players were almost last-minute choices. They could hardly have been improved upon, even had Louis B. Mayer agreed to loan them Clark Gable, Spencer Tracy and Franchot Tone, as

Hawks had hoped. Cary Grant, first offered the romantic role of Ballantine, wisely held out for the more humorous character of Cutter, a scatterbrained Cockney. Douglas Fairbanks Jr. took the less colorful Ballantine and gave the character a welcome touch of class. Big Victor McLaglen, borrowed from Twentieth Century-Fox, got what proved to be his all-time favorite role as MacChesney, the hard-bitten but lovable leader of the three.

The only logical choice for Gunga Din seemed to be Sabu, the Indian youth who scored heavily in Robert Flaherty's *Elephant Boy* (1937) and Alexander Korda's *The Drum* (1938). Korda would not loan Sabu, however, and tests were made of other actors, some of them Indians. Sam Jaffe, who had gained considerable attention for his portrayal of the High Lama in *Lost Horizon* (1937), won the role, which proved a fine piece of casting against type. Emmy Stebbins was played by Joan Fontaine, who was not destined to receive a role worthy of her considerable talents until Alfred Hitchcock cast her in his first American film, *Rebecca* (1940). The prints currently shown are lacking a number of her scenes as well as *all* scenes in which Cecil Kellaway appeared as her father.

Although the Sayre-Guiol screenplay had been okayed by the studio, Stevens didn't consider it ready at starting time. Consequently, he took the writers with him on location and they rewrote and polished many scenes as they were being set up.

Shortly after the Tantrapur Village setting was completed and dressed, a fire broke out. The crew brought it under control with wet burlap bags, a chemical truck and a water wagon. A full block of the village was destroyed along with thousands of props. Lloyd's of London paid off what was reported as the largest movie loss in 16 years. Thirty-one carpenters were rushed to the site from Los Angeles and rebuilt the damaged structures in 10 days. Freak windstorms caused further set damage.

During most of the shooting, which was scheduled for six weeks but eventually ran four weeks over, 325 actors and technical personnel lived at the site. A commissary staff of 37 – chefs, bakers, waiters, dishwashers, janitors and maintenance men – took care of the preparation of some 14 tons of meat and vegetables that were trucked in from Los Angeles each week. About 15,000 lbs. of ice per week were brought in to keep the food refrigerated.

During the last two weeks the location party almost tripled in size, as some 1,200 extras arrived for the big battle scenes. Makeup expert Charles Gemora (better known as a portrayer of gorillas in innumerable horror pictures and serials)

Part of the temple interior built on a sound stage.

In the torture chamber of the temple with Abner Biberman, left, and Ciannelli demanding troop information from the three sergeants.

Thugs ambush the "Kilties" in the Alabama Hills near Lone Pine, California.

225

found trying to make up hundreds of extras as Indians a formidable task. He had a 55-gallon drum of brown makeup rigged with a spray gun and painted six extras at a time on a wooden turntable.

Four elephants (led by Annie Mae, a famous trained pachyderm which performed in hundreds of movies), several truckloads of camels and bullocks, and nearly 400 horses also were used in the battle sequence.

It was found that the off-white costumes of the Hindus, which photographed perfectly in the Hollywood exteriors and interiors, photographed badly at Lone Pine, which is nearly 4,000 feet higher than Los Angeles. The wardrobe men bought all the available flat white goods – more than 300 yards of it – from the three stores in Lone Pine and confiscated 72 bedsheets from the location camp in order to make new costumes in a hurry for the 400-man Thuggee army.

The director of photography was Joseph August, ASC, a veteran cinematographer who began shooting Westerns at Inceville in 1911. August was William S. Hart's favorite cinematographer – he shot 59 of Hart's hard-bitten, realistic silent films. He also was an early visual effects man, specializing in miniature work, multiple exposures and matte shots. His most embarrassing moment occurred when he staged a dramatic scene of a sinking (miniature) ship in an outdoor tank at Inceville. At the screening he was horrified to see a giant cow amble into the background and take a drink from the distant edge of the "ocean."

August's work ranged from the austerity of the Hart Westerns to the rich atmospheric work in John Ford's production *The Informer* (1935), William

Fairbanks, Victor McLaglen, Eduardo Ciannelli, Sam Jaffe and Cary Grant on top of the temple. This is a sound stage mockup of a part of the set with a process projected background.

Dieterle's *All That Money Can Buy (The Devil and Daniel Webster)* (1941) and the delicate *Portrait of Jennie* (1948), his last picture.

August was a true stylist whose work often was unconventional. In an *American Cinematographer* interview (March, 1939), he mentioned his aversion to using exposure meters:

"I am not against meters, by any means. They just don't fit into my plan of taking pictures. The meters I lean on are my eyes. When I first started in this business 28 years ago I had a preceptor I then thought sort of tough: tough because he was insistent upon my learning what could be accomplished with a pair of eyes and a man with scant patience for any devices that aimed to make those organs secondary to any human invention.

"Then again, frequently I choose to make an exposure that – well, we will call it an unorthodox exposure, one aimed to produce a certain effect that may be desirable. For instance, the negative might be overexposed and underdeveloped – or the procedure might be reversed...It would be necessary to tip the laboratory if it so happened the lab were one in which a cameraman could take what some might consider liberties these days.

"I recall that same preceptor of mine down at Inceville in the beginning. There was a device at that time designed to obtain for the camerman something parallel to what a meter would provide today. I was told with considerable detail and even more emphasis just what fate would befall me if he ever found me fussing with one of those gadgets... known as the illumination system.

"It was just after that interview I began seriously to cultivate attention to my eyes with the object of learning as much as possible of what I could accumulate in the way of optical knowledge."

Photographing action among the hard highlights and deep shadows of the Alabama Range gave August's educated eyes a heavy workout. He enumerated some of the location problems in a statement to a 1939 issue of William Lewin's *Group Discussion Guide* magazine:

"The wild assortment of weather during our ten weeks on location in the Sierras gave the camera crews the most trouble. Because of the heavy expense of maintaining a large company so far from Hollywood it wasn't feasible to shoot the story in sequence. And it was our problem to reconcile the photography to keep the weather cinematically consistent.

"Here are a few weather notes on what we experienced during our work at the *Gunga Din* location:

British troops approach a Thuggee ambush.

"Temperatures which for weeks ranged from 105 to 115 degrees, beneath cloudless, empty skies.

"A pre-season snowstorm that swooped down from nearby Mt. Whitney, skirted our sets, changed our majestic background of rugged peaks to solid white. (While subsequent warm weather brought the background back to normal, we confined ourselves to closeups.)

"A freak windstorm which damaged some of the sets, and actually took the roof off a nearby mountain cabin.

"Dust storms which lasted three days, obscuring all but the closest objects. (Again we stuck to closeups till the weather cleared.)

"Several rain storms, preceded by some of the most beautiful cloud formations I've ever seen."

That damaging windstorm set a 35-foot camera tower to rocking while four of the camera crew hung on desperately. The guy wires snapped, but before the tower could topple some 40 men surrounded it, grabbed the wires and clustered around the base of the tower, holding it in check until the men were able to climb down.

One of the more unusual examples of photography occurs when two of the soldiers enter the secret valley and behold the Thuggee temple. The camera frames a closeup of one actor's right profile, then pans right to reveal details of the valley and temple in a slow, 180 degree sweep that ends on the left profile of the other actor. It provides a long moment of eerie atmosphere at once desolate and yet teeming with unseen menace.

Similarly weird are the night scenes of a torchlit procession of hundreds of Thuggees over the desert and into the secret shrine. The sequence begins at the Lone Pine location and proceeds smoothly into the sound stage interior set. Other dramatic scenes follow, lighted (to all appearances) by the flickering torches of the worshippers who crowd the big set to hear Eduardo Ciannelli exhort his fanatics to "Kill lest you be killed yourselves; kill for the love of Kali; kill for the love of killing; kill, kill, kill!"

Heading a second photographic unit in the large-scale action was Frank Redman, ASC, who had been second cameraman on 10 Pathé serials before becoming a director of photography at RKO. Other cameramen at the location were operators Charles Burke, William Clothier, Eddie Pyle and George Diskant, and assistants Charles Straumer, Joseph August Jr., William Reinhold and Ledge Haddow.

Pandro Berman, alarmed at the rapidly mounting costs as the location work extended well beyond the original six weeks schedule, ordered the company to return to Hollywood before the outdoor action was completed. Many of the remaining scenes were then shot at locations closer to the studio, such as Bronson Canyon (where a village street was erected), the RKO Ranch at Encino, and

227

The cantonment set near Lone Pine.

Lake Sherwood (which stood in for the river at the edge of the village). For the scene in which Din and the three sergeants jump from a roof atop a high cliff into the "river," it was necessary to erect a high parallel surmounted by catapults so the full-scale dummies would seem to jump rather than fall.

The interior scenes at the cantonment and in the temple were shot at this time on various stages at RKO's Hollywood studio and RKO-Pathé. In September, a rough cut was assembled and shown to the studio executives. Only the climactic battle and some post-production work remained to be done. So impressed were the officials that they decided to authorize another two weeks of shooting at Lone Pine to permit the battle to be filmed on an even larger scale than was envisioned originally. The decision was made despite the fact that the final production cost would almost certainly be more than could be recouped at the boxoffice.

The returning company was greeted by an early snowstorm and seasonal rains. The battle scenes were staged spectacularly enough to rank with the best of DeMille and Griffith. Cameras covered the action from numerous angles, capturing both the vastness of the sequence and its intimacy of minutely choreographed detail.

Producer-director Stevens said that "From a director's standpoint, the battle scenes constituted our biggest problem.

"The job was to use 1,500 men, several hundred horses and mules – to say nothing of four elephants – most effectively for scenes of utmost confusion, and still plan the action to obviate accidents and possible injuries.

"To do this we first fought on paper the entire battle, the charge, and the headlong retreat of the Thugs. Then we transferred our activities to Mt. Whitney's rugged slopes, and rehearsed the cast in small detachments and in 'slow motion' until the mechanics of the action were established. As the scene took shape the number of people and animals was gradually increased, the action speeded up until we had the scene going at top speed – then we shot it.

"Just beyond the range of the cameras were posted first-aid facilities as well as wranglers to recapture frightened, riderless animals. Behind various rocks assistant directors kept in touch with me by field telephone, and relayed my 'commands' to the groups nearest them."

Among the horsemen involved in the fighting were a number of men who were stars of Westerns in the silent era: Buzz Barton, Bob Reeves, Bob Sherwood, Tom Forman and Art Mix. About 30 stuntmen participated in these and other scenes, including David Sharpe, "The Flying Mazzettis" (Vic, Tom and Otto), Max Rose, Rube Schaeffer, Buddy Mason, Bill Lally, Clem Fuller and Walt

Robbins. Slim Hightower doubled Sam Jaffe in his heroic climb to the top of the temple and his subsequent fall.

Principal photography was completed on October 15, 1938, after 104 working days, of which 10 weeks were at the Lone Pine locations. The negative cost was $1,909,669.28 – about a half-million over the budget. Henry Berman tackled the enormous editing job, cutting most of the picture. Stevens brought in one of his old Hal Roach cutters, John Lockert, to edit the battle scenes into a cohesive sequence. Vernon Walker, ASC, took charge of special photographic effects.

Negotiations were begun to borrow Erich Wolfgang Korngold from Warner Bros. to compose an elaborate score. The Viennese composer was considered tops in the profession because of his

work in *A Midsummer Night's Dream* (1935), *Anthony Adverse* (1937), and *The Adventures of Robin Hood* (1938). The deal was made, but when Korngold learned he would have only three weeks to compose and record a score with the scope of a symphony, he refused the job.

The dependable Alfred Newman – former musical director for Samuel Goldwyn and other of the United Artists producers, soon to become head of the Twentieth Century-Fox music department – was hired at the last moment. He managed to deliver music that is among the more memorable things about the picture, capturing to perfection the frolicsome overall mood while doing full justice to the romance, suspense and mystery of the picture. Newman conducted a 32-piece orchestra for the recording sessions.

Clifford Stine, ASC, and William Collins photographed the miniatures, matte shots and back projection scenes. Mario Larrinaga executed the

Lunchtime at the hidden Temple.

matte paintings, which were utilized unobtrusively to add elements to the location settings.

The opening titles, which emphatically convey the expectation of an epic film, strongly resemble the later trademark of J. Arthur Rank Productions: a muscular man striking a large gong. In this case the gong is enormous, dwarfing the man with the hammer, who is dressed as a Hindu. Each time the tocsin is struck, a title formed of concentric ripples spreading from the point of impact, shimmers onto its face. Optical photography expert Lin Dunn, ASC, created the effect by reflecting the title letters in a pan of mercury.

Shortly after its premiere, *Gunga Din* was called back for another piece of optical work. Kipling's family had raised objections to the picture's depiction of Kipling being present at the battle scene, where he supposedly was inspired to write

Thugs and riderless horses flee the battle scene. Wranglers waited outside camera range to round up the frightened animals.

his famed poem. The poet was portrayed by Reginald Sheffield, father of Johnny Sheffield of the *Tarzan* films, and was shown standing in front of his tent while Montagu Love read his poem over the body of Din. A wagon was superimposed over the tent, effectively blocking "Kipling" from view. Both versions of the scene exist.

Gunga Din proved an immensely popular picture and has been in almost continual release over three decades. It was not popular in India, for obvious reasons, and certainly can not be taken seriously as a true depiction of that country's history. It is only what it set out to be: an exciting, outrageous, funny, suspenseful piece of pure entertainment. It was the *Raiders of the Lost Ark* of its day.

—George E. Turner

Troopers drive the Thuggees back.

An RKO Radio *picture, producer-director,* George Stevens; *executive producer,* Pandro S. Berman; *screen play by* Joel Sayre, Fred Guiol; *story by* Ben Hecht, Charles MacArthur; *suggested by the poem by* Rudyard Kipling; *music by* Alfred Newman; *director of photography,* Joseph H. August, ASC; *art directors,* Van Nest Polglase, Perry Ferguson; *photographic effects,* Vernon L. Walker, ASC; *set decorations,* Darrell Silvera; *gowns by* Edward Stevenson; *recorded by* John E. Tribby, James Stewart; *edited by* Henry Berman, John Lockert; *second unit camera,* Frank Redman, ASC; *optical photography,* Linwood Dunn, ASC; *effects photography,* Clifford Stine, ASC, William Collins; *assistant directors,* Edward Killy, Dewey Starkey; *technical advisors,* Sir Robert Erskine Holland, Capt. Clive Morgan, Sgt. Maj. William Briers; *makeup artist,* Charles Gemora; *operative cam-*

eramen, Charles Burke, William Clothier, ASC, Eddie Pyle, George Diskant, ASC; *assistant cameramen;* Charles Straumer, ASC, Joe August Jr., Ledge Haddow, Bill Reinhold; *Running time 117 minutes. Released February 17, 1939.*

Sgt. Cutter, Cary Grant; *Sgt. MacChesney,* Victor McLaglen; *Sgt. Ballantine,* Douglas Fairbanks Jr.; *Emmy Stebbins,* Joan Fontaine; *Gunga Din,* Sam Jaffe; *The Guru,* Eduardo Ciannelli; *Colonel Weeks,* Montagu Love; *Major Mitchell,* Lumsden Hare; *Bertie Higginbotham,* Robert Coote; *Chota,* Abner Biberman; *Mr. Stebbins,* Cecil Kellaway; *Mr. Kipling,* Reginald Sheffield; *Executioner,* Lalo Encinas; *Thuggee,* Richard Robles; *Thuggee,* Lal Chand Mehra; *Telegrapher,* Charles Bennett.

231

19

The Exquisite Evil of *Cat People*

Good horror movies flourished during the 1930s, a golden age for the critically despised but sometimes artistic films. By the early 1940s the gold had turned to brass. The occasional worthwhile effort that surfaced from the bog into which the genre had blundered served mostly to keep alive the hope that a worthy successor to the likes of James Whale and Tod Browning would step forth to herald a rebirth.

In 1942, during the most crucial days of World War II, the new master of horror did emerge, albeit somewhat reluctantly. He was a big, hearty man called Val Lewton. The picture that presaged the small reniassance was *Cat People,* a picture born as a consequence of one of the periodic management shakeups at RKO Radio Pictures, Inc. This upheaval, like most which preceded and followed it, was predicated upon the failure of a number of expensive productions to break even at a time when most of the studios were happily in the black.

It was at about this time that Bing Crosby, working next door at Paramount, was supposed to have said that if the threatened raid on Hollywood by Japanese bombers were to come to pass, "I'd head over to RKO. They haven't had a hit in years."

Charles Koerner, a theatre chain executive, was appointed vice president in charge of production at RKO early that year. Koerner learned that the company was losing money on its A pictures but that solid and predictable profits were being returned by many so-called B (for budget) pictures, which at RKO were made at costs under $150,000. Studying the reports from other studios he found that Universal was making so much money from

horror pictures, both A and B, that the front office called them "Midas productions." He decided to establish a new production unit that would specialize in the making of moderately budgeted horror films built around exploitable titles that could be exhibitor-tested in advance.

At a party in Beverly Hills, Koerner met Vladimir Ivan (Val) Lewton, a Russian-born former novelist and MGM publicity writer who had been story editor and research director for David O. Selznick for the past eight years. He was a pampered, precocious Columbia University graduate, the nephew of stage and screen star Alla Nazimova. Burly and good-humored, a natural raconteur, the 37-year old Lewton impressed the studio chief as a man who could put together a good show. Following his instincts, Koerner offered Lewton a four-year contract as associate producer. After much agonizing because of his loyalty to Selznick, Lewton accepted.

Lewton went on the payroll at $250 per week (with escalation to $750) on March 16, 1942. He was given a small office and a secretary, Jessie Ponitz. He happily informed his friends that he was listed in the studio telephone book as an "ass. prod." His immediate superior was an executive producer, Lou Ostrow.

Koerner handed Lewton a short story by Algernon Blackwood, "Ancient Sorceries," saying it was the kind of story he wanted Lewton to make. Lewton was impressed with his employer's taste.

A short time later he modified his opinion. Koerner had gone to another party and someone

Jacques Tourneur, sitting in front of the camera, rehearses Kent Smith and Simone Simon. The man at right is Doran Cox.

there suggested that, while werewolves and vampires had been overdone in films, "nothing much has been done about cats." Koerner dreamed up a title: *Cat People*. Lewton was appalled at the subject – he admitted to having "an atavistic fear of cats" – and the lurid title, but managed to keep his opinion to himself.

Searching for a story basis, Lewton considered Ambrose Bierce's "The Eyes of the Panther," but decided its premise of pre-natal influence would not be convincing in a movie. He then turned to a story by Margaret Irwin, "Monsieur Seeks a Wife," which he noted down as "a fetching little tale about a man who meets two sisters that are not really women, but cats." He recommended Cornell Woolrich's "Black Alibi" to Koerner as a good cat story;

Koerner bought the rights, but it became the basis of Lewton's third production, *The Leopard Man*. In mid-April, Lewton decided to drop all pretense of adapting a published work and developed an idea of his own.

This embryonic story opens in a snow-covered Balkan village as it is being invaded by a Nazi Panzer division. By day the inhabitants seem phlegmatic, unconcerned even by such a threat; by night, however, these same individuals change into great cats and turn against their captors. A girl from the village flees to New York and falls in love, but she can't escape her heritage.

Part of Lewton's initial planning was to have the girl never speak directly. "I thought we might let our cat-girl only speak in long shots; you hear the murmur of her voice, you never hear what she is saying and, if it is necessary to give her words meaning to the audience, I think we can always contrive to have some other character tell what the girl said." His bosses nixed the idea.

234

The projected ending was quite unlike the one eventually filmed. "Most of the cat/werewolf stories I have read and all the werewolf stories I have seen on the screen end with the beast shot and turning back into a human being after death," Lewton wrote. "In this story I'd like to show a violent quarrel between the man and woman in which she is provoked into an assault upon him. To protect himself, he pushes her away, she stumbles, falls awkwardly, and breaks her neck in the fall. The young man, horrified, kneels to see if he can feel her heart beat. Under his hand black hair and hide come up and he draws back to look down in horror at a dead, black panther."

Some of these initial ideas didn't survive, but important elements of the final version were suggested, such as "a man, possibly a doctor, who always gives the scientific or factual explanation for any phenomena that occurs, brushing the supernatural away with his classification and yet, who is always proved wrong by the events on the screen. This device, I hope, will express the audiences' doubts even before they are fully formulated in the audiences' mind and quickly answer them, thus lending a degree of credibility to the yarn, which it is going to be difficult to achieve." There also is a scene "in which the boy brings the girl into a pet store. Here, I'd like to show the chattering fear that arises upon her entrance. The birds and monkeys scream and chatter with fright. At the very height of the uproar, I would like to have a little black cat come down the center aisle of the store, very calmly, and rub affectionately against the girl." (As filmed, however, the cat is as terrified as the other animals).

His desire to avoid typical horror film situations led Lewton to drop the Balkan sequence, opting instead to present the entire story in the context of contemporary American settings. In a 1944 press release, he stated that "the characters in the run-of-the-mill weirdies were usually people very remote from the audiences' experiences. European nobles of dark antecedents, mad scientists, man-created monsters, and the like cavorted across the screen. With the thought that it would be much more entertaining if people with whom audiences could identify were to be shown in contact with the strange, the weird and the occult, we made it a basic part of our work to show normal people – engaged in normal occupations – in our pictures."

Ostrow, who had climbed from Monogram to Universal to MGM (where he was in charge of the highly successful Hardy Family series) to 20th Century-Fox to RKO, was not sympathetic to Lewton's ideas of cinema. He gauged Lewton as being too

pretentious and fussy to succeed as a producer of popular entertainment – a view shared (with some justification) by many others at the studio. Koerner, fortunately, liked most of the ideas.

When Ostrow, prodded by Koerner's enthusiastic response, gave a reluctant okay to the basic plotline, Lewton sent for DeWitt Bodeen, another alumnus of Selznick-International, who became the first screenwriter of the group. "Val liked a play of mine, 'Embers at Haworth,' which was about the Bronte sisters, and he hired me at Selznick as research assistant on a production of *Jane Eyre*," Bodeen said. "Before he departed for RKO he asked me to call him as soon as my work for Selznick was completed. I phoned him two weeks later and he made arrangements for me to be hired as a contract writer at the guild minimum of $75 per week. I had never written for the screen before."

Lewton and Bodeen spent a week reading whatever literature about cats they could unearth. According to Bodeen, "We used a lot of Carl Van Vechten's 'Tiger in the House,' which was all about cats throughout history. It was the source for many things we put into the screenplay. We also screened many successful horror films, mostly from Universal, intent upon eliminating the cliches."

When at last they pooled their notes, Lewton had Bodeen construct a 50-page story, not as a treatment or script but one written as though for magazine publication. Bodeen produced a first-person narrative written from the POV of Alice, a woman in love with the cat girl's husband. It included many elements important to the final script, including the outstanding sequence wherein Alice is menaced by the cat in a hotel swimming pool. The idea sprang from a personal experience: Bodeen had almost drowned once when he fell into a similar

At the Belgrade Cafe the incomparable Elizabeth Russell addresses Simon as "my sister."

Lewton's idea of "normal people engaged in normal occupations": Smith, Jack Holt, Alan Napier and Jane Randolph as ship designers.

pool from a swing-rope and nobody was there to pull him out.

"We made Irena a dress designer because we needed her to work alone in her apartment," Bodeen revealed. "She's lonely and afraid to get to know anybody – men, especially – because of her belief that she will kill whomever she falls in love with. Her sketches actually were some of Edward Stevenson's drawings we borrowed from the costume department."

Jacques Tourneur, son of the great French director, Maurice Tourneur, was hired at Lewton's instigation and arrived at RKO on May 20. He had directed four pictures in France in the early Thirties, then came to America, where he was teamed with Lewton and William Wright in staging the French Revolution sequences for the Selznick-MGM epic, *A Tale of Two Cities* (1935). During the next five years Tourneur directed short subjects for Jack Chertok's smoothly operated unit at MGM. When Chertok began producing features in 1939, Tourneur directed three of them: *They All Come Out* and *Nick Carter, Detective* (1939) and *Phantom Raiders* (1940). More short subjects followed, and a forgotten Republic feature, *Doctors Don't Tell* (1941). Under the circumstances, the overqualified and underpaid director was delighted to join the Lewton unit.

The next member assigned to the team was the film editor, Mark Robson. Robson was one of the studio's top editors and not the sort usually relegated to B product, but, as he explained: "I was Orson Welles' editor on *Citizen Kane*, and that picture cost a lot of time and money and it didn't recoup. Management tended to blame all of RKO's finanacial troubles on Orson, and those of us who worked with him had to share the blame."

Being exiled to the horror unit proved a boon, however. Robson was brought into all pre-production and story sessions from the first and made important contributions. Lewton wrote to Koerner that, "Jacques says of him that he cuts like a director, which, from a director, is praise indeed." Later, when Tourneur was promoted to A pictures, Lewton chose Robson to succeed him as director and obtained his friend, Robert Wise as film editor. When the studio promoted Robson, Wise took his place as director.

"We took the films very seriously," Robson recalled of his work with Lewton. "We worked very hard and our standards were very high. We always tried to follow any horror sequence with something really beautiful."

Lewton received valuable advice from a veteran B producer, Herman Schlom, who had learned the business at Republic in the Thirties and became one of RKO's top experts at making slick, economical melodramas. Schlom spent a day with Lewton, explaining the many ways of cutting production costs, particularly in the planning of sets. Because of wartime shortages of building materials, the government had imposed a strictly enforced limit of $10,000 per picture for set construction, which made it necessary to utilize standing sets almost exclusively. Fortunately, there was a great deal to choose from at RKO, which, in addition to the radio studio in Hollywood (now the west part of Paramount), had use of the great 40-acre backlot and stages in Culver City, Calif., at RKO-Pathé (now Culver Studio, minus the backlot) and the RKO Ranch (now a residential area in Encino). It was from Schlom, Lewton acknowledged, that he learned to alter scripts to reduce the number of sets needed and to lavish greater care in dressing one or two major sets while skimping by on the others.

The main action of *Cat People* focuses on the cat girl's studio apartment, the exterior of which was a brownstone front on the venerable Pathé New York street, a few paces from the scene of Robert Armstrong's "discovery" of Fay Wray in *King Kong*. A marvelous interior stairway built some months earlier for Orson Welles' production, *The Magnificent*

Randolph, Tom Conway and Smith on the Amberson's staircase.

Ambersons, and still standing on a Pathé stage, was altered by adding an adjacent elevator cage from the scene dock. The Central Park Zoo settings were comfortably familiar mementos of the Fred Astaire-Ginger Rogers musicals, while some offices and stairways were leftovers from the 1941 comedy, *The Devil and Miss Jones.* A standing cafe set was used as a coffee shop for one sequence, then redressed as a pet shop for another and as a Serbian restaurant for a third. A stone wall at the ranch, from *The Hunchback of Notre Dame* became part of the Central Park concourse. The majority of the other sets consisted of props set up with wild walls.

Unit art director Walter Keller artfully disguised everything to obscure any suggestion of "hand-me-down" origins. The sets were smothered in appropriate decor by decorator Al Fields, who combed the property department and prop rental houses for items significant to the development of both characters and story. Two key props of the story were made specifically for the production: a folding screen on which is painted a handsome art deco black panther slinking through the jungle, which not only dominates the apartment but is introduced as a title background; and a statuette of King John of Serbia, on horseback, with the body of a cat impaled on his lance. The latter was made in the studio plaster shop.

Casting was an important part of of the scheme to avoid conventionalities. "I'd like to have the girl a little kitten-face like Simone Simon, cute

Irena (Simon) at work in her studio apartment.

and soft and cuddly and seemingly not at all dangerous," Lewton informed Ostrow on April 9. "I took a look at the Paramount picture, *The Island of Lost Souls* and, after seeing their much-publicized 'panther woman,' I feel that any attempt to secure a cat-like quality in our girl's physical appearance would be absolutely disastrous."

Bodeen said that "Val told me from the first to write the part around Simone Simon. He seemed confident that he would be able to get her." A leading star in France, she had made a number of films in the United States but had never achieved the popularity her sponsors at Fox and RKO had hoped for. Lewton sent her a first draft script while she was appearing in a play in Chicago and she quickly accepted at rather generous terms. She proved, by all accounts, to be as charming off-screen as on.

For the ambiguous character of the psychiatrist, initially visualized as a sinister European called Mueller, Lewton's first choice was the German emigre, Fritz Kortner, who, he believed, would "add a great deal of menace and a certain conceited quality that would make audiences dislike him." He also considered Edgar Barrier and Vladimir Sokoloff. As the script developed, however, he decided to cast against type and have the character be a young and suave Britisher named Judd. Likeable, Russian-born Tom Conway, a contract player who

had recently succeeded his older brother, George Sanders, as star of Schlom's *Falcon* series, proved an apt choice.

Kent Smith, a successful Broadway leading man, who had been signed to a contract in 1941, commuted by bicycle from his home in Beverly Hills to the Hollywood studio. He was depressed, he said, because he "had been here for nine months without appearing in *anything* except some army training films." It was his second try at pictures, the first being an unrewarding stint at MGM, which cast him inconspicuously in *The Garden Murder Case* (1936) and then dropped his option. After observing the easy-going cyclist over a period of several weeks, Lewton decided he might be an ideal quiet-man hero. A brief interview and a screening of the training films so convinced him that he was willing to assume expenses incurred by Smith's contract as part of the slim – $118,948 – budget. Smith's sympathetic portrayal launched a long, solid film career.

Jane Randolph, another contract player, was chosen for the second woman role because she was *not* the ingenue type usually cast in such roles. Tall and efficient-looking, she epitomized the modern career women who had been coming to the fore since the beginning of the war. Jack Holt, venerable star of innumerable action films, was available for a few days' work before his contract expired. The other actors, even to the bits, were hand picked by Tourneur and Lewton from the contract list and Central Casting. The most striking small role is that of a cat-like woman who appears in only one sequence – an unforgettable cameo by the statuesque Elizabeth Russell.

Cinematographer Nicholas Musuraca, ASC, handsome and youthful looking despite having been in the movie business since 1909, was assigned routinely to *Cat People*. Although he had been "typed" for some years as a photographer of Western and action pictures, Musuraca's work for Lewton (for whom he shot five of the nine horror pictures) recast him as a master of highly dramatic mystery lighting. His distinctive technique not only established the prevailing style of the Lewton films but has been recognized belatedly as the cornerstone of what now is celebrated as the quintessential *film noir* style.

Actually, Musuraca had pioneered a similar "look" in an artistic RKO B picture of 1940, *Stranger on the Third Floor,* which is considered by many as the prototype of *noir* films. This picture, in fact, bears a striking resemblance in most respects to the Lewton series, which can hardly be said of any other pre-*Cat People* production. The other distinguished RKO cinematographers who contributed

238

to the Lewton films – with the single exception of J. Roy Hunt, ASC, creator of the lacy romantic images of the second in the series, *I Walked With a Zombie* – closely followed the *Cat People* style. Inescapable is the conclusion that Musuraca was the ideal collaborator for Lewton. The veteran cinematographer carried the style into a number of later atmospheric films such as *The Spiral Staircase* (1945), *The Locket* (1946), and *Out of the Past* (1947), *Blood on the Moon* (1948), *The Woman on Pier 13* (1950), and *The Whip Hand* (1951).

In the early years of the talking picture, many innovations in sound recording technique were introduced in mystery and horror films. The lessons of the masters were not lost upon Lewton, whatever his determination to eschew the conventionalities of such films. He was adamant that dialogue should be used only when the story could not be advanced through the combination of visual image and incidental sounds.

When the cost accounting office demanded to know why the recording crew worked an extra three days on *Cat People*, recording chief John Cass explained that they spent one day at Gay's Lion Farm recording the growls and roars of the big cats and two days at the indoor swimming pool of the Royal Palms Hotel recording reverberation effects. A vocal effects actress, Dorothy Lloyd, was hired to create more cat sounds. The studio bosses regarded such extras as being terribly extravagant for a B picture.

Unwilling to settle for the pastiche musical scores customarily assembled for low budget pictures, Lewton conferred with musical director Constantin Bakaleinikoff even before the screenplay was under way. Lewton said he was searching for a lullaby theme with "a haunting, memorable quality somewhat like the short bit from 'Anitra's Dance' which was used so memorably in the German picture *M*. At the same time we would like a little strain of music which is to be sung or hummed by the heroine, to have a cat-like feeling and, if possible, a sinister note of menace." (Actually, the Grieg theme referred to was from 'The Hall of the Mountain King.') Taken under consideration were Stravinsky's "Berceuse du Chat," the "Puss in Boots" scene from Tchaikowski's *"The Sleeping Beauty,"* Moussorgsky's "The Brigand Cat" and several others.

Roy Webb, who was assigned to compose the score, was brought into the story sessions to contribute ideas for linking the visuals to music. Like most film composers at that time, Webb was accustomed to being consulted only after principal photography was completed. Webb said later that by being involved in the planning he was able to provide a more effective score than was normally possi-

ble. One day on the set, Simone Simon sang for Lewton a traditional French lullaby she remembered from childhood, "Do, Do, Baby Do." Lewton took her to Webb, who listened and agreed that it would make an ideal leitmotiv for the film. A Russian writer, Andrei Tolstoi, was hired to translate the lyrics into Russian and coach the actress in the proper pronounciations and delivery.

Principal photography began July 28 and was completed 24 working days later. The budget was revised to $141,659 when shooting began, but the picture was brought in for $134,959.46. There was strong camaraderie among cast and crew. After viewing the first three days' rushes, Ostrow threatened to fire Tourneur, but Koerner came to the rescue and production proceded smoothly.

Some of the department heads grumbled about Lewton's fastidiousness, which extended even to the credit titles. He insisted that the writer's credit be changed to "Written by..." because "it might make a smoother, more tasteful title card than if we used the words 'Original Screen Play,' which have a rather dismal look and sound." Having cleared this point with the Screen Writers Guild, he arranged that the writer's card be moved from its customary position (preceding the technical credits) to appear between the producer and director credits, because he believed "the writer should receive equal recognition with the director and producer." He also insisted upon opening and closing the film with literary quotations – an uncommon delicacy even among the more pretentious films of the time. After the titles had been prepared, he requested that the director's Christian name, which had been lettered "Jack," be changed to the proper "Jacques," at a cost of $25.

Although a stringent budget did not permit a great amount of visual effects work, the excellent camera effects department, headed by Vernon L. Walker, ASC, made some important contributions to the production. Linwood Dunn, ASC, supervising optical photographer, composited a beautifully crafted dream montage of graceful, animated art deco panthers, diffused images of Tom Conway in armor brandishing a sword, and a key crucial to the story. He also supplied special transitional wipes that were deliberately soft-edged and shapeless so as to resemble amorphous shadows crossing the screen.

The most memorable optical effect shows Simone Simon seemingly beginning to change into a cat after Conway has forcibly kissed her. It had been decided to avoid any scenes showing an actual metamorphosis from woman to panther, but upon viewing the sequence Tourneur and Lewton had to agree with management that the closeup of the baby-faced actress failed to convey sufficient menace to justify the subsequent cut of Conway recoiling in horror. Dunn doctored the shot optically so that the face darkens and the eyes harden. The effect is not gruesome, yet it is superbly frightening.

"There was no preparation of any kind for the effect, otherwise it would have been easy," Dunn recalled. "It was a complicated application of density manipulation and masking. I took her close-up and dissolved it into a dupe that was of very high constrast where the face started to wash out, then increased the contrast until she changed into a horrible, dark 'thing.'" Dunn also manipulated the image so that Irena appears to move lower in the frame as she changes.

Cat People is prefaced by a quote supposedly from a book by Dr. Louis Judd, "The Atavism of Fear": "Even as fog continues to lie in the valleys, so does ancient sin cling to the low places, the depressions in the world's consciousness." At the Central Park Zoo on an autumn afternoon, fashion designer Irena Dubrovna (Simone Simon) makes sketches of a black panther as it paces restlessly in its cage. Oliver Reed (Kent Smith), a naval architect, is attracted by her kittenish beauty and intrigued by her drawing, which depicts the cat impaled on a sword. Irena has long kept to herself, but allows Oliver to court her. In her apartment, Oliver examines a statuette of a knight who holds aloft a sword upon which a cat is impaled. She explains that it depicts King John of Serbia, who in Medieval times put to death the witches of his kingdom, women who could take the form of cats. "The wisest and most wicked escaped into the mountains. Those who escaped, the wicked ones, haunt the village where I was born."

Oliver buys Irena a kitten, but it is terrified of her. When they return the cat to the pet store, the caged animals become violently agitated. The proprietress observes that "You can't fool a cat. They seem to know who is not right, if you know what I mean." Oliver exchanges the cat for a canary.

Oliver proposes marriage, but Irena is fearful. "I've fled from the past, from evil things you could never know or understand," she explains. Afraid of losing him, she later relents. Oliver's boss (Jack Holt) and co-workers hold a wedding dinner at the Belgrade, a Serbian cafe. Alice Moore (Jane Randolph), in love with Oliver, conceals her unhappiness. As the group offers a toast to the bride, a beautiful but curiously feline woman (Elizabeth Russell) arises from another table and insinuatingly addresses the terrified Irena in Yugoslavian as "moya sestra" – "my sister."

That night at her apartment, Irena begs Oliver to "Be kind, be patient. Give me time to get over this feeling that there is something evil in me." They retire to separate rooms, but in a moment Irena reaches out to the door that separates them. Hearing the nocturnal cries of the jungle cats from the zoo, she hastily withdraws her hand. The marriage remains unconsummated during the weeks that follow.

Irena often returns to watch the panther, which seems to regard her with a curious rapport. A quaint attendant (Alec Craig) observes that "No one comes to see *him* when they're happy. The monkey house and the aviary gets all the happy customers." When Irena comments upon the animal's beauty, he retorts: "No, ma'am, he ain't beautiful, he's an evil critter. Read your Bible, Revelations, where the Book is talkin' about the worst beast of all: 'And it was like unto a leopard.' *Like* a leopard, but *not* a leopard. I reckon that fits this critter."

At Alice's urging, Oliver persuades Irena to visit a psychiatrist, Dr. Louis Judd (Tom Conway). Judd refuses to believe in "women who in jealousy or anger or out of their own corrupt passions" can change into cats. Irena is disturbed by Judd's obvious desire for her and his insistence upon ascribing her fears to her mental state.

The canary dies of fright when Irena tries to pet it. Compulsively, she hurries to the zoo and feeds the bird to the panther. On another visit she sees the attendant forgetfully leave his key in the lock of the panther's cage. You resist temptation admirably," comments Judd, who has been watching, unseen. "The key. You fear the panther, yet you're drawn to him again and again... there is in some cases a psychic need to release evil into the world... a desire for death."

Oliver and Alice are drawn closer by her sympathetic interest, but Irena is enraged to learn that Oliver has confided in another woman. She spies on the co-workers as they talk at a coffee shop, a bar, and a museum. One night she tries to telephone Oliver when he is working late. When Alice answers, Irena hangs up. Later, as Alice walks toward her hotel along one of the concourses that cut through Central Park from Fifth Avenue to Central Park West, she becomes aware of a woman's footsteps following in the darkness. The unseen one keeps pace as Alice hurries from one pool of light to another. At last the sounds cease abruptly. Standing next to a high wall, Alice listens anxiously. There is a rustling sound above, and a tree branch adjacent to the top of the wall, bends. There is a sudden hissing noise – the air brakes of a bus as it lunges to a halt at the curb. Alice hurries aboard and as the bus pulls away the branch springs back.

The park shepherd discovers that several lambs have been killed savagely. In the mud he finds the footprints of a large cat leading away. Some paces away they are replaced by the prints of a woman's shoes. Irena, clutching a handkerchief to her lips, stumbles back to her apartment, brushing past the frantic Oliver to the bathtub, to wash the blood away.

Irena's sleep is plagued by images of prowling cats and of King John – impersonated by Judd – telling her to "loose evil upon the world...the key..." as his sword becomes a key. Next morning, as Irena steals the key, the panther seems to read her thoughts.

Next night after work Alice goes alone to the indoor swimming pool at her hotel. She stops to play with a kitten at the pool's edge. Suddenly the lights are extinguished and the cat flees. Unnerved by strange noises and becoming aware of a sinister presence in the shadows, Alice dives into the pool. She treads water in the center as a strange shadow prowls about the edges and the room echoes with snarling and growling. When Alice screams for help, the lights come on. Irena, standing by the light switch, smiles innocently and asks, "What's the matter, Alice?" After Irena leaves, Alice finds that her bathrobe has been torn to shreds.

Alice tells Judd she believes that Irena's fears of lycanthropy are based on fact. "The story is a product of her own fear," Judd replies. "You're both victims of fear. She fears the past and you fear the future." Alice suggests that Judd should have protection if he sees Irena again. "A gun, perhaps, with a silver bullet?" he mocks. "Of course, this isn't silver." He draws a sword from his walking stick.

"Do you sincerely believe that if your husband were to kiss you, you'd change into a cat and rend him to shreds?" he asks Irena at their next meeting. "And if I were to kiss you?" She rebuffs his advances and returns home. Happily, she tells Oliver that she now has the courage to be his true wife. Replying that it is too late, he walks out. "I love loneliness," Irena hisses as her fingernails rip the fabric of the divan.

That night Oliver and Alice, working alone in the drafting room, hear the snarling of a panther. A black shape in the shadows beneath the drafting tables moves toward them. As the beast crouches to spring, Oliver raises an adjustable T-square, which casts the shadow of a cross on the wall. "In the name of God, Irena, leave us in peace," he pleads. Instantly, the animal is gone. Alice recognizes a lingering scent: Irena's perfume. As they try to leave the

Simon fears Conway, her psychiatrist.

building, Oliver senses that something is waiting in the elevator. Descending the stairs, they find that the elevator has arrived ahead of them and the revolving door is astir.

Irena returns to her apartment to find Judd waiting. "You see, I never believed your story," he says. "I'm not afraid of you – so little, so soft, perfume in your hair and body..." He kisses her, then starts back in horror. As he draws his sword he is attacked by a snarling beast. After a savage struggle Irena emerges unsteadily from the room, the blade of the broken sword protruding from her shoulder. She hides in the shadows as Oliver and Alice arrive to find the corpse of Judd half-buried in debris.

Hurrying to the zoo, Irena unlocks the panther cage. As the cat leaps free it strikes Irena down. A moment later an auto runs over the cat. "She never lied to us," Oliver tells Alice as they stand over the body of Irena, peaceful at last in death.

Instead of the traditional end title, a quotation from John Donne's Holy Sonnet V appears:

But black sin has condemn'd to endless night
My world, both parts, and both parts must die.

The preview at the RKO Hillstreet in Los Angeles on Friday, October 6, was a great success – much to the amazement of most of the studio executives. It was decided, however, that the panther, which had been represented in the drafting room sequence only by indistinct shadows, must be shown. Trainer Mel Koontz and his panther were brought back for one day of filming. Through clever staging and cutting, the three obligatory cuts of the cat seem *almost* imaginary, yet are sufficiently palpable to satisfy the demands of the more literal minded.

241

Cat People proved to be a big moneymaker, bringing in about $4,000,000. Samuel Goldwyn, learning that it had outgrossed his big picture, *Pride of the Yankees*, wanted to hire Lewton. David Selznick, in a letter to Koerner, said, "I wish that other studios were turning out small-budget pictures that were comparable in intelligence and taste with Lewton's first film."

Lewton produced 10 more pictures for RKO, all but two of them in the horror field. All were distinctive, most were popular, several approached perfection. They were: *I Walked With a Zombie, The Leopard Man, The Seventh Victim* and *The Ghost Ship* in 1943; *The Curse of the Cat People, Youth Runs Wild* and *Mademoiselle Fifi* in 1944; *Isle of the Dead* and *The Body Snatcher* in 1945, and *Bedlam* in 1946. All were predicated on "intelligence and taste" and were exploited in the most lurid manner.

Long before the end of his stay there, Lewton had become thoroughly disenchanted with RKO. His key directors and writers were being promoted to higher budget productions and numerous promising projects initiated by Lewton were aborted. A heart attack seemed to increase his feelings of paranoia about the front office and he found it difficult to get along with Ostrow's successors, Sid Rogell and Jack J. Gross, neither of whom was in sympathy with his methods. Promises to promote him to bigger pictures were never fulfilled. His unease also contributed to a growing tension in his private life, distancing him from his wife and children.

Lewton grew increasingly difficult to deal with. "It became impossible for him to work with anybody," Bodeen revealed. "He wanted to do too much, to get his hands on everything. He became terribly nervous. The story sessions, which had been so much fun, became stormy, unpleasant." The death of Koerner from leukemia on February 2, 1946, left Lewton with the realization that he could never achieve his ambitions at RKO.

A move to Paramount resulted in more cancelled or usurped projects and the production of one mediocre A picture which he disliked, *My Own True Love* (1948) with Melvyn Douglas and Phyllis Calvert. An equally frustrating stint at MGM resulted in a comedy, *Please Believe Me* (1950), with Deborah Kerr and Robert Walker, which he considered his worst effort. An attempt to form an independent company with his successful proteges, Mark Robson and Robert Wise, failed after a series of disagreements.

Bitterly, Lewton acccepted a low-paying berth at Universal-International, where, in 1950, he produced a Technicolor Western, *Apache Drums.*

This remarkable work, directed by Hugo Fregonese, a young Argentinian director, contains the same kind of suspense, terror, psychological insight and artistry as did the best of his RKO pictures. Ignored as "another Western" by the critics, it proved a popular success.

It was the last Val Lewton production. He died March 14, 1951, at the age of 46, while engaged in pre-production work on *My Six Convicts* for the Stanley Kramer Company.

Cat People is not the perfect film; there are occasional clumsy moments and the Lewton-Tourneur team is a bit too continental to put over the desired milieu of ordinary working people with complete conviction. It is a classic, nevertheless, to be revered for its own intrinsic values – it was much imitated and rarely bettered – and as a turning point in its *genre*. Basically a story of good versus evil, it is hardly as simplistic as that. Irena is driven to evil by forces beyond her control, as are the central characters in all of Lewton's horror films, whether they be grave robbers, madmen, devil worshippers, Apaches facing racial extinction, or zealots. The Jekyll/Hyde title character of *The Leopard Man* states the case perfectly as he watches a ball dancing in the jet of a fountain: "We know as little of the forces that move us and move the world around us as that empty ball."

Simone Simon captures Irena's ambivalent nature well. Her natural child-like charm is disarming. She conveys quickly that she is fear-ridden, but it is only gradually that she betrays any hint of the sinister. Kent Smith and Jane Randolph are sufficiently down-to-earth to make the fantasy more believable. Tom Conway is convincing in a role that could have been inexplicable if less skilfully played.

The photography and sets are perfectly keyed. The interiors have the kind of chiaroscuro found in fine etchings, with rich shadows and striking highlights that take the "gray curse" out of low key photography. Exteriors are strong on atmosphere, with changes of season clearly defined, from the Indian Summer beginning through the rains, snows and mists of winter.

Sound is used creatively. The distant noises of the omnipresent zoo animals, the terrifying echoes in the swimming pool, the clacking of high heels in the chase through the park followed by a sudden hush as the pursuit becomes a silent stalking, the rustling of leaves in darkness, the nerve-jarring hissing of a bus's air brakes just at the instant one expects a panther to leap into the scene – such sounds as these are cunningly married to the visuals to inspire unease, fear, suspense and shock. The bus gag proved so successful as to be reprised

Cat People

Alice, shuddering when she senses she is being watched, says that "A cat just walked over my grave." Elizabeth Russell's moment as the cat-like woman who addresses Irena as "sister" is heightened by an ingenious touch: her voice is dubbed by Simone Simon to create a sense of kinship. The scene conveys a hint of lesbianism, which was deliberate on Bodeen's part but of which Lewton wasn't aware until someone mentioned it to him after the preview.

In a 1944 press release Lewton summed up his approach to the horror film in one paragraph. He was speaking of his fourth production, *The Seventh Victim*, but the formula applies equally to *Cat People.*

"This picture's appeal, like that of its predecessors, is based on three fundamental theories," he stated. "First is that audiences will people any patch of prepared darkness with more horror, suspense and frightfulness than the most imaginative writer could ever dream up. Second, and most important, is the fact that extraordinary things can happen to very ordinary people. And third is to use beauty of setting and camera work to ward off audience laughter at situations which, when less beautifully photographed, might seem ludicrous."

By carrying out these ideas Val Lewton, reluctant master of sophisticated horror, was able to dramatize man's natural fear of the unknown, of unseen things that – for all we know – *might* lurk in dark places. Through the arts and crafts of the cinema he expressed the primitive fears that survive, unbidden, in all of us.

—George E. Turner

An RKO Radio Picture; *produced by* Val Lewton; *written by* DeWitt Bodeen; *directed by* Jacques Tourneur; *music by* Roy Webb; *musical director,* C. Bakaleinikoff; *director of photography,* Nicholas Musuraca, ASC; *art directors,* Albert S. D'Agostino, Walter E. Keller; *set decorations,* Darrell Silvera, Al Fields; *gowns by* Renie; *recorded by* John L. Cass; *edited by* Mark Robson; *assistant director,* Doran Cox; *photographic effects,* Vernon L. Walker, ASC, Linwood G. Dunn, ASC; *executive producer,* Lou Ostrow; *orchestrations,* Leonid Raab, John Liepold; *Russian lyrics,* Andrei Tolstoi; *dialogue director,* DeWitt Bodeen; *animal trainer,* Mel Koontz. RCA *Recording. Running time, 73 minutes. Released December 25, 1942.*

Irena Dubrovna, Simone Simon; *Oliver Reed,* Kent Smith; *Dr. Louis Judd,* Tom Conway; *Alice Moore,* Jane Randolph; *The Commodore,* Jack Holt; *Carver,* Alan Napier; *Miss Plunkett,* Elizabeth Dunne; *Cat Woman,* Elizabeth Russell; *Zoo Keeper,* Alec Craig; *Cab Driver,* Donald Kerr; *Hotel Attendant,* Terry Walker; *Minnie,* Theresa Harris; *Mrs. Agnew,* Dot Farley; *Shepherd,* Murdoch MacQuarrie; *Organ Grinder,* Steve Soldi; *Bus Driver,* Charles Jordan; *Whistling Cop,* George Ford; *Mrs. Hanson,* Betty Roadman; *Woman,* Connie Leon; *Second Woman,* Henrietta Burnside; *Patient,* Lida Nicova; *Cafe Proprietor,* John Piffle; *Mounted Policeman,* Bud Geary; *Street Policeman,* Eddie Dew; *Blondie,* Mary Halsey; *Panther,* Dynamite; *Stunt man,* Louis Roth; *Cat Voice,* Dorothy Lloyd.

throughout the series: be the intruder a train, a horse, a tumbleweed, a rattletrap car, or an Apache warrior, Lewton always referred to it as a "bus."

Webb's music creates an undercurrent of menace without becoming intrusive, adding immeasurably to a gathering atmosphere of dread. It meshes well with Musuraca's cross-lighting effects (the teaming was repeated often). The deployment of Irena's childish lullaby as counterpoint to a heavy dramatic motif is ingenious. The score also employs Von Flothow's aria, "Heaven Protect Thee," as hurdy-gurdy music and Bernard Herrmann's song from *All That Money Can Buy* (1941), "Nothing Else To Do," for the zoo attendant to sing.

Subtleties are numerous. There are, for example, the cat images that permeate many scenes: the folding screen in Irena's apartment, a Goya print in which cats appear, tiger lilies in a florist shop window, a bathtub supported by claw-like feet.

20

The Mystique of *Laura*

It's a fact that during the first two decades after talking pictures began to dominate the screen, American movie studios produced more murder mysteries than any other type of film. Most were made on low to moderate budgets and weren't intended as anything more imposing than the supporting feature on double bill programs; often these were good enough to save the evening for patrons who found the bill-topper unpalatable. An occasional whodunit was something special, standing out from the general profusion of movie offerings with the conspicuousness of a Sargent portrait at an art club show.

Such a picture is *Laura,* a highly polished mystery yarn, to be sure – but it's much more. It introduces a half-dozen interesting characters and then proceeds to dissect their minds so that we see beyond their facades and get to know them rather intimately. None is spared this scrutiny. Even the hero-detective and the leading lady have certain unhealthy idiosyncrasies, while the several less admirable principals – a cruelly cynical columnist and radio personality, a gigolo, an aging socialite who is savagely possessive of a younger man, a maid brimming with hate yet obsessively devoted to her mistress – are viewed with as much sympathy as alarm. The result is one of those rare pictures in which the viewer not only observes the characters but comes to understand them.

Some, but far from all, of this multi-faceted property is inherent in the original novel by Vera Caspary and the multi-authored screenplay. Much of it can be credited to the penetrating approach of

the producer-director, Otto Preminger, who surely must have known living counterparts of all the characters. It is embodied in the unusual photographic style of Joseph LaShelle, ASC, whose camera probes restlessly to reveal not only a prevailing elegance of clothes and decor but every covert expression and secret glance. It depends strongly upon the acting of a first-rate cast: the deft underplaying of Dana Andrews, a sensitive actor portraying a rough-hewn cop; the deliberate flamboyance of Clifton Webb, a Broadway dancer turned actor, seemingly born to his role of a waspish intellectual; the alternating warmth and coolness projected by Gene Tierney, the calculated charm of Vincent Price, the grimly controlled passions of Judith Anderson, and the hard-eyed fanaticism of Dorothy Adams. Ambiguity and uncertainty are heightened by another master stroke: David Raksin's sophisticated but subtly menacing musical score, which haunts the mind long after the last fadeout.

The screen version begins on the hottest day of 1941 as Mark McPherson (Dana Andrews) visits Waldo Lydecker (Clifton Webb), critic and radio personality, in his New York flat, to question him about the murder of Lydecker's protege, Laura Hunt (Gene Tierney). The body, its face destroyed by a shotgun blast, was found in the doorway of Laura's apartment clad in dressing gown and slippers. Waldo and Laura had been close friends for five years and Waldo, conceiving himself as a mentor, had effectively managed to ridicule younger men to whom Laura was attracted.

245

Waldo (Clifton Webb) meets McPherson (Dana Andrews) on the hottest day of the year.

Waldo goes with Mark to call upon Laura's wealthy aunt, Anne Treadwell (Judith Anderson) who is "keeping" a poor, but handsome young Southern aristocrat, Shelby Carpenter (Vincent Price), even though he is is engaged to Laura. Waldo had exposed Shelby as a glorified gigolo who is Anne's lover and the lover of Diane Redfern, a model in Laura's advertising agency. Laura has gone to her country house to think and decide whether or not to marry him.

Mark keeps returning to the scene of the murder, going through Laura's belongings and letters. On the third night he dozes off in front of her portrait, painted by a former suitor. He is awakened by Laura, who threatens to call the police. When he explains, she says she has been in the country and knew nothing of the slaying. In the bedroom closet she finds a dress belonging to Diane, the real murder victim. Hiding his elation, Mark tells Laura she must not talk to anyone; he departs. She calls Shelby. Mark follows him and forces him to tell the truth.

Shelby had had a rendezvous with Diane at the flat. He remained in the bedroom while she answered a ring at the door. Hearing the shot and finding the body, he fled. Laura's maid, Bessie (Dorothy Adams) becomes hysterical when she sees Laura alive. Waldo faints at the sight of Laura. Anne is at pains to conceal her disappointment. Mark confronts the suspects, finally places Laura under arrest and takes her to the police station. He assures her that he is convinced of her innocence, and that she won't be charged, but he had reached a point where he "needed official surroundings" to see things clearly.

At Laura's apartment Waldo later argues with Mark over Laura. When Laura sides with

Mark, Waldo congratulates them on "what promises to be a disgustingly earthy relationship" and apparently leaves. Actually he hides in another room. Mark finds the murder weapon hidden in a grandfather clock given to Laura by Waldo. He had tried to kill Laura because he could not bear losing her to Shelby. When Mark leaves, Waldo reloads the gun and confronts Laura as his recorded voice on the radio talks poetically of love that lasts beyond death. He will kill her, he says, rather than leave her "to the vulgar pawings of a detective who thinks you're a dame." Mark and two cops break in and a police bullet mortally wounds Waldo just as he pulls the trigger. The shotgun blast goes wild, demolishing the clock. The camera holds on the clock as Waldo murmurs, "Goodbye, Laura. Goodbye, my love."

None of this came easy.

In 1938 Preminger had been fired by Darryl F. Zanuck, executive in charge of production at Twentieth Century-Fox, while he was directing *Kidnapped*. About four years later, while Zanuck was on duty with the Army Signal Corps, Preminger was signed to an actor-director contract at Fox by the interim chief executive, William Goetz. In June

Waldo speaks admiringly of his favorite person.

1943, Preminger convinced Goetz to pay $30,000 for rights to Vera Caspary's currently successful novel, "Laura," which had previously been serialized as "Ring Twice for Laura" in *Collier's* for October and November of 1942. Preminger soon initiated pre-production work on *Laura* and two other projects.

Preminger had become interested in the property while he was producing and directing plays in New York, where he met Caspary. Much of the novel's charm lay in its being told in first-person segments by three of the principals, the first by the acid-tongued Lydecker, the second by McPherson, the last by the supposed murder victim, Laura.

Zanuck also returned in June. Goetz, whose relations with Zanuck were strained beyond repair, quickly resigned (later to become a founding father of International Pictures, Inc.) Still nursing his grudge from 1938, Zanuck summoned Preminger to his Santa Monica beach house and, without turning to look at his guest or asking him to sit down, curtly informed him that he could continue as producer of *Army Wives, Laura,* and *Ambassador Dodd's Diary* but that he would never direct again at Fox as long as Zanuck was there. He was placed under the supervision of Bryan Foy, the executive in charge of many of the studio's medium-budget pictures. The *Ambassador Dodd's Diary* project was shelved later.

By the end of October, Jay Dratler, a New York novelist, poet, and lately, scenarist of low-budget productions for several studios, had completed the first draft script of *Laura.* It was generally faithful to the book. Preminger showed the screenplay to Vera Caspary, who angrily demanded to know why he was making her book into a B picture.

Foy's assistant, David Stevens, reported that the script was "lousy." Foy had refused to read it, but finally did so at Preminger's insistence. "The script stinks," Foy declared later. Preminger finally convinced Foy to let Zanuck read it, despite Foy's warning that Zanuck would use it as an excuse to fire Preminger. After a few days Zanuck called Foy and Preminger to his office. After listening attentively to Foy's reasons why the script should be discarded, Zanuck said, "I like the script. I have taken it home." This meant that Zanuck was taking over supervision of the picture from Foy, an honor reserved only for the studio's top product.

Zanuck offered numerous ideas for improving the characters and giving them individuality – only distinct characters like those in *The Maltese Falcon* would make the picture something more than "a blown-up whodunit," he said – and suggested that Laura's narration be dropped from the

"Is this the room of a dame?" Waldo demands.

McPherson meets Shelby (Vincent Price) and Anne (Judith Anderson). Still is from Mamoulian version.

last third of the picture. Ring Lardner Jr., talented son of the famed author, did several rewrites embodying Zanuck's ideas.

Meantime, relations between Zanuck and Preminger had thawed sufficiently that Preminger was allowed to direct *Army Wives*, which was released as *In the Meantime, Darling.* The studio chief did not relent on *Laura*, however, and Preminger continued to search for a director.

Most of the better directors at Fox were loath to do a detective movie, especially if it was being produced by Preminger. It was turned down by John Brahm, Walter Lang, and Lewis Milestone. Zanuck considered cancelling the project, but Rouben Mamoulian – the brilliant Russian-born director of *Applause, Dr. Jekyll and Mr. Hyde, City Streets, Becky Sharp, The Mark of Zorro* and *Blood and Sand* – accepted the assignment. Then he balked, saying he didn't like the script. Zanuck wooed him back, acceding to Mamoulian's wish to have the script rewritten by his long-time collaborator, Samuel Hoffenstein, and Hoffenstein's current collaborator, Betty Reinhardt.

The producer-director teaming of the abrasive Preminger and the soft-spoken Mamoulian was not made in heaven. They were unable to agree on anything, be it script, casting, costuming, characterization or photographic style.

Jennifer Jones, whose career was being guided by David O. Selznick, was first considered for the title part. She declined. Then Gene Tierney, who was under contract to Fox, was offered the part. Unhappy at being second choice and disappointed at the brevity of the role as written, she accepted

Shelby, charming but sinister.

reluctantly. Zanuck wanted contractee John Hodiak for McPherson. Dana Andrews, whose contract was split between Fox and Goldwyn, had seen the script, campaigned actively for the role and – at the last moment – got it, apparently at Mrs. Zanuck's suggestion. Mamoulian wanted Judith Anderson for Laura's socialite aunt, and this was agreed upon.

Zanuck had first considered Monty Woolley, star of the stage and screen versions of *The Man Who Came to Dinner*, for the similar role of Waldo Lydecker. Later, Zanuck and Mamoulian agreed that Laird Cregar, a fine actor but a definite "heavy," should play Lydecker, and that Reginald Gardner, who specialized in amusingly indolent drawing room types, should be the gigolo, Shelby. Preminger disagreed with such literal casting on both counts, insisting that the audience would tab Cregar as the culprit from the beginning and would never seriously consider Gardner a viable murder suspect. For Waldo, Preminger had someone much different in mind: the brittler, older and wittier Clifton Webb, who was currently starring in *Blithe Spirit* at the Biltmore Theatre in Los Angeles. A veteran of the stage, Webb had never appeared in talkies, although he had been in some silent films. Vincent Price, Preminger insisted, would lend overtones both sinister and sympathetic to Shelby's professionalized charm.

Zanuck finally agreed to the casting of Price, but remained skeptical of Webb, who was a bit prissy and mother-dominated. He finally consented to let Preminger make a test of Webb with Tierney. Webb refused, but agreed to let Preminger film his best *Blithe Spirit* monologue. Zanuck angrily refused permission for such a test, but Preminger made it secretly with a lesser known cinematographer he considered to be the studio's best, Joseph LaShelle. Zanuck was miffed, but when he saw the test he admitted he was impressed and Webb was "in."

Mamoulian, as was his habit, began extensive cast rehearsals on April 19. Lucien Ballard, ASC, whose exceptional work on *The Lodger* was receiving widespread acclaim, was assigned as cinematographer. By the time principal photography was begun there had been so many arguments between producer and director that Mamoulian had Preminger barred from the set. The players and crew, with the exception of Webb, remained loyal to the director. Zanuck, meantime, was called away to New York. Word spread over the studio that the picture was jinxed.

With each day's rushes Preminger took greater umbrage. Zanuck's assistant, Lou Schreiber,

McPherson is falling in love with a portrait.

agreed that the rushes were not good and the footage was sent to Zanuck. Mamoulian had also been in contact with Zanuck, who wired back that Mamoulian should continue the picture with no further interference from the producer. Mamoulian pressed on while Preminger smouldered.

Later, when Zanuck returned, he decided that the latest footage was no better. He called a meeting with Mamoulian, Preminger and Dana Andrews on the morning of Saturday, May 13 – 18 working days after principal photography had begun. Zanuck, gnawing his cigar and swinging his polo mallet as he paced around the room, was especially critical of Andrews' character, who was being played as an erudite criminologist a la Ellery Queen. Zanuck felt he must be a tough cop for contrast to the elegant Tierney. Vehemently, Mamoulian and Preminger each blamed the other for the misinterpretation. Andrews, who had been told by *both* men to play McPherson as an intellectual type, was excused and the turbulent meeting continued.

Just what happened then has produced a lot of speculation and few certainties. According to Preminger, Zanuck asked him at lunch later that day if he thought Mamoulian should be taken off the picture. Yes, was the reply. That afternoon Zanuck phoned Preminger and told him he could start directing on Monday. He was expected to reshoot only the objectionable scenes and complete the picture.

Preminger said that Zanuck fired Mamoulian. It was studio gossiped that Preminger had deliberately sabotaged Mamoulian in order to get rid of him and that Mamoulian elected to resign.

McPherson surprises Shelby at Laura's country hideaway.

On May 15 production resumed with Preminger directing a mostly hostile cast and crew, most of them faithful to the gentle Mamoulian. Preminger quickly replaced Ballard with LaShelle. The director's martinet approach and angry tirades, plus a sudden expansion of working hours from dawn till after dusk, soon had the cast thoroughly angered, unnerved and near exhaustion.

Vincent Price recalled the scene for us:

"Everything seemed to be going fine. All of us in the cast loved each other and we all loved Rouben. Then, after three weeks, we had a new director and a new cameraman. We all still loved each other and we – er – *liked* Otto. He always invited us to see the rushes and before long we began to realize that he was bringing something new to the picture. He was imparting an underlying sense of evil to each of our characters that hadn't been there before." Price, one of the gentlest and most tolerant of men, was more malleable than most of the others.

Anderson especially was antagonistic; she had felt great rapport with her previous director and was comfortable with her wardrobe and her performance. Preminger ordered changes in both. She watched icily as he acted out in detail the way he wanted her scenes replayed. Trouper that she was she gave him the interpretation he wanted, but she was never happy with it. The enmity between the two continued unabated long after the picture wrapped.

Andrews called Samuel Goldwyn, co-holder of his contract, hoping Goldwyn could get him off the picture. It was too late. It was a nightmarish time for Andrews, who was also working in *A Wing and a Prayer* for the equally hard-driving Henry Hathaway. One gruelling day Preminger had to halt a scene because Andrews became confused and warned Tierney that Zeros were coming in at 12 o'clock.

Physical and emotional exhaustion resulting from her dawn-to-dark schedule imperiled Tierney's recent marriage to fashion designer Oleg Cassini. She has said that Preminger seemed tireless, brimming with energy after everyone else was exhausted, but that he was always a perfect gentleman on the set. Although *Laura* is the picture for which she is best known, she never held much fondness for it or for her performance. Such is often the case with artists who have had unpleasant experiences relating to a particular piece of work. Nevertheless, her beauty and sophistication in this film leave an indelible impression on anyone who has seen it.

Webb, the only cast member who hadn't meshed well with Mamoulian, got on famously with Preminger. After production wrapped, however, he had a nervous breakdown.

Unquestionably, it was worth it. The picture brought him instant stardom and a strong career at Fox. His is the flashiest role and he has the best dialogue, clever and cutting in the Oscar Wilde tradition. He is introduced while sitting at his typewriter in a lavish bathtub. When informed that he is a suspect he is delighted: "To have overlooked me would have been a pointed insult." For Laura, he says, he tried to be "the kindest, the gentlest, the most sympathetic man in the world." Was he successful? "Let me put it this way: I would be sincerely sorry to see my neighbor's children devoured by wolves."

At Waldo's first meeting with Laura, when she visits his table in the Algonquin Hotel restaurant to explain that her career at an ad agency rests upon obtaining his endorsement of a writing pen, he tells her "I don't use a pen, I write with a goose quill dipped in venom... You seem to be disregarding something more important than your career: my lunch." She avers that he must be lonely. "In my case, self-absorption is completely justified." Relenting later, he says, "I'm not kind, I'm vicious. It's the secret of my charm." He refers to Shelby as "a male beauty in distress," and within earshot of guests at Anne's party he declares, "Laura, dear, I cannot stand these morons any longer. If you don't come with me this instant I shall run amok." When Shelby makes a lame excuse after Laura catches him breakfasting with Anne, Waldo comments that "At a moment of supreme disaster, he's trite."

250

Confronting Mark in the supposedly dead woman's flat, he snaps: "It's a wonder you don't come here like a suitor, with candy – drug store candy, of course... You'd better watch out, McPherson, or you'll end up in a psychiatric ward. I don't think they've ever had a patient who fell in love with a corpse."

Andrews is so good and subtle an actor that he is never eclipsed even by Webb's bravura performance. Initially perceived as a tough cop who sums up his love life by admitting that "a doll in Washington Heights got a fox fur out of me once," he manages to make it explicable that he is obsessed with someone he has created in his mind. Mark is unable to suppress an almost subliminal smile when Laura says she has decided not to marry Shelby and at another point he can't resist an impulse to punch Shelby in the midriff. In a sequence cut from the picture he took Waldo and Shelby to a Dodgers game at Ebbets Field while questioning them.

Price is splendid in his portrayal of a man who is virile enough to live off women and carry on affairs with three of them at once, yet is almost feminine in his knowledge of how women think. "I don't know a lot about anything but I know a little about everything," he admits to Mark. His studied Southern accent, his glib compliments ("You look very sweet – that's a lovely hat, darling"), his instinct to lie about almost anything and his occasional flashes of self-rebuke add up to a perfect portrait of a successful parasite. Most telling of all is a brief sequence in Anne's kitchen during the party as he cozens the elderly cook (Kathleen Howard) into holding out some goodies for him. A scene cut before release had him at the piano singing "You'll Never Know" for a flock of adoring young women.

The unhappy Judith Anderson is entirely convincing in her projection of an outwardly cool and reserved woman who seethes inwardly with sexual needs and admits that she "thought about" killing her favorite niece over her faithless lover.

The picture was made almost entirely in the studio. Despite the wartime set-building restrictions, an atmosphere of opulence is pervasive. There are enough expensive-looking props on display to suggest that everybody has unlimited funds for collecting art. The most famous prop is the portrait of Laura that appears under the main title and is featured prominently throughout the film. Mamoulian had used an oil portrait by his wife, Azadia. When Preminger took over direction he wanted a different sort of portrait. He asked Frank Powolny of the still department, to photograph the actress. The photo was enlarged and one of Fred

Sersen's special effects artists painted over it lightly.

The quality of luxury is furthered by the lavish costuming designed by Bonnie Cashin. Tierney has 26 complete changes of wardrobe, all of them tasteful, original and elegant. Several gowns that were ordered earlier by Mamoulian were discarded. Anderson's gowns originally were soft and flattering, but the ones shown in the final cut are much less so.

There is a nagging question as to how much, if any, of the completed film was the work of Mamoulian and Ballard. Mamoulian remained mum about it (at least publicly). Ballard opined that about three-fourths of of the picture is Mamoulian's. LaShelle said that Preminger, in addition to filming the remainder of the picture, had almost all of the Mamoulian/Ballard footage reshot, often on the sly and without Zanuck's knowledge, until only a few brief scenes remained of the previously made material. Comments by several of the players lend credence to this, as do numerous existing stills showing two versions of the same scenes with variations in the costumes.

Laura was only LaShelle's fifth picture as director of photography; its predecessors were *Happy Land, Bermuda Mystery, Take It or Leave It* and *The Eve of St. Mark.* Insiders were surprised that the discriminating Preminger had wanted such an obscure cinematographer. Actually, LaShelle had been a cameraman for 20 years, including 14 years as operator for Arthur Miller, ASC. His ability was well known among cinematographers long before he received his first screen credit.

The cinematography in *Laura* is complex because there are a great many unusually long takes in which the camera is constantly in motion. This demanded highly intricate lighting and blocking.

Waldo, Laura (Gene Tierney), Bullitt (Clyde Fillmore) and Anne are surprised when McPherson punches Shelby.

Waldo with the clock that hides the missing murder weapon.

The extra time required for this work paid off. The result is as fine a collection of perfect shots as any movie can boast. *Laura* brought LaShelle an Academy Award and put him where he belonged, among the top artists of his profession.

Preminger, who admittedly had no ear for music, knew he couldn't go wrong if Alfred Newman, head of the studio music department, would compose the score. Newman reported that he was too busy to handle it personally. Bernard Herrmann also begged off. Newman assigned the job to a staff composer, David Raksin, most of whose previous work at Fox had been done for the B units, often without screen credit. Musical direction was assigned to Newman's brother, Emil, with whom Raksin was customarily teamed.

Conferring one Friday with Preminger, Raksin learned that the director planned to have the score built around Duke Ellington's song, "Sophisticated Lady." Evidently, Jerome Kern's "Smoke Gets in Your Eyes" and George Gershwin's "Summertime" had also been considered, as well as Alfred Newman's oft-used "Street Scene, a Sentimental

Rhapsody." Raksin insisted that the picture should have an original theme with no previous connotations and was told that if he could bring in something satisfactory on Monday it would be considered.

Raksin at the time was agonizing over an unrequited love – his wife had left him. He tried a number of melodies during Saturday and Sunday and abandoned them. On Sunday night, in despair over the farewell letter he had received the day before, he conceived the bittersweet, plaintive but sophisticated theme for *Laura*. Preminger approved and Alfred Newman convinced Raksin he should build the entire score around the theme, which he did except for some brief passages.

Raksin deployed the music in a variety of ways: a symphonic arrangement plays under the titles, it is heard in an "easy listening" arrangement on a phonograph, is performed on camera by a small combo at a cafe and by a larger group at a party. Many scenes are underscored in dramatic and moody variations. It is most striking in the long sequence in which the detective is going through the "murdered" woman's possessions. This sombre arrangement for strings and solo saxophone is overlain with piano chords into which a wavering distortion was introduced.

The music haunts detective McPherson wherever he goes and succeeds in delineating for the observer the essence of Laura – McPherson can't get a woman he has never met out of his mind, and he is falling in love with a ghost. The music remains unresolved throughout, reinforcing the motifs of unrequited love and the eternal mystery of woman.

After the movie was completed, Johnny Mercer wrote lyrics to Raksin's theme and added a conventional ending. The song is not heard as such in the picture. Despite the complexity of its melodic line, it was a tremendous hit, climbing quickly to number one on the Lucky Strike Hit Parade (a popular radio show for which a national survey selected the top ten songs each week). It quickly became a "standard," spawning hundreds of recordings by male and female vocalists and all manner of musical groups ranging from Spike Jones to the National Philharmonic of London.

After a look at the rough cut, Zanuck said he disliked the picture and, with the aid of staff writer Jerry Cady, he revised the last third of the picture in an attempt to rescue it. Preminger didn't like the new scenes, but made them all. Although Preminger recalled that all of the Zanuck-Cady material was jettisoned after Zanuck's columnist friend, Walter Winchell, praised everything but the ending, the final version actually is a combination of Zanuck's and Preminger's ideas. The picture at first followed the technique of the book in being narrated by the three principals. In the revising, only the opening narration by Waldo, with its several flashbacks, was utilized.

The film received favorable reviews, although some of the more effete critics were unable to cope with its being anything more than a competent mystery yarn. The public knew a good thing when it saw it, however, and the picture, like the song, became a popular "standard." Lately it has been the subject of arguments by cineastes as to whether it qualifies as *film noir* – as if that matters a damn.

A stage dramatization by Caspary and George Sklar, which avoided all the things Caspary disliked about the film, opened on Broadway in 1947 with K. T. Stevens, Hugh Marlowe, and a properly acerbic Otto Kruger. It did not duplicate the film's success. The movie was remade in abbreviated form in 1955 as *Portrait for Murder*, a segment of The Twentieth Century-Fox Hour television series directed by John Brahm. It was intelligently cast with Dana Wynter, Robert Stack and George Sanders (a capital Waldo). Princess Lee Radziwill starred in a 1968 TV feature version which was not popular.

It is impossible to fully assess the chemistry of a great picture. Some benefit from having come about easily, their sponteneity and effortlessness enhancing their charm. Others are achieved only through painful exertions. No doubt *Laura* would have had a happier company and probably would have emerged as a memorable film if it had been directed entirely by Mamoulian and photographed by Ballard; if the portrait of Laura had been a genuine oil painting by Mrs. Mamoulian; and if the principals had been Jennifer Jones, Laird Cregar, John Hodiak, Reggie Gardner and a less tense Judith Anderson. Given this raft of talent it's difficult to imagine otherwise. Yet the *Laura* we know, born though it was of anger and contention, injured feelings, exhaustion and jangled nerves, possesses that indefinable chemistry of greatness.

—George E. Turner

Joseph LaShelle receives his Oscar from Bob Hope on March 15, 1945.

A Twentieth Century-Fox *production;* Darryl F. Zanuck, *in charge of production; produced and directed by* Otto Preminger; *screen play by* Jay Dratler, Samuel Hoffenstein *and* Betty Reinhart; *adapted from the novel by* Vera Caspary; *director of photography,* Joseph LaShelle, ASC; *music by* David Raksin; *musical direction,* Emil Newman; *art direction,* Lyle Wheeler, Leland Fuller; *set decorations,* Thomas Little; *associate,* Paul S. Fox; *film editor,* Louis Loeffler; *costumes,* Bonnie Cashin; *make-up artist,* Guy Pearce; *special photographic effects,* Fred Sersen; *sound,* E. Clayton Ward, Harry M. Leonard; *music recording,* Murray Spivack; *pianist,* Urban Theilmann; *assistant director,* Tom Dudley; *additions to screen play,* Ring Lardner Jr., Jerome Cady; *added direction,* Rouben Mamoulian; *additional cinematography,* Lucien Ballard, ASC; Western Electric *recording. Running time, 88 minutes. Released October 11, 1944.*

Laura Hunt, Gene Tierney; *Mark McPherson,* Dana Andrews; *Waldo Lydecker,* Clifton Webb; *Shelby Carpenter,* Vincent Price; *Ann Treadwell,* Judith Anderson; *Bessie Clary,* Dorothy Adams; *McAvity,* James Flavin; *Bullitt,* Clyde Fillmore; *Fred Callahan,* Ralph Dunn; *Corey,* Grant Mitchell; *Louise,* Kathleen Howard; *Detectives:* Lane Chandler, Harry Strang, Harold Schlickenmayer; *Hairdresser,* Frank LaRue; *Office Boy,* Buster Miles; *Secretary,* Jane Nigh; *Jacoby,* John Dexter; *and* Dorothy Christy, Alexander Sacha, Aileen Pringle, Jean Fenwick, Terry Adams, Forbes Murray, Yolanda Lacca, Kay Linaker, Cyril Ring, Cara Williams, Nester Eristoff, Beatrice Gray, Kay Connors, Francis Gladwin, William Forrest, Gloria Marlin, Charles Sullivan.

21

Kiss and Kill from *Out of the Past*

*O*ut of the Past was one of about 360 feature productions made in Hollywood during 1947. It was released into a booming market in which 90 million Americans were paying admissions each week at 19,207 theaters to create domestic revenues of $1.565 billion. The foreign market accounted for an additional $900 million.

RKO-Radio, which produced *Out of the Past,* released 39 features and 84 one- and two-reel short subjects that year. Although 1947 was a great year for most of the studios, RKO went into the red to the tune of $1.8 million. While this may sound like small potatoes by today's standards, it represented the production cost of three ''A'' pictures or a dozen profitable ''B's.'' *Out of the Past* was well advertised and had names that meant something at the box office, assuring it a wide enough audience to put some black ink on the books. It also has emerged from that formidable mass of pictures as one of the highlights of its time, a picture whose charm becomes more apparent with each viewing.

It is what was called, in those days, a ''hard-boiled melodrama.'' Certain pictures of this kind today represent a sort of sub-genre known as *film noir,* a designation created in 1946 by a French critic, Nino Frank, but only recently recognized by Britain and America. These films reflect the growing pessimism of the war years and their aftermath, depicting with cynicism an awareness of dark forces engendered by a world being consumed by greed and corruption. *Out of the Past* has become recognized as one of the prime examples of *noir* films.

Each of the major studios imparted to its pictures a distinctive style recognizable to even a semi-alert moviegoer. While all of the studios contributed noteworthy *noir* films, the leaders were Warner Brothers and RKO. The Warner approach – best exemplified by *The Maltese Falcon* and *The Big Sleep* – emphasized sharply drawn images photographed from often bizarre angles, fast-paced direction emphasized by rapid cutting and swift transitions, gaudy musical scoring, and strong central characterizations by the likes of Humphrey Bogart, Edward G. Robinson and James Cagney. The RKO style was almost the opposite: underplayed performances, photography themed more to convey pictorial beauty and intangible menace than startling dramatic punch, unobtrusive music that emphasizes mood rather than action, and comparatively leisurely cutting. Each approach gave us its share of masterworks.

Out of the Past was generously financed and shot in 64 working days (an unusually long schedule at the time), mostly on the sound stages at RKO's Hollywood studio and the Pathé lot in Culver City. Extensive location scenes were made in the Lake Tahoe area on the California-Nevada boundary with several of the principals. Second unit work was done in Acapulco, New York and San Francisco.

Jane Greer, Paul Valentine and Robert Mitchum.

255

Much of the excellence of *Out of the Past* can be credited to its author, Geoffrey Homes, a novelist and screen writer whose real name was Daniel Mainwaring. After a gruelling year in which he wrote a half-dozen scripts for Pine-Thomas Productions, makers of low-budget action films for Paramount release, Homes retreated from the studios long enough to write his first novel in several years, *Build My Gallows High*. He consciously gave it some of the qualities of a book he admired greatly, Dashiell Hammett's *The Maltese Falcon*. William Dozier, production chief at RKO-Radio, not only bought the property but hired Homes to develop the screenplay for producer Warren Duff, himself a screenwriter of note.

Duff, not quite satisfied with Homes' first draft, assigned James M. Cain, then America's best known writer of hard-boiled novels *(Double Indemnity, The Postman Always Rings Twice, Mildred Pierce)*, to rewrite it. Later, Frank Fenton, one of the studio's more dependable contract scenarists, revised the script further. Eventually it was Homes who wrote the final shooting script, which follows the book fairly closely.

The film opens at the town of Bridgeport, California, where Jeff (Robert Mitchum) is eking out a living running a service station. A visiting mobster, Joe (Paul Valentine), recognizes him as a former private investigator who double-crossed a big time crook, Whit (Kirk Douglas). Jeff explains the situation to his fiancee, Ann (Virginia Huston), and the story of Jeff's past is shown in flashback:

Whit was shot and wounded by his inamorata, Kathie (Jane Greer), who fled to Florida with $40,000 of Whit's money and then dropped out of sight. Whit hired Jeff and his partner, Fisher (Steve Brodie), to track her down. After finding Kathie in Acapulco, Jeff believed her story that she didn't take

Even in this plush setting there is an air of menace. Greer, Kirk Douglas, and Mitchum are equally distrustful of one another—for good reasons.

the money and that she wounded Whit in self-defense. He reported to Whit that Kathie had escaped and, blindly in love, helped her to hide out. When Fisher tracked them down and tried to make a deal for part of the money, Kathie killed him and conned Jeff into hiding the body. Kathie then abandoned Jeff, who eventually went into hiding at Bridgeport.

Ann suggests he try to patch things up with Whit. Returning to the city, he finds that Kathie is living with Whit again. Whit tells him all will be forgiven if Jeff does a job for him of stealing some incriminating papers held by a crooked accountant named Eels (Ken Niles). Jeff does the job and finds that he has been framed by Whit and a glamorous secretary, Meta (Rhonda Fleming), for the murders of Eels and Fisher. His possession of the papers makes it possible for him to make a deal with Whit to get him off the hook and let the deserving Kathie take the rap.

Whit's trigger man, Joe, stalks Jeff in the mountains near Bridgeport. The Kid (Dickie Moore), a mute youth who works at Jeff's station, sees Joe on top of a cliff, drawing a bead on the unsuspecting Jeff. Using a fly rod, The Kid hooks Joe and yanks him over the edge to his death. Telling Ann she should forget him, Jeff returns to see Whit and close the deal. He finds, to his horror, that Kathie has killed Whit. She urges him to flee with her to South America. He agrees, but secretly notifies the police. Kathie and Jeff are killed when she tries to drive through a police ambush.

The dialogue – especially that of Jeff – is terse and witty, tinged with ironic humor and flavored by a world-wise cynicism. It was tailored to fit the screen personality of Humphrey Bogart, whose performances as Sam Spade, Rick the American, and Philip Marlowe had established him as the foremost portrayer of the tough-yet-sentimental romantic. Homes personally delivered the script to Bogart, who was anxious to do the film but Warner Brothers refused to loan him to RKO. Dick Powell, who was under contract to RKO and had done a superb job as Philip Marlowe in *Murder My Sweet*, fell heir to the role and was featured in the advance advertising to the trade.

That Bogart or Powell would have created a memorable character goes without saying. However, the dialogue works superbly with Mitchum's sleepy-eyed, offhand delivery. When the beautiful but poisonous Kathie asks Jeff if he has missed her, he murmurs, ''No more than my eyes.'' When his small town fiancee opines that Kathie can't be all bad because no one is, he tells her, ''She comes closest.'' To Kathie's question, ''Is there any way to

Greer and Mitchum are lovers, but Musuraca's ominous lighting and composition make it clear that all is not well between them.

win?'' he hedges: ''There's a way to lose more slowly.'' As for the ultimate danger: ''I don't want to die, but if I have to, I'll die last.''

Jane Greer, costarred as Kathie, was a former RKO starlet (remember studio starlets? They were pretty contract players who did minor acting jobs and posed for innumerable publicity stills). She is excellent in a difficult characterization which calls for equal parts of sex appeal, seeming innocence, and malignant evil.

For the principal supporting roles of Whit and Meta, it would have been difficult to improve upon Kirk Douglas, who at the time was playing nothing but villains, and Rhonda Fleming, a statuesque beauty then under contract to David O. Selznick. When RKO reissued the picture in 1953, their names were moved to equal billing with Mitchum and Greer above the title.

The picture united for the third and final time one of the most remarkable director-cinematographer teams the industry has produced: Jacques Tourneur and Nicholas Musuraca, ASC.

Born in Paris in 1904, Tourneur came to the United States with his father, the noted director, Maurice Tourneur, in 1912. He entered the industry in 1924 as an office boy at Metro Pictures, parent organization of MGM. Later he became a continuity clerk and an actor. Returning to France, he directed several films during the early Thirties before rejoining MGM as a director of short subjects and second units. With Val Lewton he directed the siege of the Bastille sequence in a *A Tale of Two Cities* (1937). Graduating to features in 1939, he directed several minor productions at MGM before being lured to RKO by Val Lewton, who had signed a producing contract there. The first Lewton-Tourneur feature was the celebrated *The Cat People* (1942). It, too, was photographed by Nick Musuraca in a brilliant manner. *I Walked With a Zombie* – despite the crowd-teasing title, a work of real artistry – and *The Leopard Man*, which was also photographed by Musuraca, followed. The studio then graduated Tourneur to high-budget productions, of which the fourth was *Out of the Past*.

Musuraca was born in Italy in 1892 and began his film career at Vitagraph Studio in New York City in 1913, first as a projectionist, then as a cutter and assistant director. Vitagraph's co-founder,

257

A moonlit night on the beach at Acapulco simulated on a stage in Hollywood with the help of second unit background footage and a process screen. Edge of the screen can be seen in the upper right of this still.

artist and director J. Stuart Blackton, made him a first cameraman (silent picture title for a director of photography) in 1918. After several years he moved to California to join the British-backed Robertson-Cole Studio at Melrose and Gower in Hollywood. When R-C went broke, he remained with its successor, FBO Productions, shooting numerous silent Westerns starring Bob Steele, Buzz Barton and Tom Tyler. When RKO-Radio took over the studio in 1928, he shot a few "indoor" pictures before being assigned to the Tom Keene Westerns.

When the Keene series terminated in 1933, he got a chance to prove his versatility by shooting a wide variety of films, ranging from low-budget "quickies" to such prestigious productions as *The Swiss Family Robinson* and *Tom Brown's School Days*. One interesting assignment in 1940 was an artistic "B" mystery film, *The Stranger on the Third Floor*. Musuraca's striking use of chiaroscuro lighting in this unusual psychological drama anticipates the singular pictorial style he brought to the Lewton-Tourneur pictures several years later, as well as three other Lewton productions not directed by Tourneur: *The Ghost Ship, Curse of the Cat People* and *Bedlam*.

258

Tourneur and Musuraca worked well together. Tourneur, husky but mild-mannered, was usually relaxed and seemingly devoid of temperament on the set, always keeping his actors at their ease and relying heavily upon Musuraca's know-how to produce the combination of mystery and visual beauty essential to these films. The acting is deliberately underplayed, keyed to the nonchalant style of Mitchum – even that of the usually extroverted Kirk Douglas. Jane Greer has said that Tourneur's direction "was very simple to understand," and that he often asked the players to seem "impassive."

Samuel Beetley, who edited *Out of the Past*, said that Tourneur "was one of the finest directors I ever worked with. He was artistic and he knew what the editor needed." Beetley remarked upon one subtle "touch" that lent distinction in Tourneur's films: "He always insisted upon never returning to the same camera angles when intercutting scenes."

Simplicity and practicality were the keynotes of Musuraca's lighting. In an interview for *American Cinematographer*, February, 1941, he stated that "... while theories may be fine, the best way to do a thing is usually the simplest – and we can always find the simplest way if we reason things out, looking for simplicity and logic instead of technical window-dressing."

He did not agree with the cinematic convention that heavy drama must be lit in a low key, comedy in high key, and romance in soft focus, but that the style should be determined by the logic of the scene. "For example, a vast amount of real-life drama occurs in hospitals, and a modern hospital isn't by any means a sombre appearing place," he pointed out. "Everything is light-colored and glistening; what's more, everything is pretty well illuminated – trust these medical men to see to it that there's enough illumination everywhere to prevent eyestrain. So why should we always have things sombre and gloomy when ... we try to portray sad or tragic action in a hospital?

"In the same way, if there's no logical reason for it, why should comedy always be lit in a high key? Sometimes your action may really demand low-key effects to put it over! ... In making *Little Men*, we had such a scene. The scene showed George Bancroft sitting at his desk, reading; it was a night effect. While he is engrossed with his study, Jack Oakie tiptoes in through the door and hides behind the door – unknown to the professor – who calmly gets up and goes out, still unaware that anyone is in the room.

"Now if you had that scene lit in a high key, in traditional comedy fashion, even the most absent-

Mitchum falls for another Douglas scheme.

minded or nearsighted old professor could hardly ignore Jack Oakie's presence. I knew that if the scene was to be convincing, we had to make Bancroft's ignorance of the intruder plausible and natural.''

Musuraca believed that cinematography had become unnecessarily complicated. ''All too often we're all of us likely to find ourselves throwing in an extra light here, and another there, simply to correct something which is a bit wrong because of the way one basic lamp is placed or adjusted . . . If, on the other hand, that one original lamp is in its really correct place and adjustment, the others aren't needed. Any time I find myself using a more than ordinary number of light sources for a scene, I try to stop and think it out. Nine times out of ten I'll find

I've slipped up somewhere, and the extra lights are really unnecessary. If you once get the 'feel' of lighting balance this way, you'll be surprised how you'll be able to simplify your lightings. Usually the results on the screen are better, too!

"The same thing applies to making exterior scenes. One of the commonest sources of unnecessary complication is in overdoing filtering. Just because the research scientists have evolved a range of several score filters of different colors and densities isn't by any means a reason that we've got to use them – or even burden ourselves down with them. On my own part I've always found that the simplest filtering is best. Give me a good yellow filter for mild correction effects, and a good red or red-orange one for heavier corrections and I'll guarantee to bring you back almost any sort of exterior effects (other than night scenes) that you'll need in the average production . . . My own choice is an Aero 1 for the

lighter effects, and a G or sometimes a 23-A for heavier effects."

Obviously, Musuraca's deep shadows were an integral part of the atmosphere pervading much of *Out of the Past,* in which the fear of death is imminent from first to last. Even the exteriors photographed in the natural beauty of the Tahoe area convey menace as well as charm. The hard-lit textures of trees and granite in sun and shadow emphasize the danger of an assassin stalking his prey, even at an idyllic fishing stream. Jeff's comment, "You don't go fishing with a .45," echoes the ambiguity of the situation.

Several scenes are enhanced by realistic visual effects made under the supervision of Russell A. Cully, ASC, a pioneer effects cinematographer who had recently taken charge of that department at RKO following the retirement of Vernon L. Walker, ASC. Rear projection process shots were utilized to combine the Mexican location backgrounds with studio photography of Mitchum and Greer. Matte paintings provided architectural and scenic details such as the exterior of Douglas' palatial home.

Roy Webb, one of the best and most prolific composers of film music, provided the subtle underscore which helps to hold the plot complexities together. Webb's music was integral to *The Stranger on the Third Floor,* most of the Lewton films, *Murder My Sweet, Notorious, Cornered, The Spiral Staircase, The Locket, Crossfire, They Won't Believe Me* and *Riff-Raff* – in other words, most of the best of RKO's ventures into mystery and mayhem during the Forties. To say that the Hungarian-born composer had a flair for this type of music is an understatement. He created music that sounds the way a Musuraca night shot looks: suggestive, atmospheric, dramatic. While it always strengthens the visuals, it never overwhelms the senses. His work in these films was widely imitated.

After production was completed, the original title, *Build My Gallows High,* was given to Dr. Gallup's Audience Research, Inc. for testing. Their poll indicated that an overwhelming number of potential customers were put off by the morbidity of the title. The picture went into release as *Out of the Past* in November 1947 and was well received by the trade publications and the public, but there were some objections to the tragic ending. Although Jeff is a sympathetic and even praiseworthy character caught up in the machinations of others and pushed unwillingly into criminal collusion, it is doubtful that the Production Code of self-censorship would have permitted any other kind of ending. Curiously, the censors who demanded punishment for Jeff seemed unconcerned that The Kid went unpunished for killing the gunman.

Shortly after the picture was released, Musuraca complained that he was being typecast as a specialist in mystery films. He did photograph several later films in that vein, but the rest of his career in movies and TV production gave him plenty of opportunity to display his versatility with a wide variety of subjects. He died in 1975, but remains an almost legendary name – mostly because of his work at RKO.

Tourneur's career continued in high gear over the next decade, with highly rewarding assignments. In 1957 he went to England, where he made the much honored *Night of the Demon* (U.S.: *Curse of the Demon),* a return to the type of films he made with Lewton. After that his work in Italy and the United States was wasted on projects unworthy of his talents. He died in 1977.

There is a curious fact about the would-be arbiters of taste and molders of opinion: most pay lip service to originality while bowing deeply to fash-

ion. At the time *Out of the Past* was released it received only perfunctory critical attention, being viewed by all but the trade press as just one more well-made melodrama with too many killings and a story line generally characterized as "confusing." In recent years, however, it has been reappraised by many of the same critics and their successors and accorded an exalted status, not because it has changed with age but because it fits snugly into a category which – belatedly – is "in." Once removed from that handy pigeonhole labeled *film noir*, the picture is exactly what the Hollywood Reporter's critic called it after its preview in 1947: "Solid, entertaining melodrama which will enjoy a profitable box-office pay-off...For the public, this is the kind of satifsying show which for years has been the industry's bread and butter."

Mighty nourishing it was, too.

—George E. Turner

An RKO-Radio Picture; *directed by* Jacques Tourneur; *executive producer,* Robert Sparks; *produced by* Warren Duff; *screenplay by* Geoffrey Homes, *from his novel, "Build My Gallows High;" adaptation,* James M. Cain, Frank Fenton; *director of photography,* Nicholas Musuraca, ASC; *art directors,* Albert S. D'Agostino, Jack Okey; *special effects,* Russell A. Cully, ASC; *set decorations,* Darrell Silvera; *makeup supervision,* Gordon Bau; *music by* Roy Webb; *musical director,* C. Bakaleinikoff; *film editor,* Samuel E. Beetley; *sound,* Francis M. Sarver, Clem Portman; *gowns,* Edward Stevenson; *optical effects,* Linwood Dunn, ASC; *assistant director,* Harry Mancke; RCA *sound; running time, 97 minutes; released November 25, 1947.*

Jeff, Robert Mitchum; *Kathie,* Jane Greer; *Whit,* Kirk Douglas; *Meta,* Rhonda Fleming; *Jim,* Richard Webb; *Fisher,* Steve Brodie; *Ann,* Virginia Huston; *Joe,* Paul Valentine; *The Kid,* Dickie Moore; *Eels,* Ken Niles; *Sheriff Douglas,* Frank Wilcox; *Cop,* Lee Elson; *Marney,* Mary Field; *Waiter,* Joe Portugal; *Doorman,* Jess Escobar; *Car Manipulator,* Hubert Brill; *Bellhop,* Primo Lopez; *Couple at Harlem Club,* Mildred Boy *and* Ted Collins; *Waiter,* Sam Warren; *Headwaiter,* Wesley Bly; *Eunice,* Theresa Harris; *Doorman,* James Bush; *Canby Miller,* Harry Hayden; *Rafferty,* Archie Twitchell.

261

22

A Single Length of *Rope*

Many movies have been criticized as being "the same old stuff." Such a complaint could never be leveled at *Rope*, which was produced by Alfred Hitchcock more than four decades ago. *Rope* was one of a kind.

In 1946, Hitchcock and his old friend, Sidney L. Bernstein, a theater magnate, formed a producing company called Transatlantic Pictures Corp. While dining at Bernstein's London home, Hitchcock was intrigued by an idea proposed by Bernstein that stage plays should be photographed during performances for research purposes.

Hitchcock mentioned a 1929 play by Patrick Hamilton, *Rope's End*, which he believed would be ideal for such a treatment. He proposed to shoot the play, which has no time lapses and takes place in one set in an hour-and-a-half, as continuous action. "The camera never stops," he explained. But the picture should not be made on a theater stage but under sound stage conditions. The partners decided to buy the play and film it as the first Transatlantic production. Hitchcock soon debarked to America to direct the last picture required by his contract with David O. Selznick, *The Paradine Case*.

Star names were necessary to carry a picture in those days. Transatlantic decided to get one box-office star, James Stewart, and assign the other roles to dependable – but less expensive – players with stage experience. Stewart's fee – $300,000 – was a large disbursement for an independent company. The other players: John Dall, Farley Granger, Sir Cedric Hardwicke, Constance Collier, Joan Chandler, Douglas Dick, Edith Evanson and Dick

Hogan. *Rope* was the first of four pictures Stewart made for Hitchcock.

Technicolor was another sure-fire selling point. Hitchcock decided that *Rope* would be his first color picture.

The concept of shooting a picture in "real time" was not, in itself, unique. For several years following the introduction of motion pictures in 1894, short films dealing with simple situations were filmed with locked down cameras from a single vantage point. As productions grew longer, individual shots became shorter – but only gradually. After 1910, the value of editing a picture from many shots of varying lengths and angles became standard procedure, and by 1920 the average feature contained about 600 shots. The art of shooting and cutting film into a unified whole had reached a high state when, in the late 1920s, the talking picture made silent production methods obsolete.

Extremely long takes became a necessity because of the many unresolved problems of combining photography with sound. There was a general reluctance to attempt cutting during a scene, and a long scene was made more dreary by the fact that the camera was confined to a soundproof booth and the actors had to huddle around a hidden, low-fidelity microphone. The invention of the mike boom freed the sound apparatus and the soundproofing of cameras with blimps freed the cinematographer from camera booths. Cutting within a dialogue scene was achieved successfully in 1929 by Tod Browning and Merritt Gerstad, ASC – director

and cinematographer of MGM's *The Thirteenth Chair* – during the filming of a seance scene.

Hitchcock's plan was to shoot all nine reels of *Rope* with the usual variety of camera angles from closeups to long shots without cutting. The camera would be kept in continuous motion, prying into the action as an invisible visitor.

In 1947, while Hitchcock was completing *The Paradine Case*, he and Bernstein signed Arthur Laurents, a successful Broadway playwright, to write the screenplay of *Rope's End*. Hitchcock's friend, actor Hume Cronyn, had done a preliminary adaptation. The picture was to be produced at Warner Bros. for their program. The script is a unique document in that the scenes are not numbered or separated and there are very few camera directions other than some notations of positions required at certain crucial points.

Hitchcock had never worked in Technicolor before, having purposely avoided color photography because he felt that his type of story generally worked better in black and white. He decided to do *Rope* in color because, he said, ''Color will denote the change in time of day from sunset to darkness which is of vital dramatic importance in the story.''

Technicolor, at that time, was a process which utilized three strips of black and white film passing through a specially constructed camera to produce the panchromatic equivalent of three basic colors, which were printed onto a single strip of film by a dye transfer method. It was a ponderous, expensive method fraught with difficulties, but was capable of producing results surpassing those of any other available process. The three-strip process is quite extinct now, except in the Chinese film industry.

The director acquaints the cast with the script long before actual production begins. Around table clockwise are Douglas Dick, John Dall, Joan Chandler, Sir Cedric Hardwicke, Charlsie Bryant (continuity clerk), Alfred Hitchcock, Farley Granger, James Stewart, Constance Collier and Edith Evanson.

Because only 952 feet of Technicolor could be shot at one time, filming was done in segments of nine minutes or less. To hide the changes between reels it was necessary to resort to various forms of trickery. In one instance, the lid of the sinister chest is raised, momentarily blotting out the scene as it comes close to the camera lens. Sometimes the camera freezes on some part of the room not occupied by actors, picks up the same view on the next reel and continues the camera movement. Most often one of the players brushes past the camera or the camera moves in close to somebody's jacket at the end of the take.

The opening reel actually encompasses two shots. The first is a high angle looking down at a city street; then the camera swings around to show a high window with drawn blinds. A scream is heard from inside. Then the camera is in the apartment and the long take begins with an extreme closeup of Dick Hogan's agonized face. The camera pulls back to show that he is being strangled by a rope held by John Dall and Farley Granger. The boys stuff the body into a large wooden chest. The camera follows them through the hallway and dining room to the kitchen, watches them open a bottle of champagne, and returns with them to the chest. There they discuss their crime and their plans for the evening as they set the silver service on the wooden tomb in preparation for a buffet dinner to which the corpse's family and fiancee have been invited.

During the ensuing eight reels we learn that the two young men have murdered their college friend merely to prove their superiority. Amongst the guests is their former professor, James Stewart, whose teachings of the Nietzsche superman theory have inspired the crime. In their attempts to impress Stewart, the murderers arouse his suspicions. After the party he returns to confront them with their guilt and turn them over to the police.

The camera moves were not improvised to any noticeable degree. Hitchcock's method always was to pre-plan a production so intricately that the actual filming was relatively simple. A series of conferences with key production personnel to iron out technical problems began in December 1947, about one month in advance of principal photography. Among those present at these meetings were Joseph A. Valentine, ASC, director of photography; William V. Skall, ASC, a cinematographer furnished by the Technicolor Company; William Ziegler, film editor; Perry Ferguson, art director; Lowell Farrell, assistant director; Fred Ahern, production manager; and Emile Kuri and Howard Bristol, set directors.

Ziegler planned out the movements of actors and camera by rearranging the rooms of his daughter's doll house and using chess men as actors. The art director and the cinematographers used Ziegler's choreography to plan their moves, which were extremely intricate.

All action, except for a brief opening scene, was shot on a single set. The designer, Perry Ferguson, was one of the top men in his field, having done the sets for the likes of *Gunga Din* (1939), *The Hunchback of Notre Dame* (1939) and *The Secret Life of Walter Mitty* (1947). His ingenious set for *Rope* depicted a penthouse apartment consisting of living room, dining room, hallway and part of a kitchen. All the walls were wild, being hung from overhead U-tracks so that grips could move them out of the camera's way as it followed the actors through doors, then replace them before they came back into camera range. The rails' grooves were filled in with petroleum jelly so that there would be no friction as the walls were slid back and forth.

All the furniture, including a massive wooden chest which plays an important role in the story, was on wheels so it could be moved out of the camera's way. The chest, which appears to be in the middle of the living room throughout, actually was rolled away every time the camera moved across the room, then returned to its position before the camera returned.

Ralph Webb, special effects expert, and Hitchcock on the set with miniature and a spun glass cloud.

To keep such movement behind the camera noiseless, the set was built on a special floor on Warner Stage 12. Built of 1" tongue-and-groove lumber covered with soundproof celotex and a carpet, and lined with felt, the extra floor assured that there would be no creaking as the heavy Technicolor camera and dolly passed over. The floor was marked with numbered circles showing where the camera should be situated at a given time. The positions were also plotted on a blackboard. A continuity supervisor signalled the crew for each move indicated on the board. A small flashlight, suspended just under the camera lens so that its circle of light marked the exact position of each number, helped the grips to place the camera in position for each cue.

Valentine, a stocky New Yorker of Italian descent, had photographed most of the Deanna Durbin pictures, *The Wolf Man* (1941), and two of Hitchcock's earlier pictures, *Saboteur* (1942) and *Shadow of a Doubt* (1943). Skall was a specialist in Technicolor photography, whose credits included *Ramona* (1936), *Northwest Passage* (1940) and *Billy the Kid* (1941). It was his job to advise Valentine, whose specialty was black and white work, on the consid-

265

erable differences in technique demanded by the color process.

Rehearsals began on the full-size set on January 12 and continued daily until January 22, when actual photography commenced.

The camera was mounted on a special dolly invented by Morris Rosen, head grip, and called "Rosie's all-angle dolly." It was made for $1700 and consisted of a square platform, a camera post and wheels. It operated without tracks and was small enough to pass through a normal double door. The camera post would rise four feet noiselessly. Each set of double wheels was separately pivoted. A chain attached to the steering handle turned all wheels simultaneously, allowing the camera to circle a player in closeup.

Finding that it was impractical in most instances to follow the camera with a mike boom, the sound supervisor, Al Riggs, used four separate booms and two overhead mikes to pick up dialogue from anywhere on the set. Five recordists and as many boom operators were busy keeping up with the camera moves, while the mixer operated his console from a high parallel overlooking the set.

A 35mm lens, which offered a somewhat wider angle and deeper field than the normal 50mm, was used throughout, taking in 1½-foot closeups to 30 foot long shots. A Selsyn motor, calibrated to the lens, was employed to insure correct focus.

Director expresses confidence in his cast—Granger, Evanson, Dick, Dall, Collier, Hardwicke, Chandler and Stewart. The only other player, Dick Hogan, has already been tucked out of sight.

"My biggest problem was the lighting," Valentine told *American Cinematographer* (July, 1948). "Especially the job of eliminating mike and camera shadows. In the reel where we had ten mikes in operation we had to have electricians operating five dimmer panels." All lighting had to be set up overhead, television style.

Valentine and Skall kept the colors subdued throughout, except for a few moments at the end of the picture. The lighting and colors within the apartment itself are purposely undramatic and ordinary looking, with none of the sinister *film noir* look of most murder yarns. The dramatic color effects were limited to the scene outside the window, in which the passage of time had to be dramatized convincingly.

No Hitchcock picture would be complete without some use of miniatures. In *Rope,* in which there is none of the usual hectic action featured in the typical thriller, the miniature is part of the set – the view of New York City which appears beyond the windows in every reel.

It was apparent from the outset that the customary painted backdrop, however artfully lighted, would be inadequate to show the changing light and cloud formations needed to depict the passage of time from late afternoon to night. The importance of this effect to a story being told in "real time" was crucial.

The miniature reproduced about 35 square miles of the Manhattan skyline, taking in such familiar landmarks as the Empire State Building, St. Patrick's Church, the Hotel Astor, Radio City, and the Chrysler and Woolworth buildings. The 12,000-square-foot cyclorama backing was three times as

wide as the apartment and was laid out in a semi-circle so the camera could be moved around freely without compromising the background. The buildings, built in forced perspective, were similarly arranged. The closer structures were three dimensional and equipped with steam pipes inside to feed "smoke" through chimneys and stacks. It was noted initially that the steam rose too rapidly and too high for the scale of the set. Dry ice, placed over the pipes, solved the problem. The chilled steam rose lazily and drifted away.

The more distant buildings were photographic blowups shot in New York, printed up to scale and mounted as double-faceted cutouts. The farthest buildings were only 20 feet from the window, but with extreme foreshortening and effect lighting they give a proper impression of distance.

Fred Ahern, production manager, got the job of finding clouds that looked real and could be changed subtly between takes. Clouds of cotton wool were tested and rejected because they absorbed the light instead of reflecting it. Eventually, the clouds were made of spun glass ("angel hair"). Scenic artists wearing cheesecloth-lined painting masks modelled 500 pounds of the fragile substance over chicken wire forms to produce a variety of cumulus cloud shapes, which were arrived at after hundreds of photographs were studied. The clouds were mounted individually on stands or suspended from tracks on invisible wires.

Dr. Dinsmore Alter, head of the Griffith Observatory in Hollywood, was brought in to examine the clouds for authenticity. The noted meteorologist-astronomer made certain that the shapes were correct for their levels and had one group broken up because it resembled an atomic mushroom.

In the course of filming, the clouds were rearranged between reels, moving left to right according to a carefully drawn-out plan. In the opening scenes the sky is crowded with clouds, which thin out as nightfall approaches until at the end there are only two clouds in the blackened sky.

As the sky darkens, lights begin appearing in the windows of the buildings and neon signs flash on. One of these signs depicts before-and-after figures advertising a product called Reduco. The model for this was the director, whose portly figure is well known, making the token personal appearance that had been a tradition in his films since *The Lodger*, made in 1926. He had used the Reduco gag as a newspaper ad in *Lifeboat* (1943), another one-set show in which he could not logically do a walk-on.

An electrician stationed on a high parallel operated a light organ with a bank of 47 switches to

Living room, showing the numbered rings on floor which guided dolly operators to proper positions.

control the miniature lights. Some 6,000 incandescent bulbs ranging from 25 to 100 watts lit the windows and 200 tiny neon signs adorned the exteriors of the buildings, all of which were wired separately. This required 26,000 feet of wire carrying 126,000 watts of power to 150 transformers.

A full scale neon sign spelling out STORAGE in three colors – red, blue and green – was installed near the window. This sign begins flashing just at the climax of the movie, when the murderers are revealed, so to speak, in their true colors. The neon provides lurid punctuation to a film of predominantly subdued hues.

To make the light from the sign seem to flood the room and limn the faces of the killers, lights covered by gels of the same colors as the neon were set up. Shutter devices, electrically synchronized to the blinking of the sign, created the dramatic pulsing of the colors.

"Our worst calamity," Valentine said, "was the day one of the wild walls didn't move quite fast enough and the camera went crashing right into it. The crackup jimmied the friction head of the camera and we suspended filming for the day."

The *Rope* technique, Valentine said, created more problems for the crew and required more careful planning than the conventional methods, but he felt it was beneficial to the actors. "The way we usually film a scene, by making first a master shot, then a medium shot, then finally a close-up, keeps the actors waiting endlessly. By the time we get around to the close-up the stars are exhausted and the spontaneity of the scene is lost; but with this

267

reel by reel filming the actor can sustain a character-ization and maintain an even flow and pace in his work.''

A typical technical problem occurred while the first reel was being shot. After about eight minutes of a perfect take, the last camera move caught an electrician standing by the window.

Rope was completed, supposedly, in only 18 actual days of production – 10 days of rehearsals with actors, camera and crew, and eight days of shooting. Hitchcock, however, was displeased with the first version of the sunset, which was treated in a conventional movie style with an abundance of red-orange light. He decided to retake the last five reels of the picture. He sent photographers to three locations to photograph the setting sun at five minute intervals for 105 minutes. One made his shots from the top of a New York office building, another from an unfinished building on Wilshire Blvd. in Los Angeles, and the other from Santa Monica pier.

Cast and crew rehearse on Warners Stage 12. From left, Morris Rosen, Ed Fitzgerald, Paul Hill, Hitchcock, William V. Skall, Jim Porterman, Stewart, Chandler, Dick, Hardwicke, Collier, Granger and Dall.

Shooting the first version of the sunset confrontation. Note wild walls and the immense size of the Technicolor blimp.

The five reels were re-shot, using the photos as color guides. At this time, Valentine was on the sick list and Skall took charge. Nine days later the last reel was completed.

Incidentally, Hitchcock was not *entirely* convinced that his one-take approach was viable, although he had experimented with the idea in individual sequences of *Spellbound* (1945), *Notorious* (1946) and *The Paradine Case* (1947). He spent several days shooting closeups of key dialogue scenes, "– just in case."

The street sounds, including the approaching police siren at the climax, were real. Nixing the sound department's intention of utilizing library sound effects, Hitchcock had microphones hung outside a sixth story window while actors, autos and an ambulance performed to order. The effect is perfectly realistic.

The original cost estimate of *Rope* was $1.4 million, including studio overhead charges. Neither time nor money were budgeted strictly because it was impossible to anticipate what problems might arise. The 28-day completion was well under the schedule usually given important pictures, and the cost of $200,000 above the estimate was hardly excessive. There was a minimum of post-production work. The picture was released nationally on September 25.

The light of the city punctuates the climax as Stewart confronts Dall and Granger with their guilt.

The movie industry's own self-censorship board, established by the studios to keep producers from running afoul of local and state censors, rode herd on the script and production, making certain there was no direct allusion to the homosexuality of the murderers (and the bestiality of one of them), and that the murder scene was not unduly gruesome. The picture received the Motion Picture Producers and Distributors of America "purity seal," meaning it was, ostensibly, "censor-proof." However:

The Chicago censors banned *Rope* in toto. Authorities in Worcester, New Bedford, Spokane, Seattle and Memphis followed suit. Chicago later relented, with the condition that exhibitors enforce an "adults only" policy. Sioux City permitted exhibition only after the murder scene was deleted. Womens' organizations, the National Legion of Decency and other influential groups denounced it.

Fortunately for Transatlantic, *Rope* received generally high marks in the press, few reviewers remarking dislike of either the theme or the technique. A number even went overboard and proclaimed it "as important as the invention of the closeup or of sound." *Life*, selecting it as Movie of the Week, gave the sensible opinion that the "radical innovation in picture-making" was effective in maintaining suspense but that Hitchcock's effort at making his technique unobtrusive was "not a wholly successful one." On the other hand, the esteemed Thornton Delahanty, in *Redbook*, selecting *Rope* as the Movie of the Month, gave it a rave review, commented upon the "extremely effective" use of color "to dramatize the mood" and made no mention whatever of the photographic technique!

The public, undaunted by questions of technique, liked the picture well enough to make it a financial success. It put Transatlantic in a healthy financial condition and the company's future seemed secure.

Hitchcock tried a modified version of the *Rope* technique on their next production, *Under Capricorn*, interspersing several long and complex takes into more conventionally arranged scenes, but they interrupted the tempo of the otherwise exquisite film and destroyed suspense. The usually imperturbable Ingrid Bergman became so angry while wading through one nine-minute scene that she was still raving on the set after the director had gone home.

Under Capricorn, which cost a greal deal more than *Rope* and brought in a great deal less, was a fiscal disaster which forced Hitchcock and Bernstein to dissolve Transatlantic.

"I undertook *Rope* as a stunt; that's the only way I can describe it," Hitchcock said 20 years later in the book, *Hitchcock* by Francois Truffaut (Simon & Schuster, 1967). "I really don't know how I came to indulge in it...When I look back, I realize that it

Director of photography Joseph Valentine, Hitchcock, and technical advisor Dr. Dinsmore Alter.

was quite nonsensical because I was breaking with my own theories on the importance of cutting and montage for the visual narration of a story." He also referred to it as "a crazy idea."

It is, nevertheless, a fascinating show and is actually the only feature of its kind in the history of films. Its uniqueness gives it a certain monolithic stature and it is doubtful that it could have been done as well by other hands. In *Rope*, Hitchcock blazed a trail which nobody yet has followed.

—George E. Turner

A Transatlantic Pictures *production; color by Technicolor; produced by* Sidney Bernstein *and* Alfred J. Hitchcock; *directed by* Alfred Hitchcock; *adapted by* Hume Cronyn *from the play,* "Rope's End," by Patrick Hamilton; *screen play by* Arthur Laurents; *directors of photography,* Joseph A. Valentine, ASC, *and* William V. Skall, ASC; *Technicolor color director,* Natalie Kalmus; *associate,* Robert Brower; *art director,* Perry Ferguson; *set decorators,* Emile Kuri *and* Howard Bristol; *film editor,* William H. Ziegler; *sound by* Al Riggs; *makeup artist,* Perc Westmore; *musical director,* Leo F. Forbstein; *music adapted from* "Mouvement Perpetual No. 1" by Francois Poulenc; *Miss Chandler's dress by* Adrian; *radio sequence by* The Three Suns; *operators of camera movement,* Edward Fitzgerald, Paul G. Hill, Richard Emmons, Morris Rosen; *lighting technician,* Jim Potevin; *assistant director,* Lowell J. Farrell; *production manager,* Fred Ahern; *technical advisor,* Dr. Dinsmore Alter; *mechanical effects,* Ralph Webb; *continuity,* Charlsie Bryant. *Running time, 80 minutes. Released September 28, 1948 by Warner Bros. Pictures, Inc.; reissued 1983 by Univeral Classics.*

Rupert Cadell, James Stewart; *Brandon,* John Dall; *Philip,* Farley Granger; *Mr. Kentley,* Sir Cedric Hardwicke; *Mrs. Atwater,* Constance Collier; *Kenneth,* Douglas Dick; *Mrs. Wilson,* Edith Evanson; *David Kentley,* Dick Hogan; *Janet,* Joan Chandler.

A contemplative Hitchcock at the end of his Rope.

23

D.O.A., a Walk-In Homicide

A man hurries unsteadily along a dark Los Angeles street, enters a police station and stalks through the winding corridors until at last he enters a door marked HOMICIDE DIVISION.

"I want to report a murder," he tells the several detectives calmly. They ask questions: *Where did it happen?* "San Francisco, last night." *Who was murdered?* "I was."

So begins a memorable film from four decades ago, *D.O.A.* (Dead on Arrival). Certainly this is one of the more unusual and dramatic establishing sequences yet devised, worthy to rank with the arrival scene at Fort Zinderneuf in *Beau Geste*, the dream visit to Manderley in *Rebecca*, the escape from the posse in *Of Mice and Men*, Charles Foster Kane's muttered "Rosebud," or close-ups of the fishing nets in *The Pearl*. Once we have seen and heard a haggard Edmond O'Brien deliver those few lines in an emotion-drained voice that leaves no room for doubt, we're hooked for the additional 80 minutes necessary to watch him untangle a complex yarn of cold-blooded murder and a frantic race against the clock for understanding and revenge.

Harry Popkin was the producer of *D.O.A.* A theater chain operator and sporting events promoter, Popkin had entered production about nine years earlier with a series of low-budget pictures featuring all-black casts for release to specialized theaters. His first mainstream production was the successful *And Then There Were None* (1945), directed by René Clair and released by Twentieth Century-Fox. In 1949, after several years of providing financial backing for other independent producers, Pop-kin formed Cardinal Pictures, Inc., specifically to make features for United Artists release. The fourth of these, falling between *The Big Wheel* and *Champaigne For Caesar*, was *D.O.A.*, which was completed in November 1949 but not released until the following April 30. The unusual theme of the picture and the excellence of its acting and presentation won it popular and critical acclaim despite its lack of box-office star names.

The dramatic visual qualities of the story were ensured by the selection of Rudolph Maté, ASC, as director, and Ernest Laszlo, ASC, as director of photography. It was to be Maté's third directorial job, following many years as a celebrated cinematographer.

The screenplay was a collaboration of two former New Yorkers, Clarence Green and Russell Rouse, who envisioned the experiences of an average man as he plunges into a nightmarish adventure in strange – but very real – places. Most of the action occurs in San Francisco and Los Angeles, both of which abound in authentic unreality. They were able to convince key members of the Los Angeles homicide and vice squads that their story would not be detrimental to the police force and were assigned the services of a special investigator to advise them in proper police procedures and suggest appropriate locations for staging chases and action concerning gangster activity.

Watching the daily papers during what proved to be an unusually rowdy period in Los Angeles history, they deliberately introduced into their narrative places where real incidents of vio-

D.O.A.

...the strangest entry ever made on a police blotter...
the story of a man who sets out to avenge
his own murder...

Harry M. Popkin presents

D.O.A.
starring
EDMOND O'BRIEN
and
PAMELA BRITTON

with

LUTHER ADLER Beverly Campbell · Neville Brand · Lynn Baggett
William Ching · Henry Hart · Laurette Luez
Produced by Leo C. Popkin · Directed by Rudy Maté · Story and Screenplay by
Russell Rouse and Clarence Greene · Music Written and Directed by Dimitri Tiomkin
·A Harry M Popkin Production · Released thru United Artists

lence were occurring. When some mobsters were shot up in a night spot on Sunset Boulevard, for example, the writers quickly worked the club facade and adjacent areas into the story. When it was learned that some Mafia kingpins had moved into Beverly Hills, they fashioned a sequence in which the hero confronts a murderess in a hilltop mansion in the same neighborhood.

To gain a better understanding of criminal investigation procedures and absorb some underworld ambience, the writers traveled as observers with various police detectives as they called on skid row bars, pawnshops and known criminal hangouts. They observed shakedowns, arrests, booking procedures and an ambush for a murder suspect who was wounded and captured. For a time they haunted the Main Street Skid Row district, then at its post-war worst.

San Francisco supplied some of the more "normal" settings, including the St. Francis Hotel, Market Street at a busy hour, hilly streets with straining cable cars, and the wharf area. It also

provided the Fisherman Club, then a be-bop music joint, as a chaotic scene for murder.

It's a curious fact that some of the movies that utilize the American milieu most effectively are the work of filmmakers who come here from other lands and observe keenly many distinctive customs and places that we have long taken for granted. (As an example, the most authentic filmed depiction of the Texas farmer, *The Southerner,* was produced by the Hakim brothers from Egypt, directed by France's Jean Renoir and photographed by ex-Parisian Lucien Andriot, ASC.) Such was the case with *D.O.A.,* which was directed by a cinematographer from Poland and photographed by a Hungarian emigre. Both men had lived in the United States for many years – Maté since 1934, Laszlo since the mid-1920s – but they never lost their sense of wonder at their adopted land. For *D.O.A.* they achieved studio-quality artistry although they worked almost entirely on practical locations outside the studio.

Maté was born in Krakow of a Hungarian father and a Czechoslovakian mother. He majored in philosophy at universities in Vienna, Budapest and Berlin, but enlisted in the army at 17 and fought in Italy and Serbia for 26 months. After recovering from war wounds and a long bout with typhoid, Maté worked as an assistant cameraman in Budapest and Vienna before becoming a full-fledged cinematographer. During the 1920s he photo-

Ernest Lazlo.

274

In the prologue, Bigelow (Edmond O'Brien) tells detectives (Roy Engle and George Lynn) that he has been murdered.

graphed some of the greatest silent films in Austria, Germany and France, including *Samson and Delilah,* directed by Alexander Korda; *The Passion of Joan of Arc* and *Vampyr,* directed by Carl Theodor Dreyer; *Liliom,* directed by Fritz Lang; and *The Last Millionaire,* directed by René Clair. He came to the United States at the suggestion of the French watercolorist and director, Harry Lachman, for whom he had shot seven pictures in France and England and who was now working for Fox Film.

Maté's work in *Dante's Inferno,* his second picture for Fox, placed him in the front rank of American cinematographers. His distinctive touch was crucial to the success of the likes of *Dodsworth, Foreign Correspondent, That Hamilton Woman, Pride of the Yankees, Cover Girl* and *Gilda.* In 1948 he was made a producer at Columbia, and the following

year he directed *The Dark Past,* a psychological drama featuring a marvelous dream sequence shown in negative with William Holden being pelted by black rain.

Laszlo became an assistant cameraman in 1926 and got his first screen credit in 1944 as director of photography of Paramount's *The Hitler Gang,* which he shot in a *noir* fashion that won him immediate recognition as a pictorial stylist. His pre-*D.O.A.* work included *Two Years Before the Mast, The Road to Rio, Manhandled* and *Impact.* After *D.O.A.* he photographed two controversial pictures, *M* (in which he carried his artistic handling of practical settings a step farther) and *The Moon is Blue;* was awarded an Oscar for *Ship of Fools,* and received Academy nominations for *Inherit the Wind, Judgment at Nuremberg; It's a Mad, Mad, Mad, Mad World; Star!, Airport* and *Logan's Run.*

Laszlo, handsome and debonair, a man of the world with European manners, was in love with the American dream. ''Every young American should know my story,'' he told this writer several

Sam (Jeff Kirkpatrick) doesn't resent Bigelow's attentions to Sue (Cay Forester) — yet.

years ago. "If a fellow like me can come to this country and see all his dreams come true, so can anybody who really tries."

In the post-World War II years a tradition of realistic American crime pictures based upon actual police cases and photographed in authentic locales had been established: *Boomerang, Kiss of Death* (both 1947), *He Walked By Night* and *Naked City* (both 1948) are prime examples. *D.O.A.* was photographed under similar circumstances, but instead of striving for an atmosphere of semi-documentary realism, Maté and Laszlo blended actuality into the more fanciful style demanded by a strange mystery story.

Except for the framing scenes at homicide, the picture is a long flashback with minimal narration by O'Brien. Frank Bigelow (O'Brien), an overworked tax accountant in the desert town of Banning, takes a short vacation from his office and his secretary-fiancee, Paula (Pamela Britton). At the St. Francis Hotel in San Francisco, he falls in with a happy crowd of conventioneers and their wives, accompanying them to a be-bop joint, the Fisherman. While he arranges an assignation with a beautiful blonde at the bar, someone switches drinks with Bigelow. He finds that the drink tastes strange so he orders a replacement. Next day he feels ill and goes to a hospital for an examination. He is informed that he has been poisoned by an iridium substance which already has entered his system, and that he will die within a few days. He hastens to

another clinic where he is told, "I don't think you fully understand, Bigelow. You've been murdered."

Before he can be placed in a hospital, Bigelow flees in a panic, racing through busy downtown streets. At last he stops running and grimly determines to find out why he was murdered and by whom. Learning that a Los Angeles client, Philips, was trying desperately to get in touch with him, followed by news that Philips has committed suicide, Bigelow flies to Los Angeles, where he interviews Philips' brother, Frank (Henry Hart), the beautiful widow (Lynn Baggett), his chief accountant, Halliday (William Ching), and his secretary (Beverly Campbell). Bigelow's office records furnish a solid clue: he had once notarized a bill of sale for Philips, countersigned by one George Reynolds, regarding a valuable shipment of iridium. He learns that the mineral was obtained illegally by Reynolds without Philips' knowledge.

His search for Reynolds leads Bigelow to a confrontation with Majak (Luther Adler), an underworld big shot, and his deadly henchmen led by the insane and sadistic Chester (Neville Brand). Majak assures him that he had nothing to do with the poisoning, but that now he must have Bigelow killed for learning too much. Bigelow is taken for a ride, but escapes into downtown traffic, where he is hotly pursued by Chester. Cornered in a drug store, Bigelow is saved when Chester is gunned down by police. Bigelow flees – he hasn't time to get involved in a police investigation.

Bigelow finds that Reynolds also has been murdered, and that Philips was killed by Mrs. Philips and Halliday, who made it appear he had committed suicide because of his supposed involvement in the illegal iridium deal. In innocently notarizing the bill of sale, Bigelow became the one person who could prove Philips was not a part of the iridium deal and cause suspicion to fall upon the guilty lovers. They poisoned him, thinking he knew everything. Carrying a handgun he acquired during his altercations with the gangsters, Bigelow corners Halliday in his office building and, in a gun duel, kills him.

At homicide, Bigelow concludes his story: "All I did was notarize one little paper – one little paper out of hundreds." Then he dies and is booked as "dead on arrival."

There is good acting throughout, and one virtuoso performance where it counts most – that of Edmond O'Brien, who is on screen continuously. He begins as a naive, all too human small towner out for a fling in the big city before he settles down to married life. He is perfectly convincing as he is

276

Doctor (Frank Gerstle) shows Bigelow the glowing poison that permeates his body.

being dazzled by all the flashy women at the hotel (a wolf whistle on the sound track each time he gets an eyeful is a bit too cute for the situation), drinks too much, gets a bit too flirtatious with the wife of one of the conventioneers, and makes a date with a gorgeous barfly at the Fisherman. Thereafter he passes realistically through a gamut of emotions: terror when he learns that he is about to die, disbelief as he stands on a busy street and becomes acutely aware of the sweetness of the life that pulses around him, anger, obsession, suffering at the hands of a brutal gang, and a weary triumph at achieving the only goal left to him – the solving and avenging of his own murder. It's difficult to imagine another actor seeing it through so perfectly.

The second showiest part is Brand's crazed Chester, who is described by Adler (with evident affection) as, ''...An unfortunate boy...unhappy unless he causes pain. He likes to see blood.'' A highly decorated war veteran making his film debut after appearing in plays in New York, Brand over-plays the role with much leering and eye-rolling, but this works well in the context of the character's insanity. Adler, a Broadway star only recently lured to Hollywood, also stands out as the underworld chief with urbane manners and an utter disregard for human life.

The photographic treatment is cohesive, true throughout to the changing moods of the story. The framing story is in what is now called *film noir* style (although the term hadn't been coined at that time) with harsh lighting contrasts and menacing

Rudolph Maté.

shadows. The early scenes of the story proper, those in Banning and at the St. Francis, are deceptively ordinary, having been played lightly and photographed in the plain, eye-level, evenly lighted style commonly applied to romantic comedies. When Bigelow signs the hotel register, the signatures of Ernest Laszlo and Russell Rouse can be seen.

The atmosphere changes abruptly at the Fisherman, where "Jadie" Carson and his band (whose well-played be-bop music is akin to that of the better-known Dizzy Gillespie) perform fast, exciting jazz as O'Brien and the conventioneers become increasingly uninhibited. Scenes of the customers responding frenziedly to the intoxicating rhythms are intercut with extreme close-ups of sweating black musicians caught up in the intensity of their music-making. Grotesque shadows, flashing lights seen through a haze of smoke, and angular shots of lustful men and sensual women create a sense of chaos and impending danger. Incidentally, *D.O.A.* apparently was the first film to depict a be-bop session.

The flat, gray look of early morning in the wharf area is captured admirably in subsequent scenes. Later, when Bigelow learns that he is dying, he runs in terror through the city, eventually reaching the heart of Market Street during a busy hour.

Luther Adler as Majak.

278

For a few poignant moments he stands in the brightness of day, next to a newstand where a display of *Life* magazines forms an arc over his head, trying to comprehend that he is no longer a part of the vibrant life that surrounds him. He stares, open mouthed, at a little girl playing with a ball, and – as a few bars of a Viennese waltz swirl through his mind – a pair of happy lovers.

Thereafter, the photography is calculated to mirror both the nightmare world into which the hero has plunged and the torment in his mind as his fear of death itself is replaced with the fear that he will have to die without knowing why and by whose hand, and that he will be denied his right to even the score. A knowing camera searches the byways of Los Angeles, from Skid Row to lofty mansions, peering closely into the faces of well-dressed businessmen whose outward respectability hides corruption, glamorous women with murder in their hearts, hoodlums with expressionless eyes, a cultured European underworld czar who assigns killings casually while ordering cocktails and dallying with his mistress, and a childish brute who relishes torture and murder. It's a rogue's gallery worth studying.

For an early morning skid row sequence, Maté arranged for the street cleaning department to bypass the area, leaving it "unspoiled" for the camera at five a.m. Much of the picture was photographed night for night, which was a much different thing then than now, because the available film stocks were comparatively slow. Utilization of ambient light is minimal, most of the sources being as carefully controlled as if they had been set up on a stage. These scenes are dominated by menacing, opaque shadows and unusual camera placements, augmented by optical dissolves and laps, eccentric cutting and weird musical stings. The Dmitri Tiomkin score, composed in a Russian-romantic vein, is a mixed blessing. Built upon an attractive love theme which is developed through some heavily dramatic and deliberately abrasive variations, the music is very effective at times, but in several instances it becomes intrusively over-literal.

The most striking interior scenes are of the climactic meeting of the victim and his murderer in the Bradbury Building, a masterpiece of distinctive 19th Century architecture in downtown Los Angeles. The open five-story interior, with its wealth of cast iron traceries on balconies and open hydraulic elevators, is a perfect setting to showcase Laszlo's penchant for mysterious lighting effects. Here the shadows seem edged with lace, which adds a particularly sinister quality as they play over the two men engaged in a game of death. About one year later,

Bigelow slugs the tormenting Chester (Neville Brand) as Maria (Laurette Luez), Majak, and Dave (Michael Ross) watch coldly.

Laszlo photographed an equally dramatic and much longer sequence for *M* in the same building.

    D.O.A. proved to be popular with audiences, notwithstanding its downbeat premise of a hero doomed from the beginning – seemingly box-office poison in a mass entertainment whose public habitually demanded happy endings. The satisfaction of watching an underdog getting even probably accounts for this and even overrides the monstrous underlying joke that the murder was an unnecessary error, the disturbing concept that the underworld lies alarmingly close to the surface of the everyday world, and the constant reminder that the hand of fate hovers over us all. Its creators doubtless were aware of something William Shakespeare often traded upon: that revenge, in real life the most tawdry of motives and almost invariably a disappointment in fulfillment, can be devilishly satisfying in a work of fiction.

A Cardinal Pictures, Inc., *production; a* United Artists *release; executive producer,* Harry M. Popkin; *directed by* Rudolph Mate, ASC; *music written and directed by* Dimitri Tiomkin; *screen play by* Russell Rouse and Clarence Green; *producer,* Leo C. Popkin; *associate producer,* Joseph H. Nadel; *director of photography,* Ernest Laszlo, ASC; *art director,* Duncan Cramer; *film editor,* Arthur H. Nadel; *set decorations,* Al Orenbach; *assistant director,* Marty Moss; *costumes by* Maria Donovan; *makeup by* Irving Berns; *sound recording,* Ben Winkler, Mac Dalgleish; *operative cameraman,* Gene Hirsch; *assistant cameraman,* Jack Fuqua; *script supervisor,* Arnold Laven; *key grip,* Carl Gibson; *gaffer,* Jim Potevin; *still photographer,* Frank Tanner; *technical advisor,* Edward F. Dunne, MD; RCA *recording system. Running time, 83 minutes. Released April 30, 1950.*

    Frank Bigelow, Edmond O'Brien; *Paula Gibson,* Pamela Britton; *Majak,* Luther Adler; *Miss Foster,* Beverly Campbell (later Garland); *Chester,* Neville Brand; *Halliday,* William Ching; *Mrs. Philips,* Lynn Baggett; *Stanley Philips,* Henry Hart; *Maria Rakubian,* Laurette Luez; *Sam Haskell,* Jess Kirkpatrick; *Sue,* Cay Forester; *Dr. Matson,* Frank Jacquet; *Dr. Schaefer,* Larry Dobkin; *Dr. MacDonald,* Frank Gerstle; *Kitty,* Carol Hughes; *Dave,* Michael Ross; *Nurse,* Donna Sanborn; *Jeanie,* Virginia Lee; *Captain of Police,* Roy Engle; *Detective,* George Lynn; *Waiter,* Frank Conlin; *Desk Clerk,* Bill Baldwin; *Jane Carlisle,* Lynn Roberts; *Eddie,* William Forrest; *Bartender,* Peter Leeds; *Photographer,* Ivan Triesault; *Angelo,* Philip Pine; *Hood,* George Guhl; *Little Man,* Frank Cady; *Cop,* Eddie Chandler; *Bell Hop,* Jerry Paris; *Bandleader,* "Jadie" Carson.

24

The Night of the Hunter—Ritual Murder

"So, you are the *new* cinematographer to solve our complex photographic problems? Well, I am very happy to meet you, you big bastard."

These were Charles Laughton's first words to Stanley Cortez, ASC, when they met for the first time at the Hotel George V in Paris. Cortez responded:

"I am very happy to meet you, you fat S.O.B."

With this dialogue, accompanied by warm, friendly handshakes and feelings of mutual respect, began a relationship of many years which culminated in the making of Laughton's only film directorial effort, the classic *The Night of the Hunter*. Laughton's untimely death in 1962 left an unfilled void in the worlds of theater, film and literature. He was, as Cortez observes, "a brilliant, sensitive artist; a source of inspiration."

The occasion, in 1949, was a cocktail party in honor of Cortez, who had just arrived from the States to take over the photography of *The Man on the Eiffel Tower*. Production had foundered due to photographic problems. According to Cortez, "It was a strange project, put together by Franchot Tone and Irving Allen and shot on Ansco Color, a reversal process. Tone directed part of it, but when he was in a scene Charles would take over, and when both Charles and Franchot were in a scene Burgess Meredith would direct. When all three were in the scene nobody was left but yours truly, so I directed.

"Dissolving to when the picture finished, everybody left Paris to catch a ship, leaving Charles and me behind to do the finishing sequences. That's when I got to thinking that Charles would make a good director. I saw Paris through his eyes, all of Paris, and he knew Paris better than most Frenchmen."

About six years later, producer Paul Gregory put together a package for United Artists to film Davis Grubb's novel, *The Night of the Hunter*, with Laughton as director. The team had worked together on a producer-director basis on several successful plays. Laughton invited Cortez to his home in the Hollywood Hills. Gregory was there as was James Agee, who was writing the screenplay.

"The meeting took place at the pool," Cortez recalls. After the story was discussed, Cortez said, "Charles, as this is your first picture, I'm going to bring some equipment up here and I want you to study it and get yourself accustomed to the different lenses, what they'll do, and so on. Not that you should be totally absorbed, just enough to know what is going on when we get you with the crew." He brought the equipment to the house on the following Sunday.

"I became the student and Charles became the professor," Cortez says. "Not from a technical viewpoint, but from a philosophical point of view; his thoughts and feelings as an actor and a writer. He was a very fine writer. He had great cultural sense.

"The picture was to have been made for a certain amount of money and in a certain period of time. He assembled a wonderful cast and we made the picture in 36 days. That same picture today would have taken – I don't know how long, but let's say more than double.

"When a cinematographer says a certain picture is close to his heart, it's because of the fun he had doing it and in this case the tremendous feeling of *simpatico* – not a phoney veneer, but truly *simpatico* – that existed between Charles Laughton and myself. Notwithstanding the others who contribute so much to a production, on the firing line, when all the chips are down, there are two people involved: the director and the cinematographer. It was a field day for me in terms of extreme creativity.

"For this picture, a group got together every night over a couple of drinks at a restaurant on La Cienega, the Frascatti Inn. It consisted of Charles, Hilly Brown (the art director), Milt Carter (the assistant director), Bob Golden (the film editor), and sometimes Ruby Rosenberg (the production manager). The purpose of this was to sit down with Charles and help him make a great picture. And that is what it became, but it was way ahead of its time.

"In this picture I was very careful in selecting a crew. I wanted to have people in there who would have the chemistry to support Laughton – not to excite him, but to give him a boost and not create a bad situation because of Charles' lack of technical knowledge. I was there to protect Charles, and if I wasn't there my boys knew how far they could go. My choice of people was excellent and they – Bud Mautino, Sy Hoffberg and Bob Hauser – supported Charles a hundred per cent. The chemistry was there, and if there's no chemistry, brother, you're in a bad way.

"Enough credit has never been given to people like Hilly Brown, Milton Carter or Robert Golden. Hilly was a great architect and he designed his sets from a high point of view, always looking down on something. Milton Carter kept things going and made it easy to talk with Charles. Charles' sensitivity as a director – who, in my view must be the boss, and if he's a halfway decent person he'll

get our response – permeated the entire staff. Seldom have I ever seen a group of men who were so eager to come to do a day's work, tough as it was. There was never any squabble about lunch or dinner, it was a matter of 'damn it, we're going to get this out and do the best we know how.' "

The story of *The Night of the Hunter* occurs in 1930 in the Ohio River Valley country of West Virginia. Harry Powell (Robert Mitchum), a self-ordained preacher, travels the country searching for widows to marry, then to kill and rob. Arrested for car theft, he is thrown into the same cell with Ben Harper (Peter Graves), who is to be executed for the murder of a bank teller. Harper had robbed the bank of $10,000, which was never recovered. Powell is unsuccessful in trying to learn its whereabouts. When Powell is released, he goes to visit Harper's widow, Willa (Shelley Winters) and children, nine-year-old John (Billy Chapin) and five-year-old Pearl (Sally Jane Bruce). Only the children know that the money is stuffed in a doll Pearl always carries, and they were sworn to secrecy by their father.

Powell becomes popular in the small town and Willa, prodded by well-meaning townfolk, accepts his proposal of marriage. Once he is convinced that Willa knows nothing about the money, Powell murders her, disposes of the body in the river, and tells the townfolk she has run away with another man. He tries to harrass the children into leading him to the money, but they escape in a row boat. They flee down river while he follows on a stolen farm horse.

The children eventually are taken in by Miss Rachel (Lillian Gish), an old lady who looks after river orphans at her farm. When Powell finds where the children are, he tries to terrorize Rachel into giving them up. After a long seige, Rachel wounds Powell with a shotgun blast. He is arrested, put on trial, and condemned to hang. John and Pearl remain with Rachel.

Such are the bare bones of the story. It is in the fleshing out that the greater interest lies. The novel is written in a pretentiously poetic style, while the movie is built of clean-cut, simplified compositions reminiscent of the black-and-white line illustrations popular in books and periodicals of the Thirties. Despite its grim theme and relentless atmosphere of menace, the picture contains a surprising

Robert Mitchum watches his victim's house intently.

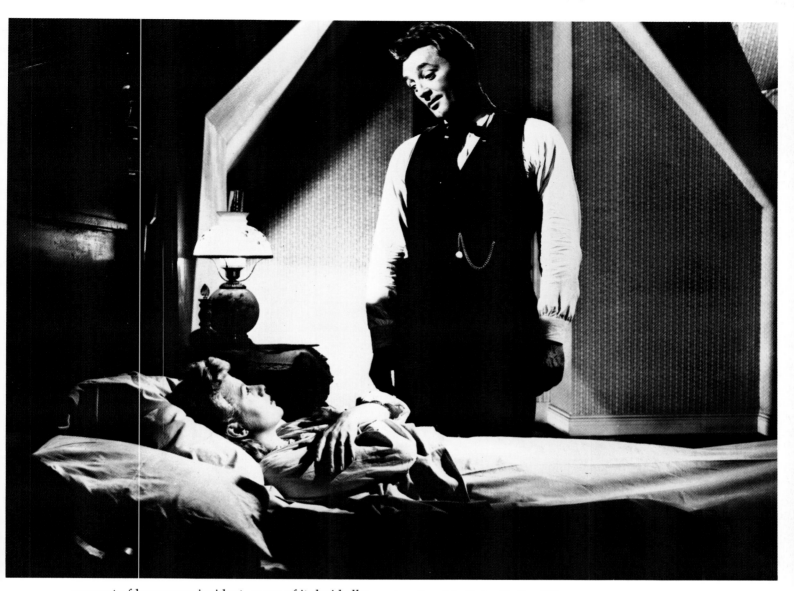

A waltz of death for Shelley Winters.

amount of humorous incident, some of it decidedly grotesque and occasionally slapstick. Aside from the quaint *patois* of the rural folk and the medicine-show con art of the evil preacher, comic bits are artfully placed at moments of suspense.

They ease the tension of the viewer and give him an opportunity to chuckle at the right places, instead of giving vent to nervous laughter at moments when it would be fatal to the mood.

One such episode occurs when Powell almost captures the children in a dark fruit cellar and a shelf full of home canned goods crashes down on his head. Later, when he is within an inch of catching the youngsters, he takes an Oliver Hardy fall into a mud hole. And when the preacher, brandishing his deadly switchblade, tries to crawl under a porch after the boy, Rachel aims her shotgun at his stern and forces him to back out.

Mitchum's performance – arguably his finest contribution to the screen – seems inspired. It takes courage for a popular romantic star to accept such a role, a situation not unlike Robert Montgomery's precedent-setting portrayal as a murderer of women in *Night Must Fall* (1936) – a superb but predictably unpopular performance. Preacher Powell is introduced as the driver of a stolen touring car. He addresses an invisible presence: ''What's it to be, Lord, another widow? Has it been six? Twelve? I disremember. You say the word and I'm on my way. You always send me money to go forth and preach your Word. A widow with a little wad of bills hidden away in the sugarbowl... Sometimes I wonder if you understand. Not that you mind the killin's. Yore book is *full* of killin's. But there are things you *do* hate, Lord: perfume-smellin' things, lacy things,

things with curly hair." His most popular sermon demonstrates the power of love over hate, which he symbolizes with a wrestling match between his right hand, the fingers of which are tattooed with the letters L-O-V-E, and the left, on which H-A-T-E is spelled out. "These fingers has veins that lead straight to the soul of man!" he tells the awed rustics. He is by turns charming, comical, grotesque and terrifying.

Equally fine is Lillian Gish as Miss Rachel, a character invested with the spiritual qualities Powell pretends to possess. Small and deceptively frail-looking, she proves more than a match for Powell – convincingly. One of the strangest scenes in any movie occurs when Powell, lurking in the night shadows outside Rachel's house, begins to sing a hymn used as a leitmotif at several points in the film, *Leaning on the Everlasting Arms*. Rachel, sitting in the dark with her shotgun cradled in her lap, joins in the singing, supplying the harmony.

Billy Chapin and Sally Jane Bruce are excellent. The stalwart boy and the innocent girl mirror perfectly the words spoken by Lillian Gish at the end of the picture: "Yes, for every child, rich or poor, there's a time of running through a dark place; and there's no word for a child's fear, and no ear to hear it if there was a word, and no one to understand it if they heard. God save little children! They abide and they endure."

Shelley Winters is impressive as the tragic widow. James Gleason is a fine river character and Evelyn Varden is true-to-life as the loudmouthed matchmaker who bullies Winters into marrying the murderous preacher and is last seen leading a lynch mob at his trial.

284

Interesting use of animal symbolism occurs throughout. The children's flight is punctuated by shots of vulnerable animals – a frog, rabbits, a turtle, sheep. The preacher, frustrated by the escape of the children, emits a wolfish growl which swells into a distorted howling. When Rachel blasts him with her shotgun, he yelps and whimpers like a wounded wolf. Rachel and her flock of children scurry singlefile down the street like a mother quail and her young.

"Charles was a great student of D.W. Griffith," Cortez recalls. "Before the picture started we ran many of Griffith's pictures, not with the idea of copying Griffith but because Charles wanted to learn from him. He wanted to do certain things Griffith did. That Griffith-like iris-in shot, where we closed down on the boy in the basement window, was a matter of sheer necessity, however. We wanted to dolly in to the boy, but we couldn't get the camera that close no matter how much we tried, and even if we could get in there it would take too long. We had no zoom lenses available, so I used an iris that we used on lights. It was about five feet square and we had to oil it up because it hadn't been used lately and was rusty as hell.

"Photographically, that picture had many problems and there were certain scenes that didn't quite come off. Like the sequence around the back stairway, when the kids are crawling as Mitchum is chasing them – there was something that wasn't quite right. There were problems because of the schedule, and, of course, it was Charles' first picture. No picture is a hundred percent; you'll find flaws in any picture, whatever it is – even *Gone with the Wind*, even in a David Lean picture.

"For certain sequences down the river with the children, Hilly did a hell of a job for us in the building of the river and the houses on Stage 15 at Pathé. The only way to get some points over was to stylize them. The skies were all lit artificially, and though it was in black-and-white it had a strange phosphorescent quality. Before the picture started, I made tests with Tri-X film to see what the film would do. The technique is one thing and the dramatic concept is something else. In my book, the dramatic aspect is far more important, because it is through the dramatic concept that communication is made to the audience, and this is the crux of the whole thing. I used Tri-X on certain sequences, not for the speed value but for the dramatic value, for the rich blacks and the luminous light I wanted. Tri-X was used in the house where the children lived, with the little stairway going up the left side, and in two other sequences. But generally we used our

Mitchum, up to his chest in the river on Stage 15, brandishes his knife. Laughton, Sy Hoffberg and Cortez are grouped around the camera.

normal film and a normal lens; nothing was pushed, nothing was forced."

Tri-X also was used in one of the more complex scenes, in which the children watch from a hayloft as Powell rides along a moonlit horizon on his stolen horse. "We built the hayloft almost to the top of the stage and had a half-moon doubled in," Cortez explains. "The stage was very small, and our idea was to give it some depth. That was a midget on a pony riding along, not Mitchum on a plow horse. It was shot from the top of the stage looking down. We used Tri-X because I wanted those blacks to go *black,* and again, it had nothing to do with the speed of the film, it was the color rendition, the tonal values. It helped us to communicate our dramatic concept to the audience. We were sort of being colorful in black-and-white."

Although most of the picture was made on sound stages, there was some location work. "Exteriors were made at the Rowland V. Lee Ranch, in the San Fernando Valley," Cortez says. "We built a street out there and at the head of the street we had a small, phony lake. For that sequence Jack Rabin, through very fine matte work, doubled in a real river steamer going across and it made that little lake look as though it were part of the Ohio River."

Undoubtedly, two of the most striking sequences in the picture are the ones in which Mitchum murders Shelley Winters and where fisherman James Gleason discovers her body sitting in a Model T Ford on the bottom of the river. Both scenes have an eerie feel that transcends the contribution of the weird lighting, the design of the set and the

Mitchum threatens Sally Jane Bruce as Billy Chapin watches.

acting of the players. According to Cortez, there is a strange reason for this.

"I am a devoted student of music, so much so that I use music a great deal to give me a clue to a given problem. While Charles was rehearsing Bob, I was making certain preparations when Charles sat down and started to watch me. He said 'Stanley, what in the hell are you doing?' I said, 'None of your damned business, Laughton' – in a nice way, of course. But he insisted. I said, 'Charles, I happen to be thinking of a piece of music right now.' And he said in a typical Laughton way, 'And pray, may I ask what the music is?' I said, 'It's called *Valse Triste.*' There was a long pause, then he said, 'Damn it! How right you are! It *has* to be a waltz!'

"Then, he did something that never happened before in my career – it may even be unique in the industry. He sent for the composer, Walter Schumann, to come on the set and see what I was doing visually so that he, Schumann, could interpret it aurally! And that's how the waltz tempo of that scene got started.

"You may wonder why I thought of that particular piece of music. Composed by Sibelius, it is a part of a saga and tells of a scene that takes place in a graveyard at one minute past midnight. Bones come to life and do a dance in sheer mockery of life, which was the exact thing Mitchum was doing because of the love and hate thing. That was what I had in my mind but I couldn't tell Charles because I was afraid he might think it was a phony thing on my part, and I thought, 'Don't tell anybody.' I've used the idea of thinking about certain pieces of music on many occasions, much as a writer might think about something that could give him a clue to the opening line and get him started. With me, it's music. Charles appreciated the musical idea. I tried, and in many instances succeeded, in using music as a key to a lighting format. It has played an important part in my career."

The *Valse Triste* motif was carried over into the underwater sequence, which was filmed in a special tank at Republic Studio. "We had to create a spiritual effect," Cortez says. "I had eight powerful Titans – the strongest sun arcs available – on a huge crane suspended over the tank." The swaying of the water weeds and the flaxen hair of the dead woman create an almost hypnotic effect in these eerie scenes.

"The visual concept of the whole picture changes in the very last sequence. It is completely different from any other sequence in the picture," Cortez points out. "It was Charles who wanted to make it like that. He said, 'Stanley, I want to get the feeling here that this is a Christmas party wrapped up in a beautiful package and off they go.' I said 'I know what you mean, Charles,' and this was our approach. The relationship between Charles and myself was extraordinary in the sense of unity of concept, of a fusion of thinking. And so, the sequence at the end was different, like night and day."

Cortez believes it is impossible to explain in so many words how the creative aspects of a film are achieved as opposed to the technical aspects. "I just did it. Either you do or you don't. You see something and you react, the juice is turned on and – boom! – you go. People ask, 'Don't you plan these shots?' I say that to a degree I do, from the standpoint of lighting, but I must be elastic, I must be open. When you read a script, that's *one* impression; but when you look at a stage, and you hear actors speak in the actual set, it becomes a completely different thing. The mature cinematographer is one who can interpret these things on the spur of the moment. A spontaneous reaction, to me, is far more important than anything else. You may say, what about the lighting? It's true the lighting is already there; it's a question of using it.

"I think the proper word is 'feel,' and that comes from you as a person and the awareness of what's happening in the world today. What happened in the world thousands of years ago is part of your psyche, in the very depths of your soul. All these things come into play and either you're sensitive to them or you're not. If you are not, you are a cinematographer who merely records instead of interpreting. Creative cinematography is the feel, the know-how; it's imagination; it's how you get the best out of nothing."

The picture was scored by Walter Schumann, who had gained widespread popularity for his work in the "Dragnet" television series. The unusual music was scored for full orchestra, mixed

Lillian Gish, prepared to protect her flock.

chorus and solo piano. Much of it was based on Ohio Valley folk tunes and some back-country themes from West Virginia. The Protestant hymn, *Leaning on the Everlasting Arms*, is utilized to fine effect. An RCA recording (1955) of the music, with narration by Laughton, has become a much-in-demand collector's item.

The Night of the Hunter was too unusual a picture to be very popular in 1955. It was in black-and-white at a time when theaters were demanding color, in standard ratio even though Cinemascope had ushered in a wide-screen "craze." It dared to depict a preacher – albeit one who says his religion is one "the Almighty and me worked out betwixt us" – as a murderer and pervert. This caused censorship problems in several states and resulted in an outright ban in Memphis. As Cortez explains, it created a worse situation in Europe. "It was banned in certain parts of the world because, although here we have many phony preachers, in Europe they don't have them. There, when you're a preacher,

The murderer at an Ohio River hobo camp, actually a stage set.

you're a man of the cloth. You represent the Guy above you. They don't know about these things so they resented seeing a guy in a white collar being a villain."

James Agee died during post-production. Otherwise, he would have received a heavy dose of the medicine he often dealt out during his years as a film critic. "Reviews were awful here," Lillian Gish wrote Paul Gregory from New York, adding: "Hope Charles did not read them." The West Coast reviews were kinder while expressing certain reservations. Variety assessed the picture honestly: "There will be no halfway reactions...Patrons will either like it...or loathe it. While it is a finely acted, imaginatively directed chiller with brooding power,

287

The runaway children follow the river.

the boxoffice draw...is a debatable matter. The controversy it is bound to stir up will help, but..."

"I think the lack of world acceptance of his picture hurt Charles' feelings to the point where it got him down," Cortez says. "He put so much effort into it and the great wit, this great talent Charles had, didn't, for some reason, come through.

"However, in contrast to that, the picture was way ahead of its time, which is why it didn't quite get over. But in later years a kind of cult developed where they had clubs – *Night of the Hunter* clubs – and it suddenly became one of the in things. As a result, it is now more understood and more popular than it was then, because we as a people have a more open mind."

Tragically, Laughton was never to direct another film. Cortez worked with Laughton and Gregory for nine months in preparation for *The Naked and the Dead*. "Something happened between Paul and the money men and suddenly the thing stopped. Later, RKO took it over and Raoul Walsh directed it."

Time has a way of catching up with pictures that were not quite in step with the fashion of the moment and bringing into focus those virtues that seemed obscure at first glance. So it is with *The Night of the Hunter*. It has gathered a devoted following of movie lovers who value experimentation above conformity, daring above security, and artistry above mere competence.

"To this day I get letters from all over, wherever it's being shown, and they want to know how we did this and how we did that. But most of all they want to know on what river the sequence of the children in the river was done. Was it back East or

288

where?" Cortez says. "I keep telling them, this is a fine compliment because we did it on Stage 15 at Pathé.

"It was a joy creating *The Night of the Hunter.*"

—George E. Turner

A United Artists release, produced by Paul Gregory; *directed by* Charles Laughton; *screenplay by* James Agee; *based on a novel by* Davis Grubb; *director of photography,* Stanley Cortez, ASC; *music by* Walter Schumann; *art director,* Hilyard Brown; *set decorations,* Al Spencer; *film editor,* Robert Golden; *wardrobe,* Jerry Bos; *property master,* Joe LaBella; *makeup artist,* Don Cash; *hair stylist,* Kay Shea; *sound,* Stanford Haughton; *production supervisor,* Ruby Rosenberg; *assistant director,* Milton Carter; *visual effects,* Jack Rabin; *operative cameraman,* Bud Mautino; *assistant cameramen,* Seymour Hoffberg, Robert Hauser; *gaffer,* James Potevin. *Running time 93 minutes. Released September 29, 1955.*

Preacher Harry Powell, Robert Mitchum; *Willa Harper,* Shelley Winters; *Rachel,* Lillian Gish; *Icey Spoon,* Evelyn Varden; *Ben Harper,* Peter Graves; *John,* Billy Chapin; *Pearl,* Sally Jane Bruce; *Birdie,* James Gleason; *Walt Spoon,* Don Beddoe; *Ruby,* Gloria Castillo; *Clary,* Mary Ellen Clemons; *Mary,* Cheryl Gallaway; *Executioner,* Paul Bryar.

Hungry and tired from the chase, orphans Bruce and Chapin peer in Miss Rachel's window.

289

Index

All films, studios, and persons in the book are listed here, with the exception of persons mentioned only in the credits at the ends of chapters, and entities mentioned incidentally. Generic subjects such as ''cinematography'' or ''lighting'' or ''music'' are not indexed. Novels, newspapers, and musical compositions are not listed by title, but authors and composers are indexed. Except for certain especially recognizable sites, locations are not indexed. Film titles are italicized; television titles appear in quotes. Illustrations are indicated with page numbers in italics.